Bringing It All Back Home

BRINGING

IT ALL BACK

HOME

ESSAYS ON CULTURAL STUDIES

Lawrence Grossberg

DUKE UNIVERSITY PRESS   Durham & London 1997

© 1997 Duke University Press
All rights reserved
Printed in the United States of America on acid-free paper ∞
Typeset in Melior by Keystone Typesetting, Inc.
Library of Congress Cataloging-in-Publication Data appear
on the last printed page of this book.

> If you prefer not to exaggerate,
> you must remain silent,
> you must paralyze your intellect
> and find some way of becoming an idiot.
> —Ortega y Gasset,
> *The Revolt of the Masses*

ontents

Acknowledgments

There are so many people to thank. Some of them allowed me to borrow their ideas—and sometimes even their words (but as Nick Lowe was purported to have once said, "I only steal from the best"). Some of them allowed me to bounce ideas and words off them, and were good enough friends to not always bounce them back to me. Some of them stood by me and others told me when to get off. Some have laughed and danced with me, others have mourned and prayed with me, and many have done both. Some have held my hand, and some have patted me on the back. Some have thanked me, and some have gone on without saying a word. Some have gotten high with me, and some have shared my lows. But all of them have taught me something, and I hope that I am a better teacher for having been able to touch so many wonderful people. I cannot thank everyone. Many are there in the notes to particular essays, and although I know it is not enough, I also know it will have to do.

My work and my life as a scholar and teacher have been shaped by three wonderful people, three of the best teachers/political intellectuals in the world: Stuart Hall, Jim Carey, and Meaghan Morris. I was fortunate enough to study with Stuart and Jim. And Meaghan has been what I used to call in graduate school a dialogic partner—every intellectual's dream. They have all been and remain more than friends and more than teachers. They have helped to shape my sense of myself as a political intellectual, and they serve as constant and powerful reminders of what an intellectual can and should be. They each continue to have an enormous impact on my work, even though I have moved in different directions, along different paths, over the past decade. They have influenced me more than I can ever say and I know that I will never find the words to express my gratitude to them. I also need to thank Catherine, Becky and Jesse, Betty, and Andre: they were generous enough to let me into their lives, and they have become an important part of my life.

I have been more than fortunate, over the years, to work with many wonderful graduate students. I have had colleagues and friends more supportive than I could possibly deserve: Chuck Whitney and Ellen Wartella (my other dialogic partner), Daniel and Barbara O'Keefe, Steve and Laurie Weidemier, Eleanor Blum and James Hay. I left them all to move with my family to warmer (and more hospitable) places, and found colleagues and friends who made us feel at home: Della Pollock and Alan Shapiro, Bill Balthrop and Nancy Keeshan, Beverly Long (and Bill Long—we will miss him), Ken Wissoker (a wonderful editor as well) and Cathy Davidson, Judith Farquhar and Jim Hevia, and more. Finally, there are other friends, around the country and the world, that I want to thank for many things: Tony Bennett, Henry Giroux, John Clarke, Jennifer Slack, Marty Allor, Jan Radway, and all the rest of you (I hope you will forgive me for not trying to list everyone).

I would not be who or what I am were it not for my parents and family, and I am eternally grateful to them (at least at those moments when I like myself).

But in the end, my life and whatever energy I have, whatever faith I have in myself and in the possibilities of a better world, rest with my wife, Barbara Anne Claypole White. Because she thinks I am better than I am, I am constantly trying to be what I can. (Thank you for loving me, and for putting up with me.) And there is my son, Zachariah Nigel Claypole White, born on Christmas Day 1994, named after the prophet who called for the rebuilding of the temple. He cannot yet read the words gathered here; he may never care enough to even bother. But he makes the future so much a part of my present, and he enriches my present so much every day. He has brought new meaning to my fears and rekindled my dreams. More than anything, I hope he will want to thank us for the world he inherits.

I dedicate this book to Zachariah Nigel, and to Barbara, and to my father, Abraham Grossberg, for the good and the bad times.

The essays in this volume originally were published as follows: "Interpreting the 'Crisis' of Culture" in *Journal of Communication* 29:56–68 (with permission of Oxford University Press); "The Ideology of Communication" in *Man and World* 15: 83–101 (with permission of Kluwer Academic Publishers); "Experience, Signification, and Reality" in *Semiotica* 41: 73–106 (with permission of Mouton de Gruyter); "Strategies of Marxist Cultural Interpretation" in *Cultural Studies in Mass Communication* 1: 392–421 (with permission of Speech Communication Association); "Cultural Studies Revisited and Revised" in Mary S. Mander, ed., *Communications in Transition*

(New York: Praeger, 1983: 39–70, with permission of Greenwood Publishing Group); "History, Politics, and Postmodernism" in *Journal of Communication Inquiry* 10: 61–77; "The Formation(s) of Cultural Studies" in *Strategies*, no. 2: 114–49; "The Circulation of Cultural Studies" in *Critical Studies in Mass Communication* 6:413–21; "Cultural Studies: What's in a Name?" in *Taboo* 1: 1–37 (with permission of Peter Lang Publishers); "Toward a Geneology of the State of Cultural Studies" in Cary Nelson and Dilip Gaonkar, eds., *Disciplinarity and Dissent in Cultural Studies* (New York: Routledge, 1993); "Wandering Audiences, Nomadic Critics" in *Cultural Studies* 2 (3): 377–91; "The Context of Audiences and the Politics of Difference" in *Australian Journal of Communication*, no. 16: 13–36; "Cultural Studies in/and New Worlds" in *Critical Studies in Mass Communication* 10:1–22 (with permission of Speech Communication Association); "Bringing It All Back Home" in Henry Giroux and Peter McLaren, eds., *Between Borders* (New York: Routledge, 1994: 1–25). I am grateful for permission to reproduce these essays here, but I am especially grateful for the opportunity, however long ago, to publish them in the first place.

Bringing It All Back Home

Introduction:

"Birmingham" in America?

"Liberals don't kick ass. And if they don't kick ass, their ass is gonna get kicked. And that is what has happened to liberalism" (Leykis, quoted in Giroux 1996, 159). I am not quite sure who the "liberals" are here, but I am pretty sure that the statement is true of many progressive intellectuals and academics in the United States. Before we run off to defend the National Endowments for the Humanities and the Arts, however, it may be useful to remember that a lot of other people are getting their asses kicked, often with much more devastating consequences. I have no doubt that we are witnessing—in fact, caught up in and contributing to—a sea change, in the classroom, in the university, in the media and consumer culture, in the nation and in the world. Too often, too many progressive intellectuals have responded to these changes politically, critically, and theoretically, with the same tactics, strategies, and assumptions, with the same theories and the same politics. In fact, often we not only end up defending what we have been doing, but we avoid the more difficult task of critically measuring our politics and theories against the challenges of contemporary trajectories of change. We seem to be content with rediscovering what we already know, with reinscribing in our institutional practice what we already do. How can we fail to understand the growing multiple hostilities toward the academy when we champion life as usual whenever it is convenient? This is unfortunately true even in the places one might hope otherwise. Let me give just a few examples:

—The canon is challenged only insofar as its new and improved form continues to legitimate the academic's power of discrimination, value, and judgment. So we either expand the possibilities of "good" or "high" art, or we reverse the valuations (making the popular "better" than the legitimate culture), or we substitute different (explicitly political/moral) systems of judgment for aesthetic ones, or we reject the very idea of the canon with the simple claim that such judgments are obviously elitist and therefore unacceptable. Unfortunately, the place of the canon in the academy is far more complicated than any of these options allows, if for no other reason than that it is largely the source of our popular cultural capital and external support.

—Consider the ways so many progressive academics and intellectuals have responded—or failed to respond—to the charges of "political correctness." Of course, the rhetoric of PC is exaggerated; it serves the strategic interests of both the conservative alliance and the media to so exaggerate. But instead of admitting in public what many of us say in private—that the internal politics of "the American Left" can be pretty atrocious at times, falling into a kind of terrorism of guilt in which suffering becomes a measure of credibility— our public stance is often one of moral self-righteousness. Despite our theoretical sophistication, we end up falling back into naïve accusations of misrepresentation.

—Too many intellectuals continue to defend the endless theoretical elaboration of difference, fragmentation, and hybridity without asking how these might be articulated into the real struggles that are changing life in the United States. Instead of challenging the unequal distribution and exchange that define the circulation of cultural theory and criticism as much as of popular culture—and asking how such discourses should be globalized—we depend on the already available if somewhat vague critique of Eurocentrism. Obviously these strategies have made important contributions, but they also have their limits.

—In too many places, cultural studies is being institutionalized in ways that merely reproduce the structure of area studies, or of the English and communication departments in which so many of us were educated and are located. One result is that "interdisciplinarity" is often used as a rhetorical weapon against the disciplines instead of as a productive challenge to build new relations and to change our own research practices. The fact is that what passes for interdisciplinarity is too often little more than cross-disciplinary theoretical dabbling.

Too often, while we are fighting a battle over here, we are ignoring other battles that may be as significant if not more so in the long run: for example, battles over the nature of academic labor and the changes that are required if we are to serve and support our students, especially graduate students, responsibly. This cannot be addressed by simply closing our doors to students because there are not enough jobs or bemoaning the inflation of expectations placed on graduate students and junior faculty. It must take us into new territory, where we begin to imagine new ways of using graduate education as preparation for nonacademic jobs. We need to be involved with notions and analyses of labor, and of the relations and possible alliances between the different forms of labor in the institution and in the general economy. We need to take seriously the expectation that we (at least those of us at state-funded universities) are supposed to contribute to the public good, an expectation that is only partly realized by the production of knowledge (or, in Gramsci's terms, knowing more than the other side). At the same time, we must not succumb to the view, common on the Right, that measures the value of knowledge only by its immediate utility. But that requires us to think about the different temporalities and effectivities of the knowledge we produce and distribute.

In fact, too often the very battles we have chosen to fight, and the ways we have chosen to fight them, have contributed to the weakening of the very institutions we are supposedly fighting for. I hope you, the reader, will forgive my rhetorical excesses here, but I think it is time that we admitted that much of what we (progressive academics and intellectuals) are doing is not working. We need to begin to seriously confront the dystopian trajectories that are leading us, all together, whatever our politics, identity, or status, into the next millennium. And we need to try to understand how the different trajectories and their different successes are being constructed. We need to understand the mechanisms and contexts of the contemporary transformations and of their articulations to specific relations of power. For example, how is it that our culture can simultaneously proliferate figures of agency in which intelligence is a liability, even as it explicitly recognizes (as the hero in one network movie, quoting Yeats, said) that "the best lack all conviction while the worst are full of passionate intensity"? While progressive political movements continue to exist as fragmented institutional organizations, the possibility of a broader movement based on shared commitments that extend beyond their everyday lives is being actively deconstructed, for particular fractions of the populace, at three sites: first, the impossibility of investing in the political (i.e., whether in the government or "the people" as agents of change or in some utopian field of political and ethical values); second, the active discouragement of any imagining of the possibility of political community (i.e., of rethinking the relation of the individual to the group and of identity to struggle); and third, the impossibility of articulating a theory and practice of agency (of reconsidering how people make history but not in conditions of their own making). These are, in the first instance, problems of everyday life, constructed in struggles in and over the popular. They are also problems at the intersection of everyday life and the tendential forces struggling to determine it. But they are also challenges for the intellectual, and I believe we will have failed if we cannot find ways to address them outside of the limits of our own theoretical and political positions, if we cannot speak, as intellectuals, through the popular, in order to connect everyday life with the very real struggles against economic and political injustice.

There are, no doubt, historical reasons that explain the situation of progressive political intellectuals. We might look at the collapse of the Popular Front and the various residual formations that remained in its wake, and how this helped to define the particular (and somewhat peculiar) shape of the New Left in the United States. We might consider the impact of the New Left's eventual self-destruction and what it meant for generations—especially of intellectuals—in the 1970s and '80s. In fact, I think it resulted in an increasingly popular feeling (which was both part of the New Left and challenged by it) that radicalism and reformism were contradictory. This enabled a general (although not universal) retreat from the politics of policy (in the broadest sense) and public debate and into the politics of theory and the theory of politics. I certainly do not mean to "bash" theory or to blame the fact that it is often (necessarily) inaccessible for the current situation. On the contrary, I think theory is absolutely necessary (and that the problem is that we do not have theories adequate to the task). But I do want to criticize some aspects of the particular practice of some contemporary theorizing.

I want to defend a different practice of theorizing, a different way of politicizing theory and theorizing politics. This is what I call "cultural studies." It is a way that leads us to reflect on where the questions driving our researches are coming from, and to refuse to take either our theory or politics for granted, as if they could be assumed in advance. Cultural studies is an attempt to answer Marvin Gaye's question "What's going on?" and theory is its tool to get a bit further along in that task. It is, to use Stuart Hall's somewhat overly heroic image, a constant effort to "wrestle with the angels," the angels of theory and of the real organizations and productions of power. It is not about interpreting or judging texts or people, but about describing how people's everyday lives are articulated by and with culture, how they are empowered and disempowered by the particular structures and forces that organize their lives, always in contradictory ways, and how their everyday lives are themselves articulated to and by the trajectories of economic and political power. Cultural studies is not about a particular theoretical position, or a particular research practice, or even a particular body of texts. It is about historical possibilities of transforming people's lived realities and the relations of power and about the absolutely vital contribution of intellectual work to the imagination and realization of such possibilities.

Practicing cultural studies involves constantly redefining it in response to changing geographical and historical conditions and to changing political demands; it involves making a home for it within specific disciplines even as it challenges the legitimacy of the disciplinization of intellectual work. But how cultural studies is to be defined and located in any particular project can only be determined by doing the work of cultural studies, by mapping/reconstructing the relations between discourses, everyday life, and the machineries of power. This is the peculiar logic of cultural studies: it begins with a context that has already posed a question; yet it always begins again by turning to discourses, as both its productive entrance into and a productive dimension of that context. But in the end, it is not interested in the discourse per se but in the articulations between everyday life and the formations of power. Thus it ends with a different understanding of the context than that with which it began, having gone through the mediations of both culture (discourse) and theory. Thus while cultural studies demands theoretical work, I would say that theory is "cheap," while politics (which is not the same as ethics or morality) are costly, since the politics of any particular study are available only after the work of analysis. I do not believe this "definition" installs a new mythology that proposes cultural studies as the new salvation for anything; rather it is a modest proposal for a flexible intellectual and political practice.

The current success of cultural studies carries with it both great promise and significant dangers, and any attempt to negotiate its identity (as the essays collected here most certainly are) must, therefore, be seen as a kind of intervention, an attempt to influence its shape, direction, and impact, for they are still to be determined.

DEFENDING CULTURAL STUDIES[1]

It is not surprising that as cultural studies has become more popular, more visible, and in some ways more successful it has also come under increasing attack. It has been described as a fad and as having succumbed to the history of theoretical fads. There are at least three criticisms that are worth considering in some detail. First, in the name of cultural studies, some scholars have called for a return to empirical researches. Of course, different people have different sorts of research in mind: textual, ethnographic, sociological, or political-economic. I have no objection to empirical research, but if it is being offered as an alternative to theory, I have my doubts. And if we are doing research to merely reaffirm that which we already know (or think we know), or to produce knowledge that is disconnected from the demands of the contemporary world, my doubts begin to seriously outweigh my sympathies. Furthermore, too often such calls are part of a larger celebration, even fetishization, of the local. I am reminded of Castell's assertion that "when people find themselves unable to control the world, they simply shrink the world to the size of their community" (cited in Gilroy 1993, 232). Such celebrations are often undertheorized, based on either a particular definition of knowledge as facts and a model of inductive empiricism, or an assumed identification of the local with the site of agency and resistance. Following Bruce Robbins (1993), we need to ask why a certain kind of work—work that identifies and celebrates the local, the specific, and agency—is valorized. Robbins concludes that this defines a technology of power that legitimates the claim of intellectual work to "public representativeness." It creates an apparent anchor in political reality while leaving the intellectual outside. It appears to give the intellectual a real audience, positioning him or her as organic intellectuals speaking for a real population. I do not mean to dismiss the importance of "the local," only its articulation to particular notions of specificity and agency within various versions of cultural studies.

The second criticism of cultural studies is that it is little more than a populist celebration of media culture, reception/consumption, and consumer capitalism, and has given up any oppositional role. The third is that cultural studies ignores economics, including the institutions of cultural production, and thus that it is incapable of understanding the real structures of power, domination, and oppression in the contemporary world. Obviously, these two criticisms are often linked. I want to be careful here. I agree that there are particular positions in cultural studies that have become too celebratory, in part because the commitment to the local and the specific has overshadowed any sense of the broader social context of unequal power relations. And I agree that there has been a tendency in some cultural studies to avoid detailed attention to the economic, in part because of the fear of falling back into reductionist models. But without a careful analysis of these developments and their place within the broader assumptive and political grounds of cultural studies, the value of such criticisms all but disappears. Often such criticisms are based on the most selective and truncated readings not only of particular texts, but of the broad range of work in cultural studies.

The criticism of cultural studies as populist is based, to a large extent, on a conflation of two positions, which, however, are sometimes embodied in the same work: on the one hand, work on consumption (and reception), which looks at the complex and even contradictory nature of consumption—and yes, often concludes that consumption can produce pleasures, that it can be, in some ways, empowering, and so on—but which need not and does not deny the exploitative, manipulative, and dominating aspects of the market. Such work attempts to place local practices into the wider context of the social structures of power, even as it attempts to see how those structures are lived and felt locally. On the other hand, there is work that, for whatever reasons, argues that any act of consumption is, by definition, pleasurable and therefore an act of resistance. While I may agree that some work in cultural studies has been caught up in a rather celebratory mode of populism, I think it is absolutely necessary to distinguish this from the more common and nuanced position of cultural studies. Moreover, similar critiques have been made by writers, especially feminists, within cultural studies itself (including Angela McRobbie, Meaghan Morris, John Clarke, Judith Williamson, and myself).

Obviously, there is more than simply rhetoric at stake here. Perhaps cultural studies has paid too much attention to consumption, but I fear that what is operating behind such claims is the tendency to dismiss consumption (or leisure) as somehow less important than production, perhaps even as trivial. Production, narrowly understood as the practice of manufacturing and abstractly understood as the mode of production, is too easily assumed to be the *real* bottom line. Perhaps cultural studies has overemphasized the pleasure, freedom, and empowerment of consumption (and reception), but again I fear that what is operating behind such claims is the desire to return to a simpler model of domination in which people are seen as passively manipulated "cultural dopes." Certainly some people in cultural studies have overemphasized the capacities for resistance in popular cultural practices, although I still see value in this work not only as a provocation in the face of a still puritanical Left, but also as a strategy for helping people see that things are not always the way authorities describe them, and moreover that things do not have to be the way they are. Certainly, cultural studies often writes more about how systems of domination are lived than about the systems of domi-

8

nation themselves, and I agree that more work on the latter needs to be done. But without such work, the Left is likely to fall back on old assumptions—and old generalizations—about the masses and everyday life.

But it is simply not true to say that, in general, cultural studies adopts an uncritical populism. Most of the work in cultural studies that I read does not equate the popular with pleasure and resistance. It does not assume that all pleasure is good or politically progressive; on the contrary, it often does recognize that pleasure can be manipulated by or at least articulated to repressive forms of power and existing structures of inequality. And it recognizes that pleasures may themselves be repressive and regressive, such as those derived from relations of domination over other groups. Certainly this is a basic premise of most cultural studies work in feminism, postcolonialism, and critical race studies.

Cultural studies does not assume that opposition, resistance, struggle, and survival (coping) are the same; but it does assume that the possibilities for the first two depend in complex ways on the realities of the last two. The question of the relations and tensions among these forms of effectivity is important and needs to be explored. Perhaps most important is the question of what it is that mobilizes opposition. But I see no evidence that those criticizing cultural studies are interested in addressing these questions, or capable of doing so. For cultural studies, the fact that people do use the limited resources they are given to find better ways of living, to find ways of increasing the control they have over aspects of their lives and so on, is significant, not only in itself, but also in terms of understanding the structures of power and inequality in the contemporary world and the possibilities for challenging them. Cultural studies does assume that people live their subordination actively; that means, in one sense, that they are often complicit in their own subordination, that they accede to it, although power often works through strategies and apparatuses of which people are totally unaware. Be that as it may, cultural studies does believe that if one is to challenge the existing structures of power, one has to understand how that complicity, that participation in power, is constructed and lived, and that means looking not only at what people gain from such practices, but also at the possibilities for rearticulating such practices to escape, resist, or even oppose particular structures of power. Cultural studies refuses to assume that people are cultural dopes, that they are entirely and passively manipulated either by the media or by capitalism. But it does not deny that they are sometimes duped, that they are sometimes manipulated, that they are lied to (and believe the lies, sometimes knowing that they are lies).

The argument that cultural studies ignores economics is more complicated, for it encompasses a number of different arguments, although they can usually all be traced back to the assertion that cultural studies defines itself by its opposition—and hence its evacuation of—political economy. But I think that the issue has always been how one thinks about the relationships or links between the different domains (forms and structures of practices) of social life. Cultural studies did not reject political economy per se: discussions of capitalism have always figured centrally in its work; it rejected the way certain political economists practice political economy.

The indictment of cultural studies is often built on a critique by absence: criticize a position for what it does not do or say. This is particularly common in the contemporary culture of the Left. Obviously, it is one thing to claim that a position *cannot* talk about something, but it is not the same to claim that it *has not* talked about it. Thus cultural studies is often accused of paying too much attention to consumption, leisure, and everyday practices and not enough to production, work, and institutions. One could simply argue that since political economists are doing this work (but not work on consumption), there is no need for those in cultural studies to undertake such work. But it is important to also point to those people in cultural studies who are working on questions of production, including Dorothy Hobson, Angela McRobbie (on the fashion industry), Sean Nixon, Jody Berland, and others. But perhaps the problem runs deeper, for what is assumed here is a rather narrow and abstract conception of production. If the very notion and practice of production are themselves culturally produced,[2] and if the relations between production and consumption are more complex and less stable than the critics of cultural studies assume, then the model of cultural analysis based on a separation of production and consumption is itself problematic, as is the reduction of production to waged labor (which ignores what Marx himself had pointed to: the production involved in consumption/reproduction).

It is in fact rather telling that production is usually equated with the "cultural industries," as if the commodification of culture were somehow complete. Part of what cultural studies has always been about is the self-production of culture: the practices by which people come, however imperfectly, to represent themselves and their worlds. Important work (e.g., by Mike Apple, Henry Giroux, Cameron McCarthy, Peter McLaren, and Patti

Lather in education; by Bourdieu and his followers; by Foucauldians looking at state discourses) has also been done on cultural production in what used to be called the "ideological state apparatuses." Production cannot simply be the capitalized manufacture of cultural commodities. Consider the decision by the African National Congress to extend the cultural boycott to people as well as commodities, apparently recognizing that the embodied and personified practice of production is as important as the commodities themselves.[3] The issue here is not whether but how production must figure into analyses of the politics of cultural practices and relations. Cultural studies rejects the assumption that production is determining in the last instance, even while it acknowledges that production has its political and discursive effects and vice versa.

A second dimension of the political-economic criticism of cultural studies involves the claim that cultural studies has foregrounded questions of identity over questions of class and economics. Obviously it is true that a great deal of work in cultural studies focuses on issues of identity and difference, of race, gender, sexuality, ethnicity, and so forth as the markers of relations of domination. But I doubt that many people in cultural studies would argue that such differences are not related to class. In fact, what they are likely to argue is that any difference, and how it is lived—whether race, gender, class, sexuality—is articulated to and by other differences. And the ways they are articulated make a difference to the formation of specific capitalisms (in particular countries, for example) rather than to some abstract capitalism. Cultural studies criticizes political economy because it often becomes ahistorical at just the points that matter: If capitalist societies (rather than modes of production) are variable, how does one understand those variations? Why is it that the U.S.A. is not the U.K. or Japan? These are not just superstructural problems but issues about the ways social relations develop beyond a simple binary distinction between owners of the means of production and wage labor. But a certain kind of political economy is unable to consider such questions precisely because it refuses to engage the question of articulation, which is of course the principal way in which the relations between production, consumption, politics, and ideology are theorized in cultural studies.

Cultural studies rejects a political economy that refuses in practice to think about the contradictory nature of social practices (except in the most abstract ahistorical form as the class contradiction) because such positions are unable to think about why things change. It rejects analyses that, whatever their declared position, operate as if capital determines in a mechanical way from start to finish. This is, in my opinion, not marxist in the least! For it cannot address the important questions about how particular forms of domination, consent, and so forth are accomplished and why they are successful, that is, how such attempts are able, sometimes, to get people to occupy the positions they want. Perhaps some people in cultural studies exaggerate the possibilities or the freedom to interpret and use popular practices. But the choice is not between freedom and determination. Certainly economic practices and relations determine the distribution of practices and commodities (although not entirely by themselves), but do they determine which *meanings* circulate and which do not? I doubt it. Those articulations are much more complex and difficult to describe. The fact that certain institutions (and individuals) would like to control how people interpret texts, or what they do with them, does not mean that such "intentions" actually determine what people do and think, that is, the effects of practices. Are the real effects determined? Of course, but in very complex ways, across a multiplicity of planes and dimensions, of codes and structures, as the result of particular struggles to articulate particular sorts of practices to particular sorts of effects. This is a crucial divide between political economy and cultural studies: the relation between origins and effects.

Political economy assumes a universal answer to the question of the nature of the determination between economic and other social relations. This avoids what McRobbie describes as the "more awkward theoretical questions such as the nature of the political relationships which can and do exist between emergent social identities . . . much of the left prefers instead to rely on the assumed centrality of class as providing a kind of underpinning for the politics of race or sexuality" (1996, 242). The fact that modern forms of race and gender relations are themselves articulated in complicated ways by and to capitalist relations (including but not only class) does not mean that they are only or even primarily economic. No one in cultural studies denies the economic realities of racism or sexism, although they are likely to think that such inequalities cannot be directly mapped by or onto class relations. Moreover they may also think that those inequalities are constructed in a variety of ways, along a variety of dimensions, besides the distribution of labor and capital, and that some of those other ways centrally involve cultural practices. The real issue is what it means to say that something is grounded or founded in something else: it need not be a description of origins, but it also need not define a sufficient condition or explanation. The fact that race and gender are articulated to economics (and may be articulated to class) does not say much about the appropriate ways of accounting for, or struggling against, structures of domination organized around race and gender.

Thus while I do agree that too much work in cultural studies reduces the field of power and politics to the terrain of culture and so fails to take economics seriously enough, I am also convinced that political economy—at least the dominant and most visible versions of it—fails to take culture seriously enough. Here we are beginning to get to the crux of the matter: Cultural studies believes that culture matters and that it cannot simply be treated (dismissed) as the transparent—at least to the critic—public face of dominating and manipulative capitalists. Cultural studies emphasizes the complexity and contradictions, not only within culture, but in the relations between people, culture, and power. Now I am sure that many political economists also believe that culture matters, but usually only as a commodity and an ideological tool of manipulation.

No one in cultural studies denies that economic relations and practices "shape in determinate ways the terrain upon which cultural practices take place" (Garnham 1995, 66); they may even help to shape the cultural agenda, but always and only in part. The question is what follows from such statements. For the fact of the matter is that for political economy, in every instance, in every context, somehow, almost magically, the economic appears to be the bottom line, the final and real solution to the problem, the thing that holds everything together and makes everything what it is. That is why, I believe, Hall (1983) argues that such reductionism and reflectionism are intrinsic to marxism (and by extension to political economy). Ironically, this suggests that political economy also fails to take capitalism seriously enough. Or at least that the way in which cultural studies takes economics seriously must be radically different from the assumptions and methods of political economy. For cultural studies does not believe that all forms of power can be explained by capitalist relations or in economic terms.[4] Cultural studies refuses to see everything locked into place by, guaranteed by, economic relations.

The question is whether it is possible to have a political economy theorized around articulation rather than strict determination or necessity. What is at stake is not so much the relations between cultural studies and political economy, but rather the ways in which questions of economics—and of contemporary capitalism in particular—are to be articulated into analyses of the politics of culture. Cultural studies rejected that version of political economy which is characterized not merely by its logic of necessary correspondences (reductionist and reflectionist), but by its reduction of economics to the technological and institutional contexts of capitalist manufacturing (with occasional gestures—and little more—to marketing, distribution, and retailing), by its reduction of the market to the site of commodified and alienated exchange,[5] and by its rather ahistorical and oversimplified notions of capitalism. After all, to describe contemporary capitalism as dependent on wage labor and commodity exchange is rather uninformative, as is the observation that contemporary culture is increasingly commodified. To point to the conditions of the existence of capitalism as providing an adequate explanation of anything is to forget that Marx described them as "what every child knows." Such a political economy seems to assume that capitalism is a universal structure that, despite minor variations (e.g., in what is being commodified), remains unchanged and stable. In fact, cultural studies did not abandon an interest in capitalism. On the contrary, contemporary work in cultural studies is, I believe, returning to questions of economics in important and interesting ways (often but not only through questions of globalization and colonization and through links with economic geography and postfordist economics). Such work needs to be encouraged and developed even further. Cultural studies will have to take account of the changing relations between the different forms of capital (and the different economic sectors), the changing nature of and competing forms of both the modes of production (and their subsequent contradictions) and the formations of capitalism (e.g., fordism, postfordism), the changing nature of labor and consumption, and the changing nature of the global relations of both political and economic power. It will have to consider how and where people, capital, and commodities move in and out of the places and spaces of the global economy.[6] What cultural studies does not need is to adopt a position it had the good sense to reject decades ago.

At the same time I would hope that we could find new ways of carrying on such internal debates and criticisms. Instead of assuming that there is one "correct" line, can we not find ways of living together, if not in the same neighborhood, at least in the same region? We might not like each other's taste or travel the same routes, but we can share a sense of the geography of power and the power of geography. We can criticize particular versions of each other's projects. More generally, we can criticize each other's assumptions; we can even criticize each other's political positions. But when we start accusing each other of evacuating politics altogether, of being traitors to the Left (i.e., playing into the Right), and so on, then we have truly forgotten who the enemies are and where our allies (who may or may not be our friends) are to be found.

The question of how economics can or should operate within cultural studies leads me to the broader question of interdisciplinarity. While many writers have talked about cultural studies' aggressive antidisciplinarity and its disruptive effects on disciplinary boundaries, few have actually specified the form of its interdisciplinarity, the reasons for it, or the nature of its disruptiveness. Raymond Williams (1989) once described the real power in the classroom as the power to ask the questions. Similarly, by allowing the context to pose the questions, as it were, cultural studies renounces the power of the institutional boundaries of disciplines in favor of doing the work necessary, wherever it is, to begin to provide better answers. As Meaghan Morris put it recently, "A literary reading of a shopping mall that does not seriously engage with questions that arise in history, sociology and economics, remains— however productive a transformation of 'the' canon of English it may enable— a literary reading, not cultural studies" (1995, n.p.). This does not mean, however, that cultural studies overthrows the disciplines, nor that it transcends them in a new unity. Rather it means that any specific project will demand work, unpredictable in advance, that crosses disciplinary lines. It means that one draws on disciplines as needed, critically and reflectively appropriating the most useful knowledge. At times it may be necessary to redo what other disciplines have tried to do but now in ways consistent with the project and assumptions of cultural studies. None of this suggests remastering the disciplines into a new megaformation; rather it suggests a rigorous and pragmatic approach to gaining whatever knowledge is necessary to map a particular context and answer a strategic question. This is its disruptive power, for this very approach to the disciplines, an approach that recognizes their legitimacy even as it refuses their power, challenges the particular disabling effects—rather than the fact—of disciplinarity.

For example, I have argued (Grossberg 1992) that understanding the "becoming conservative" of everyday life and politics in the United States requires an understanding of the state of capitalism and hence some foundational theory and empirical knowledge about contemporary capitalism. But if it is unreasonable to expect to master the highly contested field of economic discourse, it is also irresponsible to simply take a single position—usually a position we think we know and know we like before we begin—as if it were uncontested. Of course, I must admit that by my own standard, my efforts in economics were much too limited, even something of a failure. Rather than undertake the tedious but necessary work of economic detail (for example, studying changes in tax codes and revenues, and debt financing), I engaged in the easier and more abstract (and certainly more glamorous) debates within postfordist and Deleuzean theory. I do not mean to suggest that these debates are not important; I am pointing to a "failure of interdisciplinarity."

REARTICULATING CULTURAL STUDIES

At the same time, a number of more compelling criticisms have challenged many of the most basic concepts and assumptions of cultural studies. Most centrally, the very concept of culture itself has been subjected to rigorous political and analytical scrutiny. Following Bourdieu, the notion of culture as the site of the production of distinctions has been challenged, undermining our ability to assume any qualitative distinctions within the domain of culture as well as the existence of a self-contained category of cultural—creative, signifying—practices, such as literature or art, outside of their institutionalized laws and regulations. Drawing on work on colonialism and race, critics have attacked nostalgic identifications of culture and community, as well as the unproblematic assumption of *national* cultures and whole ways of life. Instead the project of constructing a singular and limited space of culture, whereby culture is located in a place, is understood to be the product of the colonizing and imperializing projects of modern Europe.

Equally important, drawing on Foucault, a number of writers have challenged romantic-aesthetic-ethical conceptions of culture as the product of specific disciplining and governmental strategies of the modern nation-state. This critique has potentially devastating consequences, for it suggests that cultural criticism is itself part of a larger technology of power. The very figure of culture locks cultural studies into structures of ethical discipline. For the notion of culture that animates much of cultural studies involves a double articulation: on the one hand, the projection of a position, constituted by a temporal displacement from some other (e.g., tradition), from which change can be comprehended; and on the other hand, the equation of that position with a standard of judgment from which one can offer a "total qualitative assessment" of such changes. "The idea of culture is a general reaction to a general and major change in the conditions of our common life" (Williams 1958, 295). That is, the very act of producing the concept of culture involves the construction of a place that allows one to both describe and judge the changes in everyday life; it requires at the very least a "court of human appeal," some locatable "higher" standard, to be set over the processes of practical social change. But this is the very foundation of the ethical discipline that critics like Tony Bennett (1993) and Ian Hunter (1988) are attacking. A partial solution may be found in Williams's refusal to locate himself within the "culture and society tradition." He argued that the concept of culture was invented as the recognition of "a practical separation of certain moral and intellectual activities from the driving force of a new kind of society," that is, that the modern is partly constituted by the separation of culture and society. For those authors Williams located in the "culture and society tradition," the separation is taken for granted; culture is simply appropriated and transformed into a position from which that very separation can be described and judged. But Williams refused such a separation. Cultural studies had to reinsert culture into the practical everyday life of people, into the totality of a whole way of life. Yet Williams was never able to actually escape this separation—both in his privileging of certain forms of culture (literature) and in his desire to equate culture with some sort of totality and/ or ethical standard.[7]

Recently, Frow and Morris have argued that such ethical conceptions of culture are simply inadequate descriptions of the ways "culture" is being articulated and deployed in contemporary politics. They argue that "changing the culture" has become "a shorthand but expansive way of challenging the conduct of other people's lives" (1993, vii). It is all about controlling people's behavior; no room for ethics or aesthetics here, except as a disciplining strategy. Culture is imagined as "a plastic medium which politically powerful social elites may remake and remould at will" (vii). In this context, for example, "culture" becomes the preferred explanation of the "failure" of particular national economies. And Samuel Huntington (1993) argues that future world conflict will be defined less by state interest or even ideology than by culture.

Such ethical conceptions of culture are closely related to a set of assumptions in cultural studies that links contemporary historical transformation, the experience of mobility, and the position of marginality. Unlike many other theories of the emergence of the modern (including the "culture and society tradition"), cultural studies is driven less by a vision of a total qualitative transformation of society (e.g., from the traditional to the modern or from community to mass society)—cultural studies was never about the destruction of community—than by a concern for the consequences of new forms and degrees of mobility. These mobilities not only created new positions of marginality but brought them into the center of the social formation.

It is not surprising, then, that cultural studies has tended to equate marginality with the very position described above, a position that culture itself can no longer define. Too often, as a result, cultural studies has romanticized marginality (the position of the outsider, the émigré) or at least ethicized it as a new standard of political and even intellectual judgment.

The weight of these criticisms has to be measured in the context of the need for cultural studies to find new ways of dealing with contemporary forms of globalization without assuming that they are simply more intense forms of older political and economic relations. These apparently new conditions of globalization imbricate all the peoples, commodities, and cultures of the world, albeit in different ways. The result is that the traditional binary models of political struggle—colonizer/colonized, oppressor/oppressed, domination/resistance, repression/transgression—seem inapplicable to a spatial economy of power that cannot be reduced to simple geographical dichotomies—first world/third world, metropolitan/peripheral, local/global. At the very least, the globalization of culture makes the cost of displacing the economic and the political too high. Globalization can no longer be confidently described from the formations of Atlantic culture as the assumed center of the global economy of space. Of course, one needs a theoretical understanding of the nature and stakes of globalization (and a theoretical vocabulary capable of describing different structures and practices of globalization) in order to consider whether the contemporary forms of globalization represent anything new and different in history (Grossberg forthcoming). Without such a theoretical framework, cultural studies is unable to recognize the multiple ways in which transnational flows and relations, in a variety of different formations of colonialism, imperialism, and so forth have been and continue to be constitutive of specific formations of power.

Cultural studies must confront the globalization of culture not merely in terms of the proliferation and mobility of texts and audiences, but also in terms of the movement of culture outside the spaces of any (specific) language. Consequently analysts can no longer confidently assume that they understand how cultural practices are working. The new global economy of culture entails a deterritorialization of culture and its subsequent reterritorialization, which challenges culture's equation with location in a place as locale. Consequently we need to ask how one does "cultural studies" in such global—spatial—conditions, conditions we as intellectuals are implicated in by, at the very least, the somewhat involuntary (albeit somewhat pleasurable) nomadic condition of our particular class fraction. I do not believe that the answers can be found simply through some acknowledgment of our locationality, or some renunciation of ethnocentrism, or some attempt to hide our ethnocentrism in more apocalyptic claims of postmodernity.

Nor can the politics of globalization be understood, in either the first or last instance, as a question of personal identity. I think it is fair to say that recently cultural studies has largely reconstituted itself around questions of the politics of identity and difference. But it also seems to have reached the limit— and hence must confront the limitations—of political struggles organized around notions, however complex, of identity and difference. In the face of globalization we need to analyze the geohistorical mechanisms by which relations have been constructed as differences and politics organized by identities. The real questions are what kinds of differences are effective and where differences make a difference; and the fact is that our theories may be incapable of allowing us to produce the answers. The category of identity needs to be deconstructed, but not necessarily in the sense that postmodernists, postcolonialists, and poststructuralists theorize. We have to locate the power of identity as a political force in the broader context of the new spatial economy, in order to ask why identity has become such a privileged site of struggle. Such a politics would have to think about the affective dimensions of belonging, affiliation, and identification in order to define the places people can belong to and the places people can find their way to. Identity becomes more a political category to be mobilized and laid claim to, a matter of belonging, of the claim to be somewhere and hence with someone. Challenging culture's equation with and location in the form of identity as a difference may enable us to think about the possibilities of a politics that recognizes and is organized around the positivity and singularity of the other.

Finally, globalization raises serious questions about the effectivities and modalities of agency (or articulation). Articulation cannot simply be explained as a matter of polysemy and decoding (notions that can be traced back to Spinoza and Descartes). Nor is it merely cultural studies' attempt to occupy a middle space between essentialist theories (which can vary from a position that asserts that all relations, insofar as they are real, are necessary, to one that simply asserts that there are some necessary relations in the world) and the anti-essentialism of certain poststructuralist theories (which denies the reality of any relation). The fact that articulation involves a kind of strategic anti-essentialism has led some to conclude that strategic essentialism provides an adequate model of agency. I prefer to think of articulation as a way of avoiding the debate altogether (Grossberg 1992, ch. 1). Gilroy's (1993) notion of artic-

ulation as anti-anti-essentialism transforms the question of the reality of relations into a matter of practices and re-places the question back onto the sites
and modes of agency, where it belongs.

CULTURAL STUDIES AND THE
PHILOSOPHY OF CULTURE

While cultural studies has made original and important contributions to our
understanding of the postwar capitalist world, I believe its attempts to respond to the changing conditions and questions of the past few decades have
been significantly less impressive. How do we account for this? On one hand,
I have already suggested that it is the result of a certain theoretical exhaus-
tion, of a failure on the part of cultural studies to theorize in response to its
project/context. It has gotten itself into something of a dead end because it
has become too entrenched in its own theoretical paradigms. In that sense, I
might say that cultural studies has failed to radically contextualize itself in
the face of these new challenges. But on the other hand, the problem may not
be as simple as it first appears, for there are reasons why, in an age of hyper-
theory, so little innovative theoretical work has been done on questions of
globalization, agency, and "otherness" (i.e., the critique of difference) and
their relationship to contemporary culture. Specifically, I believe that the
lack of such work is the result, not of any particular set of *theoretical* assumptions or positions, but of the shared *philosophical* ground of contemporary
theories of culture. I believe that almost all of the available theories of culture
can be traced back to and located within the terrain of a Kantian philosophical discourse. And the framework of the modern philosophical conception of
culture can be found in Kant's project of demonstrating that Man (*sic*), as a
self-legislating being, cannot be an object of scientific knowledge, by establishing the conditions of possibility of all knowledge and experience.

For the moment, I think that one can understand this discursive Kantian
construction of culture by identifying three founding assumptions or logics.
First, by setting up an absolute distinction between the noumena (the real in
itself) and the phenomena (the experienced real), Kant set in place a logic of
lack and mediation. In the move into various post-Kantian philosophies (including phenomenology and structuralism), Kant's formal structures are replaced by social structures of communication and signification. The result is
that culture is close to if not identified with consciousness as the middle
space of experience and human existence. According to Rosaldo, modern
thought conceives of culture within the "stark Manichean choice between

order and chaos" (1989, 98); culture is the medium of information—the supplement—which substitutes for some lack (e.g., of genetic coding, of access to the real). Culture is the agency by which the chaos of reality is transformed into the ordered sense of human reality. Without culture, reality would be simply unavailable, nothing more than James's booming, buzzing confusion. With culture, reality is always already semanticized. The logic of lack and mediation thus not only erases the real but predefines every possibility of production (or articulation) as a particular kind of social construction, and places philosophical anthropology at the center of modern thought.

Second, by separating space and time as the two a priori forms, Kant instituted a logic of dimensions. This separation, and the subsequent privileging of time over space, ensures that culture and subjectivity—since the unity of the subject depends upon the unity of time—are identified with temporality and history, and that space largely disappears as a theoretical or analytical category. Even reality itself, at least insofar as it is available to human beings (which excludes purely speculative and metaphysical discourses) is itself temporal. Third, the question of boundaries of interiority—of belonging to a singular class or set—and exteriority—or otherness—is recast as the problem of identity and difference, of essence and existence.

It is my contention, to be argued I hope in a future book, that these three logics, taken together, define the assumptions underlying the contradictory terrain of modern and contemporary theories of culture. But the issue is not merely a philosophical one, for there is another question that has to be raised: Why has this philosophical discourse had such powerful control for so long? Or, to put it another way, What relations, if any, exist between the philosophical direction inaugurated by Kant and the broader economic, political, and discursive context of the emerging European modern nation-state and all that it entailed?[8] The force of challenging what I call "the victory of culture" is, I believe, political and contextual at two levels: First, it attempts to make visible the complicitous relations between this space of culture and the structures and technologies of modern power; and second, the political demands of the contemporary world challenge the theoretical and political utility of this philosophical logic of culture. To put it differently, if cultural studies rests upon a philosophical discourse that is closely articulated into the very relations of power that it wants to dismantle, then it has to critically examine its own categories and the ways they are constrained by and articulated on this philosophical ground.

But if we are to move cultural studies onto a new ground or at least in a new direction, where it may in fact be able to respond to the challenges of the contemporary global context, we have to do more than just critique and deconstruct the Kantian foundations of the discourse of culture. We have to begin to produce cultural studies once again, this time by linking it not only with its context but also with a non-Kantian philosophical discourse. After all, if the philosophies we have don't seem to enable us to describe our reality very well, perhaps it is necessary to imagine a different philosophy—which is not to say a new philosophy since, in many ways, such a philosophy may entail a return to philosophies articulated at other times (e.g., premodern) and other places (e.g., non-Western).[9] Such a philosophy may offer a way of describing and constructing a different reality, a reality that is still ours but perhaps with a different future. But of course, every philosophical bone in our discursive body will tell us that it is impossible to escape the logic of Kantianism (e.g., mediation, temporality, identity, and difference); in fact, that impossibility is one of the products of this discourse. Obviously, modern thought/power tells us it is impossible to move outside its boundaries. But what else would you expect! While I do not believe that we can escape our social and cultural determinations, we can rearticulate them. We can challenge our inherited philosophical common sense in the name of the political struggles that must be carried on if we are to contribute as intellectuals to the creation of a better world in the face of the pressing challenges posed by the world in which we are all living, albeit in different ways and places.

In this project of elaborating what I call a "spatial materialism,"[10] I have found useful the work of Foucault and Deleuze and Guattari (and their return to Spinoza). Their philosophy comes closer than any I have found to avoiding the space of Kantian modernism. It is important, however, to remember that I want to use them to construct the philosophical ground of an alternative cultural studies; I do not want to give up the ground or the space of cultural studies. I will briefly comment on their position vis-à-vis the first two logics described above.

Their philosophy attempts to describe the modalities, the types of organizations, the "geometric mechanisms" by which different kinds of individualities (without implying identities) and subjects (without implying subjectivities) are produced in and articulated into specific configurations. The notion of geometric mechanisms, introduced by Kellert (1993) in his description of chaos theory, proposes a model of explanation that is neither causal nor predictive, and a model of agency that is neither subjective nor mechanistic. It is a matter of reality producing itself; it is both produced (contingent) and productive (real). Reality, which is nothing but the effects of its own rearticulation, cannot be bracketed out from cultural studies, nor can it be treated as if it were only and always mediated by the categories of human intelligibility.[11] Instead, cultural practices are complex technologies and organizations that produce the real as maps of power. They impose a particular conduct and organization not only on specific individualities and collectivities, but also on particular planes of effects.

Reality, then, "consists of" events that are definable and describable only by their affect, that is, by their ability to affect and their susceptibility to being affected. These "becomings" can be mapped only as lines across space, along the trajectories of their effectivities, rather than as temporal continuities and discontinuities (i.e., rather than as questions of reproduction or deferral).[12] Reality as the effect of power at every level has to be conceptualized in terms of mobilities rather than change, of lines of intensities rather than identities. It is a matter of orientations and directions, of entries and exits, rather than structures and processes. In this way, their philosophy spatializes reality so that time is no longer separated from space but is itself spatialized. The result is a philosophy in which change or transformation is more fundamental than stability or identity, and in which otherness or singularity is more fundamental than either identity or difference. More concretely, it means that we have to see cultural practices as places where multiple trajectories of effects and investment are articulated, as the point of intersection and negotiation of radically different kinds of vectors of determination—including material, affective, libidinal, semiotic, semantic, and so on.

I am aware that the language here is so awkward and foreign as to render the possibility of an alternative cultural studies suspect. Obviously this problem cannot be avoided since Kantianism has become, quite literally, our common sense and is deeply inscribed within our language. On the other hand, I do think that any effort to use such a non-Kantian philosophy as tools that will enable better analyses of some of the political dilemmas facing cultural studies will have to confront the problem of language, for it must speak beyond the audience for and the demands of the vocabulary itself.

ANOTHER STORY

The story I have just told is, of course, something of a fabrication, necessitated in part by the nature of this volume. The project of collecting my own essays, spanning almost two decades, has forced me to confront the contingency of narratives. In rereading the essays collected here (as well as all the essays that did not make it into the book for whatever reason), I was struck by the similarities and differences in the narratives and structures embodied within and across individual essays. But even more powerfully, I was struck by the fact that the essays confronted me with the contradictions in my recollection of the trajectory of my intellectual career. For it is clear that the project that arrives only at the end of the story I have just told has been there all along. I have always attempted to push the theoretical foundations of cultural studies onto new grounds so that, in fact, the appeal to Deleuze and Guattari and to Foucault has always been a constitutive part of my attempt to theorize culture.

As the essays collected here demonstrate, I have spent much of my academic life trying to define, defend, and practice cultural studies (see Grossberg 1992 and 1997). But the essays also reveal that my relationship to cultural studies (or at least to those British and American varieties in which I was educated) has always been fraught and ambivalent. My work has always been an attempt to think through the relationships among the political effects that are organized and sustained in, around, and through the popular, the (ethical) demands of progressive politics, and the philosophical possibilities of critical work.

I do not intend to bore you with my autobiography—Jewish baby boomer, etc., etc. Suffice it to say that when I abandoned my studies of science (biochemistry and genetics) at the University of Rochester, I found myself pulled in two directions. On the one hand, my real intellectual passions were philosophical, and I was fortunate enough to have professors like Richard Taylor (ethics and Greek philosophy), Keith Lehrer (epistemology), Henry Stolnitz (aesthetics), Colin Turbayne (on metaphoricity), Henry Khyberg (logic and philosophy of science), and Lewis Beck (on Kant). This passion was supplemented with marvelous professors from other departments like Hayden White (intellectual history) and Norman O. Brown (the psychoanalytical guru). On the other hand, I was encouraged by professors like William Hamilton (the death of god theologian), Gerald Ramsey (contemporary literature, who also directed my undergraduate thesis), Jim Kaufman (history), and Loren Baritz (cultural history and American studies; he taught a class on Marilyn Monroe as a cultural symbol) to think about the postwar American culture that I loved and the countercultural politics in which I was deeply invested. When it came time to write my undergraduate thesis, I was torn between writing on my philosophical fascination with Spinoza (!) and exploring the politics of popular music and generational identity. I chose the latter and wrote a series of essays, embarrassingly titled "Reflections on an Oak by an Acorn." It was in this space between philosophy and contemporary cultural criticism that I discovered cultural studies, almost accidentally, as it were. Fortuitously, the history department at Rochester had a formal (albeit rather ineffective) relationship with the Centre for Contemporary Cultural Studies at the University of Birmingham in England, and with the help of a Woodrow Wilson Fellowship, and under the pressure of avoiding the selective service system, I was able to spend part of a year (1968–1969) studying with Richard Hoggart and Stuart Hall (and visiting faculty like Andrew Bear and Alan Shuttleworth). This was, of course, relatively early in the Centre's history (it had been founded in 1964). That time in Birmingham has had a profound (and certainly unexpected) influence on almost every aspect of my life, especially my intellectual trajectory and professional career.

I appeared at the Centre, an American "hippie," yet relatively wealthy by English standards (with my Wilson money, I was one of the few students who could afford central heating). The Centre was housed on the outskirts of the campus (a location that was both significant and fortuitous), in a small Quonset hut. Life at the Centre was organized around a series of weekly seminars. The mornings were often spent with Richard Hoggart and the other graduate students learning the art—or was it a skill—of close textual reading, reading for tone and value, as Hoggart called it. Richard would bring in a mimeographed sample from some text—he started out with literature but started slipping in more popular texts—and tell us to analyze it. Inevitably, after we had done our best, both individually and collectively, he would demonstrate what we could have/should have done. The afternoons were dominated by the theory seminar, which I suppose can best be described as a collective effort to define the project of cultural studies and to find an adequate theoretical basis for its researches. During my time there, we read many of the so-called founding texts (e.g., the work of Raymond Williams), as well as interpretive and phenomenological sociology (including symbolic interactionism and ethnomethodology), structural anthropology and semiotics, humanistic marxism, rhetorical theory, and anything else we could find. It was an eclectic effort to give content to what was still perceived as a necessary but shapeless enterprise. Other afternoons were spent with an equally eclectic assortment of guest speakers or in research seminars. In these, either individual students reported on their own research—I was, for example, continuing my undergraduate thesis on the politics of postwar popular music and youth cultures—or we worked on what was the first collective research project of the Centre, an analysis of "Cure for Marriage," a short story from a "women's magazine." Unfortunately, the summary paper from this early feminist cultural studies project apparently has been lost.

I never completed my researches or my thesis. There were, I am now convinced, a number of reasons for this: I did not have the appropriate theoretical tools; I did not understand the appropriate level of analysis (or at least, the level at which I could comfortably operate); and, once again, political circumstances intervened. Through a rather strange series of events (how much of our lives are determined because we are at the right/wrong place at the wrong/right time?), I became involved in a strike at the University of Birmingham (the strike headquarters was, unbeknown to Hoggart, in the Centre) and, as a result, came under some pressure to leave the country. At about the same time, I became friends with a French-speaking Swiss itinerant anarchist theater commune, Le Treateaux Libres, who were performing in England. When they invited me to join them traveling and performing across the continent, I was uncertain. It was, eventually, a most generous evening of drink and conversation with Richard Hoggart that gave me the courage to abandon the security of my studies and join Le Treateaux. I will not try to recount my time with this group, or to conjecture about its enormous impact on me. Suffice it to say that it often made painfully obvious to me not only the contradictions in the countercultural politics of the time, but also the inadequacies in our understanding of the contemporary workings of power. It also forced me to evaluate the aesthetic and communicative basis of much of avant-garde politics and my own relationship to politics, culture, and intellectual life. And it also made me realize just how deeply middle-class I was. The group, while certainly successful (having won awards at the festival of Nancy and been featured on the cover of *Der Speigel*) eventually broke up when confronted with the prospect of financial success—not an unusual history for politically progressive groups. And since I was now free of my obligations to the selective service (again through a series of fortuitous circumstances), I returned to the United States.

On Stuart Hall's advice, I applied to do graduate studies at the University of Illinois, with James W. Carey, in the Institute of Communications Research. Actually, I don't think I realized that I was to be in a department of communication until I arrived. I studied cultural theory (and American studies) with Jim, communication theory with Jesse Delia, literary theory with Cary Nelson, social theory with Norm Denzin, semiotics with William McLean, and phenomenological hermeneutics with Paul Ricoeur at the University of Chicago. My studies began where my work at Birmingham had left off, and I spent most of my time rereading British cultural studies and reading phenomenology and phenomenological social and literary theory, marxism, and semiotic, structuralist, and poststructuralist theory. My dissertation was a failed attempt to bring philosophy and cultural studies together, by developing a hermeneutic-phenomenologically based cultural studies around the figures of Raymond Williams and Martin Heidegger. It has never seen and, god willing, will never see the light of another day. After a year teaching at Purdue University, I returned in 1976 to the University of Illinois, in the Department of Speech Communication, to teach the philosophy of communication and media studies, but it did not take long for me to redefine my classes around cultural studies and theory and popular culture. Almost immediately I also began teaching classes on rock and roll and postwar youth culture, despite the objections of many people in the university. Cary Nelson and I and a few other professors set about the task of making a space where interdisciplinary interest in theory (at the time largely literary theory and philosophy) could flourish. The result was the establishment of the Unit for Criticism and Interpretive Theory, one of the first interdisciplinary programs in the U.S. academy devoted to critical and cultural theory. And there I stayed . . . until moving to the University of North Carolina in 1994.

By replaying something of my own biography, I do not mean to claim any determinative relationship, although I do think that biographies can be deployed in ways that attempt to provide such groundings. Instead I merely want to highlight the fact that the particular trajectory of my work that is presented here and traced out in the essays collected here can be located in my own intellectual and political history. The point of this story is that my work has always tried to bring together cultural studies, philosophy, and popular culture. At the same time, I have attempted to defend and practice cultural studies' interdisciplinary project while exploring its relations with— its contribution and challenges to—the discipline of communication.

Thus I would argue that there were at least three different forces propelling my work in the same direction, within cultural studies but toward a non-Kantian (at various times, I have thought of it as postmodern, nonmodern, and countermodern) position of Foucault and Deleuze and Guattari. First, there is my abiding passion for philosophy and the sheer pleasure I have always found in philosophical (yes, abstract) argument. This may partly explain my propensity to categorize and schematize positions, for I have always found this to be a useful way to think about the relations between different assumptions (and hence to open up new possibilities), without claiming to identify the *proper* position.[13]

Second, much of my work has been driven by my ambiguous relationship to the field of communication. I have always been deeply suspicious of the concept of communication and the enormous power it has in both academic and popular discourses. I have never been comfortable with its ubiquity; its intentional vagueness, which allowed it to impose an apparent unity on radically diverse practices; its inherent circularity, grounded in a largely unexplored set of philosophical assumptions; its unfounded claim to embody a democratic impulse; and its self-presentation as the most human of practices. I was amazed by how often an appeal to the concept of communication was assumed to solve all sorts of theoretical and political problems. I was perturbed by the lack of reflection on how and why the concept has been deployed, on the genealogy of the concept itself. In fact, I quickly came to the conclusion that we were living in an organization of discursive and ideological power that could be described as "the regime of communication." Speaking as a "philosopher of communication," I found myself calling for an anticommunicational philosophy of communication. And speaking within cultural studies, I argued against the tendency to understand culture as if it were identical to (some assumed model of) communication. But I was also deeply suspicious of the "aesthetic" alternative that was being offered in poststructuralist critical theory, championed primarily by literary theorists. Not only was I troubled by its obvious elitism (an elitism that seems to be unavoidable within literary studies); I was also convinced that all it offered was a somewhat truncated model of culture as communication, for it continued to assume that culture is (1) signifying and (2) located at the intersection of text and subject—whether as encoder or decoder, whether producing or produced by the text.

Third, having failed to find a viable way of talking about the relationships between popular music, everyday life, and politics during my time at CCCS, I returned to this task after my dissertation (see Grossberg 1997). I must admit that almost everything I have written about rock music is, no doubt, too theoretical, but I was convinced that the project depended on developing a theoretical understanding of the functioning of popular music in general and of rock and roll in particular. I never really got around to the task of developing a vocabulary to describe significant differences and developments within popular music, for my attention was turned to the more specific relationship between rock and the new conservatism (Grossberg 1992). My efforts to theorize popular music reinforced my doubts about both communicative and aesthetic models of culture and led me to turn my attention to the question of affect as the energy that defines our investments in reality. I argued against seeing affect as anarchic excess threatening to disrupt the structures of power. Instead affect had to be understood as a structured plane of effects defining one dimension of human existence; moreover that structure is the ongoing product of struggles to control people's conduct. While I never equated affect with emotion (which I saw as the intersection of affect and narrative ideology), I left it rather ambiguous since it encompassed a wide range of qualitative states, including moods, mattering maps, and energization. But the point about affect was that, unlike ideology, its primary mode of existence was quantitative, for it always involved a measurable degree of intensity.

Of course, the careful reader will now realize that the attempt to develop a theory of affect takes me back to Deleuze and Guattari, although I am forced to agree with Brian Massumi's criticism (forthcoming) that I have yet to adequately link my own cultural notion of affect (as different organizations of investment) and Deleuze and Guattari's notion of affect as effectivity. This is a crucial issue and it is worth addressing here, at least briefly. I would now argue that what links the two dimensions of affect is the fact that both are grounded in a quantitative notion of intensity or energy. It is as lines of intensity that events exist (as becomings) for Deleuze and Guattari, and it is as organizations of intensity that qualitatively different planes of effects are constituted. That is, what distinguishes different modes of cultural affect (moods, mattering maps, emotions, desire, the multiplicity of pleasures, etc.) are the different ways in which they are organized, which in turn define the different manifestations of their virtual effects.[14] Thus I understand the question of "the popular" to involve a struggle to control the virtual affects that particular discourses may produce under determinate conditions.[15] In other words, it is a question of controlling the effects of particular practices by articulating them into specific affective organizations, defining the virtual quality of their effects. In fact, I wonder whether signification (cognitive meaning) and ideology themselves may be seen as affective states, organizations of intensity that have particular effects, for example, producing subjectivity/consciousness/intentionality.

In this way, human reality can be seen to be continuous and contiguous with nonhuman reality, for they are both the production and product of intensities (energy). The distinction is only a matter of the ways they are articulated, both next to and distant from each other. And through such a philosophy of affect, I find myself returning to a model of cultural practices as "busy intersections" or, more accurately, as places constructed by the multiple foldings of different affective planes—each with its own imposed organization—into one another. So it makes sense to say that culture is inseparable from a distribution of space and a distribution in space. Finally, the detour through affect brings me back to my investment in cultural studies as the analysis of the contextual relations between discourse, everyday life, and the agencies of power, so as to open up new possibilities for reconfiguring the context of power.

JUST WHEN YOU THOUGHT YOU WERE THROUGH . . .

All of the essays gathered together in this book attempt to address the question, either explicitly or implicitly, What is cultural studies? My decision to publish them now is the result, in part, of my belief that the question is more important now than ever, for as cultural studies has become more successful, it is also more susceptible to being both appropriated and attacked. Furthermore, I do believe that these essays document part of a history of cultural studies in the United States—a history to which these essays contributed—which is often ignored and sometimes erased in current discussions. Part of this history is embodied in the diverse and sometimes obscure places the essays were published. But one has to be careful not to read this distribution too quickly or literally. Sometimes what appears obscure from one discipline or paradigm might be quite central in another. Sometimes these were choices I made to support a particular journal or project. But sometimes they were the only choices available to me, for along the way I encountered lots of hostility—toward theory in general or toward particular theories, toward my politics or the politicization of academic work, toward cultural studies, toward interdisciplinarity, and toward my feeble attempts to cross disciplinary lines. It would be interesting to write an academic history of cultural studies (for example) through an analysis of letters of rejection. I remember submitting one of my first papers—it was on marxism and culture—to a major communications journal. The letter of rejection came with a two-page single-spaced list of words that the editor demanded I define for the reader. I remember wondering why he thought it appropriate to ask me to provide an introduction to theory (presumably in every paper) when similar demands were not made of every contribution. I had to fight for my right to speak, and I was not alone. I think it is important that we remember that.

To conclude, then, I want to acknowledge briefly some of the choices that I have made. After all, publishing a collection of essays written over the course of two decades poses some immediate problems. First, there is the threat of redundancy. While I have attempted to limit the amount of redundancy, redundancy after all is a fact of intellectual life, but more importantly it can be productive. It may involve elaborations or subtle shifts in emphasis and direction; it may inscribe different takes on the same theme, attempts to try new vocabularies and new frames, or to find better articulations of a problematic and a position. These essays are, after all, only provisional takes, attempts to move without ever knowing where I am trying to get to. In their very redundancies, they embody something about the exigencies of doing cultural studies in their different places.

Second, there is the choice of how to present the essays: thematically or chronologically. In some ways, I would have preferred the latter, because it would provide material evidence of the actual labor of intellectual investigation, with all of its fragility, instability, and repetitiveness. I also believe it highlights certain continuities: a commitment to a contextualist and materialist vision of cultural studies; a need to interrogate the theoretical and philosophical possibilities of cultural theory; and a project of defining a position capable of confronting the contemporary political scene. However, I have in fact chosen to divide the essays into three thematic groups (while maintaining the marks of the chronology) in the hope that this will make it easier for readers to approach these essays with their own agendas in mind.

Third, I have to think about the questions and criticisms that colleagues— both sympathetic and not so sympathetic—have raised over the years. Some of the things they have pointed to I would change if I could, but I have chosen not to do so (except to eliminate repetitions). Other things I would not change, and still others I know I cannot change. My work is admittedly abstract and speculative. Like Deleuze, I believe that philosophy seeks to make concepts that can touch and affect the real. Moreover, I want to find a way to interrupt the comfortable rhythms of narrative coherence. While I want to leap metonymically, back and forth and across the concrete and the abstract, I want to avoid the pitfalls of postmodern synecdoche, which lets the particular stand in for the general. This no doubt contributes to the fact that my writing is, too often, too difficult. I take this criticism seriously if only because I would like to think that some people might find my work useful and that it may offer some new directions for both intellectual and political endeavors. I have no doubt that many of these essays could be rewritten more effectively, but I fear that those who found them inaccessible would still find them so, even if better written. I apologize to those who put in the effort to read these essays and, in the end, do not find the effort worthwhile, but I hope that there are some out there who do find their efforts rewarded. At the same time, I do not believe that accessibility is a criterion of potentially useful knowledge, at least not in the first instance. I do not know of any correlation between accessibility and significance, which is not to claim that inaccessibility is a measure of significance. I would like to think that at least part of the difficulty of my work is the result of my project: to find a radically contextual theoretical vocabulary that can describe the ongoing production of the real as an organization of inequality through an analysis of cultural events. Moreover, such a vocabulary would have to offer a viable notion of agency without falling back on models that privilege either human subjectivity or processes of epistemological mediation. I am interested in a theory of how reality is made, but I am not willing to assume that human beings are consciously in control of the mechanisms or practices of that making.

In the contemporary political climate, where self-reflexivity is too often reduced to a litany of cultural identities—I am middle-aged, middle-class, Jewish, heterosexual, male, married, with one infant son, of Eastern European descent, and so on—pronouns have become as significant as the identities they are assumed to represent. The problem of how one may speak of and for others has become almost insurmountable. The political intellectual is caught in an impossible dilemma: either constructing or negating the other. Consequently, "we" has become one of the more dangerous words to use: Let the speaker beware! But I choose to use it and I will continue to do so, although I am constantly challenged by its exclusionary operation. After all, it is claimed, the very presumption of inclusion that "we" carries with it also entails the exclusion of significant fractions of the population. But I do not accept the assertion that "we" necessarily reinscribes the particular economy of space and identity on which so much of contemporary politics seems to be based. Apart from the fact that I am increasingly opposed to political strategies that privilege identity (and that conflate subjectivity, cultural identity, and political agency), I am also convinced that this view of the deployment of "we" depends entirely upon an unacceptable—referential—theory of language. My use of "we" is neither referential nor singular. It is intended to be

CULTURAL THEORY,

CULTURAL STUDIES

Interpreting the "Crisis" of Culture

in Communication Theory

As the number of different theories and approaches to mass communication grows, it becomes more obvious that a way is needed to talk about the relationships among them and to identify their similarities and differences. One approach that I propose to explore in this article is to compare the work of several theorists in terms of their visions of the "crisis,"[1] brought on by the processes of modernization, which faces contemporary culture.

Relating mass communication theory to the idea of a cultural crisis is not without precedent. Alan Blum (1961) suggested that there may be a strong connection between researchers' assumptions about the inherent failures of modern society and their findings about how communication functions within it. Blum, however, fails to take into account that researchers' assumptions about the nature of the failure of modern society may differ from each other, and instead assimilated all of them under "mass society theory." By examining particular theorists' underlying assumptions concerning the principal danger confronting modern society, we may be able to better understand the diversity of views offered of the nature and function of communication in society.

To begin we must identify the variety of images of the cultural crisis operative in contemporary thought. I have distinguished six views of the crisis: informational, subjective, structural, interactional, transcendental, and representational.[2] The first, a view of the crisis as one of information, is perhaps the most prevalent in our scientifically oriented culture. In this view the crisis is not located in the social changes that have taken place, but rather in our failure to respond properly to these changes. To know what would constitute a proper response one must have accurate, descriptive information about the world. Thus the crisis is located in our inadequate knowledge and in those attitudes that interfere with the acquisition of this information. This view is closely tied to an understanding of communication as a process of transmission, the movement of "pieces" of information from one place to another; it is through such a process as well that the attitudes and behaviors of individuals can be appropriately modified. Thus we find the "informational" view often conjoined with a second view of communication, as a process of persuasion.

The "subjective" view of the cultural crisis is not very influential in mass communication theory, although its influence is strong in general discussions of modern culture. Basically, according to this position, the crisis lies in the loss of "true" subjectivity or individuality in the face of some claim of commonality and equality. The great achievements, values, virtues, and creative potential of Western civilization are losing the battle (a metaphor quite common in such writers as, e.g., Ortega y Gasset) to the masses gathered under the banner of democracy and "mass culture." It is not difficult to see why such a position would contribute little to mass communication theory; it unambiguously defines it as the enemy. Nevertheless such a view embodies a commonly held view of communication: communication is the process of transmitting or sharing essentially private and subjective thoughts or meanings.

The third or "structural" view of the crisis of culture is built upon theories of symbolic structures or systems. These systems act as filters or mediating screens located between man and the world and are the source of the meanings and interpretations we give to our experiences. Thus the crisis of modern culture is understood as the domination of some particular symbolic structure and the subsequent control that structure has over our worldview. Communication, in such a view, belongs to the symbolic structures or codes rather than to the individuals who appear to use them. It is the system rather than the speaker that is the source of meaning.

Perhaps the most common understanding of the cultural crisis is what can be described as the "interactional" view. In its simplest form, this view points to a lack of shared values, norms, and meanings underlying interpersonal relationships and is closely tied to the idea that modern society involves a loss of community. Deriving from Tonnies's distinction between *Gemeinschaft* and *Gesellschaft,* this idea characterizes two forms of social organization, community and society. In community, people who are essentially alike and homogeneous in beliefs, values, and experiences are united by "reciprocal binding sentiments." The means of social control are informal and the individual is subsidiary to the social totality. On the other hand, society is built upon a formal, that is, contractual system of social control and is unified not by sharedness but through a mutual dependence necessitated by an increased division of labor. Consequently relationships become increasingly competitive and impersonal; the individual is isolated, increasingly insecure, and "alienated." In this view communication is conceived as an ongoing process of situated, symbolic interactions through which shared meanings are reciprocally negotiated and created, thus maintaining the fabric of social life.

The fifth or "transcendental" view of the crisis lays the blame squarely on the shoulders of our contemporary beliefs about the nature of being human. Insofar as we have increasingly come to think of ourselves as the masters of the universe and of our own existence, we have lost a sense of our rootedness, of our grounding in or dependence upon something outside of our understanding and control. Because we conceive of knowledge and language as tools for our projects, we use them to define the real as that which is amenable to our manipulations and control. Consequently we cut ourselves off from that other domain that has traditionally served as a wellspring or foundation on which we may ground our sense of ourselves and the world. A "transcendental" view, not surprisingly, will try to reinsert the "transcendental" (grounding) nature of communication. Communication is not merely a tool to be used for some human purpose, whether that purpose is transmitting information or creating shared meanings. Instead communication is seen as the source of social life, "a living process in which a community of life is lived out" (Gadamer 1975, 404). Almost like a deity existing outside human existence as its cause, communication is posited as a given rather than a human creation. It is the source of the possibility of social life and shared meaning, for it is only within communication that intersubjectivity becomes possible. A "transcendental" view points to communication as having already opened up the space in which interaction can occur before we can attempt to manipulate it as a medium for our projects.

The final, "representational" view of the cultural crisis has not yet entered into discussions of mass communication, but deserves to be mentioned because of its increasing exposure through the work of Roland Barthes (1972) and Michel Foucault (1970). Basically, in such a view the contemporary crisis is the result of the enduring power of a number of "myths," in particular the myth of the subject and the myth of meaning. While we have increasingly lost faith in the ability of signs to carry meaning (either as a subjective reference back to a subject or an objective reference to a world), we find ourselves unable to accept the consequences of the loss of these myths. Because these theories are relatively recent, however, it is difficult to project their possible implications for communication theory.

Using these six views of the cultural crisis, I shall next identify how they operate in a number of current theories, beginning with the so-called mainstream or effects research.

The roots of communication "effects" research are in the liberal Weltanschauung. Liberalism, it has often been noted, is historically connected with the various processes of modernization: the growth of democracy, of science, and of industrialization. It is not surprising, therefore, that its staunchest supporters have arisen within the United States. Liberalism can be characterized in terms of three basic concepts: individualism, science, and progress.

The assumption of the absolute value and primacy of the individual is most obvious in the liberal theory of political freedom that granted rights to the individual based upon the laws of nature. This belief in the autonomous self was expressed in an atomistic theory of society, that is, the view that society is created through the free agreement of individuals. Faith in science is grounded in the autonomy and ability of human (i.e., individual) reason and involves a unique combination of rationalism and empiricism. It was assumed that the individual mind could discover the laws governing the machinery of the universe through scientific observation and objective reason. Consequently, ignorance replaced sin as the great evil, information was salvation, and power the reward. A belief in progress, the inherent forward motion of human history, was necessary as an argument against both pessimistic interpretations of history and views of humans that challenged their autonomy (e.g., Freud, Darwin). It is this optimistic vision of the future, built upon a metaphysical individualism and an epistemological scientism, that gave American social thought in general, and communication theory in particular, its own unique flavor.

The liberal view of the cultural crisis serves to define significant aspects of contemporary mass communication research.[3] Although most contemporary mainstream researchers no longer recognize their debt to the liberal Weltanschauung, that does not lessen its foundational significance for this tradition.

The liberal definition of the crisis, then, would be most closely related to the "informational" view, through a belief in the efficacy of knowledge. Historically, liberals acknowledged a crisis brought on by the processes of modernization, but they tended to ascribe it to ignorance rather than social change. The crisis for them was merely a new form of a problem that has existed throughout human history: ignorance, ideology, and the tyranny of authority. It was inappropriate to locate the crisis in a new form of social organization or new modes of communication. On the contrary, for the liberal the new forms of social organization and of communications opened up, perhaps for the first time, the possibility of a society built on the free exchange of ideas and information between rational individuals. Community has not been destroyed; instead patterns of interpersonal association have become more rational and open to choice. The real crisis was located in the need for objective (i.e., nonideological) information on which to base decisions; once scientific research had gathered this information, ways of disseminating it would have to be found. The result of this would be the creation of a democracy built upon a process of rational decision making and scientific problem solving. Therefore, in the liberal view, the study of the role and effects of the new mass media was essentially to fight the crisis of ignorance and ideology under the banner of individualism and science.

The commitments to individualism and science characterize the commonality of contemporary mainstream communication research. As a result of the commitment to individualism, communication was seen in terms of its relationship to individuals rather than to social forces or institutions,[4] and mass communication theorists turned to psychology and social psychology. Behaviorism, as the dominant psychology of that time, defined much of the early research. Newer psychological theories were gradually adopted by communication theorists, but the commitment to individualism and psychology has remained.

The study of communication was seen from its very beginnings as a scientific endeavor. This was a natural outgrowth of the liberal's view of the crisis as involving a loss of certainty and a lack of objective knowledge, conditions that intensified the threat of irrationality. Science provided both the model of successful rational thinking and the means for assuring its attainment by the masses (Albig 1939, 431). Thus, for example, Lasswell argued that the function of science was to facilitate "efficient communication" where efficiency is understood as "the degree that rational judgments are facilitated" (1971, 93).

More importantly, however, the faith in science required that researchers be able to objectively measure the concepts they used and to manipulate them experimentally. Consequently the notion of communication itself had to be quantifiable and was defined in terms of its informational and influential value to provide the field with its necessary tools. For instance, Schramm, one of the leaders in the emergence of mass communication as an organized field of study, defines communication "simply by saying that it is the sharing of an orientation toward a set of informational signs" (1971, 13). While expressing the sentiment that information should be defined broadly, he nevertheless goes on to limit it to terms amenable to direct quantification: "It is any content that reduces uncertainty or the number of alternative possibilities in a situation" (13). This supported the liberal's view that what needed to be communicated were scientifically derived descriptions of the environment.

There is, however, another side of communication that had to be considered. Communication was and continued to be used to manipulate the opinions and actions of individuals. Therefore the persuasive possibilities of communication required scientific investigation as well. Such investigations would potentially inoculate people against manipulation, and, in the right hands, this knowledge could be used to help construct a more rational society, one in which manipulation via communication would no longer be required.

Thus mainstream mass communication theory can be directly related to the liberal interpretation of the modern crisis as essentially an informational one. The connection resulted in a series of methodological, normative, and definitional decisions that still ground the mainstream tradition of theory and research.

Cultural theories, while united in their opposition to mainstream research, differ in their understanding of communication and the cultural crisis. Harold Innis was one of the first to include the relationship of communication and culture as a key element in his worldview. Innis saw the crisis of culture, in this case for Canada, in terms of the threat of cultural domination. As has been persuasively argued by both Theall (1975) and Carey (1975b, 28–29), Innis saw Canada as poised between the then two largest empires: Britain and America. In addition to the socioeconomic ties with Britain and America, which dated back to Canadian origins, the time at which Innis wrote was marked by the increasing effectiveness and sophistication of American communication systems. Built upon an economically based technology, U.S. communications, he felt, struck "at the heart of cultural life in Canada" (1952, 19). It is not surprising, therefore, that Innis articulated an interpretation of the role of communication in cultural life built upon the central images of empire and bias.

His reading of economic history led him to focus on the role of communication (and transportation) through the lens of a technological determinism. Culture came to be seen as dependent upon, derived from, even "epiphenomenal of" (see Carey 1975b) communication technology. Concerned with understanding the significance of the threats represented by the two empires, Innis looked to the "biases" of communication in its various technological forms. He argued that particular biases of communication were partly determinative of particular forms of social organization; the forms of social organization themselves, in turn, could be interpreted as distributions of political power based upon technologically determined "monopolies of knowledge."

Innis identifies two forms of bias: time-binding and space-binding. The British empire, with its great burden of tradition and history, was seen as embodying a time bias, and the American empire, so conscious of its spatial freedom and so committed to control and unity across that space, as embodying a space bias. As Canada was precariously located between these two empires and between these two biases, it was natural to interpret the uniqueness of the Canadian experience in the possibility of mediating between them. Innis clearly believes that the ideal culture would be one in which the two biases are balanced (see 1951, 85). Innis thus provides a striking example of the way in which a theory of communication can be understood in the context of a perceived crisis at the heart of cultural life.

It is but a short step from Innis's rich and complex theory of communication to McLuhan's global observations. McLuhan (1967) inherited from Innis a view of technological determinism, but he places it within the context of a global crisis of the alienation of consciousness and perception. McLuhan defines culture using three terms: oral, print, and electronic media. The first two correspond generally to Innis's time and space biases. But while Innis sees the ideal as a mediation between opposing forces of technological determinism, McLuhan tends to see it as a return to many of the characteristics of the oral culture—the recreation of the whole human and community life. McLuhan's solution rests upon a concept of communication defined solely in terms of technology. The crisis results from the inability or unwillingness of contemporary cultures to flow with the historical forces of technological communications. The decreasing influence of McLuhan in communication theory may be due in part to his essentially passive rendering of the role of the individual in the crisis of culture.

Both Innis and McLuhan, then, hold a variation of a "structural" view of the crisis of modern culture. Communication is seen as a filter that organizes and interprets our social existence. The meaningfulness of our experience is not within our control, but is determined by the structure of a particular (in this case, technological) system. And for both, the crisis of culture is understood in terms of the domination of one system over other potential systems.

The Chicago school of social thought, rooted in pragmatism, is another uniquely American tradition, best represented in the works of John Dewey. For Dewey and all the members of the Chicago school, the crisis of contemporary culture was at the very core of the American experience. Responding to Turner's "frontier thesis," Dewey (1927) argues that the true source of the American promise was embodied in the creation of communities in the Midwest and New England. It was here that the very spirit of democracy was made active in both political and everyday life. The crisis for Dewey was the eclipse of community and democracy resulting from the forces of modernization. Thus the problem of community became central; his work focused on the role of language and communication in the creation of community.

Belman (1977) has argued that the work of the Chicago school, and of Dewey in particular, can be seen as three distinct but interrelated projects. First, like his colleague George Herbert Mead, Dewey was concerned with articulating a philosophical anthropology built upon the perception that language is the distinctively humanizing element: language gives humans the capacities of empathy and foresight. Second, he interpreted the social changes wrought by technological advances in communication and transportation as a move away from the shared experiences of community. These social changes meant that we could no longer have knowledge of the world and our fellow citizens from face-to-face interaction required for foresight and empathic understanding. Instead technology had made individuals dependent upon strangers who were separated from them by space and cultural experience. And for Dewey the idea of community life defines democracy; it is the political face of the community, the idea born of association. The new communication technology, then, caused the demise of face-to-face communication and with it the demise of community and democracy.

Dewey is not content, however, to conclude on such a pessimistic note. His third project dealt with the viability of democracy in the modern era. Ironically, it is the technology of communication that provides Dewey with hope for a rebirth of democracy. Although the new media elided face-to-face communication, they also could create a new kind of empathic understanding among all citizens and present the public with the information it needed to make rational decisions once again. The new technology, wedded to an unfettered social science, provided the remedy for the disease it had spawned.

This tension in Dewey's work—communication is both the cause of and the cure for the loss of social community and political democracy—is characteristic of the Chicago school. Communication is understood simultaneously as technology and the process of communication. Within the context of this "interactional" view of the crisis, Dewey refused to accept the possibility that these defined antagonistic views. The liberalism of pragmatism gave him a fundamental faith in both communication and science, while his own historical interpretations showed that these were the enemy.

Although their faith in science has often linked the Chicago school to the mainstream effects tradition, there has been a recent attempt by James Carey (1989) to purge the scientism from their theory. In Carey's interpretation, the meaningfulness of language is no longer seen in terms of foresight and consequences. He focuses instead on its symbolic content. Consequently the problem of interpreting the meaning of symbols and cultural rituals becomes central. However, like Dewey, Carey draws an indivisible link between communication and community. The crisis of the age is still the decline of community, but Carey resists making technology the villain. Although he accepts Dewey's historical arguments, Carey asserts that community and democracy are in eclipse because of the models of communication we assume in our lives. In other words, as a result of conceiving of communication in particular ways, we have created forms of social relationships precluding the possibility of community life. Carey seeks to articulate a theory of communication allowing us "to enlarge the 'human conversation' by comprehending what others are saying" (1975c, 189).

Carey sees communication as the process whereby "we first produce the world by symbolic work and then take up residence in the world we have produced" (1975a, 16). Thus Carey avoids the tension, within pragmatism, of seeing language and communication both in scientific/technological terms and in terms of the symbolic construction of reality. On the other hand, his commitment to social democracy as the political form of community life and his perception that "problems of communication are linked to problems of community, to problems of the kinds of communities we create and in which we live" (19), are clearly built upon a vision of the crisis he shares with Dewey. By purging communication of its scientistic overtones, Carey avoids the potential reduction of communication to technology. This move is necessary if only because Dewey's faith in the processes of communication technology and science proved to be unwarranted. If viewing the cultural crisis as the eclipse of community is not to result in pessimism, Carey's attempt to unite communication and community in a theory of the symbolic creation of reality is indispensable. It also makes clear the connection between an inter-actional view of the crisis and a particular way of talking about the process of communication.

The work of Raymond Williams, like that of Dewey, can be seen as a direct response to the experience of modernization. Williams also experienced mo-dernity in terms of mobility and recognized the problem of community as central. "What community is, what it has been, what it might be . . . these related themes are the dominant bearing. For this is a period in which what it means to live in a community is more uncertain, more critical, more disturb-ing as a question both to societies and to persons than ever before in history" (1973b, 12).

But Williams never experienced, as did Dewey, the *loss* of community life, the slow and invisible destruction of the community under the constant pres-sure of the forces of modernization. Rather he found his life dislocated, exist-ing between *two* communities, between cultures in a "border country . . . between custom and education, between work and ideas, between love of place and an experience of change" (1973b, 197), and, we might add, between intelligence and fellow feeling, between education and class. The questions he asked were drawn from his own experience of existing between two com-munities, the working-class culture of his family and the middle-class intel-lectual community of the university, and being unable to belong to either because the cultures defining them were so far removed from one another.

As a result, Williams sees the crisis of contemporary culture in terms of the "knowable community" and a "common culture." It is increasingly difficult for us to understand the concrete experience of community life, he argues, for we must move between communities. Each has its own social relationships and language; each has its own way of seeing the world. As long as one remains outside a culture, one cannot fully participate in the community life. The problem of the knowable community is that of "finding a position, a position convincingly experienced, from which community can begin to be known" (1978, 17). For Williams, the crisis of culture is not the absence of community but the absence of understanding and of appropriate ways to share that understanding. This points to the need for a "common culture" as a "position" or grounding process from which communication and under-standing between cultures is possible (1970, 316–17).

But a common culture could not merely be another way of seeing the world, imposing itself upon the cultures of existing classes and communities. Williams's view of a common culture would not reduce cultural diversity.

Instead he sees it as "a common process of participation in the creation of meanings and values" (1974, 34). Culture is, then, simultaneously the particular structure of experience defining a particular community ("the structure of feeling") and the general activity of offering, evaluating, and sharing new meanings and experiences within the context of already shared meanings (the "community of process"). Seen in this way, the problem of common culture is identifiable as a "transcendental" view of communication.

The crisis of contemporary culture, then, resides in precisely the fact that such a common culture does not exist. There is no point (or process) outside of particular communities that allows us to communicate. Williams finds the reasons for this absence in an analysis of the actual conditions of communication and culture. As a marxist, he finds that community is also "a social system containing radical inequalities and conflicts of interests" (1976, 149). The interests of one group dominate those of others—defining their own forms of experience and social relations as the only legitimate ones. We must, therefore, attend to "the interests and agencies of communication" (120).

Insofar as culture is dominative, communicative forms and practices will embody relationships of inequality and passivity; the possibility of participation in the process of culture is denied by the hegemony of the dominant culture. Communication, then, must be studied in the context of its role in the processes of culture and domination. To the extent that communication is a creative act of individuals, it cannot be reduced to technology, objects, or structures. It must be seen as forms of activity that define the possibilities of community. To the extent that the contemporary forms of communication exclude people from participation in the cultural process and inhibit the creation of a common culture, they are in the service of some dominative culture. And the problem of communication becomes "the problem of revolutionary politics" (1974, 297). It is this "long revolution" leading toward a "transcendental" common culture that underlies the entire theoretical structure of Williams's view of communication.

Like Williams, Jürgen Habermas (1976) sees the crisis of contemporary culture in terms of domination and communication. At the social level, Habermas sees the contemporary crisis within the sphere of motivation and culture. The crisis has been displaced, he argues, from the social spheres of economics and politics to the individual domain of social interaction. The crisis of capitalism in the modern world results from its demand for and lack of legitimation as it increasingly fails to meet the needs of the members of society. This "legitimation crisis" has been transformed into a crisis of motivation, in which the individual can no longer find norms and values to sustain his or her everyday decisions. According to Habermas, the solution proffered by the state is to demand loyalty by restricting the possible criteria of truth.

In one of his early works, Habermas (1968) identified three "quasi-transcendental" interests underlying human knowledge and activity. The *technical* interest underlies material labor as purposive-rational activity, the *practical* interest underlies communicative interaction, and the *emancipatory* interest underlies critical reflection and revolutionary praxis. Each is conceptually tied to a particular form of knowledge and truth. The capitalist solution to the crisis of the modern age, Habermas argues, has been to attempt to make technical rationality the only acceptable form of truth, thus denying the possibility of the practical and critical conceptions. Rational life, on the other hand, requires the recognition that each of the three interests has a legitimate place in human affairs and that each provides a check on the claims of the others by providing the grounds for a particular set of activities and social relations.

Habermas's discussions of communication are an attempt to justify the demands of these alternative conceptions of truth. He has attempted to do this by developing a "theory of communicative competence" (1970) in which he demonstrates that communication presupposes claims of truth and validity outside the conventions of technical rationality. Rationality within human affairs assumes the possibility of an ideal speech situation, that is, of an interaction within a structure of undistorted communication. Communication will be undistorted when all participants have the abilities to engage in the various forms of communicative action equally.

On a first reading of Habermas, it seems that he holds a "structural" view of the crisis: modern society is characterized by the domination of a scientific worldview and rationality. A closer examination, however, reveals that the three interests serve as necessary grounds from which communication is possible. It is not merely a question of one system dominating others, but of one "quasi-transcendental" interest negating the other two.

In this article I have tried to suggest that there is a close connection between how a theorist conceives of communication and his or her image of the crisis of culture. This relationship between communication and culture has implications for the ethical dimensions of communications study. Numerous writers reject the notion of a value-free social science and raise instead the possibility of evaluating and discussing various theories on the basis of their ethical implications. For example, Carey has argued persuasively that "the wide-spread social interest in communication derives from a derangement in our models of communication and community . . . Our existing models of communication are less an analysis than a contribution to the chaos of modern culture" (1975a, 20). For Carey, the study of communication must not only attempt to describe and analyze the processes of communication in everyday life, but must also locate itself in a broadly based ethical concern to find "a way in which to rebuild a model of and for communication of some restorative value in reshaping our common culture" (21).

In fact, the study of communication seems to have obvious ethical dimensions as soon as the researchers face questions of policy and normative concerns. But it is often difficult to draw the ethical implications of theoretical positions directly out of the more descriptive writings. The notion of cultural crisis, however, allows us to look at the ethical dimensions of theories less directly. It accomplishes this in two ways. First, it locates the notion of culture at the heart of communication theory; and the concept of culture includes a moral dimension at its very core. Williams has demonstrated this in his attempt to trace the historical development of the meaning of the term. The concept of culture, in his view, originally pointed at an attempt by a literary elite to argue that the new forces of change have been divorced from the critical processes of critical and moral evaluation. Consequently they sought to find some criterion, source, or locus of value that could serve to render judgment on the rapidly expanding forces of modernization. Thus, in Williams's analysis, the very idea of culture represents "a general reaction to a general and major change in the conditions of our common life. Its basic element is its effort at total qualitative assessment" (1958, 295). The continuing presence of this normative dimension of culture is still obvious in the complexity of meanings surrounding the concept.

Second, the question of the crisis facing modern humans and culture raises a normative question in terms of the future survival of human and humane existence. The notion of a cultural crisis implies some image of an ideal culture, or at least of a culture not in crisis. And since culture is, broadly speaking, the framework within which an individual lives, the notion of a cultural crisis must have a conception of an ideal form of human existence underlying its judgment. Of course, this is not to say that such an ideal must or even can be explicitly articulated. Thus an understanding of the relationship of communication and cultural crisis raises the ethical question in terms of the ethical foundations rather than implications of communication theories.

Moreover there is a theoretical reason making the identification of such normative dimensions desirable, namely, that of raising the possibility of making comparative evaluations of alternative perspectives. Such evaluations are difficult, if not impossible, on the basis of the epistemological, methodological, and metaphysical assumptions of theories. One is no more likely to gain agreement on the criteria to be used in judging such assumptions than on those used to judge the theories themselves. Similarly comparisons on the basis of the ethical implications of theoretical positions do not fare much better. The notion of a cultural crisis, however, might provide a partial solution to this problem. One could reasonably attempt to compare and evaluate alternative conceptions of the cultural crisis. Such conceptions are neither purely normative nor descriptive. Certainly their descriptive claims are open to question. We can inquire into (a) the adequacy and accuracy of the description of the modern age and (b) the comprehensiveness of the description. For each theory we can ask whether there are good reasons to accept or reject its characterization of the crisis and whether its characterization can be encompassed by or can encompass other conceptions of the threat to culture.[5] The very possibility of such critical comparisons is a potential contribution to our reflections on communication theory.

The Ideology of Communication:

Poststructuralism and the Limits

of Communication

There has appeared, recently, an interest in the philosophical implications of communication. This concern has taken two forms: First, "communication" has provided a foundation for accounts of other aspects of human life (e.g., language, human nature, social reality). Such work assumes that it already understands the nature of communication. Second, alternative theories of communication have been generated from particular philosophical perspectives (e.g., phenomenology). Such work substitutes theory for philosophical investigation: its major thrust is to produce new research programs and critiques of other communication theories. One never asks if the grounding philosophy is built upon an unquestioned understanding of communication. In both cases, "communication" itself is not problematized. The first section of this paper will argue that the theoretical discourses on communication available to us, paradoxically, reproduce communication within their very account of it, thus defining communication tautologically (see Lyons 1977; Rommetveit 1978; Lanigan 1979).

My reading of communication theory will show not only that we have failed to undertake a philosophical exploration of communication, but that such reflections have been effectively blocked. We must, therefore, confront these effective prohibitions on and within our discourse. I will argue that they are constituted by our assumption of the transcendental reality of both subjective and intersubjective meaning. "Communication" articulates the mediation in which the individuality of meaning is transcended in an experience of intersubjective meaning, and thus claims transcendental status for itself—that is, that it is a universal and constitutive condition of our humanity.

This has at least two significant consequences. First, we are unable to distinguish communication from other forms of signification, since all human reality is seen as significant and all signification is understood on the model of communication. The "discipline" of communication is unable to define its own boundaries since every object or event is potentially "communication," and the interpretation of messages as communication has no grounded methodology. Second, we have ignored questions about the ideological and political power of communication itself. This lacuna is intensified by recent calls for radically new models of communication to deal with new technological possibilities and new political realities, and by the increasing importance that models of interpersonal communication play in our relational and political ideals.

But if the transcendental status of communication results from the transcendental dualism of subject and object reproduced within the concept of meaning, a philosophical investigation of communication forces us to rethink some of the most basic assumptions of our philosophical tradition. For example, the task of philosophy is taken to involve a transcendental account of experience; experience itself is taken as innocently given; consequently the categories apparently present in experience are used as a resource. Even Wittgenstein's reconceptualization of philosophy failed to challenge this transcendental status of experience: discourse is the culprit leading us to look for things that aren't there.

If the assumed innocence of experience is the real culprit, a philosophy of communication will require that we recognize experience as both real and deceptive; that is, while our experiences are real in that they are the surface on which we live out our lives, they are the product of social and historical processes. Other positions, because they fail to question the innocence of experience, assume the transcendental status of at least certain moments of experience outside of the determination of history: for example, the self as creative subject and the meaningfulness of reality (apart from any particular structure of meaning). The result is that communication is assumed and granted a transcendental status as the motor force of the production process itself. The alternative that I am proposing fragments and problematizes the production of experience. Furthermore, these processes are themselves implicated in complex ways with investments of power and desire rather than being innocent human capacities. Thus the categories that appear to be inherent within our experience and are consequently recreated as primitives within our theories must be seen as codes and practices, penetrated by relations of desire and power. These are neither hidden behind our experience nor present within it. They exist on the surface of our experience as that which effectively determines and produces experience itself. By refusing experience its innocence and transcendental status, by locating any phenomenon within a context in which it is "overdetermined" by and effective within a number of interpenetrating but fragmented contexts, such a discourse allows us to question the status of communication as a necessary mediation of the transcendental dualism apparently present in our experience.

At this point, the project of a philosophy of communication has been reconceptualized. Rather than searching for some essential and universal characteristics of communication, it addresses the determining and determined relations between communication and other aspects of our lives. What are the particular involvements and investments of communication in real historical social formations? Why and how is communication posed as a space of particular, yet central, problems? How have we come to see the "truth" of our existence as necessarily implicating us within a discourse about communication? Without rejecting the everyday understanding of communication, it questions its status—the assumption of the "natural" importance that it has in social existence. Our task is to "denaturalize" the role of communication itself in our lives.

THE TRANSCENDENTAL STATUS
OF COMMUNICATION IN MODERN THOUGHT

The first task, then, is to demonstrate that there is, effective within our theories of communication, a prohibition against problematizing the concept of communication itself; that is, that our accounts of communication work only insofar as they assume communication as a given. Furthermore, its nature is specified beforehand—it is the process by which the individuality of meaning is transcended. Thus the paradoxical status of communication within communication theory is produced by its location within the transcendental dualism of subjectivity/objectivity or, when this is located within meaning, of individual and social meaning.

Obviously this task cannot be accomplished inductively. A detailed reading of all of the various communication theories, taking into account their particular differences, would be an overwhelming task. Instead I shall propose a schema organizing the images of communication underlying currently available communication theories (see Grossberg 1982b, 1982c). The six images of communication proposed are not meant to correspond with particular communication theories. Although I will often use particular theories as examples to clarify the images, the more common situation is that particular theories combine a number of images. The images are discursive codes or theoretical vocabularies available as resources for the articulation of communication theories within the present historical-intellectual situation. The schema is organized around three basic images of intersubjectivity, expressing alternative views of the relationship of the individual and the social. Consequently each of the three images poses the question of how communication is possible in different terms. In this section, I will briefly summarize the three images of intersubjectivity and the resulting six views of communication and argue that none of them is able to question the nature and transcendental status of communication.

Communication as Sharing. The first image of intersubjectivity—"coming together"—involves an absolute, metaphysical distinction between the individual and the other. This may be expressed as either a radical isolation of individuals or an opposition (gulf) between the subjectivity of the individual and the objectivity of the social world. Such an image of intersubjectivity presupposes a *causal* relation between the individual and the social. Thus either individual acts, events, meanings, and so forth produce the social or vice versa. Communication is seen as a moment of sharing, enabling us to escape the very real threat of solipsism. But there must be a meaning that is shared, an objective or social meaning that is not the exclusive property of any specific individual. Given this minimal condition for describing communication as sharing, there are two options. Either the dualism between the individual and the social is inserted into the very structure of particular meanings, or the subjective aspect of meaning is denied.

The latter, "objective view" of communication fails because it gives meaning a status inherently independent of the subject without accounting for the role or contribution of the individual to the process of communication. The presence of the individual in communication as, minimally, an apparent ground for change, creativity, and particularity (i.e., for the specification of concrete meanings and the introduction of new meanings) can be questioned and even denied. The objective view of communication, however, merely ignores such questions and assumes, a priori, that communication is describable without accounting for such aspects of the process.

On the other hand, if one begins with the subjectivity of meaning, then the transcendental duality of subjectivity and sociality must be recreated in the account of communication. This is the function of the concept of the sign, for it gives stability and objectivity to particular meanings that would otherwise be individualized and unknowable by the other. Insofar as the sign involves a real (i.e., a nonsubjectively constituted or social) connection between a material vehicle and a meaning, the meaning is present and available to any number of subjects. The inability of such a view to question communication is obvious: it works only by postulating as given that which it seeks to ground. The problem of communication appears as the need to share essentially private meanings, to escape the subjectivity of meaning. It is solved by postulating the objective presence of meaning within the sign. The sign is the recreation of the question of sharing itself, that is, the question of communication between isolated and subjective individuals. The apparent paradoxical movement of subjective entities is merely translated into an equally paradoxical transformation of subjective entities into objective or social entities.

This "subjective view" fails to address the relationship between the meanings within the speaker's consciousness and those of the shared sign system. That signs are the means by which we escape the solipsistic subjectivity of meaning is clear; the question of how they perform this function is typically explicated in terms such as conventionality that, once again, merely recreate the assumption of intersubjectivity. The appeal to the sign, within a view of communication as sharing, constantly postpones the question of communication itself, for the sign carries within itself its own meaning and thus introduces a third term into the model (a nonsubjective or intersubjective meaning), whose relation to the subject and the medium of signs remains problematic. One consequence of this constant postponing of the question is that such views are actually unable to account for the creative moment of communication through signs even though they start with the subject as the creative source of meaning. Thus the image of intersubjectivity as "coming together" and the resulting views of communication as sharing are unable to address the question of communication without assuming or recreating communication within their solution.[1]

Communication as Emergence. The second image of intersubjectivity—"belonging with"—defines the relationship between the individual and social (or between individuals) as a process of partial and mutual determination. Rather than separating the two terms initially and absolutely, they are held to depend upon each other, at least in part, for their identity and existence. Individuals are actors constantly engaged in interactions with other actors within an already existing context of social reality and relationships. Each of the two terms has a dual existence, at once partly determined by the other and partly self-determining. The domain of the social exists, on the one hand,

only insofar as it is continuously reaffirmed by the subject in particular interactions; on the other hand, it is a structure of stability and transindividuality.
The social world is the context within which particular interactions between
individuals occur and are possible. Consequently it serves to partly determine the particular interactions that partly determine its identity. Similarly
the individual is both determined by the social and determinative of it. Such
views directly address the question, merely raised by the image of sharing, of
the relationship between individual meanings and the socially shared meanings of signs. Such an image of intersubjectivity presupposes a *functional* relation between the individual and the social; that is, individual acts, events,
meanings, and so on function to reproduce, maintain, and change social reality; or alternatively, the social system functions to make possible individual
acts, and so on.

The question of communication—of the transcendence of the individuality
of meaning—is redefined. Rather than trying to unite two distinct domains of
meaning, one talks about a directed process of relationship and development,
a continuous emergence of creativity within a context of tradition or a process
of contextualization and decontextualization. Although meanings exist only
within particular speech acts defined by the projects of the interactants, the
possibility of understanding (or concretely realized intersubjective meaning)
depends as well on the stable structure of meanings and relationships preexisting and determining those particular interactions. The simultaneous emergence of understanding and creativity in any concrete interaction is a function
in part of a taken-for-granted, shared stock of knowledge of intersubjective
meanings: the decontextualized existence of the social world. If individuals
are continuously immersed within their own projects, they are also immersed
within a field of meanings that transcends and determines those projects. This
immersion defines their existence as socially determined beings, but because
individuals are also self-determining, they are able to transcend that social
context (tradition) to bring new meanings and projects into it. The individual
creatively engages in a process of communication through which the social is
continuously reaffirmed, reproduced, and changed (transcended).

There are two views of communication as a process of emergence. A structural view describes particular speech acts as expressions or manifestations
of a social structure of meanings or rules. An interactional view, on the other
hand, focuses on the processes of interaction and emergence, describing communication as the ongoing interactional production of understanding (intersubjective meaning). Neither view, however, questions the nature or status of

communication. Communication is assumed to require the presence of a real intersubjective meaning transcending the perspectives and projects of the individual. In contrast to previous views, which seemed unable to account for communicative success, the question of emergence makes communication inevitable; the possibility of failing to communicate is jeopardized.[2]

Communication still functions as a transcendental term in such views, undermining the possibility of a radical examination of the concept. In fact, communication is reproduced within each of the two terms—individual and social—as the emergence of meaning from a context of determinateness and self-determination. Consider the social realm: On the one hand, it is a stable body of taken-for-granted meanings that has been determined by a previous history of interactions and determines, in turn, future interactions. On the other hand, it is an ongoing context of interactional emergence. This emergence is not totally determined by the individual projects that set it in motion, nor by the already taken-for-granted social meanings. This real emergence of new understanding or intersubjective meaning, partly determined and partly undetermined, is both the assumption and guarantee of communication.

This social location of the emergence of understanding does not escape the transcendental dualism that protects "communication" from scrutiny. Communication is still assumed to involve a transcendence of individuality. Such views continue to presuppose and reflect a particular image of the individual as subject; this image incorporates within the individual the split between determinateness and self-determination and thus, like the image of the social, merely reproduces the question of communication. To the extent that the individual exists in part outside of the social context as a self-determining agent, communication must involve a relationship between the intentions and meanings of this agent and the social context of interaction within which emergence is possible. This undetermined aspect of individuality is an expression of pure subjectivity, an essential and universal characteristic of human nature. This transcendental assumption—of an undetermined moment of individuality—is necessary if one assumes that communication, creativity, and the possibility of misunderstanding all imply both a subjective definition and strategic control of the particular interaction and a determinative context of intersubjective emergence.

Within an image of intersubjectivity as "belonging with," the problem of communication is postponed into that of the relationship between these two moments of the individual's existence. And this transposed problem is solved only by postulating communication as an innate potential. Consider, for example, the paradoxical notion of competence that is often central to an interactional view of communication: it is a capacity that is determined by the social context and yet is the precondition for all interactions within that context. The individual must already be competent if he or she is to participate in those interactions that will make for a competent interactant. This dilemma is solved only by assuming that subjectivity can be described as a set of essential and inherent capabilities for engaging in just those sorts of processes and relationships that universally characterize communication (e.g., negotiation, perspective taking, foresight, empathy). The determined and self-determining aspects of the individual are related to each other by making the latter the locus of an assumed communicative competence that is actualized in the former. The possibility of engaging in communicative processes must exist prior to any interactional involvement.

This innate potentiality is understood differently in the structural view, where the subject is an unstructured but potential domain of meaning waiting to be organized by the structure of the social sign-system. Again, a moment of innate potential must be introduced to connect this undetermined subjectivity and the determined existence of the individual; yet the relationship between these two moments of subjectivity is problematic and, once again, only a particular understanding of communication and its transcendental status can reconcile the subject to itself. The paradoxical fission of the subject—as potentiality and agency—can be overcome and accounted for only if communication is imported as a third term into the individual between its moments. The concept of communication is protected from scrutiny by locating it within a framework of transcendental dualism. Whichever term—individual or social (meanings)—is primitive, there remains an insupportable residue or surplus; the two terms ground and determine each other, but never completely. Neither term is able to give stability to the other and each makes the other partially unstable. Consequently a third term—communication—is assumed, and the dualism appears mediated in the achievement of understanding or real intersubjectivity. This assumption already locates communication as a relationship between two moments or domains of meaning, resulting in communication defining its own definiendum; none of the terms can be radically questioned within this network of assumptions!

Communication as Constitution. The phenomenologically articulated image of "sociality" represents a refusal to assume the reality of both the individual and the social. The issue is no longer the "real" relationship between these terms, but the meaningful experience of such a relationship; experience is the new transcendental term. The phenomenologist hopes to avoid the traditional dilemmas by arguing that our experiences are always and already presented to us in a particular way; that is, they are always interpretations or meaningfully present. And in particular the self-presentation of our experiences is apparently structured as that of an isolated individual separated from and related to a social world. Intersubjectivity is both an attribute and a product of our experience; it is the sense of the experiences themselves and not some given state of reality independent of those experiences. The question then becomes how such interpretations are constituted or accomplished within our experience. Such an image of intersubjectivity presupposes that the relationship between the individual and the social is one of *representation* or *signification:* while each term has a different status, there is an isomorphism between the two domains, albeit an isomorphism that can be understood only in terms of the mediating processes of signification or constitution. Similarly the question of communication concerns the processes by which both individual and social meanings appear as real within our experience.

Two views of communication have been articulated within such an image: the phenomenological and hermeneutic. Both begin with experience and the presence of the sense of intersubjectivity within experience. And both, whether explicitly as in phenomenology or implicitly as in hermeneutics, postulate a transcendental subject as (at least the partial) source and/or locus of such experience. They differ on the structure of experience and on its relationship to the human subject. Despite significant differences, both locate the question of communication in the examination of the interpretive processes by which intersubjectivity is constituted.[3]

A phenomenological view of communication asserts the primacy of the individual subject and sees communication as the individual's accomplishment of intersubjectivity. The reality or presence of social meanings is an interpretation constituted within the individual's experience. Communication does not accomplish any real transcendence of individual meaning but is itself a moment of the individual process of meaning, the result of the particular interpretive processes through which we make sense of our experience with others. The question of communication is that of our interpreting the actions of others within a context that has already been constituted by our perception of the need to coordinate lines of action to accomplish some project.

If, however, the intersubjectivity of meaning (the apparent production of real social meaning) is determined by each individual's interpretive processes, we are thrown back into a solipsism as threatening as that of the first, subjective view. The phenomenologist must address the question of how we coordinate our situated interpretations with those of other actors. The most promising response thus far has been that the constitution of our experience as communicative is a result not merely of our interpretations, but of our actions in the public world as well. We act in routinized ways that are themselves constitutive of the sense of intersubjectivity and of the reality of social meanings. Communication is an accomplishment of the individual engaged in public and routinized performances of coordinated interaction.

However, the phenomenological view falls back into transcendental dualism as soon as it questions the status of such public routinized performances, of the relationship between these performances and individual interpretations, perspectives, projects, and strategies, and of "coordination." Let us consider each of these related questions.

Although the phenomenologist must deny that socially available practices form an objective social context (a structural view), the nature of these practices remains uncertain. By describing them as routinized and socially available, the phenomenologist implies that they are, in some sense, present independently of the individual, to be strategically chosen and situationally performed. Then they must have some sort of limited objectivity, a transcendental existence different from that of the individual and his or her projects.

Furthermore, it is obvious that the individual's strategic management of such practices is motivated by an attempt to make their perspective manifestly available to others in order to accomplish their project. It is not obvious, however, how such practices make the individual's perspective present. We have returned to signifying systems and the question is whether they manifest an inherent meaning. Thus the question of the relationship between individual projects and socially available practices recreates the question of the relationship between the individual subject (subjective meaning) and the social domain (social meaning).

Finally, if communication is tied to the notion of a real coordination among individually performed, routinized actions, then the notion of coordination seems merely to be a substitute for intersubjectivity. It involves a domain of meaning as well as a point of judgment that is not reducible to the perspective and interpretive processes of the individual. The phenomenological view, like earlier views, finds it necessary to postulate two irreducible moments of meaning: subjective and pragmatic. If they are mutually constitutive, that process remains opaque. At best, the phenomenologist replies that it is in communication that they are reconciled. Communication still involves a transcendence of meaning, from individual projects to coordinated interactions (or vice versa) and remains a transcendental assumption of the framework. The attempt to escape transcendental dualism by "reducing" the reality of intersubjectivity to a question of its presence within the subject's experience fails because its assumptions about the reality of subjectivity and the operation (or "effectivity") of meaning remain unquestioned. Like previous views, it ends by recreating the transcendental argument.

The image of sociality has given rise to a second view of communication—the hermeneutic—in which experience is constitutive of the subjective as well as the social. The hermeneutic view begins by equating experience with understanding as the transcendental (i.e., transcendent and constitutive) condition of both the individual and the social. Within the moment of understanding, they exist together in a relationship of "belonging-together" that is prior to the possibility of any absolute separation between them. (Consider two ice cubes that have melted together, or a wishbone: we are not sure where they will break or if there is some inherent line dividing the two entities.) Within this relationship, the individual and the social belong together and are made present to each other. The experience of dualism must be located within the transcendental moment of understanding. Hermeneutics looks behind the apparent duality of experience to find the transcendental unity of the moment of understanding.

But a radical reflection on communication is effectively prohibited because the model of understanding in hermeneutics is the dialogue or communication itself. While disagreements arise whether all experience has this structure or whether there may be distorted experiences, and whether "distortion" is to have normative weight, all hermeneutic positions make speaking (dialogue) the fundamental term and the transcendental condition of human existence. Such views obviously cannot question either the status or the nature of communication. The hermeneutic view is the completion of the tradition of our thinking about communication. It not only raises the mediation—communication—to the pinnacle of its edifice by making it the root, it reaffirms that such mediation involves a relationship between two terms (the individual and the social) that are given equal, albeit now secondary, metaphysical status. Communication is still assumed to involve transcendence; the hermeneutic view merely locates the moment of transcendence prior to that of immanence.

The hermeneutic view, furthermore, fails to avoid the dualism generated from the assumption of a transcendental moment of subjectivity (i.e., of a universal human nature that may be historically concretized). This assumption operates at two levels. First, the model of the dialogue carries with it the speaking subject as a creative origin of meaning. Second, by beginning with experience, hermeneutics assumes an agent of the experience. If that experience is transcendental, then the agent must be as well. Heidegger recognized that phenomenology and phenomenological hermeneutics merely replaced the subject-object dichotomy with that of the logos and the phenomenon. Similarly the claim to address transcendental questions seems to require that the philosopher occupy a position outside of the processes of historical determination. Thus hermeneutics fails to allow us access to the concept of communication because it too assumes a transcendental framework, albeit one in which the transcendence of communication is opposed to the *apparent* immanence of subjectivity, an immanence that inevitably transcends itself.

The Question of Communication. The transcendental status of communication is protected by and thus requires a certain stability of the relationship between the subject and the sign and of the two terms themselves. The stability of these terms represents the postulation of an origin and presence of meaning within the subjective and social realms, respectively. The latter makes communication possible. The former makes it necessary. Communication presupposes a split within the givenness of meaning: a subjective and a social moment, an immanent and a transcendent moment, and neither term can be totally constituted or determined by the other. Both terms are transcendentals which, along with a term of mediation or transcendence (intersubjectivity, understanding, communication), define the basic constitutive structure of human existence. It is only within this context that communication is opposed to miscommunication, that it operates within a dichotomy of success and failure.

My critique of the situation in communication theory echoes the more general critique of transcendental philosophy articulated by Heidegger in his later writings and by the poststructuralists.[4] Both have attacked the "homocentrism" and the "myth of presence" in Western thought, without being confident that they could escape. "Homocentrism" refers to the assumption of a transcendental subject that is transparent to itself, that is, a subject that can separate itself from and reflect upon its contextual experience and existence. Subjectivity becomes transcendental when one postulates an essential and universal human nature apart from the determining processes of the individual's sociohistorical existence. The "myth of presence" refers to the assumption that there is a meaning or set of meanings that properly belongs to a particular sign and that, therefore, is in some way present alongside the material aspect of the sign.

The status of communication can be questioned only by refusing any appeal to either a stable and universal subjectivity present in each individual or a system of signification in which material signs and meanings are stably connected. The two terms—subject and sign—are intimately connected. If the sign is a relationship between a vehicle (signifier) and a meaning (signified), the subject stands in a particular relationship to this divided unity. It can be said that the subject (the "I" of speaking) stands at the bar between the two and constitutes the particular relationship between them. It is this edifice that has dominated our reflections on communication, prohibited us from questioning it, and condemned us to seeing it as sharing, emergence, or constitution. I say "condemned," although such views are not wrong; communication does appear to play such roles. We do in fact experience ourselves as free subjects creating meaning ex nihilo (albeit within limits), living in the presence of stable meanings located within signifying media, systems, and contexts. That we experience ourselves in such terms is, however, not the issue. The implication of this brief series of critiques is that the demand for a radical philosophy of communication can be accomplished only within a *broader* philosophical project, namely, the general critique of the transcendental status of experience in philosophy and its associated philosophies of the subject and meaning.

DECONSTRUCTIVE MATERIALISM AND THE PHILOSOPHY OF COMMUNICATION

In this section I will suggest the contours of a social contextualist approach to communication, within certain limits. First, the position is not an alternative view of communication as it is experienced. It is a rethinking of the questions that concern the philosophy of communication and it is an intervention into the social discourses of communication at a specific historical moment. In particular this investigation attempts to interrogate communication from within a "regime of communication"—a social formation in which communication has come not only to define the truth of human existence but, increasingly, to preoccupy our interpersonal and social resources. Rather than the nature of communication, I am concerned with its power or effectivity within a broader social context. Second, I assume that there are significant differences among the various social practices that are given an apparent unity within the category of communication. Consequently I shall limit my reflections to one particular concrete form of communicative practice: the dialogue or interpersonal. This choice is not serendipitous, for it is this practice that has established a hegemony within the category of communication and hence within the social discourses on communication.

Third, the interrogation will be conducted only in terms of the problematic relationship between communication, subjectivity, and signification (or discourse). "Deconstructive materialism" focuses on the production of subjectivity within signifying or discursive practices, without reducing reality to discursive practices, signification, or even to signified reality (experience). Discourse does not encompass the Real; rather it traverses and is traversed by it; each sends "lines of flight" into the other, inscribing its codings onto the other. Thus questions of biological needs, physical constraints, unconscious desires, and social power must all eventually find their place within a philosophical investigation of the effectivity of concrete communicative practices; in the present context they will appear only marginally. Finally, I do not claim that the present reflections are complete or even that they can be generalized to contain all communicative practices or all of the questions that need to be raised. The particular questions I want to address concern the productivity of communication within discourse and subjectivity and the production of communication with a particular status in the contemporary social formation. I have argued that such questions are effectively blocked by the location of communication within a transcendental framework of subjectivity and signification. We must, then, deconstruct these terms if we are to interrogate communication. Deconstruction, in this context, is an attack on transcendence; the apparent unity of any category of experience is fragmented by locating its concrete articulations within its contexts of determination.

The Deconstruction of Subjectivity. The deconstruction of the subject does not deny that we experience ourselves as subjects but rather that this experience can be taken at face value. The apparent givenness of a stable subjective unity that remains indeterminate and uncontaminated by the structures and processes of its sociocultural existence is denaturalized. No one denies that parts of our individuality are determined socially, historically, and psychologically. Mead described these as the various "Me's" that constitute the social individual. But there is always more—a surplus or supplement: an essential moment of autonomy that Mead called the "I." The I is the source of creativity, the locus of inherent rights and responsibilities, and that which determines and stabilizes the meaning of any particular signifying event.

The first moment of the deconstruction of the subject (the I) is obvious: the I is itself socially produced or determined; the I is another Me. In certain contexts we experience ourselves as subjects, but it is the context itself that determines that experience. This is not to suggest that subjectivity is an illusion or epiphenomenon, nor a mechanical cause, simple expression, or functional bearer of a prior, externally existing, stable system of determination.

Two characteristics of the deconstructed subject distinguish it from other notions of the socially determined subject: it is "in process" and productive. To say that deconstruction describes a subject-in-process refers to the concreteness of the processes of determination. The way in which an individual exists as a subject depends upon the determinations of the particular context. Each context defines a space within which the individual can exist as subject, and so each context installs the individual as subject in a particular and potentially different position; the position is not chosen by the individual, for it is only by already assuming a position that the individual can have its own effectivity within the context, nor is it simply describable as reproduction, although this may be a tendency in certain social contexts. Yet the individual never enters into a context "innocent," devoid of a historical context of subjectivity. Thus the subject is always a "subject-in-process," constantly determined and constantly determining.

And this refers us to the second distinctive feature of the deconstructed subject: its productivity or effectivity even while it is produced and effectively determined. As Coward has stated, somewhat paradoxically, "the subject is absent until it produces itself, decentered in the structure which already includes it" (Coward 1977, 102). Thus the individual as subject is an effective determinant within the context in which it is effectively determined. Deconstruction does not reject creativity and change; rather these are integrated into the processes of determination themselves.

The deconstruction of the subject is, however, still incomplete, for this social subject appears to retain its unity, singularity, and simplicity; it has become another Me, added to other social selves. We must then fragment this subject; not only is it denied autonomy, decentered and dispersed into its context, it is itself seen as a complex and contradictory multiplicity. Although we typically assume, for example, that the single subject is the locus of meaning and insight, of legal responsibility and political freedom, of economic action and interpersonal intentions, and so on, deconstruction questions whether these experiences are all determinations of the same posit-ionings within any context. Thus rather than having a single I that is deconstructed into a single, corresponding Me, we are given a complex, contradictory structure of poten-tial determined and determining posit-ionings of the individual as a social subject. The situation is even more complicated since the individual exists within a variety of contexts at any moment as well as within the historical context of its own positions as subject. We can assume that these multiple social subjective positions exist in complex relationships to one another as well as to other aspects of the determining context. In fact, various subjective positions may have a determining effect on others; some may dominate in particular contexts (without necessarily negating the effectivity of other con-tradictory positions within the same context); more importantly, some may dominate across a wide range of determining contexts. It is this that will eventually provide my account of the regime of communication. We must first ask how subject-positions are determined within concrete contexts.

The Deconstruction of Signification. Materialism responds that social prac-tices constitute the context of determination, and so it is to particular forms of social practices that we must turn our attention. Social practices are modes of the material transformation of contexts that both determine and are deter-mined by social subjects; that is, forms of social practices both require and install the individual in a specific position vis-à-vis the material context and the practice itself. I have already argued that the particular social practices that concern us are signifying practices: we must, at this point, deconstruct the sign in order to investigate the particular posit-ionings of the subject determined by those signifying practices referred to as communicative.

Wahl has argued that there are two dimensions defining the sign: function and structure (Wahl 1979). Functionally the sign connects two disparate realms (e.g., ideas and things, individual and social) by serving as an agency of transcendence. The structure of the sign reproduces this transcendence; the sign is a divided unity involving a symmetry or correspondence between, for example, content and expression, or signifier and signified. Consequently signification is assumed to involve a stable meaning or set of meanings be-hind or alongside the material appearance of the sign-vehicle—"a unit of pure intelligibility, thinkable in itself, independent of that which expresses it, immediate and transcendental" (352). If we fracture the transcendental claim of the sign's function (i.e., the stability of a preconstituted goal), the sign is effective precisely insofar as it contextually produces meaning. This move simultaneously deconstructs the structure of the sign. The effectivity of the signifier produces the experience of a transparent correlation between itself and some nonmaterial entity, a meaning. This productivity of the signifier is a process, itself the product of the contextual articulation of a chain of signifiers. Meaning is, like the subject, a determined and determining effect of a material context. The apparent presence of meaning is not an illusion since meaning is itself effective within the context, but it is the product of practices that arrest the potentially unending movement of signifiers.

The signified is a moment in the chain or sliding of signifiers; the signifier is always inserted into and functioning within the signified. In fact, the signified is a signifier installed in a particular position within the chain. If we could allow the sliding to continue, we would be confronted by the infinite possibilities of meaning of any text (i.e., the effective absence of meaning). It is at those moments when the sliding is stopped—points of "punctuation" in the chain—that particular signifiers are produced in determined positions vis-à-vis the chain itself. A simple but useful analogy to the determined production of meaning is a game of musical chairs: those signifiers that find a seat, that slide under the chain of signifiers, appear as meanings.

But how is the sliding of the signifiers stopped? While the productivity of signification is contextual work carried on in and by discourse, the question of the concrete production of meaning within a particular context remains unanswered. That is, what determines the moment at which the process of structuration is stopped? Obviously we cannot appeal to a subject existing outside the material context of discursive articulation. Individuals do not bring anything into such a context nor take anything away from it that is not already structured by discourse. Furthermore, the determination must be defined immanently within the context itself.

Actually, talking about chains of signifiers is misleading, for it implies that material signifiers are stable and self-identical across contexts. Instead signifiers are constantly being articulated and determined in different ways, in different relations to other discursive and nondiscursive features of the context. Materialism replaces the notion of signifiers with that of signifying or discursive practices: discursive practices produce signifiers in apparently stable relationships to one another and in a particular position vis-à-vis the others. Discursive practices produce meaning at the same instant that they articulate signifiers.

By recognizing that interpreting discourse through the notion of the sign masks the effectivity of discursive practices, we can now provide an answer to the question of how the praxical context produces the effective experience of meaning. The production of meaning can be replaced by the effectivity of practices. Discursive practices produce meaning; how they do so concretely and contextually is determined by and determines the position of the individual as subject in relation to the signifying chain. In particular, the individual is installed as a "transcendental signifier" within the chain itself; this is both its determination and the possibility of its discursive effectivity (as that which stops the reading, punctuates the chain). Consequently the description of the concrete and contextual effectivity of discursive practices requires that we recognize that each of the moments—for example, practice, posit-ioning of the individual as subject, and the production of meaning through the posit-ioning of signifiers—is both determined by and determines the other moments. They are all articulated together. This complex situation in which a number of praxical codings are mutually determined and determining is "overdetermination."

The Overdetermination of Communication. Returning to a philosophical interrogation of communication, I will describe the productivity of dialogic communication. Then I will briefly address the question of the ideological function and status of such practices within the context of the contemporary social formation.

My description of communication assumes that it is a particular form of discursive practice. To summarize, the individual exists within social practices, in a complex, fragmented, and changing space of determination, constantly worked and traversed by contradictions and having its identity as a subject overdetermined by the conjuncture of practices within which it is installed. Any particular identity is a particular subject-ion or posit-ioning (a positing that is a position) of the individual within the praxical context. But overdetermination is neither simple nor mechanical; the individual and forms of social practice articulate the context within which they are mutually effective. That is, the productivity of discursive practices involves a particular installation of the subject that is, simultaneously, the determination of the practice as discursive. In general, most discursive practices are effective by producing the subject as language user (as the "I" of speaking) (Lacan 1977). The question remains whether there may be discursive practices that in fact do not close off the endless productivity of discourse. In this way, the subject-position serves to punctuate or stop the sliding of the signifying chain and thus closes off the infinite possibilities of meaning. Discursive practices produce the subject as a transcendental signifier within the signifying chain, a position that effectively appears to be an origin of meaning in general and the author of any particular meaning. Discursive practices, for the most part, install the individual as the authority of meaning.

To specify the effectivity of *communicative* practices, we must recognize that some discursive practices place the subject, in addition, within a space of social relations. There is a dual determination of the subjectivity of the individual, an overdetermination of signifier, self, and other. The position of the other as subject is then itself a determined and determining moment within such discursive practices: in communication "you talk to yourself from the place of another" (Coward and Ellis 1977, 79). Communicative practices position the speaker in a particular subject-position, which I will call "conversed subjectivity," but they do so only by positioning the listener in the same place. The conversed subject is produced at the same moment as a "conversed intersubjectivity." However, this intersubjective moment exists only as a particular relationship between two transcendental signifiers within the signifying chain. There is no meeting of minds, no emergent sociality, and no phenomenological constitution.

The claim that communication positions the other as a conversed subject says that the other is articulated in the same relationship to the signifying chain as the self; the other is the mirror image of the self and vice versa. This "double speculary" structure (an imaginary structure [Lacan 1977]) structures the signifying chain and closes off the space within which the signifiers can move. The space of communicative practices is elliptical; its closedness is defined by its having two equal centers so that neither is an absolute author-ity or both are. The individuals are set in a circuit of exchange. Communication produces and represents concrete relationships as relations between equals; the communicative practice itself is responsible for making the interaction work, without producing understanding as it is traditionally interpreted by hiding (naturalizing) its own overdetermined effectivity and constituting our experience as dialogic.

Communication and Ideology. In conclusion, I want to turn to the question of the relationship between communication and ideology. Here again I must distinguish two issues. First, I will suggest that communicative practices are inherently ideological. Second, I will briefly examine the ideological function of communication—the regime of communication—within the contemporary social formation. Poulantzas (1975) has recently argued that ideology operates through a process of separation (the fragmentation of real social relations) followed by a reuniting of these fragments into new, imaginary wholes. In this way, real processes of social power and determination are masked and displaced into ideologically determined representations. Althusser (1971) has similarly argued that ideology is the form of representation through which people live the imaginary relation between themselves and their real conditions of existence. Ideology then naturalizes its own productivity, presenting its representations not only as the way things are but also as the way they must be through the imaginary or speculary structure of its representation. By locating experience within a mirror structure, ideological practices ensure that the ideologically produced representations are articulated and experienced as the Real. This speculary structure operates, in turn, by producing a subject who stands in a particular relation to the meaningfulness of reality presented in ideological representations. "The individual thus lives his subject-ion to social structures as a consistent subject-ivity, an imaginary wholeness" (Coward and Ellis 1977, 76).

The parallels between this description of ideological practices and my own description of communicative practices are obvious. Certainly communicative practices fragment the real social relations of determination (within which we exist with the other as overdetermined and effective products of material practices) and then reconstitute the relationship in an imaginary form—the apparent accomplishment of a real intersubjectivity of the dialogue. Producing communication as a relation in which each individual is the mirror of the conversed subjectivity of the other masks the institutions and relations of power within which communication is produced and the unconscious as the scene of a desire that is never totally discursive. Yet if power and desire escape, in part, the determinations of discourse (and stand as the Real), discourse and communication can never escape their determining productivity. Furthermore, increasingly dialogic communication masks real relations of power, determined by nondialogic communicative practices such as mass communication.

Althusser suggests that all ideological practices place "the subject in the position of a homogeneous subject in relations to meaning, a subject who thinks himself/herself to be the point of origin of ideas and actions" (Coward and Ellis 1977, 77). Once again, this is quite similar to my description of discursive effectivity in general and would certainly include communicative practices. However, it is not clear that ideologically produced subjectivity must always take this form. In fact, I would argue that Althusser has discovered something of the unique form in which ideology is effective in the contemporary world.

This leads me to the final question I will raise regarding the particular ideological effectivity of communicative practices in the contemporary social formation where it is increasingly valorized. While communication and conversed subjectivity have always been a moment of social existence and human subjectivity, within the present context they have been articulated at a particular position, with a particular status. If discursive subjectivity is required for the reproduction of the contemporary social formation, then the fact that discourse and, increasingly, communication have come to define the essence of human nature, social life, and the real locus of our subjectivity is itself a further ideological representation. Thus the very importance and power of communication is a form of domination, for particular interests, articulated within a context of ideological practices. It is this question—of the ideological role of communicative practices and the ideological production of the status of communication—that has resisted and blocked philosophical interrogation.

The real question is how and why this has come about. What is the determining context within which communication itself has apparently become determining? This would involve concrete social and historical research. This "genealogy"[5] would investigate the overdeterminations of communicative practices, discourse, and subjectivity on the one hand, and on the other the effectivity of desire and power (the Real) invested in material practices (discursive, ideological, political, economic, sexual, familial, etc.). I have attempted only to denaturalize communication to open the possibility of examining the ideological complicity of communicative practices.

Experience, Signification, and Reality:

The Boundaries of Cultural Semiotics

The terrain between phenomenology and poststructuralism is a land in which few have traveled. The two discourses incorporate radical critiques of each other. Experience, which the latter distrusts, is foundational for the former. Consequently there seems to be little hope for a truce, not to mention cooperation. But there are occasional voices suggesting that the relation may not be as antagonistic as it seems: Barthes's (1975, 1978) playful hopscotching between the two, Schrag's (1980) and Giddens's (1979) efforts to reground social theory, Jameson's (1981) and Aronowitz's (1981) search for a contemporary marxist discourse, and Nelson's (1976, 1978, 1980, 1981) rethinking of the relation between literature and criticism with a voice that combines features of both phenomenology and poststructuralism. All of these works accomplish, with varying degrees of ambition and success, an integration of the two discourses that should not be possible given their self-descriptions. The issue has been raised recently by Hall's (1980c) characterization of the present moment in "cultural studies" as a conflict between two paradigms: experience and structure.

By framing the issue in these terms, however, the concrete relationship between these two discourses remains unexamined. Two questions need, then, to be raised. First, Is the poststructuralist's refusal to accept experience as an innocently given foundation for knowledge sufficient or does s/he still locate experience in a foundational role? Second, Is the deconstruction of presence sufficient to avoid the dualism of transcendental philosophy and to articulate a "philosophy of immanence"? In the first section, through a brief critical discussion of the work of Derrida and Kristeva, I will suggest that the response to both of these questions is no. If semiotics, even in its poststructural form, is implicated in the transcendentalism of phenomenology, a philosophy of immanence requires a rupture with semiotic as well as phenomenological discourses. The second section of the paper will discuss the work of Deleuze and Guattari as offering a discourse that scrupulously avoids any moment of transcendence. Finally, Foucault's project of a microphysics of power can be read as attempting to use this discursive strategy in the context of history and social relations.

POSTSTRUCTURALISM AND EXPERIENCE[1]

Poststructuralism is a particular discursive strategy and experience has a particular role within it. That strategy—deconstruction—rejects any appeal to the categories of experience as foundational for a description of human existence. Experience is itself the product or expression of the determining forces that constitute its particular appearance. For example, the fact that we experience ourselves as subjects and act effectively from such a position—as creators and manipulators of meaning who stand outside of discourse—does not justify accepting subjectivity as the definition of a universal human nature. Deconstruction addresses questions of how particular facts or features of human existence have been produced and interpreted in transcendental terms and what functions this particular transcendental discourse serves in relation to other social and discursive structures.

The strategy of deconstruction can be described as fragmentation or multiplication. It refuses the claim of any term to constitute a self-identical and self-sufficient center that is expressed in or is directly determinant of other, more peripheral events. No single term can define the origin or essential nature of the various constitutive moments of concrete human existence. Instead, any particular feature is located within an "indefinite multiplicity" of relations. The indefiniteness implies a never-ending possibility of fragmenting each term into its concrete determinants or constituents, and hence a real undecidability. Deconstruction is an activity of "free play" that inversely reflects the indeterminacy of the deconstruction. But as Deleuze and Guattari suggest, "unity is endlessly thwarted and impeded in the object, while a new type of unity triumphs in the subject . . . a higher unity of ambivalence or of overdetermination, in a dimension always supplementary to that of its object" (1981, 52). That is, deconstruction itself, in the form of its agent, retains a unity that escapes deconstruction. Moreover it leaves the trace of the unity that has been deconstructed within its own discourse.

Although the categories of experience and their referential reality are questioned and reduced to the determined contextual effects of discourse, it is those categories that provide the starting point for deconstruction and that always leave the traces of their unity and necessity. Experience is questioned, its innocence and priority rejected, but it remains as an originary discourse, the trace of phenomenology on poststructural discourse. This may become clearer if we consider the broad parameters of the deconstruction of subjectivity. Deconstruction explicitly locates human existence within discourse understood as textual processes. I have elsewhere summarized this view:

> Deconstruction sees all human experience as an ongoing reading within which the individual is implicated and determined. The ongoing reading, the "textuality" of existence, is a semiotization of experience, for it is the experience of signification. The context of experience is replaced by the ongoing production of an intertextuality. That is, the process of signification no longer involves a relation between two discrete domains (the signifiers and the signifieds). Rather, it is a process, within discourse, of the continuous articulation—a laying out as a production—of differences. Meaning is merely the trace of difference, but because that trace is always a supplement as well since it is constantly dispersed into the discursive process, meaning is always undecidable. (Grossberg 1982b, 197)

This is an important notion, meaning is more than difference; to say that it is a trace or supplement suggests both that it is effective within the context of its production and that the indefiniteness of the fragmentation—the possibility of its always being continued—means that one can never account completely for its existence or nature. A process in which difference is constantly deferred (and deferred to) describes discourse as *différance*. Everything, including the individual's identity and subjectivity, is an effect of discourse. What does it mean to say that the individual is an effect of discourse? The deconstructionist says that discourse "positions" the individual; the identity of the individual is dispersed or fragmented into a context of determining discourse or *différance:* the individual as intertext. Moreover the form of one's identity as an individual is determined by the place in which one is positioned or located by and in relation to the reading or discourse. Our existence as subjects is the product of the way in which various discourses locate us within an essentially discursive context. Subjectivity is a particular relationship to discourse produced within discourse. And while different discourses fill the place of the individual differently—hence the unique identities and histories of individuals is itself a textual production—and the reality of our subjectivity is only the trace of discourse, discourse necessarily positions the individual as a subject. That is how discourse is able to "have" a meaning and avoid the possibility of an indefinite generation of meaning (Eco 1976). Thus there is always necessarily an individual implicated as a discursive subject. The individual, then, functions as a unity existing outside of discourse, but its identity and effectiveness as an agent depend upon discursive determinations. The subject-object distinction of transcendental philosophy is replaced by an individual-discourse dichotomy that always locates the former at some place within the latter.

I will now concretize this reading of poststructuralism by first considering the objections that have been raised against Derridean deconstruction and then discussing Kristeva's attempt to salvage deconstructive practice.

The Critique of Derridean Deconstruction.[2] Derrida's presentation (1976) of deconstruction as a reading practice problematizing the "logocentrism" of Western culture represents the theoretical starting point of poststructuralist reflection, but the particulars of his position have been widely attacked, including the project itself, the form of his practice, his "idealism," and his failure to escape the problematic of representation.

Derrida's project is a continuous problematizing of any transcendental term; he attacks any assumption of a "presence" existing outside of the determination of *différance.* In practice, Derrida is content to deal only with moments of subjectivity and meaning, but more important, he is satisfied with *merely* problematizing them. As Coward and Ellis (1977) point out, it is a long way from this destructive task to the more positive articulation of a nontranscendental theory of signification, subjectivity, and the relation between them. These are crucial questions that Derrida's project continuously raises but from which his discourse constantly retreats. The problem is crucial because the problematizing of the subject, for example, is not its negation. To undermine its foundational role as an origin of discourse and meaning is not to deny its real effects within our lives. Without such an alternative account, the subject remains as an active principle—albeit only as a trace—within his discourse. Poststructuralism seems to demand an account of how the subject is both produced and produces its own effects. Kristeva's critique of Derrida makes this failure explicit:

Modern philosophy concurs in recognizing that it is the transcendental ego that has the right to represent the *thesis* which sets up signification (sign and/or proposition). But it is only since Freud that the question can be posed not only as to the origin of this thesis, but as to the process of its production. If one simply stigmatizes the thetic as the basis of meta-physics, one is liable to be merely its antechambre unless one specifies the conditions for the production of this thesis. Freud's theory of the unconscious and its development by Lacan seem to us to be a revelation of the fact that thetic signification is a phase that is producible in certain definite conditions during the process of "signifiance," that it consti-tutes the subject without being reducible to its process, because it is the threshold of language. (1974b, 43)

The second objection involves Derrida's practice of deconstruction, the particular way in which he fragments unities into determining structures. Using Jameson, we might say that Derrida mistakes the Imaginary for the Symbolic: "We will however come to learn that this process of definition by binary opposition is itself profoundly characteristic of the Imaginary, so that to allow our exposition to be influenced by it is already to slant our presenta-tion in terms of one of its two objects of study" (1977, 350). Derrida, perhaps not quite so naïvely, stops the process of fragmentation too quickly, always finding a pair of mutually opposed and mutually constitutive terms. Conse-quently, the "supplementarity" of deconstruction is doubly necessary: not only is it the result of the indefiniteness of a polyphonic determination, it is that which in addition transcends his binary constitutions. Thus, for exam-ple, Derrida privileges the notion of discourse and fails to subject it to the same deconstructive strategy he applies to subjectivity and meaning.

This leads us to the third criticism: the underlying idealism of his philo-sophical and political commitments. The privileging of discourse as *dif-férance* results in the inability to talk about the historical determination of particular texts, either those Derrida reads or those constituted by his read-ings. That is, discourse as a sliding of signifiers remains undetermined, rely-ing on nothing other than chance or the traces of an intertextuality. Texts appear as acts of free play, determined only by the logocentrism of Western civilization. This is reflected in Derrida's choice of texts, a choice that often reconstructs the "canon" of great masters.

This lack of reflexivity results from Derrida's idealism, his underemphasis of the materiality of discourse as practice in the reduction of everything to *différance*. The result is that Derrida ignores nondiscursive practices that would incorporate questions of interpersonal desire and institutional power. This is Foucault's critique of Derrida, whose practice he describes as the reduction of discursive practices to textual traces; the elision of the events produced therein and the retention only of marks for a reading; the invention of voices behind texts to avoid having to analyse the modes of implication of the subject in discourses; the assigning to the originary as said and unsaid in the text to avoid replacing discursive practices in the field of transformations where they are carried out. (1979b, 27)

Foucault asserts that Derrida has instituted a "little pedagogy" that reestablishes an origin and gives authority to the "master's" voice, that is, to Derrida himself. This critique is reiterated by Coward and Ellis when they describe *différance* as "movement without matter, in which everything is finally unknowable. This is ultimately idealist. Idealist thought appropriates the constraining factor that Lacan analyses [positionality] and fixes it as a point of origin, thus affirming 'presence and identity,' and repressing the process of construction. That is why this process can be found in certain idealist philosophers or writers as an excess" (1977, 126).

Derridean practice condemns us to an endless reading, an endless problematizing in which everything is reduced to a trace of *différance,* to a supplement (without there being something identifiable of which it is the supplement). Derrida describes (1976) an infinite tracing of Arche-writing and claims that, in some way, this is revolutionary, that it potentially unleashes a great "monster" upon the logocentric world. But his discourse is easily assimilated into the traditional institutions and practices of criticism. Derrida's readings might be described, in Kristeva's terms, as "experience texts" that "can show the annihilation of the unity of consciousness" but "fail to show the objective material relations which engender the conflict" (Coward and Ellis 1977, 150).

The last criticism of Derrida that I will consider questions the very notion of the "primacy of the signifier," a notion that is often used to describe the fundamental break between Derridean deconstruction and more traditional views of structuralism. Derrida's argument, that by seeing the signifier already insinuated into the signified we can escape the transcendental problematic of representation, has been challenged by Deleuze and Guattari: "Does the signifier take us beyond the question, 'What does it mean?' Is it anything other than this same question, only this time barred? This is still the domain of representation" (1977, 179–80). A philosophy of the signifier, in refusing to define language by what it says (the signified), defines it by "What makes it a signifying thing." Derrida fails to see discourse as production because the signifier asserts a unity and identity where there are only "point-signs," moments of production interpenetrated by other productive practices. A linguistics of the signifier gives it a privileged reference so that it manifests a moment of transcendence through which language becomes the expression of the effects of the signifier. The primacy of the signifier as a doctrine forces discursive practices to exist within a philosophy of the sign and signification. Even though the signifier in Derrida always presents itself as a lack in the face of an absence—whether as the trace of an Arche-writing or the erasure of the signified—it implicates itself within a philosophy of transcendence, of meaning and presence.

It may be objected, against my rather harsh treatment of Derrida, that I am demanding a theoretical position of what is offered only as a form of critical practice. In fact, Derrida seems to problematize the very possibility of theorizing. Such an attempt to rescue Derrida is untenable for two reasons. First, not all theorizing is static and reifying and claims for itself some privileged position. While Derrida certainly undermines such notions of theorizing, this leaves open the question of theory as discursive strategies. Second, there is a dialectic between theory and practice: every practice implicates other practices, some discursive and some nondiscursive, some theoretical and some not. The relationships among them are certainly complex and perhaps even contradictory, but there is no practice that does not implicate itself within a theoretical discourse.

Kristeva and Materialist Semiotics.[3] Kristeva, perhaps more than any poststructuralist, has attempted to describe the processes by which subjectivity is produced by as well as implicated within discourse. She responds, in her work, not only to the inadequacies of the Derridean project, but also to the failure of Althusser's marxism to account for the possibility of a "revolutionary subject." Althusser (1971) sees subjectivity as a "positing" that positions the individual vis-à-vis an ideological representation of reality. By "hailing" the individual as a subject, ideological practices subject individuals to and make them complicitous with ideology's naturalization of meaning. The subject is the bearer of ideology, the pillar supporting it. The result is, however, that Althusser's subject is merely the necessary fulfillment of an empty space, a static installation that makes the possibility of revolutionary action extremely problematic. It is the dialectic of determination and transgression—without postulating a transcendental subject—that defines Kristeva's project.

She accomplishes this by placing psychoanalysis (Lacan 1977) between semiotics and marxism. The discursive determination of the subject must be
located within the context of sociopolitical structures and psychoanalytic
drives (Kristeva 1973, 1975a, 1975b).

Kristeva views the production of the subject as the result of a bipolar economy constituting the space of a reinterpreted process of signification that she
calls *signifiance*. *Signifiance* or signifying practice is describable as two separate but functionally interrelated moments: the symbolic and the semiotic.
The symbolic is the signifying space of the transcendental subject and the
signified. It is the apparent functioning of discourse as communication between intending subjects, a domain in which subjects exist in relation to and
separated from both discourse and its objects. Within the symbolic, the subject is functionally split into the subject expressed in language (the "I" of
speaking) and that which is responsible for the production of the sentence
and therefore absent from language. The symbolic is the domain of Derrida's
discursive subjectivity.

The semiotic is a signifying but not symbolic moment of *signifiance*. It is
logically prior to the sign and representation, to meaning, to the production of
the subject, and to the social (i.e., the relation to the other). It precedes even
the earliest stages of the constitution of the ego (e.g., Lacan's mirror stage),
and while it precedes the symbolic, it can only appear as that which returns
in the symbolic as the repressed. The semiotic is precisely that which is
constantly transgressing the symbolic, the arena of Freud's primary processes. It is the unconscious as already implicated within signifying practices. Correspondingly, Kristeva replaces the traditional Freudian notion of
the unconscious with the "semiotic chora," which she describes as the space
of the articulation of drives and the arrangement of instincts. Moreover, like
Freud, Kristeva argues that the chora is ruled by the death instinct as a principle of negativity that "engenders" the semiotic. That is, the semiotic as the
articulation of an arrangement or structure of the drives is the product of the
material contradictions of the chora that are expelled from the chora by its
negativity to transgress the symbolic.

Since the semiotic and the symbolic always presuppose each other and
exist only in relation to each other, Kristeva's *signifiance* defines a space
within which desire, discourse, and subjectivity are mutually implicated. It
is within this context of *signifiance* that Kristeva provides an account of the
production of subjectivity as a domain of positions within which the individual is momentarily located and transfixed. She argues that the thetic or tran-

scendental subject is real, but neither the product solely of the symbolic nor a static and permanent structure of existence. While Lacan is correct in asserting that the unified thetic subject is produced in the movement into the symbolic (beyond the "Imaginary" ego of the mirror stage, it is the Oedipal experience that is primary), Kristeva disagrees with Lacan that the subject exists only in opposition to that which is simultaneously produced in the Oedipal propulsion into the symbolic—the unconscious. Lacan argues that subjectivity is the product of the "splitting" of the subject into the unconscious and the "I" of speaking. Furthermore, he locates the "truth" of the subject in the former. Kristeva brings the entire process of the production of subjectivity into *signifiance.* The production of the thetic subject cannot be located only within the symbolic; it is the product of the relationship between the two moments of *signifiance.*

Since every signifying practice partakes of both modes of *signifiance,* subjectivity is not a fixed positioning but an ongoing production. Thus rather than describing the subject as a fixed product, one is describing the production of a "subjectivity in process," a heterogeneous subject always displacing itself and its own established positions. Since there is never a moment in which the unconscious is innocent, free of any symbolic contamination, its effects cannot be read merely in terms of the opposition to or undermining of the production of subjectivity. Instead the symbolic order fixes the subject in process: the Oedipal event and, in particular, the threat of castration that opens the child to the Law (the name of the father), engenders a lack that discourse is called upon to fill. It is here that the other enters into the place of the subject as the signifier, and the subject is produced in a position vis-à-vis discourse itself.

But this thetic subject is unstable, perpetually reconstituted in signifying practices. Just as the symbolic is always contaminating and determining the semiotic, so the semiotic continues its negation, its constant expulsion of drives even when the symbolic has become effective. In fact, the semiotic is constantly transgressing the symbolic, challenging the law of its organization and authority, and undermining the stable fixation of the thetic subject. Consequently, the subject in signifying practice is constantly being reconstructed and restructured in the struggle between the two orders of *signifiance* and reinserted into the symbolic as a fixed moment of the subject in process. In this struggle, neither the symbolic nor the semiotic remains constant and unchanged. As White summarizes it,

It is the way in which the semiotic relates to and disfigures the symbolic, as well as the way in which the symbolic reasserts its unifying control of the semiotic which gives us the basis of subjectivity as a process. From the mirror phase onwards the semiotic and the symbolic involve each other in a shifting process of dependence and rejection, the spreading reticulation of syntactical and nominal order are informed and some- times broken, by the power of the semiotic: the signifying power of de- sire, aggression and pleasure. (1977, 12)

It is obvious that Kristeva's theory accounts not only for the production of the thetic (discursive or transcendental) subject, but also for the possibility of new and even contradictory subject-positionings and hence for the possibil- ity of revolutionary action despite discursive and ideological determination.

Despite the broad implications of this theory, Kristeva (1974b, 1976, 1980) has been primarily concerned with reading the dialectic of *signifiance* in lit- erary texts. Thus she distinguishes between the text as a system of signs (the "pheno-text") organized by semantic and syntactic codes and the text as the site of an abstract semiotic functioning that precedes and exceeds the system of signs and their organization into sentences (the "geno-text"). While tradi- tional semiotics is content to analyze the phenotext, she proposes a "sem- analysis" of texts that examines the relationships of constraint and trans- gression that exist between the phenotext and the genotext. Obviously the genotext is related to the semiotic as opposed to the symbolic order of *signi- fiance,* although the two vocabularies arise at different points in her career. The genotext is the space of discourse as an infinitely productive practice, transgressing the constraints of meaning coded within the phenotext. The text, then, as the site of a dialectic of genotext and phenotext studied in sem- analysis, is an articulation of the process of *signifiance* itself. Texts represent a particular kind of discourse—poetic—that makes visible the contradictions between the semiotic and the symbolic operating within *signifiance* itself. The other forms of discourse—narrative, metalinguistic, and theoretical— remain essentially imprisoned within the structures and constraints of the symbolic.

Since it is only in poetic discourse or textuality that the semiotic transgres- sion of the symbolic is allowed to a great extent, it is apparently only, or at least primarily, in poetic discourse that revolution can be articulated. That is, only texts call the social structure into question. Because the text is characterized by its productivity it refuses to reify either subject or object; it is the site of an ongoing production of the subject in process. The text is neither the product/expression of its author, nor is it a representation of a reality outside of *signifiance*. Its only "reference" is to itself as signifying practice, as *signifiance*.

It is in her readings of poetic discourse, and especially particular avant-garde poets (e.g., Lautréamont and Mallarmé), that Kristeva has attempted to draw the connection between her theory of the subject in process and a theory of society, power, and revolution. It would be unfair to suggest that poetic discourse defines the parameters of her political interest: along with others associated with the journal *Tel Quel*, Kristeva has evidenced a continuous concern with dissidence and revolution as embedded within a wide variety of social practices. And she has certainly written about matters political and cultural outside the boundaries of aesthetic practices. But it is in her consideration of such discursive practices that she has most explicitly attempted to come to grips with the theoretical issue: What is the structure by which the subject in process is implicated in political and social structures? Only when one has addressed this issue can the question of the possibility of revolutionary subjectivity be answered.

Basically, Kristeva follows Sollers in seeing all of reality as a play of negativities, that is, as contradictions. She assumes that there are three fundamental levels of contradictions: the socioeconomic mode of production, the process of *signifiance* (the subject-in-process), and the semiotic chora itself. Thus Kristeva sets up a model of desire opposed to power, mediated through the production of subjects, where each level is characterizable in terms of concrete contradictions. The crucial intervention—the establishment of the subject in process as the locus of potential revolutionary action—demands that Kristeva give an account of how the various levels of contradiction are articulated together, through the mediating process of the production of subjectivity. Unfortunately the metaphor of levels leads her into all of the dilemmas of searching for correspondences; materialist semiotics retains a hermeneutic quality as it recreates in a revised form the model of signifier and signified. Kristeva's goal is to describe a basic and intrinsic unity, but her theoretical position leads her to separate levels of individuality (desire) and power (mode of production) that demand reconciliation. Consequently, while it is obvious that the symbolic order is worked through, penetrated, and upheld by the socioeconomic and familial forces of the sociopolitical order, and that the semiotic is the result of an expulsion from the chora, this is insufficient. One is left only with the notion of transgression: individual desire opposing social power. *Significance* would, according to such a theoretical position, merely reproduce the contradiction between desire and power, individual and social, without mediating it.

The solution for Kristeva is to follow Lacan and his students in recognizing that desire itself is structured by the contradictions and relations of an outside, social world, even prior to the child's biographical accession into the symbolic. The semiotic chora itself is always and already operating according to structuration defined not only by the constraints of the symbolic but by the contradictions of the sociopolitical world as well: "Discrete quantities of energy traverse the body, later to be a subject and in the course of his or her becoming, arrange themselves according to the constraints imposed upon this ever semiotizing body by the familial and social structure" (Kristeva 1975b, 21).

The problem remains, however, that all of this is supposed to occur within and be mediated by the dialectic of *significance,* and it remains a problematic assumption that political questions can be reduced without an excess to questions of the constitution of subjectivity within discursive practices. Kristeva is, apparently, acutely aware of this dilemma. In her reading of avant-garde texts, for example, she describes a discursive practice that involves a continuous and radical fracturing of the syntactic and semantic structures of the symbolic order, a radical transgression of the symbolic by the semiotic. But of course, if the semiotic is already defined by the symbolic and by the socioeconomic level as well, then the political implications of this transgressive practice are not clear-cut. Compare the following statements: First, "What the theory of the unconscious looks for, poetic language practices, within and against the social order: the ultimate means of its mutation or subversion, the condition for its survival and revolution" (Kristeva 1974a, 381). Second, "the nineteenth century avant-garde text serves the dominant ideology since it supplies it with the means of making up for its lacks, without directly challenging the system of its reproduction in representation" (186). Thus politics appears, finally, to be undecidable within the limits of a discourse on discourse. That desire transgresses social power is clear; it may even be true that this process is able to account for the production of the subject and for the possibility of different subjectivities. But it can go no further. It cannot reconcile what are essentially two distinct discourses: that of desire and that of power. And consequently, in reducing political effectivity (i.e., revolution) to a discursive process of mediation, it fails precisely at the point of articulating the relation between subjectivity and that which is always a discursive supplement: power.

The question underlying my conclusion is whether Kristeva's semiotic materialism expunges the traces of phenomenological discourse from post-structuralism and succeeds in defining a vocabulary with which to talk of desire and power together: that is, a philosophy without transcendence or surplus. I would argue that she has not, and the reasons are summarized in the following statement by Guattari

> The distinction proposed by J. Kristeva, at the heart of the process of signifiance, between a so-called "semiotic chora" level and a symbolic level, could have been able to constitute an interesting exit door from linguistic semiologies. But besides the fact that this distinction "perennializes" and universalizes the signifier, it also has the disadvantage of closing around itself the diagrammatic transformation, to make of it once again a sort of deep structure, a sort of archi-ecriture. With J. Kristeva, the innateness of universals leaves the symbolic in order to emigrate towards the semiotic. In these conditions, the pragmatic risks both to slide into an interminable textual practice (comparable to the psychoanalytic practice) and to wander infinitely between a symbolic pheno-text and a semiotic geno-text. Despite the fact that this latter concept (semiotic genotext) is extricated from the personological polarities of communication, it still remains caught in the hypothesis of a signifying unconscious subjectivity encircled by itself. (1979a, 34)

What Guattari points to are two interrelated moments of phenomenological unity: signifying practice and the unconscious. Individuality remains an effect of textuality or *signifiance* and that which is outside discourse appears only as a contradictory other.

The transition from Derrida's textual process to Kristeva's discursive practices, while making discourse material rather than abstract, still maintains the abstract unity of *signifiance.* The semiotic and the symbolic exist only in an anaclitic relation, constituting a unity within which both the subject and the real (abstract sociopolitical context) are implicated in a way that implicates the reader as well: it is the reader who must produce the unity of the concrete discursive practice. On the other hand, Kristeva's semiotic chora suggests some originary drives that are constantly displaced into a desire worked over by discourse. Apparently Kristeva follows Lacan's view that desire involves a retrospective constitution (*Nachtraglichkeit*) of some originary, irrecuperable need, a constitution that always discursifies it. The unity of *signifiance,* furthermore, brings together the discursive subjectivity of the symbolic and the oppositional subjectivity of desire. No longer homogeneous, the subject remains a fractured unity of potentially contradictory moments. On the one hand, the chora defines an individuality that both precedes and resides within *signifiance.* On the other hand, *signifiance* defines a unified process of subjectivity.

Kristeva's discourse merely retraces the unities of transcendental phenomenology and thus excludes the other as the nonsignifying from its discourse. Like Derrida, Kristeva begins with the categories of experience and subjects them to a fragmentation built upon distrust. Nevertheless these categories continue to provide the constitutive structures of human existence. The categories define the beginning and end of semiotic analysis, an analysis that is assimilable to a phenomenology of suspicion, to echo Ricoeur (1970).

BEYOND THE SEMIOTIZATION

OF EXPERIENCE

Rhizomatics and the Philosophy of Immanence[4]. If poststructuralism describes the production of experience, Deleuze and Guattari have turned from the idealism and transcendentalism inherent in the notion of experience to articulate a materialism connecting human existence back to the real. If poststructuralism starts with a singular term—*différance* or *signifiance*—rhizomatics begins with a plural term: lines of intensities. Their position is admirably summarized in the following statement by Guattari:

> Everything that's written in refusing the connection with the referent, with reality, implies a politics of individuation, of the subject and of the object, of a turning of writing on itself, and by that puts itself into the service of all hierarchies, of all centralized systems of power, of what Gilles Deleuze and I call all "arborescences," the regime of unifiable multiplicities. The second axis (according to which everything that is written is linked to a political position), in opposition to arborescence, is that of the "rhizome," the regime of pure multiplicities . . . the pattern of . . . breaks in reality, in the social field, and in the field of economic, cosmic and other flows . . . What is in question in the rhizome is a rapport with sexuality, but also with the animal, the vegetal, with natural and artificial things, all different from the arborescent rapport . . . An arrangement in its multiplicity forcibly works both on semiotic flows, material

flows and social flows ... There is no longer a tripartition between a field of reality, the world, a field of representation, the book, and a field of subjectivity, the author. But an arrangement places in connection certain multiplicities taken from each of these orders ... The book is an arrangement with the outside, opposed to the book image of the world; a book-rhizome. (1979b, 65)

Rhizomatics is a strategy of drawing lines or connections. What these lines represent are the productive links between points within a multidimensional and multidirectional field. Each of these terms, however, requires some elaboration. "Lines of intensity" map out reality in terms of the productive relations between the points linked. Productivity is synonymous with effects or, more accurately, "effectivities." That is, something exists as an object related to other objects only in its multifarious effects at other points and their effects at the point of its apparent locus. To ask what something is, is to ask how it is produced and how it functions. But the description of any point cannot be confined to a particular "regime" or domain of effects, such as the signifying. Lines must always be drawn between disparate regimes of effects.

If poststructuralism excludes the other from its discourse, rhizomatics is entirely a philosophy of the other; there are only others, only the real. A particular point—a "partial object"—is defined by its externality, by the connections it has with other points, by its field of effects. And this assemblage of lines traverses the traditional boundaries with which we claim to carve up the real. Thus, contrary to Jameson's claim (1977, 380) that rhizomatics overestimates the (Lacanian) Imaginary, it rejects the distinction: "The true difference in nature is not between the Symbolic and the Imaginary, but between the real machinic elements [the production of lines of intensity] ... and the structural whole of the imaginary and the symbolic, which merely forms a myth and its variants" (Deleuze and Guattari 1977, 83). Consequently rhizomes cannot be treated as signifying or even significant systems, since their existence traverses the real as well. This means that rhizomes cannot be described with generative or structural models, since these merely retrace the indefinitely repeatable lines of a previous signification upon concrete assemblages.

Rhizomes are acentered, nonhierarchical, and nonsignifying (Deleuze and Guattari 1977, 65) systems of lines mapping out concrete effects or productivities. Objects, always partial and temporal unities, are the loci of particular assemblages of effects. Of course, some of these effects—"lines of articulation"—produce hierarchies, locate centers for particular regimes, define master structures purporting to define and control the entire assemblage. Lines of articulation draw boundaries between particular regimes of effects and exclude the external as they produce identity within difference. Rhizomatics undermines any such tracings of lines of articulation by drawing "lines of flight." The multiplicities of rhizomes are the result not of fragmenting the unity of a given category or assemblage (which leaves the trace of the unity), but rather of subtracting unity from the assemblage (and its discourse). Moments of transcendence (unity) are replaced with maps of concrete relations or effects. Rhizomatics draws lines of flight connecting a point to its external, and thus cuts across and dismantles unity, identity, centers, and hierarchies. It "deterritorializes" regimes and undermines any claim of essentiality. Rhizomatics is a strategy of immanence, a monism of plurality. It rigorously expunges from its discourse all trace of the categories of experience as it maps out the connections of lines of effects within the real. Perhaps the best way to clarify this strategy is to describe the point at which the "subject" appears in Deleuze and Guattari's critique of psychoanalysis, *Anti-Oedipus: Capitalism and Schizophrenia.*

Obviously, rhizomatics must scrupulously avoid any vocabulary that brings with it the baggage of Western transcendental philosophy: subject and object, sign and representation, experience and signification. They use, instead, a discourse of the "machinic," embodying a materialism without subjectivity, embracing discontinuity and partiality without transcendence. The machinic exists only in terms of its production and productivity. Their basic terms, then, are energy (libido, flows) and desiring machines (partial objects as the productivity of connections and breaks within the flows of energy). They begin by rethinking the notion of desire itself as desiring production:

> The three errors concerning desire are called lack, law and signifier. It is one and the same error, an idealism that forms a pious conception of the unconscious . . . From the moment lack is reintroduced into desire, all of desiring production is crushed, reduced to being no more than the production of fantasy; but the sign does not produce fantasies, it is a production of the real and a position of desire within reality. From the moment desire is wedded again to the law . . . the eternal operation of eternal repression recommences, the operation that closes around the unconscious the circle of prohibition and transgression, white mass and black mass; but the sign of desire is never a sign of the law, it is a sign of

strength (*puissance*). And who would dare use the term "law" for the fact that desire situates and develops its strength, and that wherever it is, it causes flows to move and substances to be intersected . . . ? From the moment desire is made to depend on the signifier, it is put back under the yoke of a despotism whose effect is castration, there where one recognizes the stroke of the signifier itself; but the sign of desire is never signifying, it exists in the thousands of productive break-flows that never allow themselves to be signified within the unary stroke of castration. It is always a point-sign of many dimensions. (Deleuze and Guattari 1977, 111–12)

There is no lack behind desire, no signifier structuring it, no law controlling it. Desire is a plenitude of production, producing a multiplicity of connections between partial objects or assemblages that are as likely to be subindividual or social aggregates. Desire is, in fact, always social, irreducible to any unity. It is not constrained to the psychic, the property of the individual, or structured as the subjective.

Psychoanalysis is, consequently, involved in the repression of desiring production by defining it according to its own lines of articulation. Schizoanalysis, on the contrary, seeks "to analyze the specific nature of the libidinal investments in the economic and political spheres and thereby to show how, in the subject who desires, desire can be made to desire its own repression— whence the role of the death instinct in the circuit connecting desire to the social sphere. All this happens, not in ideology but well beneath it" (Deleuze and Guattari 1977, 105). Schizoanalysis draws the lines of flight that map out and reopen the productivity of desire. It explores the relations between social production and desiring production to show that the former are institutions of desire and that desire itself is already part of the social infrastructure. Social production and psychic desire are the same process, operating in different regimes but always already infiltrated by the other. Desire cannot be located within a particular regime of effects; its productivity is precisely to make connections regardless of the boundaries psychoanalysis would construct.

The idea of the unconscious must similarly be revised, for it can no longer be conceived of as the domain of individual drives or desires. Again, the psychoanalytical notion of the unconscious stops the flows of desiring production by codifying it within a system of representation that reduces the factories of the unconscious to a theater stage—Oedipus, Hamlet—and traces desire onto family coordinates. Psychoanalysis sees the unconscious as always and already constituted, structured, and expressive. It is an ideological or symbolic theater in which the familial narrative—*Oedipus*—is constantly reenacted. The schizoanalytic unconscious, alternatively, is above all else productive and it is constantly producing itself as the ongoing production of lines. It is schizophrenic, material, machinic, "an unconscious finally that is molecular, microphysical and micrological rather than molar or gregarious" (Deleuze and Guattari 1977, 109–10).

Schizoanalysis attempts to describe the particular effects of desiring production. Most obviously, it connects assemblages, including desiring machines, to one another along the paths of the breaks and flows of desire (or libidinal energy) itself. The productivity of desire is an attraction that links and produces partial objects as breaks in the flow of desire. That is, the objects of desire are "sliced off" the continuous flows of desire at the points of disruptions or detours. Thus desire as desiring production is constantly reproducing itself: it connects desiring machines and thus reproduces as well the unconscious as the factory of such production. But desire also produces its own contradiction in the form of a principle of antiproduction: the body without organs (or within the social regime, the socius). The body without organs is that which resists desire and connections, that which is itself nonproductive but into which desiring production sends its lines of flight. It is, presumably, that which disrupts and interrupts the flows of desire, a principle of pure passivity, materiality, or resistance that is itself the product of the desire. It is the other that desire must constitute as its antithesis, a produced abstraction of a totality of materiality unmarked but traversed by the lines of desiring production.

The analytical and theoretical importance of the body without organs lies in the space it opens between desiring machines and the body without organs, a space that calls into existence and is traversed by other forms of production juxtaposed to desiring production itself. If desiring production can be understood as connective lines, Deleuze and Guattari propose as well disjunctive and conjunctive lines or productivities. Disjunction produces partial objects that attach desiring machines (and their partial objects) to the body without organs. It produces breaks in the flow of desire that, rather than being objects of desire as connection, detach themselves from desire and inscribe themselves on the surface of the body without organs. Disjunctive productivity is the articulation of chains of objects, structures that record and define boundaries upon abstract materiality itself. It is a territorialization, the production of a grid or coding, disconnected from both desire and materiality, and yet it disjunctively relates desire back to the body without organs. It thus produces a circuit of relations among the partial objects of desire through which desire is directed and distributed. This statement, however, is not meant to suggest that disjunction is always the production of lines of articulation, a production that represses and even halts the flows of desire.

For each of the three modes of production, Deleuze and Guattari identify both an immanent and a transcendent use, the former allowing desiring production on its way, the latter controlling, directing, and even stopping desiring production. Thus it is "a disjunction that remains disjunctive, and that still affirms the disjoined terms, that affirms them throughout their entire distance, without restricting one by the other or excluding the other from the one . . . Either . . . or . . . or, instead of either/or" (1977, 76). Disjunction, then, though it defines paths for the flows of desire, need not constrain it. Disjunction produces heterogeneous codings that trace upon the surface of the body without organs the lines of flight of desiring production. That is, insofar as desire itself connects partial objects from disparate, heterogeneous regimes, disjunctive lines inscribe paths of differentiation and externality rather than of identity and repression. As long as the circulation of desire as attraction is permitted in structures of "either . . . or . . . or . . ." and desiring production is allowed in its flows, it continues to produce lines of flight. It is only when the pathways are rigidified and exclusive, forcing desire to flow into particular circuits, that the inscription of differences (codes or chains) becomes a reterritorialization.

The third mode of productivity—conjunction—accounts for the production of the subject. Conjunctive lines produce a reconciliation between the assemblages of desiring production and the body without organs, a reconciliation that goes beyond a merely disjunctive production. Conjunction produces lines between circuits of distribution and the surface upon which they are inscribed. It too produces breaks in the flow of desire, partial objects that break off from the circuit and wander over the surface of the body without organs. These residuals or "qualities" exist independently of desire and of the codings of desire, apparently; they exist adjacent to any concrete partial object or chain, "with no fixed identity . . . peripheral to desiring machines" (Deleuze and Guattari 1977, 16). The productivity of conjunction is the becoming of identity through the breaking off of intensive qualities that, though apparently independent, have no proper place or identity.

The subject is, then, a particular effect of the productivity of desire—an assemblage with no concrete identity other than its effect in conjoining desiring production and its partial objects with that which resists desire and over whose surface desire travels. The subject—like capital (another quality)—is a surplus reality that flows in and out of the circuit of distribution, a domain of emotion and affect, of potentials and consummations, providing the link between desire and matter, between productivity and that which, while being a product, resists production. This subject—as the product of conjunctive links between partial objects—is clearly neither Kristeva's thetic subject nor Derrida's discursive subject. These are, instead, the products of the transcendental uses of conjunctive production involving the familization of desiring production and the oedipalization of the unconscious. Nor is the nomadic subject the same as Kristeva's subject in process, for this assumes a primordial and individual psychic reality out of which the subject is continuously emergent. But this view is already a particular social investment of the regime of desiring production that brings that production to a halt in the image of transgression. Oedipus is not an individual event or fantasy but a social reterritorialization of an already social desire: "The social field, where everyone acts and is acted upon as a collective agent of enunciation, an agent of production and antiproduction, is reduced to Oedipus, where everyone now finds himself cornered and cut along the line that divides him into an individual subject of the statement and an individual subject of enunciation. The subject of the statement is the social person, and the subject of the enunciation, the private person" (Deleuze and Guattari 1977, 265). The thetic or discursive subject of experience is the social territorialization of the surplus reality of desire rather than the necessary product of linguistic and/or psychic processes.

If the subject as a residue of conjunctive production is a nomadic quality, an "image" that provides the measure of desire and distribution, then the experienced subject that preoccupies the poststructuralists is only an image "of the second order, images of images, that is, simulacra that are thus endowed with an aptitude for representing the first order images of social persons . . . They are nothing more nor less than configurations or images produced by the point-signs, the break-flows, the pure figures of capitalism" (Deleuze and Guattari 1977, 264). The subject as the private subject, even if socially determined, is no longer a category within rhizomatics; the subject of schizoanalysis is not individual, not discursive, and not ideological. It is produced before the significations of ideology at the level of the breaks and flows of material desire, not merely in process, but nomadic and polyvocal. It provides a measure and consummation of that which produces it as a residue.

I have worked through some of the details of Deleuze and Guattari's schizoanalysis to illustrate a strategy avoiding the remnants of phenomenology within poststructuralism: the idealism of subjectivity and discourse is subtracted from the complex reality of a network of effects. I want, finally, to read the recent work of Michel Foucault as a more general, rhizomatic analysis of human existence. Foucault, like Deleuze and Guattari, disclaims the attempt to describe or explain the structures of experience. Their work, taken together, represents a significant attack on the pretensions of discourse to totalize itself, to locate life and desire, history and power within itself. With Foucault, the dichotomies of desire and discourse, individual and social, phenomenological and semiological discourses are put aside in favor of a new discourse on effectivity.

Michel Foucault and the Effectivity of the Concrete. The paradox of schizoanalysis both as practice and especially as a discursive strategy is that it introduces a binarism implicating transcendence. Although Deleuze and Guattari maintain that binarisms may be used to undermine the effects of other dualisms (1981, 64), the division between deterritorialization and reterritorialization, between arborescence and rhizomes seems absolute and the basis of a normative/political position. This is most obvious in their utopianism of schizophrenia. It is interesting to consider, in this context, Foucault's introduction to *Anti-Oedipus*: "I would say that *Anti-Oedipus* (may its authors forgive me) is a book of ethics . . . (perhaps that explains why its success was not limited to a particular "readership": being anti-oedipal has become a life style, a way of thinking and living). How does one keep from being a fascist, even (especially) when one believes oneself to be a revolutionary militant?" (Deleuze and Guattari 1977, xiii). What Foucault has accomplished is to change the effectivity of their discourse because it is no longer to be read as theoretical, even though the text claims a theoretical power for itself. Foucault's strategic intervention recontextualizes the text as a practical guide to the nonfascist life. He gives it a local and concrete existence within the particular context of the contemporary French Left. Deleuze and Guattari present a strategy of theorizing that fails to negate the transcendence of theory itself. Foucault, on the other hand, eschews theorizing. If Deleuze and Guattari present a theory calling for "bricolage," Foucault presents theorizing itself as "bricolage," a practice for the analysis of the concrete. Foucault makes rhizomes while always locating the analysis within the concrete as well, albeit necessarily a different historical concrete. Thus Foucault can write about the birth of the prison or the clinic as concrete events—facts—locating them within a network of other facts, all of which can be analyzed in terms of power and resistance, and at the same time relating the analysis to the context of his own implication within a network of power. His writing becomes neither theoretical nor utopian but a fact of strategic intervention. It is Foucault's apparently simultaneous acceptance of historical determination, political choice, and "positivism" that has troubled so many of his American (U.S.) readers.

I want to summarize, then, the strategy that Foucault uses in his more recent work on power and that he has, to some extent, described in various interviews and short pieces. Foucault's project is clearly to describe and explain the existence of a particular event within a concrete context of events. The key to my reading is that, depending upon the particular point at which his discourse intervenes into that context, events are described in terms of facts, strategies or techniques, effectivities (power and resistance), or conditions of possibility and that, from a theoretical perspective, all of these terms function equivalently. All of them attempt to describe events as existing within an assemblage of lines of intensity, to use a rhizomatic vocabulary.

Foucault rejects any transcendent or transcontextual appeal, even if it is only to some content-free process such as intentionality, ideology, *différance*, or *signifiance*. He refuses any term that reduces the concreteness of an event, that effaces its specificity in the name of understanding, explanation, or theory. For example:

> it seems to me that the specificity of the question of the Gulag must be stressed against any theoretical reduction (which makes it an error readable from the texts), against any historicist reduction (which makes it a conjunctural effect isolatable on the bases of its causes), against any utopian dissociation (which would place it, along with "pseudo-socialism," in opposition to socialism "itself"), and against any universalizing dissolution into the general form of confinement. All of these operations . . . have the same role: to continue . . . to keep a certain form of leftist discourse circulating among us. (1979a, 51)

He even refuses the reduction of human existence to labor, proposing instead that "the life and time of man are not by nature labour, but pleasure, restlessness, merry-making, rest, needs, accidents, desires, violent acts, robberies, etc." (62).

Foucault sees poststructuralism as a philosophy of the signifier still locked into a discourse of representation and hence transcendence. It still looks for the meaning of the text, albeit a determined but undecidable meaning. In fact, poststructuralism, while denying *a* meaning to the text, explodes it into a playful sliding of the signifiers, seeing meaning always as a surplus to the processes of determination. Only Barthes (1974) seems to have realized that the lack of innocence of a particular reading does not negate that reading; it merely implicates the text as an event within a context of power, desire, and truth-effects. Foucault opposes to the poststructuralist's practice of reading texts an accumulation of texts. He is concerned with the signifier's place or existence within a concrete historical context, an existence that is never innocent, innocently possible, or merely a question of meaning. This suggests that the signifier or text is an event whose place is broader than just discourse itself.

For Foucault, not everything is discourse; reality encompasses more than discursive practices, more than the signifying, and more than the significant. This idea reaches out in three directions. First, there is a material reality, and consequently there are nondiscursive (not prediscursive) practices that cannot be described or explained with a theory of signification.[5] Second, chance or accident is itself part of the context of human existence. Third, all human practices function in a material context in which there are many different types of effects and determinations: desire, power, and truth are those most central to Foucault's project. And although these all intersect with and have their effects on discourse, they cannot be analyzed in the language of representation or signification. Consequently Foucault is not particularly interested in providing critical readings of text, even deconstructive ones. When he uses texts—and he does so frequently—it is almost as if their meaning were clear so that they can be used as "documentary" evidence. It is more accurate to see that their meaning is not the issue. Texts exist as particular discourses, factual events embodying particular strategies, related to other specific events, only some of which are discursive. Texts are not accountable within their own terms, nor within the terms of an intertextuality. They are not dissolved, dispersed, or fragmented into a play of discursive codes or practices. Rather a text is identified with its particular existence within a context, with its particular functions and conditions of possibility:

I do not question the discourses for their silent meanings but on the fact and the conditions of their manifest appearance: not on the contents which they may conceal, but on the transformations which they have effectuated; not on the meaning which is maintained in them like a perpetual origin, but on the field where they coexist, remain and disappear. It is a question of an analysis of the discourses in their exterior dimensions. From whence arise three consequences:

1. Treat past discourse not as a theme for a *commentary* which would revive it, but as a *monument* to be described in its character-disposition.

2. Seek in the discourse not its laws of construction, as do the structural methods, but its conditions of existence.

3. Refer the discourse not to the thought, to the mind or to the subject which might have given rise to it, but to the practical field in which it is deployed. (1978b, 15)

Foucault's practice is to always deny any "molar" term of unity and transcendence, whether it be, for example, sexuality as a universal human condition, or even a text as a constituted whole. Thus Foucault is as likely to be concerned with a word, a sentence, or a rhetorical figure as with a text "in its entirety." Foucault emphasizes the diverse, the concrete, the discontinuous, the molecular. He is concerned with the individuation of practices or events, an individuation defined by the particular effectivity of the event both within and outside of discourse, and by its conditions of possibility.

In particular, Foucault's concern thus far is with the existence or nonexistence of the discursive event "within the true," that is, with the fact that some discursive events produce "truth effects." Because that production is itself conditioned, the particular effectivity of such events cannot be accounted for within purely discursive terms. Truth effects are not a measure of epistemological validity; they rather describe the inclusion and exclusion of concrete discursive facts from exerting particular effects. It is, then, a question of power—of the power of some discourses that we describe as true, and of the power of contexts to determine which events have such power. But it is not only discourse that can have truth effects; the "regime of sexuality" as an organization of the body, material and discursive practices, for example, has its truth effects. Foucault's project, then, is to explore the "political history of the production of truth," where truth is no longer a property attached to discourse but the concrete effects of particular practices.

In his earlier work (1970, 1972), Foucault appealed to the concepts of episteme and archive to describe the existence of discourse. The former pointed to an open field of relations and successive displacements, a space of dispersion. The latter referred to an anonymous system of rules accounting for the appearance, formation, and transformation of discursive practices. Together these terms defined the domain of an "archaeology" of knowledge. However, since his lecture "Orders of Discourse," delivered in 1970, the question of power has displaced that of knowledge. The discursive field is seen as the difference between what could be said correctly and what is actually said, and thus defines a space within which power is operative. Archaeology explores "the law of existence of the statement, that which has rendered them possible—them and none other in their place: the conditions of their singular emergence: their correlation with other previous or simultaneous events, discursive or not" (1978b, 14). The meaning of discourse is supplanted by the conditions of its emergence, insertion, and functioning, what Foucault calls its mode of existence or effectivity.

The turn to power as the central concern in Foucault's writing is crucial, for it marks as well a change in Foucault's theoretical strategy. Power is not a category with a fixed significance, but a description of concrete techniques, effects, and conditionings. There is no fundamental principle—power—grounding all of the various manifestations of power. Rather one must analyze the concrete mechanisms through which power is exercised and the contexts of historical events and strategies that condition that exercise. The problematic of power has led to two important changes in Foucault's discourse: the metaphor of war and the vocabulary of events. Foucault rejects the view that human life and history is like a dialogue, asserting instead that it must be seen as a constant battle or struggle and thus in terms of strategies and techniques of power. Further, he has proposed (1981a) a view of his own method as an "eventalization." The "event" has increasingly replaced talk about codes, rules, and discontinuities, but it is not offered as a singular, metaphysical term:

> It is not a question of putting everything on a certain plane, that of the event, but of seeing clearly that there exists a whole series of levels of different types of events, which do not have the same range, nor the same chronological breadth, nor the same capacity to produce effects. The problem is to both distinguish the events, differentiate the networks and levels to which they belong, and to reconstitute the threads which connect them and make them give rise to one another. (1979a, 33)

The strategy of eventalization represents a "monism of practices" that, because of Foucault's politicotheoretical intervention, takes the form of an investigation of truth and power together.

The notion of practice brings together regimes of "jurisdiction" and of "veridication." The former prescribes what can be done: procedures and strategies. The latter provides reasons and principles justifying these ways of doing things through a production of "true discourses." These two regimes develop together and condition each other. Within these terms, one can address questions of how particular practices emerged and were accepted as natural, at a particular moment, within a larger context of practices.

Regimes of practices, then, define particular technologies or "programmings of behavior," which coexist and interact with other regimes. The notion of an "apparatus" describes such heterogeneous ensembles of practices: "discourses, institutions, architectural forms, regulatory decisions, laws, administrative measures, scientific statements, philosophical, moral and philanthropic propositions—in short, the said as much as the unsaid" (1980a, 194). The apparatus brings together disparate discursive and nondiscursive events, regimes of jurisdiction and veridication, all of which condition and modify each other's functions and effects. It is a network of techniques of power.[6]

Despite this contextual determination, particular techniques and apparatuses always emerge in response to a particular historical need: they are strategic. But their existence is not completely conditioned by this "origin," for they continue to exist through "functional overdetermination" and "strategic elaboration." Because a technique enters into a context of complex relations in which it conditions and is conditioned by other techniques, its effects demand that the apparatus readjust itself. And further, the technique may have effects that demand the elaboration of the technique itself, extending it beyond the original need but nevertheless completing its effectiveness. To put it simply, the effectivity of techniques extends well beyond their intended or even imagined possibilities because they enter into larger apparatuses.

Particular techniques, then, are neither natural nor arbitrary, but rather connected with a "multiplicity of historical forces." In order to analyze a technique, one must break through its façade of naturalness and necessity. Eventalization begins with a "breach of self-evidence," through which the singularity, concreteness, or positivity of the event is made visible. With no historical constants, essences, or universals, Foucault's position is an extreme nominalism, not only of events but of contexts as well. Given the singular event, one must "rediscover the connections, encounters, supports, blockages, plays of force, strategies, and so on which at a given moment establish what subsequently counts as being self-evident, universal and necessary" (1981a, 6). Through a process of "causal multiplication," the archaeologist constructs, around the event, a "polyhedron of intelligibility." Analysis is rhizomatic, connecting the event with other events that constitute it and its effects: drawing lines of effectivity and determination! This reassembling of historical contexts is somewhat analogous to constructing a jigsaw puzzle without knowing how many pieces are needed, if they are all present, or what the puzzle is a picture of. What one finds as the apparatus is the inscription of lines of power upon its surface, but the lines need not correspond to the breaks between the pieces of the puzzle, that is, to experienced categories and relations. It is only by constructing the puzzle that one maps out the relations of force that are operative.

It is important to recognize that this project, despite superficial similarities, is not comparable to the search for the underlying codes governing and determining human behavior. And despite the similarities between Foucault's description of the apparatus and, for example, Williams's "structure of feeling" (1965), it is not a description of experience, of what it felt like to live at a particular time and place. Foucault's project is radically different from the phenomenologically motivated attempt to capture a context of experience or, as he puts it, of "grasping a 'whole society' in its 'living reality'" (1981a, 11). Foucault is not concerned with how we experience everyday reality but with how we live and act in ways over which we may have no control and about which we may be unaware, experientially as well as consciously. Experiences are to be treated as facts among other facts.

Foucault's recent work on sexuality seems to raise two distinct questions: First, "how has sexuality come to be considered the privileged place where our deepest truth is read?" (1977, 152). And second, "how [are] the relations of power . . . able to pass materially into the very density of bodies without even having to be relayed by the representation of power?" (1979a, 69–70). In fact, the two questions are not distinct; an answer to the first requires an answer to the second, yet that can only be provided by concretely examining the techniques by which a particular apparatus of sexuality has been constructed and made effective.

Foucault's "theory" of power refuses to define and limit its effectivity to particular forms: either as prohibitory/repressive (on the model of juridical law and the monarchy) or as positive/constitutive of desire: "They both rely on a common representation of power which, depending on the use made of it, leads to two contrary results: either to the promise of a "liberation," if power is seen as having only an external hold on desire, or, if it is constitutive of desire itself, to the affirmation: you are always-already trapped" (1978a, 83). Nor is power merely equivalent to effectivity; it is, however, an omnipresent form of effectivity. Foucault's "microphysics" of power focuses on, first, the mechanisms of power and second, power in its "capillary existence: the point where power reaches into the very grain of individuals, touches their bodies and inserts itself into their actions and attitudes, their discourses, learning processes and everyday lives" (1980a, 39). Power does not exist outside of the concrete and local mechanisms by which it is exercised. It is the inscription of relations of force on the surface of our lives, our bodies, institutions, and discourses. And it operates directly, without the mediation of consciousness, representation, or ideology, for these are already the effects of power. In fact, power is the fact of an "organised hierarchical, coordinated cluster of relations" (1980a, 198). The domain of power is coextensive with that of social relations; power exists between every point within the social field, always connecting it to a political field that both constitutes and is constituted by the "myriad powers, effects of power and issues of power." Macrostructures of power (e.g., the sovereign or the court) are real and may have their own effects, but they arise out of and act back upon an entire context of minute strategies and relations of power.

The analysis of power must begin, Foucault contends (1980b), with the relations themselves, since power itself determines the elements on which it bears. Consequently, like Deleuze and Guattari, Foucault is unwilling to assume that the primary term of strategies of power (e.g., that which it infiltrates) is always individuals or groups of individuals. The individual, in fact, like the "subject," is itself an effect of power (1980a, 99). Power may seek to control particular facts of material existence with no consideration of their "belonging to" individuals. Thus when Foucault was asked "would [this] mean that there are only ever transitory coalitions, some of which immediately break up, but others of which persist, but that strictly speaking individuals would be the first and last components?" he responded, "Yes, individuals or even sub-individuals" (1980a, 208). The question was intended to shatter the stable unity of social aggregates such as classes, but Foucault takes it a step further to shatter the unity of stable individuality in power relations. Foucault's nominalism is, then, not of objects or individuals, but of events and relations of power. Foucault has summarized this microphysics in a series of hypotheses (1978a, 94–95): Power is local, multiple, mobile. Power relations are immanent in other relations. Power relations are productive. Power is fragmented and infrastructural. Power relations are intentional and nonsubjective. And finally, where there is power, there is resistance.

The notion of resistance is crucial and yet particularly problematic, since it apparently introduces a second principle into Foucault's discourse. Thus when Foucault attempts to locate the basis of resistance to power, he talks about the "pleb":

> Without doubt, the "pleb" must not be conceived of as the permanent foundation of history, the final objective of all subjections, the never totally extinct hearth of every revolt. The "pleb" undoubtedly has no sociological reality. But there is indeed always something which in some way escapes the relations of power; something in the social body . . . which is not at all the more or less docile or reactive raw material, but which is the centrifugal movement, the inverse energy, that which escapes. The "pleb" undoubtedly does not exist, but there is "plebness" . . . it is that which responds to every advance of power by a movement to disengage itself; it is therefore that which motivates every new development in the networks of power. (1979a, 52)

There are two ways to read this and avoid the assumption of a transcendental principle of resistance, both of which would see resistance in material terms as an effect of power. First, one might identify plebness with the socius (the social form of the body without organs), an abstract principle of resistance that is the product of power. Second, one can argue against Foucault that one need no more account for the abstract possibility of resistance than one need describe a universal principle of power. Power relations are never simple, causal, isolated, and unidirectional, but rather operate under conditions of material and strategic contradiction. Thus power produces its own material relations of resistance, which have their own local effects, including perhaps the apparent absence of any real effects. Resistance is not always effective. Plebs do exist as concrete relations of force; plebness does not exist! Resistance is merely the drawing of lines of flight.

Finally, one must locate Foucault's work as an intervention into a particular field of power and question its own status. Foucault's strategy is intended to support any resistance to what he sees as a particular apparatus of power that is rapidly being extended and elaborated: "biopolitics,"[7] or the regime of disciplinary practices (1978a). Thus his description of the "deployment of sexuality" is not built upon a utopian image of a liberated sexuality, nor does it assume some innocent albeit irrecuperable organization of sex preceding all relations of power. The "erotics of the body" which he opposes to "sexuality" also exists within a network of power; its attractiveness is its resistance to the biopolitics of contemporary Western society. While he acknowledges that we live in "a state of sexual misery . . . the problem is to know whether the misery should be explained negatively by a fundamental interdiction, or positively by a prohibition relative to an economic situation ('Work, don't make love'): or whether it is not the effect of much more complex and much more positive procedures" (1977b, 153).

If we return to Kristeva's concern for the revolutionary subject, Foucault obviously faces an "enigma of revolt." If there is always power, with no transcendental term defining a utopian justification for revolution, what are the grounds for locating points of political intervention and resistance? Foucault refuses to answer the question of whether it is useless to revolt:

> There are revolts and that is a fact . . . A delinquent puts his life into the balance against absurd punishments; a madman can no longer accept confinement and the forfeiture of his rights; a people refuse the regime which oppresses it. This does not make the rebel in the first case innocent, nor does it cure in the second, and it does not assure the third rebel of the promised tomorrow . . . One does not have to maintain that these confused voices sound better than the others and express the ultimate truth. For there to be a sense in listening to them and in searching for what they want to say, it is sufficient that they exist and that they have against them so much which is set up to silence them. A question of morality? Perhaps. A question of reality? Certainly. (1981b, 8)

This brings us back to Foucault's view that certain discursive events produce truth effects. But as some discourses are "in the true," others are thereby excluded. Truth and politics demand that we return to the "local character of criticism and struggle," for only then can one understand Foucault's theory as a political intervention asserting its own truth. Foucault has recently redescribed his project as "genealogy":

> Let us give the term "genealogy" to the union of erudite knowledge and local memories which allows us to establish a historical knowledge of struggles and to make use of this knowledge tactically today . . . If we were to characterize it in two terms, then "archeology" would be the

appropriate methodology of this analysis of local discursivities, and "genealogy" would be the tactics whereby, on the basis of the description of the local discursivities, the subjected knowledges which were thus released would be brought into play. (1980a, 83, 85)

Foucault's strategy, then, both analytically and politically, is to return to those contexts in which particular technologies not only emerged and were incorporated, but were made to appear natural and inevitable. This process always involves struggles between competing discourses and strategies. In the historical production of particular apparatuses, some regimes of practice and knowledge are denied their place within the true, and thus their right to exist and function. By returning to these struggles and recuperating these local knowledges and techniques that have been silenced, we denaturalize the existing apparatus and open up potential points of resistance and contemporary struggle. For example, Foucault raises the discourse of an "erotics of sex" opposed to the deployment of sexuality as a local discursivity through which we might intervene and resist the regime of biopolitics; there is no claim that it defines a purer, more innocent, or even happier sexuality. Similarly, his attack on science is not predicated on the form of scientific discourse or its appropriateness to a particular object of study, but rather on its particular power to exclude other discourses from the true, its negation of the local and political reality of all knowledge. Foucault's position is describable, oxymoronically, as a social anarchy, that is, a politics of temporary and pragmatic coalitions attacking particular regimes of power at specific points that have been identified as the site of an ongoing struggle in the mutual conditioning of knowledge and behavior.[8] As a theoretical discourse, Foucault has described his work as a tool box (1979a, 57), continuing this image: through his own genealogies, he has made some rhizome from the vantage point of his own theoretical and political context. The reader is free to take some of that rhizome into his or her own analysis, implicating and prescribing both different analyses and different strategies of resistance.

But in what sense does Foucault claim a "truth" for his discourse, and what of his troublesome combination of determination and positivism? Foucault's response is typically to say that he writes fictions or constructs fabrications, but such fictions are neither innocent—they are conditioned by their context—nor necessarily outside of the true:

It seems possible to me to make fictions work within truth, to induce truth-effects within a fictional discourse, and in some way to make the discourse of truth arouse, "fabricate" something which does not as yet exist, thus "fiction" something. One "fictions" history starting from a political reality that renders it true, one "fictions" a politics that doesn't as yet exist starting from an historical truth. (1979a, 74–75)

After all, the fact that history itself is problematic because the distinction between the true and the false is itself a product of that history does not mean that history is not real, nor that our descriptions of it, fictions always, are not true and effective. Foucault's claim that he produces fictions is not set in opposition to the possibility of a nonfictional discourse on history. Foucault's discourse locates itself within the network of power and knowledge that it analyzes: if history is a war, then the subject who speaks is already implicated in the struggle, speaking from one side or the other. One seeks victory not within the abstract idealism of a theory of representation or signification, but in terms of a local struggle—political and discursive—over truth effects. Foucault's discourse locates itself within the local historical fact of struggle it seeks to analyze: "What we have here is thus a political and historical discourse which lays claim to truth and right, but excludes itself explicitly from juridico-philosophical universality . . . [a discourse] which deciphers the permanence of war in society, and in which truth functions as a weapon for partisan victory; it is a sombrely critical yet at the same time intensely mythical discourse" (1980b, 17–18). Foucault has provided us with an analytic strategy that is simultaneously psychic and social, historical and political, relative and true.

CONCLUSION

I have tried to distinguish the project of poststructuralism from the search for a philosophy or strategy of immanent analysis. I am not claiming that the work of Foucault, for example, is a complete break with the tradition of Western philosophy; if anything, it is a return to the pre-Kantian concern with the real. Through this comparison, I hope to have clarified the relation between poststructuralist discourse and the discourse of experience. My argument can be summarized by saying that poststructuralism continues to exist with the Kantian problematic of mediation. The split between structure and experience exists only within the space mediating between the subject and the object. Poststructuralism reconstructs a context of experience without a subject as origin or center by substituting a context of signification or connotation for that of experience. But the substitution does not displace the problematic, it merely changes the terms of the discourse. Thus, despite its rhetoric, poststructuralist readings of texts exploded into con-texts serve only to reconceptualize the terms within which the experience of texts provides the "given." It remains situated within the "between" that is the place of experience. The poststructuralist escapes the subject-object dichotomy by locating his or her activity as a context of readings, a context that already implicates the reading subject and transforms the text into an experienced reality. Rather than avoiding the dilemmas of relativism that such a procedure raises, poststructuralists lovingly play with relativism. Hence the most compelling feature of their readings is the absolute uniqueness of the critic's voice, the sheer irreproducibility of the reading. The implications of relativism in the politics of truth are ignored.

Barthes's reading of "Sarrasine" (1974) makes this explicit: he presents and deconstructs a realist text, that is, a text that has already been read. It is a variation on Althusser's view (1971) of ideology constituting experience so that experience may now be read within a discourse of textuality. The poststructuralist project resembles, more closely than they would like to admit, Williams's attempts (1965) to reconstruct and deconstruct structures of experience, merely substituting an anonymous field of signification for the humanistic, personological discourse of experience. I am not suggesting that this is not an important difference with real consequences, but rather that the failure to recognize the relationship may be a stumbling block to poststructuralist research. For example, when Morley (1980) constructs two discourses on the same text, one a poststructural/ideological reading and the other composed of audience members' comments on their experience of the text, he is apparently unable to reconcile the two, for they are *about* different things. On the contrary, they are two discourses about the same thing—the experience of a particular discursive event—and Morley merely fails to recognize his own implication within any reading. The deconstruction of texts is, in some way, the mirror image of the phenomenological reading of experience.

This conclusion is not a critique of poststructuralism. Any semiotic theory concerned with describing structures and contexts of signification is located within a transcendental framework of experience. Poststructuralism is not condemned to find phenomenological traces within its discourse; rather it should seek ways to more effectively understand and utilize the mirror provided by the discourse of experience.

Strategies of Marxist Cultural Interpretation

There is a growing recognition and acceptance of what is often euphemistically called "critical" or "materialist" theories of communication and culture. If we are to believe the cumulative description offered in *Ferment in the Field* (Gerbner 1983), we have not advanced very far since Lazarsfeld first introduced the conflict between administrative and critical research into the canonical constitution of the discipline. First, each side is still attacked as if it held the same positions and faced the same theoretical quagmires as when Lazarsfeld attempted a liberal rapprochement between them. Second, each side continues to attack the other as if the "enemy" were a monolithic, theoretical, methodological, and political monster. Third, and most importantly, each side often presents itself in similarly monolithic terms, ignoring not only their differences, but the contributions that such differences make to their alliance. The origins of such "reductionist" strategies are complex. To be sure, they are a risk of any interdisciplinary endeavor, and they seem, too, often, to be the almost inevitable effects of the self-nominations, "science" and "marxism."

Given the increasingly confusing proliferation of models for marxist communications research, it should be useful to document some of the differences that exist. There are, however, a number of ways to divide the terrain; the framework constitutes as well as describes the differences. Positions are "necessarily" misrepresented because they respond to different issues. The framework I propose focuses on the practice of interpreting specific messages or cultural forms, rather than centering on any theory per se. On the other hand, I will "read" such practices as responses to two related theoretical questions: (1) the politics of textuality, and (2) the problematic of cultural studies.

The *politics of textuality* signals the changing meaning and function of the category "text" (or "message"), both within everyday life and in the specific work of intellectuals. The analysis of the functions[1] of a text depends in part on how one conceptualizes the nature of signifying practices and structures and their relations to processes of creativity, determination, and interpretation. In more traditional marxist terms, the interpretation of texts also depends upon how and where they are inserted into the circuit of production and consumption. These terms are reproduced in a model of communication as the circuit of the exchange of meanings, information, or signifiers. Consequently, the investigation of the text is divided into questions of encoding—the relation between production and text—and decoding—the relation between text and consumption or reception.

The second issue, the *problematic of cultural studies,* concerns the division between culture and society within the social formation. It questions the difference, as well as the relations, between signifying and nonsignifying practices. The "culture/society" couplet brings together the Chicago school pragmatists, marxist models of base and superstructure, and contemporary theories of ideology and power. In fact, there is a third term implicit in the question: not only cultural meaning (forms, practices, etc.) and social structures (processes, forces, etc.), but also experience or the domain of everyday life. This third term slides between culture and society. Williams (1958) identifies the ambiguity *in* the concept of culture, although he then projects it into the social. Culture refers to both the anthropologically constituted notion (with its liberal democratic politics) of a "whole way of life," and the critical humanistic notion (with its sharply demarcated class politics) of a special set of signifying activities. The latter can be "cleansed" of its inherent elitism by broadening the institutional sites of such practices beyond the narrow domain of art to include the entire range of "ideological state apparatuses" (Althusser 1971); in other words, the forms and practices of interpersonal and mediated communications.

Just as the question of textuality creates an analytical, if not theoretical, gap between encoding and decoding, the problematic of cultural studies produces a gap between culture and society in describing how particular structures of meaning determine or are determined by social processes. The task apparently requires both a hermeneutics of faith and a hermeneutics of suspicion (Ricoeur 1970). The latter sees the text determined by a context and functioning in part to hide that determination. The former treats the text as transcending that context, its message potentially universal. A "hermeneutics of faith" interprets the meaning or message of a text; it reaches into literary, symbolic, and semiotic theory. A "hermeneutics of suspicion" connects that meaning to a determinate context; it must already have described the social realm and the organization of power and domination within it. The intersection of these two hermeneutics defines the "ideological function" of the text, and it is often in terms of "ideology" that the problematic of cultural studies is theorized.

The questions of the politics of textuality and the problematic of cultural studies, taken together, provide one way of defining the task of marxist interpretation: to describe (and intervene in) the way messages are produced by, inserted into, and function within the everyday lives of concrete human beings so as to reproduce or transform structures of power and domination. I will describe ten different positions (organized into three larger categories or approaches) to the study of cultural texts or communicative messages coexisting within the space of a marxist theory.[2] For each position I will briefly describe its methodological practice and the (often implicit) theoretical responses to the two questions described above. While I will provide at least one example of an interpretation for each position, the mix of abstract and concrete analysis will vary depending upon the availability and accessibility of the work. I will conclude with a schematic summary of this admittedly partial and oversimplified map of the marxist terrain.

THE CLASSICAL APPROACH

Under this heading, I describe three different positions sharing a number of assumptions: *false consciousness, critical theory,* and *economism.* All three positions seek to find direct relations between cultural texts and social/economic realities. Not surprisingly, they often find intentional and malevolent voices speaking in the messages, voices seeking to protect their own positions of power and economic domination. Thus we might describe all three as "reflection" or causal theories. Finally, such classical positions describe both the social and cultural practices of capitalism in terms largely derived from Marx's earlier, humanistic rhetoric: Capitalism creates false needs; modern experience is built upon standardization, the sensationalization of everyday life, dehumanization, escapism, and fragmented if not false understandings of the world. Both the economic interests behind particular texts and the processes of production are always hidden.

Classical approaches, then, never question textuality. The text is assumed to be a transparent medium, or it is erased, or it is simply a conduit that determines the necessary modes of its own consumption. A confrontation with the text is strategically avoided by bracketing decoding processes. Such analyses focus on the relationship between the producer and the text, implying that consumers are passive and unaware of the ways in which messages act upon them. Mass communication becomes a process of the self-colonization of the individual. Culture cannot be the site of a struggle for power unless there are radically alternative and competing economic and political systems of media production. The result is that change can only occur through action upon the economic and political systems that determine the media messages.

False Consciousness. This position assumes that texts are collections of images that can be extracted from the text and treated as isolated, ideological representations of reality; that is, they are motivated by and function to protect the class interests already structured into the economic relations of capital. How the critic reads this meaning/ideology in the text is mystified within the critical practice, and there is no consideration of how the critic is able to escape the ideological machinations of the text. These meanings are then projected back into the processes of production (as intentions) and forward into the everyday lives of its audience. The unexamined practice of text-interpretation defines both the origin and effects of the text.

Perhaps the most compelling and important example of this approach is Dorfman and Mattelart's *How to Read Donald Duck* (1975). They interpret the comics as a series of image-codes that organize and define the characters and the relations among them. Using techniques as diverse as semiotics and psychoanalysis, the authors describe the structures of social identity and social relationships that constitute the world of Donald Duck. They assume that these meanings are found in the text by its diverse Latin American audiences. The text becomes a simple link between the producer and the consumer. The meanings "transmitted" by the text are placed there by the producers and directly determine their own reception in ways that support the interests of the producers. The text, then, is determinately univocal. For example, they argue that the comic texts consistently re-present a particular familial politics predicated upon an absent father (and an absent mother), creating a relationship between international capitalism and imperialism on the one hand, and familial and gender politics on the other.

Their reading is based on two assumptions: (1) that people take the media to be a realistic representation of reality which then reflects back onto it to reproduce systems of distorted knowledge (ideology); and (2) that people consume such messages by a determined and direct identification with a single (set of) character(s). For example, their interpretation is predicated on the child's identification with his (the authors do not seem to acknowledge the importance of the gendered determination of consumption) counterpart in the comics. Their practice is manifested and exhibited in the conclusions they draw throughout the text:

> It is the manner in which the U.S. dreams and redeems itself, and then imposes that dream upon others for its own salvation. (Dorfman and Mattelart 1975, 95)

> The bourgeois concept of entertainment, and the specific manner in which it is expounded in the world of Disney, is the superstructural manifestation of the dislocations and tensions of an advanced capitalist historical base. In its entertainment, it automatically generates certain myths functional to the system. It is altogether normal for readers experiencing the conflicts of their age from within the perspective of the imperialist system, to see their own daily life, and projected future, reflected in the Disney system . . . Behind the Coca Cola stands a whole structure of expectations and models of behavior, and with it, a particular kind of present and future society, and an interpretation of the past. (97)

This ability to, as Blake might say, "see the world in a grain of sand," is based on a vision of the culture/society couplet as a system of reflexes, moving from the base to the superstructure, through the audience, and returning to the base. Thus the complex and necessary ideological mechanisms of economic and political domination are "part of the metabolism of the system" (56).[3]

It may be useful to provide a second, more widely accessible example of this approach—Gitlin's The Whole World Is Watching (1980). Gitlin examines how the "routine practices" of news organizations define the structures of, and possibilities for, the production of news messages. Although Gitlin's theoretical framework suggests a "hermeneutic" position built upon Williams (1973a) and Gramsci (1971), his methodological practice contradicts this. Like other classical positions, his assumes that the media have the power to "orchestrate everyday consciousness" (2) in rather unproblematic ways, and that the structures of meaning that the media impose upon the audience can be simply read off the surface of the texts themselves. Ideology is "distributed by the media," which "bring a manufactured public world into private life" (1). Although he argues that critics must pay attention to the symbolic contents of the media before questions of concrete effects can be raised, Gitlin assumes that the texts are univocal. Consequently he is not compelled to offer any theory of how one is to discover the "frames" within which the media place events. They are there, on the surface, available to anyone who looks for them, that is, who has the proper political awareness. But most importantly, Gitlin's analysis of the ideological encoding in news production raises questions of its consumption. While he wants to allow for an active audience, that activity is limited to the ability to disagree with the ways in which media have framed a particular event or to respond to the textual framing in future activities. The frames are the meaning of the text, and they apparently determine the terms within which the audience can respond to the message, either in sympathy or in opposition. That frames themselves may take on different functions, or that audiences may respond to the messages according to an alternative reading of the encoded frames, does not enter into his argument.

Critical Theory. The work of the Frankfurt school has, for a number of reasons, been one of the most influential interpretations of marxism in communication studies. Critical theory sees cultural texts as an imposition of the categories of mass production onto the domain of consciousness, imagination, and thought. That is, the text becomes a conduit through which practices of production determine practices of consumption. The text is critically evaluated in terms of the ways in which it demands to be consumed. Thus once again, the relations between encoding and decoding, and between society and culture, are assumed to be simple reflexes or reflections.

This can be seen most clearly in Adorno's discussions (1941) of popular music. This critique, typical of the Frankfurt school, is enacted in ways that are qualitatively different from the analysis of "art." Adorno condemns mass or popular music as a standardized industrial product (commodity) which determines an infantilized (fetishized) mode of consumption. He acknowledges that, while the manufacturing, distribution, and marketing of the music are industrialized, the production itself must retain some artisanal character, but this merely functions as a rationalization of the music's commodification; it provides the illusion of individuality and masks its standardization. This contrasts sharply with Adorno's modernist vision of art as a transcendental, autonomous activity which, by projecting utopian possibilities, opens up a space for social critique.[4]

Critical theory assumes, first, that there is an abstract process of the "colonization of consciousness" by economic, industrialized forms which defines the power of the media; second, that there are direct relations between socioeconomic and sociopsychological processes; and third, that these can be read off the surface of the text, not as a particular signifying form but as an exemplar of an abstract category of cultural practices. By assuming that the text is a mere exemplar of a superstructural commodity, Adorno collapses the distinction between production and consumption, making the consumer's alienation the same as the laborer's. Thus while he recognizes that the consumer is an active coproducer of the cultural text, his view of the text as nothing more than a commodity form leads him to see this work as the production of the (economic) success of the text. That is, the consumer's work is the production of pure exchange value. The superstructure has not only been industrialized; it has collapsed into the forces of production. For critical theory, the cultural object is pure exchange value, with no use value whatsoever, except perhaps as an ideological mystification in the service of the already existing structures of power:

> To be sure exchange-value exerts its power in a special way in the realm of cultural goods. For in the world of commodities this realm appears to be exempted from the power of exchange, to be in an immediate relationship with the goods, and it is this appearance, in turn, which alone gives cultural goods their exchange value . . . The appearance of immediacy is as strong as the compulsion of exchange-value is inevitable. The social compact harmonises the contradiction. The appearance of immediacy takes possession of the mediated exchange-value itself. If the commodity in general combines exchange-value and use-value, then the pure use-value, whose illusion the cultural goods must preserve in completely capitalist society, must be replaced by pure exchange-value, which, precisely in its capacity as exchange-value deceptively takes over the function of use-value. The specific fetish-character of music lies in this quid pro quo. The feelings which go to the exchange-value create the appearance of immediacy at the same time as the absence of a relation belies it. It has its basis in the abstract character of exchange-value. Every "psychological" aspect, every ersatz satisfaction, depends upon such social substitution. (Adorno, cited in Bradley n.d., 28)

This results in a rather odd view of consumption and the consumer, as well as of signifying practices and processes of encoding. In the *Grundrisse* (1973), Marx struggled with the problem of consumption, though unsuccessfully. He finally concluded that consumption involves the "gratification of needs" that exist in a sphere of individual appropriation. Adorno psychologizes this need, and reduces the object of that appropriation to exchange value (in which both text and consumer are alienated and reified). This forces Adorno to confront the ultimately undecidable question of whether this need is real and unsatisfied, or illusory and produced by capitalism.

However, critical theory need not take that particular turn. John Berger (1972) has provided a reading of the "language" of publicity. Following Benjamin (1968), Berger argues that, in the age of mechanical reproduction, the meaning of such visual language is no longer *in* the representations themselves. Thus while publicity is "about" social relations, the message is embodied in its consumption—in how it is used, who uses it, and for what purposes. Publicity is a language that, in its very consumption, produces its message: it is both the "life" of capitalism (as the necessary condition of consumption) and the "dream" of capitalism (as the celebration of future possibilities over present realities). Publicity is a "way of seeing" that proposes the possibility of transformation by consumption, a transformation that is measured by the "happiness of being envied" rather than by the actual possession of commodities. Berger makes the assumption, constitutive of critical theory, that there is a correspondence between social use and meaning. The text embodies a way of seeing only insofar as its appropriation is already defined by the moment of production or encoding. However, consumption is neither psychologized nor explained simply in terms of exchange value.

Economism. The third classical approach to the interpretation of cultural texts is perhaps the most difficult to fit into the framework of the present discussion since its "interpretive practice" negates the practice of interpretation. It responds to neither the question of the politics of textuality nor to the problematic of cultural studies. Instead, it erases any textuality by treating the cultural text as (just another) commodity; it not only refuses to consider the relation of encoding and decoding, but denies the specificity of cultural practices. And hence the question of the relationship between culture and society is replaced by questions of determination within the economic sphere.[5] There is, in a sense, no necessity for cultural interpretation to ever look at cultural texts.

Economism looks behind the messages to see the mode of economic forces and relations, the systems of production and distribution. Consumption is monolithically determined by production, and hence both cultural texts and decodings are epiphenomenal products of the "economic base." At its most extreme, economism proposes that a concern with specific textual and consumption practices is itself a mystification of the actual relations of power in which cultural commodities are implicated. However, such reductionism is not inherent in the practice of economism. On the contrary, it is obvious that economic and technological practices not only determine cultural texts in part, but also insert them into already existing social relations of power. And there may be features of such texts, or moments in the history of particular cultural forms, that depend crucially on such factors.

Economism assumes a series of correspondences or identities between the cultural text, its status within the circuit of production and consumption, the economic relations embodied within that circuit, and the social relations of power. Most frequently, it analyzes the economic structures of media industries (e.g., modes of production, patterns of ownership, systems of distribution). But such "political economy" does not, by itself, constitute "economism" as an interpretive practice. Economism is based on implicit responses to the two questions discussed above, which allow it to read such analyses as making significant statements about the social functions of cultural texts, without any further interpretive mediations. For example, as Shore (1983) demonstrates, the six so-called major record companies control an enormous share of the records produced and sold in the world. But, as he recognizes, the issue is what this tells us about the music being produced, the constraints that the system imposes upon the concrete production of particular records, how the record is consumed, and what the relations are between this "economic" power and forms of ideological and political domination. On the other hand, Smythe's article, "Communications: Blindspot of Western Marxism" (1977), is certainly correct to argue that the product of the media, which they then sell for a profit, is the audience itself. Advertisers buy time only to obtain the real commodity: an audience. The interpretation, however, slides from the commodity status of the audience to claims about the media's concrete functions in structures of social power. To do so, it must equate the accumulation of capital (surplus value at the expense of labor) with the particular organization of political, ideological, and moral power (Murdock 1978). And it must negate the ability of the text, as a cultural practice, to enter into the equation in specific (e.g., ideological) and even contradictory ways.

In summary, classical approaches can take a number of different forms. All of them refuse the problematic of cultural studies by making culture at best a reflection or mechanical reproduction of the social. They are thus able not only to erase the specificity of cultural practices (even when talking about ideology), but also to refuse to raise the question of production and consumption in terms of encoding and decoding. By identifying the determining moment of social life with economic forces and relations, they establish a correspondence between production and power. The text is nothing more than an impediment that must be shattered if its real functions are to be constituted within this equation. The differences among classical positions depend largely upon the assumed status of the epiphenomenal text: as a distorting but representational mirror, as alienated consumption, as another form of capital accumulation.

THE HERMENEUTIC APPROACH

Within this approach, I want to describe a number of positions that give cultural or signifying practices a more active (ideological) role in the construction of power relations. Such positions assume that the relationship between cultural texts and social reality is always mediated by processes and structures of signification. Thus texts reveal their social significance not on the surface of images and representations, but rather in the complex ways that they produce, transform, and shape meaning structures. Texts orchestrate social reality, producing a symphonic experience that is not reducible to the cumulative contributions of each social determination. A text is not a simple reflection of a social reality, even a distorted one, nor is it a reflex response to the material conditions of its production. Thus the interpretation of a text requires an appreciation of the specific rules of its formal existence as a signifying practice.

Furthermore, according to such positions it is not primarily the factual, material social structure itself that is reworked and reshaped by the cultural text. Rather society itself is already mediated through signifying practices. The question of the relationship between culture and society is answered by appealing to the third term—experience—which already locates the social within the cultural. Thus social power is always to be viewed through the mediating structures of social experience, defined and determined, in the last instance, by class position. The "raw material" represented in cultural texts is social experience, and only indirectly then, social structures of power and domination. The critic, using the resources of literary theory, must look at the complex ways in which the text codes, reworks, and potentially transforms the very fabric of lived experience.

The result is a practice that seeks to find homologies or correspondences between the workings of the text and the social structures of experience; relationships embedded within the concrete mediations performed by the text. They exist only at a deeper level of textual meaning. At the level of this deep structure, points of correspondence can be identified and meanings that comment upon and enter into the experienced social reality of consumers and producers can be uncovered.

Structural Mediation. Perhaps the most significant figure in the emergence of marxist cultural studies has been Raymond Williams. For Williams, the crucial mediation by which cultural text and social reality are linked is defined by the notion of the "structure of feeling" (Grossberg 1977; Williams 1965). This concept identifies a series of homologies between cultural texts as organizations of meaning, social reality as lived experience, and the "objective" structures of social organization and power. One can see the force of this concept in Williams's interpretation of television as a text (1974) in which he seeks to uncover the common structure underlying television's existence within multiple social and cultural dimensions. As an economic-technological system, television was marketed as a privately owned commodity for the home, receiving messages from centralized transmitters outside the home, in the public world. There are, obviously, political and economic interests "behind" these historical production/marketing decisions. More importantly, this insertion of the technology according to a particular structuring of the world connects it to, and corresponds with, other dimensions of television's existence: "The technical possibilities that were commonly used corresponded to this structure of feeling: the enclosed internal atmosphere; the local interpersonal conflict; the close-up on private feeling. Indeed these emphases could be seen as internal properties of the medium itself, when in fact they were a selection of some of its properties according to the dominant structure of feeling" (Williams 1974, 56).

This dominant structure of feeling, which apparently emerged in the nineteenth century to organize the experience of modernization, is described as "mobile privatization." For Williams, it organizes particular television texts, as well as other cultural texts, and provides the central images defining the "feel" of contemporary life: waiting inside the home for the outside world to be "transmitted" into one's private life. Moreover Williams uncovers it as well in the very social experience of television broadcasting, which he describes as *planned flow:* "This phenomenon, of planned flow, is then perhaps the defining characteristic of broadcasting, simultaneously as a technology and as a cultural form" (1974, 86). And even this flow of programming, comprised of diverse cultural forms as well as advertising, previews, and so on, can itself be read as embodying the same structure of feeling:

> The apparently disjointed "sequence" of items is in effect guided by a remarkably consistent set of cultural relationships: a flow of consumable reports and products, in which the elements of speed, variety and miscellaneity can be seen as organising: the real bearers of value. (105)

> Yet the flow of hurried items establishes a sense of the world: of surprising and miscellaneous events coming in, tumbling over each other, from all sides. (116)

> This, essentially, is how a directed but apparently casual and miscellaneous flow operates, culturally, following a given structure of feeling. (111)

The structure of feeling is produced and responded to at the level of experience. Even when Williams finds, within a particular structure of feeling, the intentional roots of its production (in structures of class power), such intentions are neither conscious nor individual. That is, the structure of feeling—mobile privatization—organizes the television text, its form, its technology, and even its socioeconomic institutions, not by some conscious design nor as a simple reflection of those class relations, but only through the mediating interventions of the production, within signification, of homologies between society and culture.

This explains, in part, the apparent slippage of production and consumption, encoding and decoding, in Williams's work. One cannot draw direct links between the structure of feeling and the conscious interests of the agents of production, nor can one assume that the structure of feeling defines the terms within which the texts of television are immediately consumed. Yet neither relationship can be denied. Certainly the dominant structure of feeling has become dominant precisely insofar as it supports the interests (both political and economic) of the ruling classes. Similarly the structure of feeling sets limits and exerts pressures on how the audience is able to interpret the television text. Yet it functions below the surface, mediating these moments. The dominant structure of feeling defines the experiential context within which both the production and the consumption of particular meanings are to be grounded.

Thus Williams has collapsed the difference between encoding and decoding by simultaneously collapsing the social into the cultural. The relation between society and culture (a hermeneutics of suspicion) is accomplished through an analysis of the common textuality of both (a hermeneutics of faith). Society, now understood as the structure of social experience (which can be read off the surface of class position) is part of the same dialectical processes as culture; both are symbolic productions of meaning. The two are interrelated and homologous processes. Their relation is defined at the point of their intersection: the structure of feeling. Their correspondence is guaranteed by the necessary relation between class position and social experience through which class can be defined simultaneously as a structure of feeling and, in the last instance, as a set of economic and political interests.

Let us consider more carefully Williams's solution to the question of the politics of textuality, that is, the relation between encoding and decoding. As the discussion of Adorno demonstrates, merely accepting an "active" audience does not necessarily guarantee that the issue is acknowledged. One can take that active audience to be producing the text according to the interests of the dominant class, interests preprogrammed into the text itself. The issue is linked directly to the possibility of "political" struggles over and within cultural processes. In Williams's work, when we find the existence of different structures of feeling (embodying and producing different class experiences/positions), the clash between them is distant and global, having little to do with the concrete text. The reason for this is clear: the struggle is not in and over the text, as an attempt to impose a structure of meaning from one class position onto another (Volosinov 1973). Rather, since there are two competing cultures, the question is deferred into the process of mediating between alternative structures of feeling.

While Williams maintains the possibility of struggle in his analysis of television, the question of the source of that struggle and its relation to the texts is submerged within his description of the dominant structure of feeling embedded within the texts. This is not simply a submission to the pessimism so often characterizing classical positions. It is, rather, the point at which the totalization implicit in the "dominant structure of feeling" and its necessary correspondence to social position breaks down. For if this simple correspondence is ruptured, as it clearly is in his actual practice (which recognizes the complexity of interests within the media), then Williams can only locate the source of resistance and struggle in some place outside of the already constituted class relations: hence the importance of residual and emergent formations, each with its own structure of feeling. But such notions bring the question of decoding back to origins, forcing consumption to reproduce the model of production. Origins replace effects, and the question of decoding is indefinitely deferred.

Mediation through Appropriation. This dilemma sets the agenda for the next position to be discussed. This position attempts to understand the ways in which the struggles between different social groups are enacted within the domain of culture, as a contradiction between different meaningfully organized formations. The major representative of this position is the work of the Centre for Contemporary Cultural Studies, under the leadership of Stuart Hall (Hall 1980a; Grossberg 1983).

As the Centre attempted to move beyond Williams's assumption of a single correspondence between class position, experience, and culture, much of their work focused on the phenomenon of subcultures and subcultural styles (Hall and Jefferson 1976). Style, in fact, provided a new mediating term between the social and the cultural. Rather than beginning with two separable realms, each embodying a common structure, this position locates the homology within the subcultural formation itself. Style is a representation of, and an imaginary solution to, the experienced contradictions within the everyday lives of the members of the subculture. Such experience is "overdetermined," so that it can no longer simply be read off the class position of the members. In fact, the experienced contradictions are often the result of the contradictions between various social registers of determination and identity. Furthermore, the "fit" between the pieces that are appropriated by the subculture and constructed into its style defines the homology. It includes, as a part of its very structure, the experienced contradictions as that to which the style responds by presenting itself as a "magical" solution. Thus the relationship between culture and society is not a structural homology but rather the homology of question and answer, of an "imaginary" solution to experienced contradictions. The correspondence cannot be read off the text itself, even as a deep structure. It can only be uncovered by placing the text within the social experience of its producers and consumers. Thus the question of textuality is partially shifted (but only partially) from origins to effects, only partially because the text is still inserted into a pregiven structure of experience. (I will forgo giving an example of such subcultural analysis until the discussion of Hebdige below.)

By changing the grounds on which the relation between culture and society was understood, the Centre found itself directly confronting the question of the relationship between encoding and decoding. For if subcultures could appropriate cultural practices into their own constructed style, then one has to begin by acknowledging that cultural texts can be read and used in different ways. Drawing upon semiotics, Hall (1980b) argued that texts are polyvocal and that there is no necessary correspondence between language (the surface of the text) and signification. The question then becomes that of identifying the relations between the origins of alternative readings and the possibilities for struggling against the interests of the existing structures of domination. On the one hand, Hall argued, processes of cultural production encode particular meanings into the structure of the texts. Such "preferred meanings" attempt to represent experience in ways that support the interests of those already in power, both economically and politically. Such encoding is, however, often the product of, and could be read alternatively through, "negotiated codes" that constitute particular social and professional identities (such as the "routine practices" of newsmaking). Thus one cannot assume that the intentions behind the production of news are simply those of the ruling class; the question is rather how journalists, operating with professional codes seeking to produce objectively neutral reports, nevertheless consistently produce texts that encode the preferred meanings of the existing structures of power. Finally, the fact that texts encode certain preferred readings does not guarantee that they are read accordingly; that is, we cannot assume effects simply from origins. Rather there are alternative and even oppositional codes, derived from their own subcultural formations, which allow audiences to decode texts in ways that are not only significantly different from, but even opposed to, the preferred readings.

However, because it remains within a hermeneutic approach that seeks correspondences between experience and textual meanings produced through particular decoding practices, this position ends up with an abyss that threatens to sunder the relation between culture and social structures of power. In one of the clearest applications of this theory, Brunsdon and Morley (1978) undertook a semiotic reading of the *Nationwide* television program. Their analysis focuses neither on a simple explication of meanings or images, nor on the uncovering of an underlying structure of the text. Instead they are concerned with the codes which the text seems to offer for its own interpretation, revealed in such semiotic features as modes of address (which determine the status of actors and the formality or informality of the presentation), and the ways in which the text defines it own "ideological problematic." For example, they conclude that the "persona" of the programme, then, is a professionally formulated reconstruction based in and on "popular speech" and its sedimented wisdom. The use of this linguistic register is one of the ways in which *Nationwide* constructs "ordinary people" as the subject of its particular kind of speech. This "populist ventriloquism" is a crucial strand in the way the programme attempts to forge an "identification" with its audience. (8–9)

Here we can clearly see the shift in interpretive interest, no longer focused on the text as an isolated and autonomous cultural object, but as part of a specific cultural-social formation in which strategies encoded into the text attempt to define the ways audiences bring these texts to bear on their own social experiences—according to the encoded, preferred reading.

In a second part of the study, Morley (1980) attempted to describe how different groups within the audience of the program actually decoded the text. He argues that it is through the mechanism of identification that the audience is brought into the circuit of meaning of the preferred reading, but if these identifications are ineffective or challenged, alternative decodings become possible. Thus "we must assume that there will be no necessary 'fit' or transparency between the encoding and decoding ends of the communication chain" (11). "We need to see how the different subcultural structures and formations within the audience, and the sharing of different cultural codes and competencies amongst different groups and classes, 'determine' the decoding of the message for different sections of the audience" (15). Using Bourdieu's idea (1980) of "cultural capital," Morley argues that how a text is decoded depends upon the codes available to the interpreter. Codes function within the domain of culture much as capital functions within the domain of economic production; they allow for the generation of surplus meaning. But while capital is defined only by its circulation through the circuit, Morley fixes cultural capital within the individual, defined as the intersection of social identities or experiences. That is, a particular experiential position within the social formation predetermines the availability of particular resources for decoding. Once again the interpreter is seen as appropriating the text into the already constituted space of his or her cultural formation, understood as a structure of experience. And, once again, the question of effects is postponed into that of the origins of such resources.

Morley found, not surprisingly, very little relationship between the "preferred meaning" encoded into the text and the diversity of alternative decodings made by the audience. He also found it impossible to specify the cultural resources of a particular group as a function of their social experience. In the end, the two studies together foregrounded the very real gap between encoding and decoding, origin and effects, production and consumption. He could find relations between the social and cultural within both the production and the consumption of the text, but he could not bring the two sets of relations into relation. While he begins by arguing that the "key question" is "exactly what is the nature of the 'fit' between, say, class, socio-economic or educational position and cultural/interpretive code" (1980, 20), he concludes that "social position in no way directly correlates with decodings" (137). His conclusion questions the very assumption of a distinction between the social and cultural, and he argues that experience itself must be located within the field of discourse: "This is to insist on the social production of meaning and the social location of subjectivity/ies—indeed it is to locate the production of subjectivity within specific discursive formations" (157). But such a move would make the assumption of a homology between social experience and cultural meanings fortuitous. This apparent contradiction between the two issues originally described grounds the shift into "discursive approaches" to cultural interpretation (Morley 1981; Coward 1977).

Mediation through Signifying Practices. If hermeneutic positions seek correspondence, homologies, or fits between structures of signification and experience, the Centre's work attempted to reproduce this structure on top of the split between encoding and decoding. But they sought to describe both signification and experience at the level of meaning, or signifieds. There is another tradition in marxist thought, rooted in the work of Brecht, Benjamin, and perhaps Bakhtin, which locates meaning within its specific cultural mode of production. Consequently, the relation between culture and society and that between encoding and decoding are reconceptualized as competing forms of signifying practices.

One example of this strategy is Hebdige's *Subculture: The Meaning of Style* (1979), which combines the hermeneutic subcultural theory of the Centre with certain ideas taken from a discursive approach. For Hebdige, style is not merely an alternative construction of meaning, but an alternative mode of production. It does not merely offer different "cultural capital," but challenges the very way in which the signifier and the signified, language and meaning/experience, are connected. Subcultural styles deny and disrupt "the deceptive innocence of appearances" (19) on which dominant structures of meaning are built and maintained. This "naturalness" of the meaning of reality, of the world of experience, of the circuit connecting object and sign, is not only problematized but ultimately rejected by the practice of style. The social processes of production, reproduction, and consumption, depending as they do on the processes by which objects are given meaning and transformed into signs, are contradicted by the very production of style as a signifying practice.

Hebdige fails to see the implication that style is the de-construction of the possibility of any representation of reality as natural (i.e., of both ideology and experience). This would move style outside of a hermeneutic approach, for one would no longer be comparing structures of meaning. The relation between culture and society and the struggle between encoding and decoding would be located within the contradictions between competing modes of (symbolic) production. Hebdige, however, continues to see style as a representation of, and an imaginary solution to, experienced contradictions. Thus, following the Centre's model, the first half of the book is an ethnographic description of the experience of particular social groups. But in the second half—a description and elucidation of subcultural styles—it becomes clear that we can not seek structural homologies or cultural resources. One is, if you like, still comparing these two planes, but the relationship between them is only describable in terms of the reproduction of the same constitutive signifying practice within each.

Hebdige continues the Centre's hermeneutic position: "The succession of white subcultural forms can be read as a series of deep-structural adaptations which symbolically accommodate or expunge the black presence from the host community . . . We can watch, played out on the loaded surface of British working class youth cultures, a phantom history of race relations since the War" (1979, 44–45). Hebdige argues that subcultural styles construct "forbidden identities" that reflect the experience of the group. This representational identity provides the appearance of a magical resolution, within experience, of the contradictions. But because this identity is the product of signifying practices, it is always open to reappropriation and is, at best, temporary.

When the analysis turns to modes of symbolic practice, it opens up wider and even more disparate readings. For example, on the one hand, punk involved an "open identification with Black British and West Indian Culture," which antagonized not only the dominant culture, but other youth subcultures as well. On the other hand, "despite the strong affinity, the integrity of the two forms—punk and reggae—was scrupulously maintained, and . . . punk music, like every other aspect of punk style, tended to develop in direct antithesis to its apparent source" (1979, 67–68). Here we have an origin that is negated by the signifying practice of punk; it is this transformation of origins into effects that characterizes, above all, the punk style:

> punk style had made a decisive break not only with the parent culture but with its own *location in experience.* This break was both inscribed and re-enacted in the signifying practices embodied in punk style. The punk ensembles, for instance, did not so much magically resolve experienced contradictions as represent the experience of contradiction itself in the form of visual puns. (121)

Punk style does not so much "fit" within and answer to experience as reproduce within itself the practice of contradiction, a practice that constitutes the signification of that experience. Punk style is the deconstruction of all meaning in a world in which meaning is already deconstructed.

Punk has become an emblem for Hebdige's argument that all style is "a semiotic guerilla warfare." But when he seeks the representation of experience in style, the emblem forces him beyond his own descriptions: "The safety pins and bin liners signified a relative material poverty which was either directly experienced or sympathetically assumed, and which in turn was made to stand for the spiritual paucity of everyday life" (1979, 115). Accounting for a particular style, Hebdige moves from a particular contradiction to a general one, from a phantom history of race relations to a general history of the deconstruction of experience, of the collapse of the future, and with these, the end of all spiritual meaning. The "homology" between culture and social experience is reconstituted by making the signifying practice of style "represent different signifying practices" (120).

The issue has slid from what style signifies to the homology between the way in which it signifies and the very structure of experience within the class formation: as reality has lost its meaning (i.e., as social signifying practices have been altered, whether or not this is experienced as such), so the subculture constructs a style that is defined by its practice of intentionally collapsing all meaning. The collapse itself—the production of the very reality it represents—is not the issue. Rather the focus is on the relation between the practice of style and the practice by which experience is dismantled within a subculture's reality. The correspondence, so to speak, is located in a common signifying practice, represented in both style and experience.

Mediation through Narrative. Before leaving the hermeneutic approach, I want to briefly discuss positions that use narrative structures as the basis for cultural interpretation. Such positions read the narrative structure of a cultural text as an attempt to represent or work out the contradictions of social life. There are many sources for contemporary narrative theory (Rimmon-Kenan 1984), including Propp (1968), Lévi-Strauss (1963), Barthes (1974), Bakhtin (1981), Greimas (1966), Frye (1957), and Burke (1945), as well as theories of historical narrative. Furthermore, the different positions describe the narrative structure and its relation to the social world differently (e.g., mythic narratives, narrative structures that reconcile contradictions, psychoanalytic processes of identification through which the reader is carried through the narrative, and semiotic circuits of transformation).

Perhaps the most significant contemporary use of narrative theory within marxist cultural interpretation can be found in the work of Fredric Jameson (1981). Although this is only part of his larger theory of interpretation, its centrality is evident in his description of his project as the attempt to "restructure the problematics of ideology, of the unconscious and of desire, of representation, of history, and of cultural production, around the all-informing process of narrative" (13). In fact, the subtitle of his most recent book, *The Political Unconscious: Narrative as a Socially Symbolic Act,* is somewhat misleading, for narrative is *the* social-symbolic act, the very structure and production of history, the mediation of reality and fantasy, and the nature of the "political unconscious." Jameson wants to rescue the possibility of a hermeneutic reading of history as narrative which would also rescue the utopian projects of culture and marxism.

Jameson has a unique, indeed postmodern, view of the relationship between culture and society. While he argues that the social has collapsed into the cultural, this is the product and sign of the "consumer society" and its associated modes of production:

> I will say that culture, far from being an occasional matter of the reading of a monthly good book or a trip to the drive-in, seems to me the very element of consumer society itself; no society has ever been saturated with signs and messages like this one . . . until the omnipresence of culture in this society is even dimly sensed, realistic conceptions of the nature and function of political praxis today can scarcely be framed. (1979a, 139)

By both accepting (as a historical fact) and refusing (as a theoretical position) this collapse, Jameson reconstitutes the hermeneutic correspondence between particular narrative structures, narrative (and culture) as a mode of production, and social modes of production (with their associated class contradictions).

The assumption of this series of homologies grounds Jameson's attempt to understand the utopian possibilities of history and the ideological functions of culture. According to Jameson (1981), while history is a real materiality never reducible to the symbolic, it is available to us only as texts. The real is always mediated to us through interpretive paradigms ("ideologemes"). Culture, then, involves an ongoing transformation of these received texts and defines the intertextual existence of history by constructing and transforming the narrative paradigms within which we have received history. History is constantly displaced into and created within the semiotics of narrativization, that is, the practice of organizing particular narratives.

This narrativizing process, however, does not dissolve the distinction between society and culture, base and superstructure. Rather it allows Jameson, following Lévi-Strauss, to reconstitute the relationship. Culture transforms and provides resolutions in the realm of the symbolic or ideological to more basic political and economic contradictions:

> This is why a book like *The Nether World*, . . . is best read, not for its documentary information on the conditions of Victorian slum life, but as testimony about the narrative paradigms that organize middleclass fantasies about those slums and about "solutions" that might resolve, manage, or repress the evident class anxieties aroused by the existence of an industrial working class and an urban lumpenproletariat. (1981, 186)

The function of the political unconscious is to seek "by logical permutations and combinations to find a way out of its intolerable closure and to produce a 'solution,' through the semiotic transformation of the narrative" (167). This "intolerable closure" is the particular and often contradictory desires, determined by social position and class struggles, that are unavailable to us except through such symbolic mediations. The function of the narrative apparatus, then, is to rechart these libidinal investments at the site of competing and multiple modes of production, in order to open up the multiplicity of generic narratives—both ideological and utopian—within the text.

The ideological function represses the contradictions, as well as the real possibility of their resolution, by the projection of an imaginary solution, for example, by the symbolic construction of a semiotic position within the logical possibilities of the "combinatoire" of characters (see Jameson's reading [1979c] of the fascism of Wyndham Lewis's narratives). On the other hand, the utopian function of such narratives is to offer the symbolic possibility of a real (i.e., utopian) transformation of history through compensatory structures.

Consequently, we must "grasp mass culture not as empty distraction or 'mere' false consciousness, but rather as a transformational work on social and political anxieties and fantasies which must then have some effective presence in the mass cultural text in order subsequently to be 'managed' or repressed" (1979a, 141). Unlike Adorno, Jameson argues that "the works of mass culture cannot be ideological without at one and the same time being implicitly or explicitly utopian" (144). We can see this method at work, briefly, in Jameson's readings of contemporary popular films. For example, concerning *Jaws* he writes:

> We are thus authorized to read the death of Quint in the film as the twofold symbolic destruction of an older America—the America of small business and individual private enterprise of a now outmoded kind, but also the America of the New Deal and the crusade against Nazism, the older America of the depression and the war and the heyday of classical liberalism.
>
> Now the content of the partnership between Hooper and Brody projected by the film may be specified socially and politically, as the allegory of an alliance between the forces of law-and-order and the new technocracy of the multinational corporations: an alliance which must be cemented, not merely by its fantasized triumph over the ill-defined menace of the shark itself, but above all by the indispensable precondition of the effacement of that more traditional image of an older America which must be eliminated from the historical consciousness and social memory before the new power system takes place. This operation may continue to be read in terms of mythic archetypes, if one likes, but then in that case it is a Utopian and ritual vision. (1981, 143–44)

Similarly, concerning *The Godfather* Jameson argues that its ideological function is to displace the problem of the "deterioration of daily life" from the economic to the ethical realm. On the other hand, its utopian impulse lies in its projection of the family as the fantasy of a resolution, a fantasy because it is located in the terms of an alien (non-American) other. That such solutions are the product of narrative acts is made even clearer in Jameson's reading of *Dog Day Afternoon,* in which it is the construction of a crucial narrative place—that of the FBI agent—which provides the resolution, within which "the whole allegorical structure of *Dog Day Afternoon* suddenly emerges in the light of the day" (1979b, 88).

We have now returned to the dilemma that Williams's hermeneutic reduction of the social to the cultural made obvious: the reading of a particular text assumes that the positions of producers and consumers vis-à-vis the text are identical within the common intertextual space of culture. This dilemma suggests that marxist interpretive theory must rethink the question of the relationship between culture, society, and experience.

THE DISCURSIVE APPROACH

Within this category of interpretive practices, I want to describe a number of positions that refuse the hermeneutic binarism of text and experience while even more radically sliding the social into the cultural. Within such positions, textuality is a productive practice whose (imaginary) product is experience itself. Experience can no longer serve as a mediation between the cultural and the social since it is not merely within the cultural but is the product of cultural practices. As Hall (1980c) suggests, this move can be traced to Althusser's interpretation (1971) of ideology as the unconscious system of representation of the imaginary relationship between people and their real conditions of existence. That is, the way in which we experience our relationship to the world is precisely that which ideological signifying practices manufacture. Ideology works as a practice not merely by producing a system of meanings which purport to represent the world, but rather by producing its own system of meanings as the real, natural (i.e., experienced) one. Thus the issue of ideology is not merely the conflict between competing systems of meaning but rather the power of a particular system to represent its own representations as a direct reflection of the real, to produce its own meanings as experience. It is a question of signifying practice and representation rather than signification alone.

Experience can no longer be seen as something pregiven, outside of particular cultural or textual practices. It is already inherently implicated with structures of power. Power is no longer outside of culture (in the social) but within the very structures of signifying practices themselves. This radical negation of the binarism of culture and society implies as well a reconceptualization of the gap between encoding and decoding. For the subject, whether producer or consumer, cannot be defined by resources or experience existing outside of the network of cultural practices. Neither the production nor the consumption of particular texts can be approached as if the already socially constituted subject comes to the text from somewhere outside of the intertextual cultural environment. The issue is reconceptualized in terms of competing forms of signifying practices, or the different ways in which the text locates the subject within its construction of experience. Thus it is the cultural practices themselves that define identities for their producers and consumers by inserting them into the fabric of their discursive spaces. It is this power of the text to locate the subject by producing its intertextual domain of experience that becomes the object of critical interpretation. It cannot be read off the surface of the text as a system of meaning, nor is it to be found by a hermeneutic excavation of some deeper structure of signifieds. It is rather to be found in the ways in which the text produces meaning through its practices of structuring signifiers around the subject. The issue is not so much the particular knowledge of reality (true or false, mystified or utopian) that is made available, but the way in which the individual is given access to that knowledge and consequently empowered or de-powered. Rather than seeking a series of mediations or correspondences, discursive positions seek the processes of encoding and decoding as a series of discontinuities and ruptures that are woven together, by signifying practices, around the sites of social identity and subjective power.

Positioning the Subject. Althusser, drawing upon the structural psychoanalysis of Lacan (1977), argued that ideology works by producing or positioning the subject within its circuit. Lacan argued, more generally, that language (signification) is made possible only by a "splitting" of the subject. One accedes to language and enters into the cultural only by representing oneself in language (I), but this entails the repression of the speaking subject as the absent source (the unconscious). The subject within language is, then, already a position within a system of cultural power. Althusser identifies the specificity of ideological practices precisely by the specific point at which the subject is inserted into signification, a point from which the apparent givenness of experience cannot be problematized. Ideological practices locate the individual language user within language as its absent source who is therefore responsible for the meanings produced, the transcendental agent of experience. The individual as a subject becomes complicitous with his or her own insertion into the ideological production of an imaginary but lived reality. Ideology accomplishes its task, on such a view, by having already defined the phenomenological relationship of subject and object, and thus the possibilities of power and knowledge.

This position is most clearly and influentially exhibited in the work of *Screen,* a British film journal, in the seventies (Heath 1981). Their analyses of films focused on the ways the camera functions to produce a particular series of identifications for the viewer. For example, they argued that in the classic Hollywood cinema, one is positioned by the cameras as if one were seeing the scene of the film from an omniscient position outside of the scene of action itself. That identification with the camera slides into the particular characters within the film, through the way in which the camera relates to the positions of the characters themselves (as agents of knowledge). Consequently, the viewer is "stitched" or "sutured" into the text. Furthermore, the camera of the Hollywood film identifies with the male protagonists and renders the female the object of the voyeuristic sight/site of the camera, the male characters, and the spectator. Alternatively, the avant-garde cinema often places the camera within the mise-en-scène, imposing a reflexively limited point of view on the spectator and dispersing the viewing subject into a multiplicity of positions, no longer claiming a privileged point of entry into or existence within the text, and thus declaring no single access to its truth.

The implications of this position, thus far, are apparently not that different from those of the classical positions (Allor 1984). If the subject is totally the product of the encounter with the filmic texts, which create a monolithic identification with the camera, then the audience is once again merely the object of a (now textual) manipulative practice. The simplest solution is, of course, to allow for a multiplicity of contradictory subject positions and their different accessibilities to different audiences. A text may in fact embody different textual practices and thus produce fractured subjectivities. But more importantly, the consumer of the text is already a subject; he or she has a history of textual or ideological existence. Thus, rather than speaking of experiences, codes, or resources that the individual brings to the text, we can talk about the intertextuality of the practice of consumption itself, a discursive history in which both the text and the subject have already been determined and through which they are reinserted into that process of determination. As some feminist film critics (Kuhn 1982) have argued, many Hollywood films cannot totally render the female into the passive object of the camera's male gaze. Rather there are points in the text itself in which the female cannot be coded within the dominant signifying practices and consequently ruptures, or threatens to rupture, the text. There are then alternative and resistant readings already coded into the text, insofar as the text always exists only within the larger intertextual context of encoding and decoding.

While this position seems to ignore the question of encoding, it is actually raised as the constitution of the terms of decoding. That is, such readings must identify the particular relations of power that are coded by the production of particular subject-positions. The dominant practices of the Hollywood "cinematic apparatus" produce subject-positions that are identified with the preexisting categories of domination: capitalist, male, white, and so on. This assumed correspondence allows those practices that differ to be comfortably identified with the opposition or dominated other (e.g., socialist, female).

Of course, such identifications are not as serendipitous as they may appear. Obviously, one might appeal to the marxist maxim that, at the very least, the dominant culture will attempt to reproduce the dominant relations of power. There are, however, other dimensions to the practice of such positions, which ground its ideological readings and which are already implicit in its semiotic and psychoanalytic foundations. The former depends upon the film's production of signifiers in particular ways that leave "structured absences" within its narrative or surface textuality. By locating particular characters and events within a connotational chain, the film must attempt to hide the particular moments that it is unable to code according to its own ideology.

A more powerful critical tool of such practices is based upon a psychoanalytic narrative theory that focuses on the ability of cultural practices to "stitch" the consumer into the structure of signifiers itself. For example, by using our identification with the position of the camera and its own narrative structure, the film can displace that identification, making it slide through a series of identifications within the narrative practices of the representation. We identify not only with the camera but with the narrator, and even further, as a result, we enter into the narrative itself by virtue of the narrator's own identifications within the text. Thus we are not only positioned within the circuit of signifier and signified (whether as a unified or fragmented subject), but in the narrative movement of the signifiers themselves. This use of narrative theory constructs the film's power not only in terms of its subject-positions, but also in terms of how it uses such identificatory processes to code and render acceptable the contradictions and movements of resistance that threaten to disrupt the ideology of the particular textual system of power.

Articulating the Subject. The question of the positions which ideology creates for the individual as a subject does not, however, exhaust the concerns of marxist criticism, nor is it the only use that has been made of Althusser's critique of experience. Recent work has returned to the relationship between signifying practices and social reality, without appealing to the humanistic assumption of a pregiven social experience. It focuses on the construction of social positions or identities and the "articulation" of particular practices and meanings as belonging to these identities.

This position has been defended in the more recent work of Stuart Hall (1983, 1986b) as well as by a number of marxist feminists such as Angela McRobbie (1982a). Arguing that experience is the product of complex processes of overdetermination, Hall transposes the question of cultural criticism from the search for necessary correspondences (whether direct or mediated) between culture and society, to the analysis of the specific ways in which different practices, meanings, and identities are "articulated" together. The critic can no longer assume that there is a necessary relationship between a text and a particular meaning, or between a practice and its representation in signification, or between a particular social position and a structure of experience. But there are always relations or correspondences *produced* between practices, texts, and identities. The problematic of cultural studies is transformed, concerned with how a particular practice—signifying or social— is located in a network of other practices, at a particular point, in particular relations.

This reconceptualization of the relation between culture and society is accomplished by rejecting the gap between encoding and decoding. The question of power is transposed from origins to concrete effects. If the ideological significance of a cultural text cannot be read off the text itself, the task of the analyst is to examine how the particular text or practice has been "inflected" or inserted into its context in such a way as to have identifiable ideological consequences.

While acknowledging the existence of the real (e.g., as the nonsignifying social practice), Hall (1983) argues that the effects of such practices are always articulated within the cultural regime of signification. The critic cannot escape ideology, and so must always talk about the politics of the representations of the social. Cultural criticism becomes the study of the connotational codes within which a particular term (such as "nation" or "democracy") or a particular point of social identity (such as black, female, or adolescent) are located. We examine the specific ideological inflections or effects that, while not inherent in the texts, are produced for the text by its insertion within a set of connotational codes, its articulation to other signs.

Althusser (1971) argues, in essence, that the question of ideology is how particular significations appear as the natural representations of reality, so that individuals accede and consent to their explicit organizations of reality and their implicit structures of power and domination. Rejecting a psychoanalytic theory of subject-positioning, Hall (1980e) turns to Gramsci's theory (1971) of hegemony. Hegemony is the ongoing process by which a particular social bloc (made up of various class fractions) maintains its position of power by mobilizing public support for its social projects in a broad spectrum of social life. Hegemony is a question of leadership rather than explicit domination and control, containment rather than incorporation. It involves the colonization of popular consciousness or common sense through the articulation of specific social practices and positions within ideological codes or chains of connotational significance.

The fact that hegemony must operate on a broad terrain of social and cultural life means, for Hall, that the politics of its articulations cannot be assigned to preconstituted structures or categories of power. One cannot explain particular ideological moments by reducing them to a single contradiction within the real. Rather such effects are determined by a multiplicity of power relations that can only be identified within the particular context of the articulation. Thus Hall (1983) argues that the contradictions of race and gender are at least as fundamental as, and certainly irreducible to, the economic contradictions (whether in terms of class—capital versus labor—or of modes of production—forces versus relations of production) that have preoccupied marxists. These three planes on which power is organized may have different relations to each other at different points within the struggle for hegemony.

Angela McRobbie's study of the ideology of adolescent femininity within a mass circulation magazine, *Jackie,* is one of the best examples of this approach:

> It will be argued here that the way *Jackie* addresses "girls" as a monolithic grouping, as do all other women's magazines, serves to obscure differences, of class for example, between women. Instead it asserts a sameness, a kind of *false* sisterhood, which assumes a common defini-

tion of womanhood or girlhood. Moreover by isolating out a particular "phase" or age as the focus of interest, one which coincides roughly with that of its readers, the magazine is in fact creating this "age-ness" as an ideological construction. "Adolescence" and here, female adolescence, is itself an ideological "moment" whose connotations are immediately identifiable with those "topics" included in *Jackie*. And so, by at once defining its readership vis à vis age, and by describing what is of relevance to this age group, *Jackie* and women's magazines in general create a "false totality." (1982b, 265)

The appearance of this totality allows the significations of *Jackie* to function ideologically, to appear as representations of the real. It allows no space for alternative constructions of identity around adolescence and femininity. The ideological significance of any text within the magazine can only be understood in terms of its inflection by its existence within the larger cultural and social context of the magazine and adolescent feminine culture, that is, in terms of the project of constructing a "false totality" around the particular identity.

A second example is provided by Hall, Critcher, Jefferson, Clarke, and Roberts in *Policing the Crisis: Mugging, the State, and Law and Order* (1978), which examines the ideological articulation of the crime of mugging within a larger crisis of the social formation, defined by issues of both race relations and "law and order." By looking at the complex intertextuality within which mugging was given an ideological significance, the authors attempt to describe the ways in which this particular construction participated in the production of a hegemonic formation.

Perhaps most radically, and unlike the other positions I have discussed, this position locates, within its own analysis of the relationship between culture and social power, the possibility of and the sites for resistance. For, corresponding to the struggle for hegemony, the struggle against it must involve the struggle to disarticulate the ideological inflections that are produced on a broad number of issues and social identities.

Thus, rather than being concerned with the production of subjectivities within texts, a discursive theory of articulation examines the ways in which particular sites of social identity are articulated (and hence the experiences to be associated with them produced) in an intertextual context of ideology. In the end, the question of encoding and decoding becomes, if not irrelevant, a misleading way of framing relations of cultural power. Rather the question is the existence of particular inflections of social identities and practices within the articulating cultural environment and the gaps within this network that allow for struggle and resistance. While previously discussed positions must, at best, find it difficult to find an optimistic place for the broad range of actively struggling social groups, within this position it is precisely the actions of such groups that articulate particular messages with particular meanings or inflections into particular connotative networks. But this decoding process, if we are to continue referring to it in this way (since it includes resistance to, and the reproduction of, existing structures of domination) is not the product of already available cultural capital, preconstituted social identities, or domains of experience that necessarily correspond to positions of power or powerlessness. Both encoding and decoding are only artificial moments within the struggle for and resistance to hegemony, defined by the particular context of the text itself. Nevertheless, because it locates social reality or power within culture, this position continues to see power in terms that escape signification and the differences it constitutes (e.g., in various social and economic positions of domination).

Power and the Materiality of Culture. This final position is best represented in the work of Michel Foucault and reverses the premise of a discursive approach by collapsing culture into the social (Grossberg 1982a). Nevertheless, given the primarily methodological interest of this inquiry, Foucault's position bears important similarities to the two discursive positions previously described. Like these, Foucault's refuses to begin either with experience as an innocent measure of social reality, or with an appeal to a transcendental, autonomous subject (i.e., the determiner of its own determinations, unified and transparent to its own self-reflection). But unlike other discourse positions, Foucault refuses to assume any absolute distinction between culture (the signifying) and society (the nonsignifying locus of a power that is represented in and maintained through signification). Finally, Foucault refuses to define questions of culture and power around the central issue of subjectivity or identity—as the primary sites or vehicles for the production of power-effects.[6]

This position attempts to describe the contextual articulations of discursive and nondiscursive events together. Like the previous one, it is concerned with the particular network of effects and rejects the assumption that any event has inherent within it its own meanings or effects or even political implications. But Foucault is not willing to limit the category of effects to the production of connotational webs or codes of meaning (i.e., ideology). Rather the very fact of a text's existence at a particular social site—its materiality—is the occasion for multiple planes of effects beyond the ideological. Hence power can be located neither entirely within this plane, nor entirely outside of it (as if merely the reproduction of external relations of power upon the organization of meaning).

Rejecting the separation of culture and society, Foucault (1979a, 33) locates any event in a multiplicity of interacting planes or regimes of power within the social formation. We can see this demand for specificity in Foucault's own use of "event." The materiality of events points to the ways in which we live and act, ways over which we have no control and about which we are unaware. This is not simply the ideologically constructed plane of experience, for experience itself (phenomenologically understood) is merely another set of events or facts, to be included within the analysis of the network of effects.

The identity of an event is only given in its contextual specification; it is fractured and dispersed into the multiplicity of its effects. These effects define the "conditions of possibility," operating in either direction, of the particular practice. In a sense, Foucault (1978a) carries the theory of overdetermination to its logical conclusion, and this has important methodological consequences for cultural criticism. If any event is articulated at a particular point in a network of effects, whether its existence is primarily determined by its production of meaning-effects is an empirical question. That is, a text may be more than or other than its meaningfulness, depending on whether its most powerful effects are mediated by processes of signification.

Of course, once we have allowed that our concern is with the multiplicity of effects that may both exceed and absent the meaningful, then the issue of encoding and decoding is itself called into question. For Foucault, this dilemma embodies marxism's inability to confront the reality of power as the very microstructure of effects or relations. The dilemma, by recreating the duality of culture and society, always locates power as something outside of an event, something brought into it (intentions or interests) or something taken away from it (hegemonic consent). Power is, instead, the intricacies of the particular network in which events make possible other events; it is a "capillary action," organizing and extending the possibilities of its own existence. Thus power is always located in "apparatuses" that are built upon "technologies," programmings of behavior (Foucault 1981a). An apparatus not only emerges at a particular site, it is also located within or excluded from "regimes of jurisdiction and veridication" (8). The former prescribes what can be done: procedures and strategies; the latter justifies these ways by producing particular discourses as "true."

If Foucault refuses to locate power outside of the apparatus itself, he also refuses to center or hierarchize it. He rejects notions of ideology, hegemony, the state, or capitalism, as if these could explain the materiality of power. For example, in his consideration of the Gulag (1979a, 51), he refuses any category that reduces its specific structuring of power: for example, treating it as a structure of meaning to be read off texts; or as a single effect, perhaps with multiple causes; or as a specific instance of a repeated historical phenomenon; or as the negation in practice of its explicit ideology. Foucault, in fact, refuses any reductionism; human life itself is not merely labor, nor the production of meaning (1979a, 62). Life is both chance and determinations, both power and pleasure. It is the complex interweaving of power, knowledge, and desire that defines the politics of an event.

The analytic task (Foucault 1980c) is to provide a "genealogy" of specific practices and apparatuses, mapping out the conditions of possibility into which they emerged and out of which they elaborated new (and even unintended) effects. And the political task is similarly transformed; no longer seeking to identify the conspiracy or structure of power behind the surfaces of everyday life, Foucault seeks instead to locate those voices and practices that have been excluded by the contemporary technologies of power, and to struggle to open a space within which their resistance can be heard. It is then the already existing history and context of struggle that needs to be organized, not as the attempt to develop alternative or counterhegemonic strategies but as the ongoing struggle against all moments of power and domination.

My own work on rock and roll (Grossberg 1983–84, 1984a) attempts to use this position to analyze rock and roll as a set of apparatuses within which a variety of events are empowered as sites of pleasure for youth cultures. These are, simultaneously, both the condition of possibility of rock and roll and yet deconstructed by the very technologies it organizes. We can see another example of this position in the recent work of Hebdige, who, in a series of articles (1981a, 1981b, 1982, 1983), has sought to describe the complex "effectivities" of particular cultural texts: the motorscooter, pop art, and the products and discourses through which "America" was constructed as an "imaginary" category within the British social formation. To consider one example in more detail, Hebdige has begun a "genealogy" of youth in England, pointing to the complex and productive relations between a range of discourses, social institutions, and technologies of surveillance: "The vectors of power I want to trace cut across a number of heterogeneous sites—discursive categories, institutions and the spaces between institutions. Those sites are youth, sexuality, fashion, subculture, display, and its corollary, surveillance" (1982, 71). He draws three conclusions. First, youth only exists when it is posed as a problem, and consequently the power of youth is precisely, through a variety of practices, to pose a threat. Second, the resistance or "insubordination" of youth can only be understood as a "micropolitics of pleasure" which exceeds the current boundaries of "legitimate" political practice. And third, the politics of youth is enacted on the material surface, at the interface between surveillance and the evasion or transformation of surveillance into pleasure (i.e., as style). Although Hebdige attempts to return this politics of style to the space of the sign, it is clear that it exceeds the question of signification and representation. It is the production of youth as difference, in the gaps between the signs, in the leaks within hegemony, in the contradictions within institutions, and in the heart of the capillary existence of power. Further, if we accept Foucault's (1978b) argument that the contemporary technologies of power articulate a "biopolitics" in which the body of the population—the very materiality of human existence—becomes the object for new strategies of control, then Hebdige seems to be suggesting that youth—its construction, emergence, and elaboration—is both a product of and a resistance to this apparatus.

CONCLUSION

In conclusion, I will attempt to provide a useful schematic summary of the ten positions described above, emphasizing their methodologies of cultural interpretation. I have tried to point to the necessity for a more reflective consideration of the theoretical, methodological, and political assumptions that organize the ways in which we interpret cultural texts.

Classical approaches: culture reflects society; decoding is unproblematic.

1. False consciousness: the text is a distorting mirror that acts directly upon its audience.

2. Critical theory: the text imposes forms of consumption that reflect their industrialized modes of production.

3. Economism: the text is erased in favor of the forces and relations of its production.

Hermeneutic approaches: culture represents society; decoding is problematic.

4. Mediation through structure: the relation between the text and social experience is defined by a common "structure" or organization of meaning that links the encoded interests and the decoded interpretations.

5. Mediation through appropriation: the relation between the text and social experience is defined by the former's ability to be "fit" into the codes that structure interests (encoding) and experience (decoding); the absence of any necessary relation between the two sets of codes results in a gap between encoding and decoding such that the homology between text and social experience must be examined at each end of the circuit of the communication.

6. Mediation through signifying practices: the relation between the text and social experience is defined by the cultural mode of production of the former, which is a response to the structures of the latter. Encoding and decoding are differentiable as embodying different forms of response.

7. Mediation through narrative: the relation between text and social experience is defined by the narrative structure of the former, which provides, in its own narrative trajectory, possibilities for the resolution of experienced and unconscious social conflicts. Both encoding and decoding, albeit not necessarily equivalent, are constructed within the narrative through processes of identification.

Discursive approaches: culture produces not only the structures of experience but experience itself, which functions within social structures of domination; the question of encoding is one of the dominant forms of decoding.

8. Positioning the subject: the text creates a space within the experience it produces into which it inserts the reader as the subject or source of that experience, and thus of its claim to be true knowledge of reality. The possibility of different decodings points to the existence of different positions that may be taken up within the text.

9. Articulating the subject: the text is inserted into a network of other texts that define the particular ways in which it produces the meaningfulness or experience of particular social identities. Decoding is precisely this intertextual articulation understood as a struggle over the power to constitute experience.

10. Materializing power: the effects of the text are defined by its existence at a particular place within a network of other practices which it both enables and is enabled by. Neither the subject nor the terms in which power is organized exist outside of this fabric of material effects.

My own biases are, I am sure, painfully obvious in the summary, if only by the trajectory of the presentation. Nevertheless, I want to emphasize that I think that all of these positions have made, and will continue to make, important contributions to our understanding of communications in the contemporary world. The point is not so much to choose between them, although one inevitably must do so, but to define new forms of alliance and cooperation among them.[7]

2 LOCATING

CULTURAL STUDIES

Cultural Studies Revisited and Revised

"Communications in transition" (the title of the volume in which this essay originally was published): the ascription is a seductive one, and perhaps, for that very reason, it is worth interrogating. Its appeal may be in part the result of its apparent innocence, which leaves unspecified not only the direction but also the substance of change. At the same time, it constructs the illusion of autonomy and occludes the sociological, political, and discursive determinations implicated in the process. Whether that autonomy is located in the "natural logic of the subject matter" or in the dialogue among individual scholars, both the specificity and the determinateness of theoretical interventions are glossed over. My own preferred characterization is that communications is the site of a discursive struggle.

My aim in this essay is twofold:

—To bring to the center a rather expansive discourse that has been largely marginalized and ghettoized. Cultural theory, which is a particularly lively field of theorizing in Britain and Europe, exists for the most part in the gaps and cracks in the American disciplinary apparatus. (The fact that it does exist is evidence that "hegemony is leaky.") Moreover, I want to outline the trajectory of theorizing in contemporary cultural studies.

—To locate the conjuncture of two questions. The first is an epistemological one: How does one understand communication? The second is a political one: How does one acknowledge and intervene in the relations of power involved in contemporary communicative practices? By following the trajectory of cultural theory into what has been called "postmodernism," I will suggest that the struggle in communications theory is not, as is often claimed, between theories of effects or influence and theories of signification or interpretation, but between theories of signification and theories of power (which reconceptualize the notion of effects).

The specificity of cultural theory can be seen in part in the context from which it emerged and into which it reinserted itself: namely, an interrogation of the nature and value of the intersecting social, economic, and political changes constituting "modernization." The uniqueness of its intervention was to locate these processes within culture, taken broadly as the structures and production of meaning. Thus cultural theory set for itself a double problematic: on the one hand, the primacy of a theory of signification and interpretation; on the other hand, the foundations of a theory of community and politics. As a result, it implicated its own discourse, as cultural, within its sphere of concern. This particular conjunction has not only provided the site for a broad series of theoretical and political arguments, it has also circumscribed a discursive space through the structure of its analytic practice (as the construction of homologies) and the identification of the culture/politics couplet with that of relativism/legitimacy. For just as the issue of interpretation problematizes any epistemological or cultural claim of truth, the confrontation with modernization threatens to undermine the political possibility of community and democracy (Rorty 1982).

The relationship between cultural theory and communication theory is a complex one. Historically, the former was one of the founding discourses from which communication, both as a unified object of study and a discipline, was constituted. Moreover, as communication theory has increasingly turned to questions of meaning, this new theoretical hegemony has attempted to incorporate some of the terms of cultural theory. While communication theory radically segregates questions of signification and politics (even the so-called critical communications theorists rarely threaten this boundary), cultural theory is located at the point of the intersection of these two problematics.

I shall begin by briefly comparing the "founding discourses" of John Dewey and Raymond Williams. While their positions are initially quite similar, the two traditions to which they give rise differ significantly because of Williams's eventual incorporation of the problem of politics into the moment of signification or culture. Thus, rather than understanding power as an external intervention into the processes of culture, the British school of "cultural studies" argues that power is a struggle within and over meaning. As a result, cultural studies have drawn upon contemporary theoretical developments in marxist theories of ideology and semiotic theories of signification. After outlining these recent developments, I shall briefly discuss some of the work of the Centre for Contemporary Cultural Studies. Raising a number of objections to this work on both theoretical and political grounds, I will suggest the possibility of a cultural theory that reverses the primacy of signification over questions of power. Rather than seeking the truth of politics, I will attempt to locate a politics of truth. Rather than seeking an interrogation of culture and communication through the problematic of signification, I will propose that signification itself be taken as merely one moment within the organization of power and desire.

DEWEY AND WILLIAMS

Given the temporal, geographical, and philosophical distance between John Dewey and Raymond Williams, it is somewhat surprising that they each articulated very similar theories of culture and communication. Of all the contributors to the Chicago school of social thought, Dewey (1954) spoke most directly to problems of communication and culture. The particular way in which Dewey described these was, of course, partly determined by his philosophical commitment to pragmatism, which, as a naturalist theory of meaning, argued that meaning was worked out in action or, more accurately, in transaction with the other. In fact, all of life was characterized transactionally: in relation to the world at the biological level, to people at the social level, or to language at the level of the generalized other. For Dewey, the model of all such transactions, at whatever level of human complexity, was ultimately communication.

The pragmatists' commitment to transaction or process was further defined by their acceptance of the evolutionary model (not surprising, given when they wrote). They assumed a hierarchical series of evolutionary levels characterized by homologous processes: Organism is to the world as self is to the social self as individual is to the social as forms of communication are to forms of social life. That is, the structure of the various levels was taken to be the same, a basic process common to all the levels. This assumption was common to the pragmatists, and thus what it meant to be human demanded an answer in terms of some particular form of a more general process. Basically, the pragmatists offered three views of this process. At one extreme, Peirce (with his logical semiotics) and, later, Morris (with his behavioral semiotics) located human meaning as the product of a semiotic system (signs/structures) as a way into the problem of interpretation. At the other extreme, James grounded his work on a theory of the stream of experience. G. H. Mead seems to have positioned himself somewhere between James and Morris, looking to the analysis of what came to be called "symbolic interactions." There is a clear trajectory in his work from the behaviorism of *Mind, Self and Society* (edited by Morris, coincidentally) to the phenomenology of *The Philosophy of the Present*. Only Dewey, located somewhere in the middle as well, began explicitly with notions of communication and sought to elucidate the relations between *forms* of communication and *forms* of social life (the notion of forms presumably existing somewhere between structures and processes).

Furthermore, for Dewey this process of communication was teleologically defined, inevitably leading toward consensus, shared meaning, and community. Thus the process of communication is the same as the process of community and, even more fundamentally, of social life. The two moments—communication and community—each reinforce each other and locate themselves in a continuing circle, since communication presupposes the community that it creates and recreates.

Consequently, if the processes of communication and community were not working, this could not be due to something inherent in the process itself but rather must be due to the interference of some external force(s). For Dewey, the twin faces of the failure of modernization—the destruction of community (culture) and the eclipse of the public (politics)—were both manifestations of the same breakdown of the natural human processes of communication due to the intervention of outside forces blocking the flow of necessary communication. The problem was not inherent in the process itself. While the new media of communication were apparently to blame for the economic, social, and political dispersion of American culture, the solution was to be found in those same media. The real enemy was simply the misuse of the possibilities of the communication media, and the solution was to restore the process, a question of providing the knowledge that was needed for people to interpret successfully and act upon reality in shared, rational ways once again.

Thus the result of Dewey's attempt to think through the relation of culture, communication, and social life was a particular vision of the mediating function of meaning, through which the cultural and political realms were describable as homologous or corresponding processes. Furthermore, the idealist view of process (albeit a naturalism) assumed a teleology that grounded and directed political optimism and, apparently, intervention. The failure of the process could be understood only as the result of some foreign and external agent or structure blocking the flow of communication; the solution lay in setting the original processes back in circulation.

This position is similar to the early position of Raymond Williams, but there are important differences that have defined the divergent traditions that have arisen out of each. I will return to this shortly. In an obvious way, the most significant difference between Williams and Dewey is the starting point. Williams (1958) raises the question of judging "modernity" by constituting a tradition of British critical thought—the "culture and society tradition"—in which both conservative and populist authors approach the task of judging the new social organizations and relationships through the explicit mediation of the category of "culture." Like Dewey, Williams was a part of a specific generation of writers, working-class children who entered into the intellectual elitism of the British university system. They existed in a "border country," living with two conflicting and competing identities, and thus they located at the center of their interrogation of modernity questions about the nature of cultural identification and understanding. Williams in particular began by identifying the specific ambiguity of the concept of "culture": it refers to a particular social sensibility, a special kind of activity (for example, the arts) and the notion of a whole way of life. As is his wont, he then argues that the changing meaning of the term is related to other historical changes and that underlying these diverse significations—historically and therefore semantically—is the notion of a special (agricultural) process: the tending for natural growth. Williams thus interprets the idea of culture as a continuous process by which shared meaning is established by common effort. Culture becomes the "community of process" and the process of community is that of communication. Social reality as a shared meaning production is accounted for as a dialogue, not merely between individuals nor between rigidly isolated individuals and reified society but between systems of meaning constantly interacting. Reality is the product of a dialectic of creativity and tradition within the space of the production of shared meaning.

When we turn to the political implications that Williams draws from this view, we find that he continues the impulse of the various writers in the culture and society tradition to locate in the concept of culture itself a standard or measure of social life. For Williams, the ideal of the "community of process" is the measure. He rejects both the conservative defense of art or of some (mythical) organic community and the populist defense of working-class culture for its own sake. Rather what Williams extols is the "long revolution" embodied in the course of modernization, what today we might call the beginnings of a populist social democracy. The problem then becomes one of participation in and access to the media by which the process of community is realized. Thus Williams attempts to identify both the positive and the negative contributions of modernization to the realization of the ideal of culture.

However, Williams (1965) takes another direction that results from the complexity of the concept of culture and that takes him into radically different questions and directions. Understood as either a sensibility or a way of life, "culture" refers to the social construction of reality through the processes of meaning production. This is also clearly the function in part of those privileged expressive activities that we also label as cultural (for example, art). Yet this does not account for the latter's special position, their privileging, or their special role in social and cultural life. Generally speaking, Williams proposes to find a way to speak about the relationship between this one unique mode of human activity and the rest of our social lives, understood in terms of our lived experience. Williams then sets out to understand the relationship between art and the totality of lived experience of a particular social moment.

What Williams proposed, as did Richard Hoggart (1957) at the same moment, is that the foundations of cultural studies lie in the intersection of literary and sociological theory. Both suggest that the specifically literary analysis of culture offers a unique insight into the understanding of culture as the whole way of life of a particular social formation. In a sense, the project of cultural studies, as it arises in England, is to understand what it felt like to be alive at a particular time and place through the interpretation of cultural (that is, artistic and communicative) texts (Hoggart 1970). How this is to be accomplished is, then, the unique problem posed by British cultural theory. Williams's solution is somewhere in the gaps of the pragmatists: in the notion of the "structure of feeling." It is this notion that opened up an analytics of interpretation in Williams's work that remained unexplored in the corpus of the Chicago school. It is meant to provide a principle of structure to that which is to be interpreted and which is, apparently, structureless (that is, feelings). Like Dewey, Williams assumes a principle of homologous structures, but his is even more encompassing. The "structure of feeling" describes both the "objective" whole way of life and the coherent totality of lived experience. That is, it provides a description of the way in which all of the "pieces" of social existence fit together into an apparently rational whole, both from the objective and the subjective sides. It is precisely this assumption of a homology between these two perspectives that has made Williams's criticism so powerful.

Thus in order to examine the social significance of any one element in social life it is not sufficient simply to relate it to one of the remaining pieces (for example, literature to the economic). Rather the interpretation of any moment of social life requires that it be related to the totality of the structure of feeling. Williams's interpretive analytic directs one to look at the relations among all of the elements in a whole way of life. Of course, there is still a problem when one turns to the question of the interpretation of artistic texts, for their relation to the general structures of feeling remains unexplicated. Here Williams uses the assumption of homologies to replace less sophisticated casual models of the relationship. Williams argues that artistic texts embody, perhaps more clearly than any other form of social practice, the structures of feeling of the social moment of their origin and reception. This is not, however, simply a reflection of an already constituted external structure; rather artistic texts both refract and constitute the structure of feeling of their social contexts. It is for this reason, according to Williams, that art is so highly valued. It is not only the most articulate entrance into and presentation of the structure of feeling, it is also the most potentially honest and reflexive production of that structure of feeling.

The notion of the structure of feeling, however, problematizes the political implications of the community of process. A consideration of the latter alone led Williams to agree with Dewey that the failure of this process must be due to external agencies interfering with the natural movement of history; similarly, the political task was one of removing blocks to access and restoring natural flows. But this model is undercut to some extent by the competing moment of the structure of feeling, for this seems to suggest that the contradictions and inequalities of a particular social moment are an integral and constitutive moment of culture. It is, however, only as Williams (1974) begins to examine the concrete structures of communication—the actual material processes by which the community of process is both carried out and undermined—that the implicit break with the politics of the Chicago school becomes explicit. Increasingly, Williams began to argue that if the forms of communication and their mirror image in the structures of relationship both produce and reproduce social reality, then these must be seen as concrete human activities. As a result, one must identify the intentions and interests that structure communication itself behind the apparently innocently given communication environment. Such intentions are neither personal nor psychological, however; rather they are constituted within social structures and represent economic and political positions within the social formation. Further, Williams argued that such intentions could be read off, interpreted within, the communicative texts and practices themselves.

Thus the community of process constantly is contradicted and distended by "the community of culture." The latter points to the necessary materiality of the processes by which social reality is produced, a materiality that incorporates into the process itself questions of power and inequality. These are not two separate processes but two moments—*telos* and *ursprung*—of the same process, the social production of meaning. Thus Williams concludes that the question of politics must be raised within the issue of signification, rather than as the result of external interference. Politics is a moment of the cultural process itself; politics is itself an interpretive issue.

The interpretation of culture and communication, then, rests upon the assumption of homologies explicated in the notion of the structure of feeling. Now, in addition, one must find a way of describing these processes not only in terms of the social production of meaning (or of reality as meaningful) but also in terms of the social displacement of reality in processes of meaning production. Once we recognize that all of culture refracts reality as well as reproducing it as meaningful, then we are committed as well to examining the interests implicated in particular refractions. If both the production of meaningful reality and the displacement of reality within that production are integral moments of the process of culture, then cultural studies must interrogate the ways in which communication not only produces but also distorts or deviates from the homologous structuring of culture and social experience.

Thus despite the fact that both Dewey and Williams began by exploring the same intellectual and historical terrain, each opened up a different discursive space. This has had significant implications for the development of cultural studies in the two countries. Both apparently confronted two distinct problematics. The first (signification) questions the nature and production of meaning. It points to, in Ricoeur's terms (1970), a hermeneutics of faith. The second issue (power) questions the possibility of distortion or misrepresentation, pointing to a hermeneutics of suspicion. As long as the two problematics remain separated, however, there is the third question of the relationship between the two theories offered in response. Williams's most significant contribution was to recognize eventually that the theories of communication and miscommunication had to be articulated together, that the question of how texts mean is intersected by the question of how texts relate to and distort reality. This insight suggested that cultural studies fruitfully might locate itself at the site of the intersection of semiotics and the theory of ideology.

On the other hand, the U.S. tradition of "culturalism" that developed out of the work of the Chicago school (Carey 1975a, 1977) has taken a very different path. This was the result, in part, of the particular marginalization of this tradition, not only in social theory but in the study of communications as well. Because of its narrower focus on the processes of mass media, American cultural theory has devoted an inordinate amount of its energy to defending itself against the claims of the more "scientific" effects tradition. Furthermore, Dewey's naturalistic idealism provided little direction for concrete theoretical and interpretive practice.

Rather vague and often contradictory notions of the symbolic construction of reality have led to the celebration of epistemological and cultural relativism, and at the same time have undermined the possibility of coherent political critique. While this tradition often provides some of the most sensitive readings of American culture, it does so in an apparently atheoretical way, without any interpretive analytic. In a rather unique paradox, it assumes the mediating function of signification without offering any theory of how this is accomplished or of how it can be dismantled and described. Nor is there any theory of why the production of meaning is itself effectively produced as a representation of the real. Because the role of concrete social and material relations in this process remains unconceptualized, there is no way of addressing the relationship between processes of meaning production and "intentional displacement." Because the two problematics remain essentially unconnected, there is no apparent place for a theory of the political management of the production of meaning. Despite its impeccable humanistic credentials, the American culturalist tradition seems a less fruitful alternative than the British school of cultural studies, which attempts to link signification and social processes, communication and miscommunication, together.

CULTURAL AND STRUCTURAL MARXISM

The traditional reading of Marx suggests that the social formation could be represented as a dialectic between the base and the superstructure. The former is characterized by the particular mode of production, defined by the dialectic between the forces and relations of production. In capitalism at least, this is determining, and its internal contradictions provide the potential source of revolution. The latter consists of the various political and cultural institutions of the social formation. While the base is often reduced to only the mode of economic production and the superstructure is seen as a mere reflection of the determining base, there are those who would argue that this is an oversimplification of Marx's theory. Nevertheless, in this traditional view ideology is defined functionally as a representation of the interests of the dominant or ruling class, as the body of "ruling ideas," or as the ideal expression of the dominant material relations. It is, in other words, a hierarchically imposed false consciousness whose function is to hide, via a distortion of reality, the contradictions and interests constituting the social formation in general and the class relations in particular.

Such views have been made a little more sophisticated by recognizing the dialectical nature of the relationship between the base and the superstructure. Furthermore, the simple class analysis on which it initially was based has given way to a more open view in which ideology need not reflect the interests and position of a single dominant class. Instead ideology can be understood as the site of a struggle and, in particular, of the conflict inherent in the class struggle. However, the real lacuna in this view of ideology is any analysis of how ideology works, of the mediation of reality that it produces, and of the medium through which it is empowered (that is, language).

There have been two major responses to this lack of an adequate theory of either ideology or, more generally, the superstructure. Hall (1980c) has described them as "cultural" and "structural" marxism. In contrast to the traditional conceptions of marxism, both of these approaches are theoretical and are primarily concerned with the superstructure and its role in constituting power and domination through the operation of ideology. Both are opposed to the economic reductionism of earlier marxisms, although they retain the basic assumption that the economic is determining in the last instance. Rather than seeing the superstructure or culture as a mere reflex or reflection of economic determinations, however, they argue that culture and ideology have their own real determining role in the social formation. Furthermore, they suggest that the relationship between economic and political processes on the one hand, and superstructural processes on the other, always is mediated by other refracting levels of determination. Finally, both are opposed to the totalitarianism of the Stalinist reading of Marx, and both seek to reclaim the political fecundity of marxist practice.

The argument between them is over the status of experience as a possible beginning point or standard. This issue is not, however, reducible to a simple argument over the primacy of the individual versus the social, since even culturalists like Williams would argue that experience is always social. While it does have implications for issues of subjectivity and the possibility of oppositional practice, the real issue is, I believe, whether one starts with a theory of reality (experience) and distortion or a theory of signification and the production of experience.

The culturalists' revision of marxism (Williams 1973a) emphasizes the

"humanistic" rather than the "economistic" side of Marx's writings, especially the earlier Hegelian works. They point to Marx's concern with describing social reality in terms of lived experience. They focus their analysis on
the social subject as an active agent who makes history through "praxis," the
essential form of creative human activity. Furthermore, they argue that any
particular practice must be located within the totality of social life, both as an
actuality and as a totalization to be achieved. They maintain a teleological
image of history explicated through the eventual resolution of the class struggle. Thus they continue to describe social experience in terms of class experience, although classes no longer are seen necessarily as homogeneous to-
talities but rather as an alliance of particular "class fractions," which are
determined ideologically and politically as well as economically. The result
is, of course, that particular class alliances may themselves embody contradictions among the various fractions. While class position determines the
consciousness with which individuals confront, for example, ideological
forms, the model that the culturalists propose for this process is significantly
revised in a number of ways. Attempting to escape the limits of the base-
superstructure model, they suggest that both of these terms must be seen as
processes and as complex sets of often contradictory practices. For example,
Williams (1973a) prefers to say that "social being determines consciousness,"
that is, that the structures of human material practices determine the structures and contours of human consciousness.

Further, the relation of "determination" is seen as a dialectical process of
shaping and influencing, rather than the simple production of mirror images.
It is the exertion of force that tends to push the other in a certain direction.
The processes of determination rarely operate directly; they are mediated
through a variety of moments that necessarily distend the possibility of any
causal relationship. One of the consequences of this view is that the category
of the economic is largely absent from culturalist analyses, except in terms of
class experience.

Finally, the concept of ideology either is replaced by or supplemented with
Gramsci's concept (1971) of hegemony. Whereas ideology suggests the distortion of reality through a stable system of representation, a content that can be
compared to experience, hegemony points to a constant process by which the
dominant class alliance wins the consent of the dominated classes by creating representations of reality that are taken as reality itself. Hegemony
is a continuous struggle to dominate through consent rather than coercion,
through representation rather than falsification, through legitimation rather

than manipulation. In the struggle for hegemony, representations of reality are offered in the place of the real and come to be taken as reality, and thus they provide the natural and reasonable limits of "common sense." On the surface this view of the production of meaning as the social construction of reality bears a striking similarity to the theories of American culturalists; but its location within the context of a theory of the class struggle opens up an entire analytic of the concrete processes by which particular interests are tied to particular representations, and the struggle to produce and maintain consent is carried on concretely. However, because the cultural marxist's final appeal is to the category of experience, there still remains a moment of distortion within the theory of hegemony, and a moment of correspondence between ideology and reality. Thus the culturalist's project is to compare the ideological representations, now located within the ongoing struggle for hegemony, with the lived experience of particular classes. Cultural marxism seeks homologies between class positions and systems of representation.

On the other side of the current debate in British cultural studies is structural marxism, based largely upon the work of Althusser (1970, 1971). Althusser explicitly rejected Marx's early writings as idealist and ideological. He proposes both a new model of the social formation as well as a new theory of ideology, resulting in a radical undermining of the base-superstructure model that he still sees operating in the culturalist's search for homologies. Given the complexity and difficulty of his views, I can provide only a brief outline.

First, according to structural marxism, the social formation is to be described as a "structure in dominance." It is composed of four levels or ensembles of social practices: the political, the economic, the ideological, and the theoretical. This last level—Althusser's failed attempt to describe the scientific status of marxist critique and thus to avoid the conclusion that marxism is itself an ideological practice—need not concern us here. Any social analytic must begin, then, with the complexity of the unity of a structure. This requires that we recognize both the specificity of the levels and their relations, that we identify the contradictions within each level as well as those between them.

The relations among the levels are described in the concepts of "structural causality" and "overdetermination." Althusser distinguishes three kinds of causality. Mechanical causality is the identifiable operation of one isolatable entity on another (the billiard ball model). Expressive causality is the expression of an internal or central principle (such as the spirit of an age or the structure of feeling) in all of the surface phenomena. Structural causality is a cause that exists only in its effects, or, more accurately, in the structuration of its effects. Structural causality rejects any appeal to an external agency or to an internal principle. There is no essential structure (or even any particular contradiction) that can characterize and explain the social formation. Structural causality operates by overdetermination; that is, every moment in the social formation determines and is determined by every other moment. One cannot, therefore, isolate individual causal relations as if they could exist outside of the structured context. And yet one cannot reduce any level entirely to the determinations of the other levels, since each level of practice is characterized as well by a semiautonomy. This is not an appeal, however, to some notion of absolute freedom; rather it points to the fact that each level is determined partially by its own history and its own internal logic. As a result, there is and must be a necessary noncorrespondence between the levels in the social formation.

While the culturalists define the social in terms of class experience and structure, Althusser returns to the more traditional marxist view of the social as defined primarily by the mode of production. Each of the levels, however (political, economic, ideological), as a form of practice is productive. Thus one must specify the hierarchical relations among the three levels. This is what Althusser calls the "structure in dominance." At any historical moment, one of the three levels is dominant (that is, most directly and powerfully determining) within the social formation. Which of the three serves this function is itself determined by the economic level in the last instance. But as Althusser quickly adds, the last instance never comes, and it can never come if we are to avoid falling back into economic reductionism. Thus the structural marxist view of the social totality within which ideology and culture are effective is significantly different from that of the cultural marxists: Overdetermination replaces homology.

Althusser's theory of ideology (1971) is also significantly different; it denies that there are homologies between representations and experience. For structural marxism, ideology is in fact the process by which experience itself is produced. It is the unconscious system of representation of the imaginary relationship between people and their real conditions of existence. It is the production of the meaning, not of reality, but of the way in which we live our relationship to reality, that is, of our experience. In what Althusser describes as a "double specular relation," ideology is a mirror structure within which the individual and reality are produced in a relationship to each other, as subject and experience, respectively. That is, ideology works by positioning the individual in a particular relation to the system of representation. Ideology "hails" or "interpellates" the individual as a subject. It makes the subject apparently responsible for those meanings and hence for his or her own experience. The result is that the system of representation appears to be innocently given in the immediacy of our own experience, whereas, in fact, it is that experience itself that has been produced. Ideology is not a mediation between subjectivity and reality. The subject, which is the transcendental assumption of all humanists, is "deconstructed" and shown to be a necessary product of ideological practice, that which ideology constructs as its own support or bearer. One of the more controversial results of this particular functional theory of ideology is that ideology is a necessary moment of any social formation. There must always be ideology, embodied within the material practices of signification. This would seem at least to problematize the assumption of any utopian reading of history insofar as such readings must appeal to an image of human nature (subjectivity) as universal and essential.

There is an apparent similarity between the structural theory of ideology and the concept of hegemony. Both identify the operation of ideology with the processes of signification and naturalization so that meaning is offered in the place of reality/experience. The power of the structuralist view, however, lies in its explicit articulation of a theory of signification that brings together the moments of representation and misrepresentation. In order to see this more clearly, one must examine the semiotic foundations of Althusser's work and, in particular, his debt to structuralism and poststructuralism.

STRUCTURALISM AND POSTSTRUCTURALISM

The theory of structuralism is built upon distinctions: langue/parole, synchrony/diachrony, paradigm/syntagm, and signified/signifier. Structuralism brackets questions of language use (parole) and history (diachrony) in order to study the underlying system or codes that make possible the concrete usage. It analyzes the system in terms of relations of substitution (paradigms) and contiguity (syntagms). Most significantly, the basic unit of signifying systems—the sign—is described as a unity of signifier and signified. While it is tempting to describe these as a material vehicle and a concept or meaning, respectively, this is not quite accurate, for the concept of the sign (and all of structuralism) is based upon the assumption of constitutive difference.

Saussure (1959), often regarded as the founder of structuralism, argued that the sign is always arbitrary, that is, that the relationship between the signifier and the signified is neither necessary nor externally defined. The sign does not refer to some external referent nor to some subjective intention; both reality and subjectivity are excluded from structural analyses. Instead the sign is defined by a series or system of differences. Both the signifier and the signified exist only as spaces within such systems of differences; thus meaning (or more accurately, since we are in the realm of langue, value) is immanent within the system. Any particular signifier is not a concrete matter but a position that is differentiated and therefore given value within the system itself. Similarly, the signified is not a concept in the mind but a place carved out from an amorphous conceptual space. Either one can be filled by a multiplicity of variants or concrete embodiments, but this would take us into the realm of parole. Finally, structuralism argues that there is a necessary correspondence between the system of signifiers and that of the signifieds. It is as if these two distinct domains existed on opposite sides of a common plane; the way in which one inscribes differences on the plane of the signifier determines the inscription of differences on the plane of the signified. Thus, according to structuralism, language structures conceptual space and the only place for the subject is as a prisoner in the house of language (Jameson 1972).

While Althusser's theory draws heavily upon structuralism, he also draws upon the structural psychoanalysis of Lacan (1977). Together they represent the transition from structuralism to poststructuralism in their attempt to account for the production of meaning (the signified) and subjectivity in signifying practices. Lacan argued for both the primacy of the signifier and the implication of the subject in language, both of which serve as the foundations for contemporary poststructuralist work. Briefly, Lacan located the origin of desire as a lack that results in the infant's need to become the object of desire of the mother—the phallus. This lack is filled only (and only apparently so) in the Oedipal stage, which involves the child's accession into the domain of language, or what Lacan calls "the Symbolic." By representing oneself in language—the "I" of enunciation—the moment of Oedipal resolution produces a splitting of the individual: the one who speaks and is represented in language and that which can neither speak nor be spoken, the unconscious. Thus, according to Lacan, language is responsible not only for the production of the subject but also for the production of the unconscious (and hence the possibility of repression and all that entails psychoanalytically).

This connection of signification and subjectivity opens up a radically new space of critical discourse. No longer content merely to bracket questions of subject and reality—a strategy that inevitably leaves them in their taken-for-granted place—the focus of poststructuralism has turned from signifying structures to processes and practices of structuration. It is, then, a philosophy of the signifier. It takes for granted that signifying practices involve the production of signifiers in relations. Interestingly, this is quite similar to Peirce's pragmatic semiotics in which signification is to be analyzed as the continuous production of material signs. The poststructuralists argue that there is no need to assume the existence of signifieds or meanings within some sort of conceptual space. Rather language (no longer distinguishing between langue and parole) is a constant sliding of one signifier into another, the production of a chain of signifiers. Meaning is the (imaginary) product of this movement, the result of the need or desire to stop the infinite generation of signifiers and to rest somewhere with an apparently natural meaning. It is, metaphorically, a game of musical chairs in which meaning is simply the product of our bringing the music to a halt. At that point, particular signifiers appear to be in special places (the chairs) or to have special effects that we take as meanings. Thus there is no "conceptual space of the mind" in which meanings preexist and are organized by the signifying system. Signification is not a mediating function at all.

If there is no conceptual or phenomenological space of meanings, then there is similarly no moment of subjective existence that escapes the determination of signifying practices. The subject—as one who uses language for his or her own projects or as one who creatively binds the signifier and signified together into the sign—is an imaginary product of the very practices the concept seeks to control. This "I" is, simply put, another socially produced reality (Lukacs 1971).

It is important at this point to be clear about the precise claims that are being made. Poststructuralists do not deny that we experience ourselves as subjects, nor that we experience the world as meaningful, nor that these experiences are effective and have real material consequences in the world. Rather they are suggesting that experience itself must be problematized and destabilized. The categories of experience cannot provide the beginnings of a theory of signification nor the standard for a theory of representation and misrepresentation, for it is these very categories that are the product of signifying practices. Appeals to experience, as if it existed outside of the production of meaning, and appeals to subjectivity, as if it were not positioned by and within signifying practices as the source and locus of meaning, are at the very root of our inability to theorize the processes of meaning production and their relation to power (Coward 1977).

The practice of poststructural criticism takes a number of closely related forms. Basically it attempts to "deconstruct" any apparently transparent, given, essential, totalizing, or transcontextual moment; such moments may be categories of experience, philosophically privileged concepts, or particular texts. Deconstruction destabilizes the claim of any term to contain its own meaning within itself by dispersing its apparently given unity and meaning into the processes of its production. The result is that meaning always becomes "undecidable."

Such deconstructive practices have taken two basic forms (Coward and Ellis 1977). The first form of deconstruction involves a kind of philosophical critique by which any attempt to identify a stable meaning in a particular concept is undermined. This does not entail the denial of meaning or of the effectivity of the experience. Rather it is a constant deferral of one's ability to locate such a meaning. Even the structuralists' claim that meaning is constituted in relations (often binary) of difference is undermined by destabilizing the very category of difference; the ability to locate a stable moment of difference within which one can describe the particular constitution of meaning is again deferred. It is this notion of a difference that is constantly deferred, thus always pushing meaning away from us, that Derrida (1976) calls *différance*. Difference and hence meaning constantly are produced and deferred, always pushing themselves further into the infinite possibilities of such production, leaving only traces of their operation for us to find. *Différance* is the ongoing inscription or articulation of differences, and hence it is that ongoing movement of the production of meaning that cannot be said to exist outside its concrete products.

The second form of deconstructive practice also disperses meaning into the processes of its production. However, such processes are located in concrete reading practices. The result is that the explosion of meaning is not given in a deferral but rather in the infinite possibilities of the continued generation of meaning in readings. Focusing generally on texts, such "dissemination" (Derrida 1981) explodes the very category of "the text" in general and any particular text into the context of reading. If meaning is a product of the various codes that traverse the text, then the text always exists and is carried beyond itself into a domain of intertextuality. The meaning of a text is undecidable outside of particular readings; hence the text cannot be said to have a meaning or even a closed set of possible meanings. But this does not mean that one can claim that texts have no meaning, for this would merely be to substitute a void, an absence, for the assumption of a presence. Deconstruction, then,

dissolves the boundaries of the text by continuing the connotative reverbera-
tions and webs of its discourses. Meaning is not the product of some reified
text nor of some privileged "perspective" belonging to the reader. Rather
meaning is a function of the context produced by particular reading practices,
and the possibility of new readings opens the text to an infinite possibility of
meaning.

There are a number of problems, however, with such deconstructive practices. First, they continue to privilege experience by defining their project as
accounting for the production of the categories of experience. Thus they fail
to radically problematize the semantic boundaries of such experiences and
thus question only their claim to primacy and stability. The alternative would
be to take experience itself as one material fact among others. Second, they
actually do not give an account of the production of the subject in concrete
terms and appeal instead to universally necessary processes. Neither Althusser's theory of ideology nor Derrida's theory of *différance* gives an adequate account of how these processes work to produce the subject. In fact,
everything ultimately is reduced to a trace of these processes. This suggests
that they may in fact be functioning as new transcendentals, that is, universal
processes that determine but are not determined by historical contexts.

However, it is not only the existence of the subject that needs to be explained; it is also the possibility of the breakdown or failure of the production
of the ideological or discursive subject. For it appears that both Derrida and
Althusser reconstitute a unified subject. It is, on the one hand, the necessary
and almost mechanical result of the operation of signifying practices. On the
other hand, it is the assumption of their own critical practices: in Althusser's
claim for the scientific (that is, nonideological) status of marxist analysis, and
in Derrida's apparently innocent, undetermined, and playful reading subject.

This raises a significant theoretical and political problem. If the subject (as
it is experienced within the terms of Western culture) is the product of signifying practices (either ideological or discursive), then how is it possible to
move beyond the mechanical reproduction of this subject? How is deconstructive practice possible? And how is revolutionary action (even in terms of
the production of revolutionary discourse) possible? If one cannot explain
the necessity of the production of the subject, how is one to explain the
possibility of the revolutionary subject? For example, in Derridean terms,
why do the reading practices in which we are implicated function in the way
they do? Derrida's attempt to incorporate some moment of historical and

political determination—in his appeal to logocentrism—would throw us back into an expressive theory of causality.

The poststructuralist response to these problems largely has come from the work of the group associated with the journal *Tel Quel*, in two related interventions. The first proposes a critical vector that moves in the opposite direction from the playful and infinite possibilities of dissemination. It interrogates the moment at which the productivity of the sliding of the signifiers is halted; it looks at the ways in which meaning is determined by reading practices and the contextual constraints within which readings are accomplished. Thus reading in itself seems to be the determined product of textual, intertextual, and cultural codes. For example, Barthes's reading (1974) of a realist short story offers something other than an explosion of the meaning of the text. On the one hand, he argues that the realist text is read precisely as a realist text, that the chain of signifiers is structured, directed, and ultimately stopped in determined ways. This determination is the operation of codes that can be located only in the intertext of our socially determined reading practices. This determination of meaning cannot be accounted for in terms of some stable structuring of the text, nor in terms of the subjective appropriation of the text. Yet on the other hand, Barthes argues that this particular text also deconstructs the very possibility of its own meaningfulness as realism by constantly playing off, against its own codings of language and sexuality, the image of that which resists all attempts at coding: the image of castration. The result is that Barthes exhibits both the intertextual determination of meaning and the instability if not impossibility of any such meaning. Similarly, in *A Lover's Discourse* (Barthes 1978), he demonstrates how a particular intertextual set of discursive practices carries the speaker along, constructing not only a highly emotionally charged language but the speaker as the subjective source of such emotions: To be a lover is to exist within a web of clichés.

The second intervention into a politics of and for poststructuralism derives from Kristeva's attempt (1975b, Grossberg 1982a) to appropriate and rework both Althusser and Lacan. Both of these end up suggesting that the individual is inserted into an already defined space of subjectivity that leaves little room for either political or discursive oppositional practice. Kristeva seeks to theoretically locate the possibility of multiple and even contradictory subject-positionings. While Barthes apparently is satisfied to ascribe this to the effects of competing reading practices, Kristeva argues that it is the result of the conflict between language and desire that takes place within the production of meaning or *signifiance*. There are two moments to this process, two lines of force and determination: the symbolic and the semiotic. The former points to the Lacanian, Althusserian, and Derridean view of signifying practices and their necessary production of a particular subject-position. The second moment, the semiotic, which is also signifying, implicates the unconscious in its opposition to the constraints of social codings. The semiotic is the eruption of libidinal drives into and through the structures of the symbolic. It is also an interruption, an articulation of that which cannot be articulated symbolically. According to Kristeva, the subject is constantly produced in the struggle between these two moments within *signifiance*. Although symbolic practices seek a stable subject position, semiotic practices constantly disrupt and destabilize the possibility of any such mechanical reproduction. If the subject is never produced once and for all and if there is, at the very heart of the production of meaning and subjectivity, a moment of opposition, then the possibility of a revolutionary subject—one that would disrupt the stability of the ideological and discursive subject—always exists. Obviously, this view is not incompatible with that of Barthes. The strongest poststructuralist position will be one that combines a theory of the relationship of desire and discourse with the recognition that the subject is determined by the multiplicity of signifying practices available to him or her. The result is that subjectivity is not produced as a stable unity but rather is always being produced in fragmented and contradictory ways. The subject (even of experience) is not a single position but always a determined structuration of multiple positionings.

THE RETURN OF CULTURAL STUDIES

While U.S. cultural and communication theorists have, for the most part, ignored these theoretical arguments, they have had a decisive impact on the development of cultural studies in England, through the work of the Centre for Contemporary Cultural Studies (Hall 1980a). While the Centre's initial problematic involved the attempt to examine the relationship between social practices and the ways they are represented in discourse (and ideology), its developing theory has led it to question this dichotomy. Rather than separating questions of representation and determination, the Centre has attempted to think these two moments together at the intersection of structuralism and marxism while focusing on questions of the relative autonomy and the specificity of cultural practices.

At the same time, while the concerns of the Centre have always been much broader than those of traditional communication studies, their work increasingly has attempted to bring these two discourses together. For example, Hall (1982) has rewritten the history of communication theory through the history of the Centre. He argues that the problem of communication theory is that of consensus, and he identifies three historical moments in the theoretical elaboration of the discipline. In the first stage, consensus was understood in terms of shared norms. Those not participating in the structure of shared norms were characterized as deviant and their experience as anomic. The second stage was constructed upon the recognition that the world is meaningful and that most people act according to operative definitions of the situation. The deviant was placed into a subculture that offers its own construction of meaningful reality. The third stage, defining the current position of the Centre, argues that the world "has to be made to mean." Not only is meaning produced, but the claim to representation is also produced. The definition of the situation is neither given nor innocent but rather is the product of an ongoing "struggle over meaning" (Volosinov 1973). Consequently, subcultures must be located within the social and cultural struggle to produce consensus.

This has led the members of the Centre first to critique and then to extend Althusser's theory of ideology and to locate it within the concept of hegemony (Hall 1977). First, they reject the pessimistic conclusion that ideology always functions to reproduce the conditions of the existing social formation. Consequently they tend to underemphasize the notion that ideology works by producing subject-positions (Coward 1977) and substitute a process of the negotiation of and struggle over identities. Second, since meaning itself is never given in language but is always a product of social practices of signification, and since the production of consent takes place within a struggle over meaning, the Centre has attempted to use contemporary semiotic theories to explore the "articulation of ideology in and through discourse" (Hall et al. 1980). This entails rejecting Althusser's apparent identification of ideology and language. This has significant implications and had led to an extension of Althusser's argument that ideology always must be located within the ensemble of practices of the social formation. For if the ideological import of any particular text cannot be read directly from the text itself, then one must explore the social practices that enter into the determination of the ideological effect. Using the work of Laclau (1977), the Centre has argued against the culturalist reading of hegemony in terms of class experience and suggested instead that there is no necessary "class-belongingness" of specific ideological practices. There is no simple correspondence between class position and ideological practice, despite the fact that there may be "traditional" couplings

the end the question of the relationship between the two moments of encoding and decoding. There is no concrete analysis of the struggle between representation and determination embodied within this particular context of social relations and practices. This has led some of the Centre's contributors (Corrigan and Willis 1980) to question the analysis of reading practices in terms of experience and to seek a semiotic description of cultural resources. They argue that one cannot assume a correspondence between practice and identity (that is, between role performance and role internalization). Using semiotic theory, they suggest that the multiple and contradictory positionalities of the social subject determine differential relations (openness and accessibility) to different discourses. The problem for cultural analysis is to find ways of describing the relations between discourses and the noncoded, extradiscursive resources of the working class. Such knowledge, albeit not articulated, is embodied within "cultural forms" that are amenable to semiotic reading.

The notion that the cultural resources can be deciphered as signifying practices underlies Hebdige's study (1979) of subcultural style. It is worth considering his position in some detail since it is perhaps the most complete example of the Centre's work. Hebdige offers the concept of "style" as the mediating term through which the interpretation of any concrete subcultural form must pass. In essence, his argument is that a subcultural style is a representation of and an imaginary solution to the particular experienced contradictions within class culture. Let us begin by asking, first, how subcultural styles work to signify and, second, what it is that they represent. One must ask what distinguishes a subcultural style from the systems of representation of the dominant culture. Hebdige's response is that styles are obviously fabricated and display their own codes. Consequently they deny and disrupt the "deceptive innocence of appearances" on which the hegemony is built and maintained. The naturalness of the meaning of reality, of the world of experience, of the circuit connecting object and sign is problematized and ultimately rejected. The social processes of production and reproduction, depending as they do on the processes by which objects are given meaning and transformed into signs, are contradicted in the very practice of style. Here we can begin to examine the function and operation of style: as communication, bricolage, homology, and signifying practice. Style primarily communicates "a significant difference" and thus a group identity. It marks its members as different from the rest of the world as it simultaneously defines and represents a "forbidden identity." The remaining three terms of the series explain how this function is carried out. Style is a form of bricolage that uses the commodities of a conspicuous consumption culture in a particular way, as a form of what Baudrillard (1978) calls a "semiotic guerilla warfare" against the innocence of the surfaces of hegemonic reality: "These humble objects can be magically appropriated; stolen by subordinate groups and made to carry 'secret' meanings: meanings which express, in code, a form of resistance to the order which guarantees their continued subordination" (Hebdige 1979, 18). Style fits these objects together in a particular "symbolic fit" or homology that forms a unity, not only with other stylistic objects but also with the group's relations and situations. Subcultural style exhibits a consistency and coherence that can only signal that "the objects chosen were, either intrinsically or in their adapted forms, homologous with the focal concerns, activities, group structure, and collective self-image of the subculture" (114). There must then be an underlying level of style at which it is able to generate this appropriation of objects into a homology: style exists finally as signifying practice. Different styles embody different modes by which objects are transformed into signs. Such signifying practices not only produce the circuit between object and sign in various ways but also that between sign and subject. They position individuals and group in language and thus represent identities in the last instance.

However, we can take this last point further and ask what it is that is represented in style or, from the other direction, how style is determined. Hebdige's most general response is that subcultural styles represent "group experience," but the group is, at least initially, apparently broader than the subculture: style is "a coded response to the changes affecting the entire community" (80), which in turn is defined largely in terms of class experience. However, drawing upon Althusser, Hebdige argues that style represents the way in which class is lived (74). A subculture is "a form of resistance in which experienced contradictions and objections to [the] ruling ideology are obliquely represented in style" (133). Avoiding the obvious appeal to the material conditions of class existence, Hebdige argues that style gives expression to the particular contradictions within the way in which a group lives its relationship to the economic reality (class structure).

Yet Hebdige refuses any such simple correspondence; instead he argues that the experience responded to in style is overdetermined. It responds to a number of other moments within the historical social formation, including hegemonic attempts to represent and appropriate its own existence. Further, the particular experiences coded and responded to within subcultural styles in England are predicated upon the assumed identification of the position of blacks and working-class white youth. Their styles can be interpreted as a "series of mediated responses to the presence in Britain of a sizeable black community" (1979, 73). Finally, there is a particular "generational conscious-ness" that responds to the more general "breakdown of consensus" in post-war Britain. Youth cultures, while confronting and experiencing the class contradictions of their working-class roots, attempt to define a position for themselves that can "negotiate a meaningful intermediate space somewhere between the parent culture and the dominant ideology: a space where an alternative identity could be discovered and expressed. To this extent, they were engaged in that distinctive quest for a measure of autonomy which characterizes all youth sub- (and counter)cultures" (88).

The final stage in the argument is to address the issue of the relation be-tween style as signifying practice and as a representation of lived contradic-tions. Hebdige's answer lies in the "obliqueness" with which these contradic-tions are represented: style can be read as "maps of meaning which obscurely re-present the very contradictions they are designed to resolve or conceal" (1979, 18). That is, style represents experienced contradictions in an eternal circle so that the representations themselves appear as an (imaginary) solu-tion. The signification of style is a magical one by which the identity it pro-duces provides the appearance of an experiential resolution of the contradic-tions. Because this resolution is only magical, that is, because it works by appropriating commodities into a "spectacular" style, it is always open to re-appropriation. It can always be reincorporated into the hegemony, either through the mass production and recommodification of its signs or through an ideological renomination of the subculture. Because of its oblique and magi-cal effectivity, it is impossible to maintain this as an absolute distinction. Sub-cultures remain based in leisure activities and, consequently, the gap between an appropriated and a reappropriated commodity cannot provide the basis of a reading of style. However, because every subculture moves through a "cycle of resistance and defusion," the interpretation of style must focus on the "outrageous" spectacle, that moment in which style transforms objects into subcultural signs, rather than on the signs as "objects-in-themselves." Heb-dige's argument then would suggest an interpretive practice built upon the structuration of identities in response to experience rather than the search for homologies between texts and experience.

Nevertheless, his actual reading belies his own argument and points to the contradictions within the Centre's theoretical practice. First, the fact remains that Hebdige assumes a series of homologies and structures his analysis accordingly. There is a correspondence between any particular moment of a subcultural style and the general characterization of that style, and between the style and the lived experience of the subculture. This double homology, re-presented in the undecidable relation between style as communication and as signifying practice, throws us back into the search for phenomenological correspondences. Second, not only are the descriptions of the two regimes—experience and style—radically separated, but each is also problematic. The experience of the group is described in essentially interactionist terms and, apparently, taken as an innocently given starting point. What appears to be its overdetermination is merely a description of a part of its conjunctural specificity (class, age, race). Its ideological production, which would implicate style itself in the process, is ignored in favor of the class determination of experience. In fact, Hebdige's description of the style is phenomenological. It depends on his prior description of the experience behind and represented within it; style is represented as part of the subcultural experience so that its description is in phenomenological rather than material terms. The result is that Hebdige fails to specify the particular nature of the struggle over meaning within subcultural style. He is satisfied with glossing over this theoretical problem in the notion of an "imaginary" solution, but this serves only to reiterate its place within an ideological struggle.

There have been at least two responses within the Centre to the inadequacies of Hebdige's reading despite its richness. McRobbie (1980) has pointed to the "structured absence" of any consideration of the place of women within subcultures. Indeed she seems to argue that questions of sexual power cannot be dealt with adequately within the Centre's current theoretical position because it lacks a theory of pleasure. The result is that there is no theory of leisure, and hence there is a serious flaw in their reading of subcultures. We can identify, however, at a deeper level the Centre's inability to deal with the challenge posed by feminism and sexual politics. For the question is, fundamentally, whether cultural power can be conceptualized on the model of hierarchical domination and the ideological production of experience (Foucault 1978a; P. Adams 1978). Can the relations of power organized around the distinction between male and female be theorized within a framework of signification and experience? If the oppression of women is not merely a question of symbolic meaning, then the call for a theory of desire and power challenges the phenomenological roots of any theory of the social production of the real as meaningful. What if behavior is not just a function of the interpretation of the situation and if the effect of social practices is more, or actually less, than the meaning of the practice?

The second response to the gaps in Hebdige's analysis emphasizes overdetermination and the materiality of social practices. Thus, in his recent work, Hebdige (1981a, 1981b) increasingly attempts not only to treat the object as an image but the image as an object to be located in an overdetermined historical moment:

> It is perhaps only in this way by outlining the connections and breaks between groups of separate but interlocking statements that we can begin to imagine the particular dimensions of a language which is now largely lost to us and to appreciate not only the historical conditions under which that language was originally constructed but also the social conflicts and shifts in power which were registered inside it and which ultimately led to its dispersal and decline. (1981a, 40)

Similarly, Chambers has argued that specific cultural texts must be seen as constituting "an active, contradictory, cultural practice whose choices, relations and possibilities are being continually forged and transformed by the social relations that traverse it" (1981, 39). Thus the cultural power of such texts—their implication in a struggle over meaning—demands an analysis of "the interlocking effects of cultural powers, and institutional apparatus . . . and the social relations that invest them" (37). What is significant in these arguments is, ultimately, the absence of any appeal to experience as the other side of the cultural production of meaning. Implicit in their position is a critique of the Centre's fundamental assumptions. In particular, instead of reconciling notions of hegemony and the structural theory of ideology, the Centre falls back into a model of expressive causality and reconstitutes the division between base and superstructure. There remains, at the core of its position, the contradiction between experience as the product of an ideological struggle and as the articulation, however displaced, of class position. This contradiction is reproduced in the ambiguity of their critical practice: seeking to describe overdetermined cultural practices, they conclude by uncovering homologies. In Hebdige's recent work on the image and Chamber's analyses of popular music, we find the theory of overdetermination clearly displacing the search for homologies. Both argue for an examination of the specific articulation of social practices onto other practices. Yet both continue to decipher the meanings of a symbolic form. It is this (the primacy of signification) that, I would like to suggest, is at the root of the inability of cultural studies to construct a practice adequate to the theory of overdetermination. This is, in turn, the result of beginning with the question of the relationship between culture and society, for this inevitably privileges and differentiates cultural practices as essentially significatory. In the concluding section of this essay, I would like to propose an alternative approach to the issues of communication and culture based on the project of postmodernism. Rather than thinking of our task as the interpretation of meaning, or even as the deconstruction of meaning, I want to suggest that meaning itself must be located as an effect within a broader theory of power and desire.

CULTURE, POWER, AND DESIRE

The irony of cultural theories built upon the reduction of the real to the meaningful is that they are unable to argue for either the truth of their own interpretations or for the validity of their political interventions. Structuralists struggle to find an adequate description of "theoretical" or critical practice that will enable them to ground their politics in a comparison of experience and reality. Culturalists are forced to appeal to transcendental utopian principles while at the same time acknowledging that these are themselves the product of ideological practices. Questions of power and determination are, for both, conceptualized as either coercion (violence, oppression) or consent (reproduction, the struggle over meaning).

The attempt to understand both culture and politics within a theory of signification is a result of the modernist assumption—at the center of philosophical thought since Kant—that the world is only available to us as already and always meaningful. But the fact that there are no uninterpreted phenomena is not sufficient to argue that, therefore, the real exists only as the meaningful. Even the marxist supplement that the world must be made to mean is taken as the limited claim that there is a politics implicit within any particular signifying practice. However, it can also be read to suggest that the world—the real—is always other than the meaningful and that signification is one strategy for the production of the real in terms of particular relations of power. Thus there is a politics of the problematic of interpretation or signification itself (Baudrillard 1980). To speak as if one were not always and already implicated in a universe of significations may appear to be nothing but self-delusion. The task, however, is to find a way of talking about the real without falling into either positivism or relativism, without either sounding naïve or becoming trapped within the discourse one uses. Obviously, I can only begin to suggest the possibility of the project in this limited space.

Such an argument against meaning is at the root of the postmodernist project: the search for an immanent critical practice that would not appeal to any transcendental terms (as ground, origin, or essence). This, of course, demands that one seek new writing practices as well. Consequently it denies any apparent unity or totality and emphasizes discontinuity, difference, fragmentation, and rupture. Rejecting teleology, it makes history the very context and substance of our existence. Disrupting metaphors of depth (and hence the problematic of meaning), it imprisons itself within the materiality of surfaces. Excluding any claim of transparency, innocence, or freedom, it contextualizes all of reality in terms of processes of chance, change, and determination. This all may be summarized by saying that the postmodernist begins by rejecting the appeal to the givenness of experience and, consequently, argues that subjectivity, meaning, and truth are produced effects that may, in turn, have their own effects.

There are, of course, a variety of postmodern practices. Poststructuralism, for example, attempts to fragment the categories of experience and multiply the possibilities of meaning. However, it consequently relocates itself within a philosophy of signification refusing any connection to the real (Grossberg 1982d). It is content to define its task in terms of the problematizing and production of the categories of (signifying) experience. An alternative postmodern practice (Deleuze and Guattari 1981) subtracts such transcendental moments and adds more connections and effects and functions. One asks not what the event means, but what it does and what are the conditions of its existence as a material fact. Events may have effects that contradict or even occlude each other. Such effects need not take place through the mediation of meaning, consciousness, or ideology. In fact, the production of particular meanings (or struggles) can be treated as one such material effect. This is not the same as the behaviorist's attempt to substitute effects for meaning, nor the rhetorician's reduction of effects to particular domains of individual response. Thus cultural practices must be located not only in a context within which social facts determine interpretations and vice versa, but in other regimes in which texts have asignifying effects and are determined through asignifying practices. The result is that, rather than locating power in the context of signification, signification is to be located in the context of relations of power.

While a theory of signification totalizes itself and represses the real, this postmodernism describes a reality that is always pluralizing itself. The real is like crabgrass (not just metaphorically, either), constantly extending itself by producing effects at some place other than itself; its existence is only in the tangled web of often inseparable lines ("rhizomatic flows"). Reality is its own production—"a monism of plurality"—as lines of "effectivities" (Foucault 1981a), "desiring productions" (Deleuze and Guattari 1977), or "intensities" (Lyotard 1977a, 1977b). If the existence of an event is only the plurality of its effects, located in its others (that is, its contextuality), analysis is no longer interpretive. The analysis of an event, instead, maps the connections or relations between that point and all of the other points that effect or are effected by it. Defining the nature of the event beforehand (for example, as the unity of a signifying practice) results in simply retracing the boundaries of the particular "regime." For in fact reality is "territorialized." Lines of effect (desire) are not only continuously erupting to and from multiple points; desire apparently flows in ways that continuously transgress and (re)constitute particular structures and organizations. We might describe the real, then, as a "machinic apparatus" producing and extending itself but also inscribing boundaries upon its surfaces that direct the flows of desire and the possibilities of the real. Power, always local and plural, is the struggle over the configuration of effects included within and producing the contours of the real. Power territorializes, deterritorializes, and reterritorializes the vectors of effectivity; it defines "the real" as the places at which effects can be produced and circumscribes the possibilities of connections.

The analysis of a cultural practice, then, examines its functioning within a material context of desire and power. Drawing a map of its network of effects (that is, its place in a particular machinic apparatus that is never totalized), one interrogates the conditions of its existence: the emergence of its particular effectivity. Its specificity is shattered into the plurality of regimes of effects traversing it and its place within an organization of power. While some of its effects may be mediated through the production of meaning, it does not follow that the description of these effects requires an interpretive detour. Moreover while there may be effects that are precisely describable as the production of meaning and thus raise the problematic of signification within analysis, we should not assume a unity of signifying practices and effects, nor a homogeneity of interpretive procedures. In fact, both the multiplicity of signifying practices and the inscription of regimes of signification can be examined through the ways in which they modify the structurations of desire. So that, for example, the existence of the individual is always fractured and contradictory, determined not only as multiple subjectivities within the regimes of signification, but also as multiple objectivities of desire and power within asignifying regimes (Foucault 1978b).

The cultural analyst is confronted with the task of constructing a machine with apparently only one instruction: Include this particular piece understood as a conjuncture of specific effects. The analyst then produces an analytic machine that maps the real by drawing lines connecting the specific practice to and locating it within multiple regimes. One will necessarily transgress some of the boundaries already inscribed upon the real, and at the same time will inscribe or reinscribe others. The analytic machine not only maps but also reaches into and intervenes in reality. Its truth is not representational but political. Because it itself is connected to some of reality, the analytic machine is always a deterritorializing and reterritorializing of desire. Consequently the truth of any statement is its existence within a particular regime of effects. Not only must these truth-effects be seen as a form of power, but the fact that any particular statement has a place within this regime is itself an effect of power. The regime of truth is a particular production of boundaries that privileges particular discursive practices. Within its borders, statements are empowered and protected in specific ways; they are both allowed to intervene and protected from intervention.

The production of analytic machines may be likened to a topography of cultural practices. One reconstructs the complexity of a multidimensional surface only by mapping the various planes that traverse the surface. Insofar as each singular place inescapably is implicated with the others, it carries traces of the multiplanar existence of any of its points. Topography, beginning as cartography, draws the lines within a regime; but by invoking those traces, it seeks to dissolve the boundaries of the regimes and map the multiple and contradictory connections among the points across regimes. For example, Hebdige has begun to examine the place of "youth" in society:

> The vectors of power I want to trace cut across a number of heterogeneous sites: discursive categories, institutions and the spaces between institutions. Those sites are "youth," "sexuality," "fashion," "subculture," "display" and its corollary "surveillance" . . . many of these sites are themselves quite clearly "superficial" . . . A conventional presentation of history in which selected themes are carefully pursued along a single line leading from a finished past to a yet-to-be completed present will have to be abandoned. Instead I want to posit each site as a terminus

in a circuit within which a different kind of knowledge, a different kind of truth can be generated; a knowledge and a truth which can't be encapsulated within the confines of a discrete historical "period," one which sets out, instead, with the best of intentions: to pull the Father's beard. (1982, 69)

Similarly, I have proposed an analysis of rock and roll (Grossberg 1983–84) that maps its contradictory functions at particular conjunctural moments in order to describe the specificity of its relationship to youth cultures. Thus one begins by fracturing the cultural form and locating its effects within a determinate multiplicity of social regimes, both signifying and asignifying. By beginning with the fact of its popularity, the particular machinic functioning of rock and roll can be described: it is an affective organization of and resistance to the contradictory demands of desire and power made upon and constituting postwar youth culture. Importantly, only a part of this existence can be explained by appealing to rock and roll's intermittent site within signifying regimes. Rather it is only by locating the multiple sites of its effectivity that one is able to invoke its particular affective politics.

If the result of such analysis is to inevitably implicate cultural practices within relations of power, it also restructures the possibility, indeed the necessity, of political intervention. For on the one hand it suggests that every description not only defines a site of intervention but is itself already an intervention. Moreover it directs that such interventions cannot be grounded upon either utopian teleologies or opposition to general structures of domination and repression. Nor can particular interventions be justified from a place outside the analysis of the particular context of power. If power is always local, then struggle too must be defined locally: one resists particular structurations of reality within relations of power. But if resistance always seeks to deterritorialize, its success always threatens to reterritorialize. Hence one must continuously seek to intervene in ways that undermine the propensity of any "truth" to reinscribe relations of domination, oppression, and so on. It seems reasonable to suggest that any particular intervention be located within an alliance of ongoing resistance in what might be described as a network of "social anarchy" (Grossberg 1983).

I have described only the outlines of a postmodern theory of cultural studies, which reinscribes the problematic of signification and communication within the context of an analytic of the real. As a theoretical project it is paradoxical, since it would replace theorizing with concrete analysis. As a political project its conclusion records an undecidability that can be escaped only in the concreteness of political struggle. That is, it demands that political action and goals be defined within the particular context of struggle rather than by an appeal to theoretical or utopian principles. As a theory of communication, it opens new possibilities for the discipline by interrogating the place of communication within the production of the real, a place that we recently have begun to take for granted.

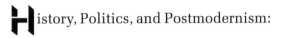

History, Politics, and Postmodernism:

Stuart Hall and Cultural Studies

STUART HALL ON IDEOLOGY, HEGEMONY,
AND THE SOCIAL FORMATION

Living with Difference. It is both surprising and understandable that British marxist cultural studies, in the work of the Birmingham Centre for Contemporary Cultural Studies, has recently had a significant and influential impact in the United States, especially for communication scholars. (Bits and pieces of it have been appropriated before by other disciplines, such as education and sociology.) There are many reasons for the resistance in the past: the publications are dispersed and often difficult to find; the language is often explicitly defined by its links to and debates with contemporary continental philosophy and theory; and the "position's" commitment to the ongoing and practical nature of theorizing contravenes common notions of theoretical stability in the social sciences. There are also many reasons for the sudden interest: the dissatisfaction with available theoretical paradigms and research programs, the increasing politicization of the academy, the slow incorporation of continental philosophies into the graduate curriculum, and perhaps most powerfully, the recent visibility of Stuart Hall in the United States. Those who have been working in this tradition for some time might, understandably, be a bit suspicious of this current interest, even as it is welcomed, for like all intellectual traditions, marxist cultural studies, even in the work of a single author like Hall, is a complex and contradictory terrain, with its own histories, debates, and differences.

It is difficult to identify a single position, concern, tradition, or method in Hall's work, or to assign specific arguments to a single theoretical level or "empirical" arena. The "multi-accentuality" of his work is magnified by his commitment to modes of collective intellectual work and authorship (1988d). His "author-ity" extends far beyond those texts he himself has authored; he is as much a teacher and an activist as a writer. As a founding member of the "New Left" in England and the first editor of the influential *New Left Review,* as one of those crucially responsible for the definition and institutionalization of "cultural studies" during his tenure at the Birmingham Centre for Contemporary Cultural Studies, and as a leading figure in the attempt to forge a new marxism—both intellectual and practical—since moving to the Open University, his work embodies an ongoing project, realized in an explicit dialogue with others and characterized above all by a modesty and generosity, as much in his descriptions of people in concrete historical situations as in his considerations of other positions. Anyone who has had the pleasure of hearing or meeting Hall knows the special quality of his presence, a presence that combines his political and intellectual passion with the commitment to human decency that pervades all his interactions.[1]

In fact, Hall's own discursive practice exemplifies those commitments. His engagement with other writers embodies a "critical dialogue": he simultaneously borrows and distances himself from them, struggling with their texts, reinflecting them into his own understanding of history as an active struggle. History and theory—both enact an ongoing process of what Gramsci called "destruction and reconstruction" or, in Hall's terms, "de- and re-articulation" (although Hall tends to use "articulation" when talking about cultural or signifying practices). While many increasingly acknowledge the need for theoretical complexity, Hall elaborates and concretizes that demand as he moves from the more abstract to the more concrete. He rarely claims that the questions he addresses are sufficient, merely that they are often ignored. He does not offer his answers as authoritative; he seeks rather to open up new fields of exploration and critical reflection, to put on the agenda of the Left whatever is being kept off, to challenge that which we take for granted. His theoretical advances are offered not as the end of a debate, but as the ongoing attempt to understand the complexity, contradictions, and struggles within the concrete lives of human beings. Yet the model of his practice—as a writer, teacher, theoretician, cultural critic, and political strategist—and the middle ground he constantly tries to occupy, can be extended beyond the debates he addresses. It is this commitment to struggle, at all levels, that constitutes the center of his current position and the theme of his latest work.

Nevertheless, Hall does write from a particular position, defined in part by his own social and intellectual history. The latter is likely to be unfamiliar to many communications scholars. Hall works within both marxist and semiotic discourses which attempt to understand the nature of contemporary social life and the central place of communication within it. To try, in the name of generalization, to eliminate either his fundamental concern with power and historical change or the real theoretical advances, over a broad range of issues, accomplished in his vocabulary would be a disservice. Moreover it would be a distortion of Hall's work not to recognize that his position has changed, over time, in response to new theoretical and historical questions; old concepts and strategies have occasionally disappeared from his writing, but more commonly, they are reappropriated into a new theoretical formation that rearticulates not only their significance but their political challenge as well. In what follows, then, I will try to move between the abstraction and the detail, offering a map of Hall's own current strategies and struggles.

For Hall, all human practices (including communication and communication theory) are struggles to "make history but in conditions not of our own making." He brings this marxist maxim to bear upon at least three different, albeit related projects: (1) to offer a theory of ideology that sees communicative practices in terms of what people can and do make of them; (2) to describe the particular historical form of contemporary cultural and political struggle (hegemony); and (3) to define a "marxism without guarantees" by rethinking the "conjunctural" nature of society. At each of these levels Hall connects, in complex ways, theory and writing to real social practices and struggles.

There can be no radical separation between theory, at whatever level of abstraction, and the concrete historical context which provides both its object of study and its conditions of existence. This is not merely a political position (although it is that); it is also an epistemological one. Hall extends the marxist attempt to "reproduce the concrete in thought" with Benjamin's comparison of the magician and the surgeon: the magician acts upon the surface of reality, the surgeon cuts into it. (It is not coincidental that Benjamin's metaphor describes the new media technology, specifically photography.) Rejecting the "magical incantations" of the empiricist who claims to have secure access to the real (even in its marxist forms: e.g., theories of false consciousness), Hall (1976) seeks "concepts with which to cut into the complexity of the real, in order precisely to reveal and bring to light relationships and structures which cannot be visible to the naive naked eye," relations of power and contradiction, of domination and struggle. Hall disclaims abstract and universal theory; rather, his epistemology derives from a reading (1974) of Marx that sees the relation between conceptual and empirical reality as a constant movement between different levels of abstraction. Hall also refuses the relativism of rationalism: although theories and descriptions are always ideological, their "truth" is measured in the context of concrete historical struggles, their adequacy judged by the purchase they give us for understanding the complex and contradictory structure of any field of social practices, for seeing beyond the taken-for-granted to the ongoing struggles of domination and resistance.

At whatever level of abstraction, Hall's fundamental commitment is to a structuring principle of struggle, not as an abstract possibility, but as a recognition that human activity at all levels always takes place within and over concretely "contested terrain." For example, against those who would reduce the politics of culture to a simple economic relation of domination, Hall argues that

> we must not confuse the practical inability to afford the fruits of modern industry with the correct popular aspiration that modern people know how to use and master and bend to their needs and pleasures modern things . . . In part, of course, this is the product of a massively capitalised swamp advertising campaign. But more importantly, it is also a perfectly correct perception that this is where modern technology is, these are languages of calculation of the future . . . Not to recognize the dialectic in this is to fail to see where real people are . . . (1984a, 20)

By identifying the possibilities of struggle within any field, Hall occupies the middle ground between those who emphasize the determination of human life by social structures and processes and those who, emphasizing the freedom and creativity of human activity, fail to recognize its historical limits and conditions: a middle ground in which people constantly try to bend what they are given to their own needs and desires, to win a bit of space for themselves, a bit of power over their own lives and society's future.

Hall seeks to define a nonreductionist theory of determination and social practices, of ideology, culture, and politics. The concept of "articulation" signals his attempt to rethink the dialectic of determination as struggle; it marks his movement of this marxist problematic onto the terrain of structuralist theory while simultaneously registering the limit he places upon the "riot of deconstruction" (1985a), a movement that is determined in part by his more recent nonhumanist rereading (1986c; cf. Hall et al. 1977) of Gramsci. Structuralism argues that the identity of a term is not pregiven, inherent in the term itself, but rather is the product of its position within a system of differences. Thus, as Hall himself has said, it was structuralism (and particularly Althusser) that taught him to "live with difference." For Hall, the meaning and politics of any practice is, similarly, the product of a particular structuring of the complex relations and contradictions within which it exists. "Articulation" refers to the complex set of historical practices by which we struggle to produce identity or structural unity out of, on top of, complexity, difference, contradiction. It signals the absence of guarantees, the inability to know in advance the historical significance of particular practices. It shifts the question of determination from origins (e.g., a practice is defined by its capitalist or working-class genesis) to effects. It is the struggle to articulate particular effects in history that Hall seeks to find at every level, and in every domain of social life.

Marxism without Guarantees. Although Hall is best known for his work in cultural theory and ideological analysis, the power of the concept of "articulation" is perhaps more clearly illustrated by his "conjunctural theory" of the social formation. Here Hall's middle ground between "culturalism" and "(post)structuralism" is explicitly theorized (1980a, 1983). What is the nature of society and of the structural determinations operating within it? In the "culturalist" position, the coherence and totality of a particular social structure (and the nature of the power relations within it) are already given, defined as a series of correspondences between different levels of social experiences, cultural practices, economic and political relations. Society is an "expressive totality" in which every practice refers back to a common origin. A chain of equivalences is constructed: for example, a particular class = particular experiences = particular political functions = particular cultural practices = particular needs and interests = a particular position in the economic relations of capital. That is, a particular social identity corresponds to particular experiences, defines a particular set of political interests, roles and actions, has its own "authentic" cultural practices, and so forth. What determines this network of correspondences, what defines and guarantees this system's existence is—whether in the first or the last instance—the economic. Culturalism is a theory of necessary correspondences in which the meaning and politics of every action are already defined, guaranteed in the end by its origin in the class struggle or by its stable place in the contradictions of capital. As a theory of power, struggle and contestation are possible only by appealing to an abstract principle of human nature: the question of agency is necessarily transformed into one of creativity; the subject is somehow determining but indeterminate.

On the other hand, in the "(post)structuralist" position, structural unity and identity are always deconstructed, leaving in their place the complexity, contradictions, and fragmentation implied in difference. There are no necessary relations, no correspondences; that is guaranteed outside of any concrete struggle. What something is (including the social formation) is only its relations to what it is not, its existence in a nominalist field of particular others.

Any structure or organization is to be dismantled: one can build neither theory nor struggle upon it. With any unitary nature denied, society can only be seen as a network of differences within which power operates "microphysically" (i.e., absolutely nonhierarchically). Similarly, the identification of the historical agent with a creative subject is broken. The actor is fragmented and its intentions "decentered" from any claim of origination/determination. Agency is nothing but the product of the individual's insertion into various and contradictory codes of social practice: the speaker is always already spoken. Thus the social totality is dissolved into a pluralism of powers, practices, subject-positions. This is a theory of necessary noncorrespondence, in which the lack of identity and structure is guaranteed, in which there can be no organization of power (as either a system of domination structured by certain more fundamental contradictions or a coherent structure of resistance.) Resistance itself is comprehensible only by appealing to an abstract principle of the unconscious or the repressed.

At this level, the concept of "articulation" marks Hall's unwillingness to accept the necessity of either correspondence or noncorrespondence, either the simple unity or the absolute complexity of the social formation. He argues that correspondences are historically produced, the site of the struggle over power. Society is, for Hall, a complex unity, always having multiple and contradictory determinations, always historically specific. This "conjunctural" view sees the social formation as a concrete, historically produced organization—a "structure-in-dominance"—of the different forms of social relations, practices, and experiences. Each form of social practice (political, economic, and cultural) has its own specificity or "relative autonomy"; each has its own specific field of effects, particular transformations that it produces and embodies. But the effects of any concrete practice—its conjunctural identity—are always "overdetermined" by the network of relations in which it is located. For Hall, the struggle is over how particular practices are positioned, into what structures of meaning and power, into what correspondences, they are articulated.

Hall (1983) offers a "marxism without guarantees," a theory of "no necessary (non/) correspondence," in which history is the struggle to produce the relations within which particular practices have particular meanings and effects, to organize practices into larger structures, to "inflect" particular practices and subject-positions into relations with political, economic, and cultural structures of domination and resistance. Hall's marxism demands that we seek to understand the concrete practices by which such articulations are accomplished and the contradictions around which struggles are and can be organized. The theory of articulation is the assertion of struggle over necessity, struggles both to produce structures of domination and to resist them. (It is perhaps also meant to remind the left of an important lesson: "pessimism of the intellect, optimism of the will.")

It offers a different version of determination, a rigorously antireductionist model of the production of social life as a field of power. Furthermore, Hall argues that these systems of power are organized upon contradictions not only of class and capital, but of gender and race as well; these various equally fundamental contradictions may or may not be made to correspond—this is yet another site of articulation and power. Hall's theory offers, as well, a nonessentialist theory of agency: social identities are themselves complex fields of multiple and even contradictory struggles; they are the product of the articulations of particular social positions into chains of equivalences, between experiences, interests, political struggles, and cultural forms, and between different social positions. This is a fragmented, decentered human agent, an agent who is both "subject-ed" by power and capable of acting against those powers. It is a position of theoretical antihumanism and political humanism, for without an articulated subject capable of acting, no resistance is possible.

Culture and Ideology. These same principles and practices define Hall's contribution to the theory of culture and ideology (1977, 1982, 1983, 1985a). Culture is never merely a set of practices, technologies, or messages, objects whose meaning and identity can be guaranteed by their origin or their intrinsic essences. For example, Hall argues that

> there is no such thing as "photography"; only a diversity of practices and historical situations in which the photographic text is produced, circulated and deployed . . . And of course, the search for an "essential, true original" meaning is an illusion. No such previously natural moment of true meaning, untouched by the codes and social relations of production and reading, exists. (1984b, 2)

Cultural practices are signifying practices. Following Volosinov as well as the structuralists, Hall argues that the meaning of a cultural form is not intrinsic to it; a text does not offer a transparent surface upon or through which we may discern its meaning in some nontextual origin, as if it had been deposited there, once and for all, at the moment of its origin. The meaning is not in the text itself but is the active product of the text's social articulation, of the web of connotations and codes into which it is inserted. Hall writes: "The meaning of a cultural symbol is given in part by the social field into which it

is incorporated, the practices with which it articulates and is made to reso-
nate. What matters is not the intrinsic or historically fixed objects of culture,
but the state of play in cultural relations" (1981, 235). The text is never isolatable; it is "always caught in the network of the chains of signification which
over-print it, inscribing it into the currency of our discourses" (1984b, 6). We
can deconstruct any text, disseminating and fragmenting its meaning into its
different contexts and codes, displacing any claim it makes to "have" a meaning. Yet particular texts are consistently read with the same meanings, located
within the same codes, as if they were written there for all to see. Thus every
sign must be and is made to mean. There is no necessary correspondence
between sign and meaning; every sign is "multi-accentual." Culture is the
struggle over meaning, a struggle that takes place over and within the sign.
Culture is "the particular pattern of relations established through the social
use of things and techniques" (1984a, 20).

But it is not only the sign that must be made to mean, it is the world as well.
For meaning does not exhaust the social world: for example, "Class relations
do not disappear because the particular historic cultural forms in which class
is 'lived' and experienced at a particular period, change" (1984a, 18). Culture
is the site of the struggle to define how life is lived and experienced, a struggle
carried out in the discursive forms available to us. Cultural practices articulate the meanings of particular social practices and events; they define the
ways we make sense of them, how they are experienced and lived. And these
already interpreted social practices can be, in turn, articulated into even
larger relations of domination and resistance. It is here—in the question of the
relations between discourses and the realities they purport to represent—that
Hall locates the question of ideology.

Ideology is articulated (constructed) in and through language but it is not
equivalent to it. There is, in fact, no necessary correspondence between a text
and its politics, which is always a function of its position within an ideological field of struggle, the struggle to achieve an equivalence between language
and reality. Particular ideological practices are not inscribed with their politics, any more than particular social identities are inscribed with their ideologies "on their backs." Practices do not intrinsically belong to any political
position or social identity; they must be articulated into it. The meaning and
political inflection of, for example, "democracy," "freedom," or "black," or of
a particular media practice, technology, or social relationship are not guaranteed by its origin in a particular class structure. It is always capable of being
de-articulated and re-articulated; it is a site of struggle. Hall writes that "The
meaning of a cultural form and its place or position in the cultural field is not

inscribed inside its form. Nor is its position fixed once and forever. This year's radical symbol or slogan will be neutralized into next year's fashion; the year after, it will be the object of profound cultural nostalgia" (1981, 235), or, one might add, it may be rearticulated as a symbol of opposition. Moreover, "it depends . . . on the way concrete practices are used and implemented in concrete historical conditions, the [strength] with which certain codes are constituted as 'in dominance,' the relations of struggle within the social relations of representation" (1984a, 20). It is the struggle to articulate certain codes into a position of dominance, to legitimate their claim, not only to define the meaning of cultural forms but to define the relation of that meaning (and hence the text) to reality as one of representation, that defines the specificity of the ideological. That is, ideological practices entail a double articulation of the signifier, first to a web of connotation (signification) and second to real social practices and subject-positions (representation).

Ideological practices are those through which particular relations, particular chains of equivalences, are "fixed," "yoked together." They construct the necessity, the naturalness, the "reality" of particular identifications and interpretations (and of course, the simultaneous exclusion of others as fantastic, contingent, unnatural, or biased). Ideology is the naturalization of a particular historical cultural articulation. What is natural can be taken for granted; it defines "common sense." Ideology "yokes together" particular social practices and relations with particular structures of meaning, thus anchoring them in a structure in which their relations to social identity, political interests, and so on have already been defined and seem inevitable.

We cannot live social reality outside of the cultural forms through which we make sense of it. Ideology involves the claim of particular cultural practices to represent reality. Yet it is not reality that is represented (and constructed); it is rather our relation to it, the ways we live and experience reality. Ideology constructs the field and structures of our experience. It is, then, a contradictory field in which we struggle to define the systems of representation through which, paraphrasing Althusser, we live the "imaginary" relations between ourselves and our real conditions of existence (Hall, 1985a). The necessity that it inscribes upon particular interpretations is grounded in the "immediacy" of experience and in the ways we are located within it. Ideology links particular social identities with particular experiences, as if the former were the necessary source of the latter. While the individual is positioned—his or her identity as the author/subject of experience defined— within ideological practices, the individual is never a tabula rasa seduced into a simple ideological structure. The ideological field is always marked by contradictions and struggles. Moreover the individual is already defined by other discourses and practices. Ideologies must attempt to win subjects already spoken for into their representations by articulating various social identities into chains of equivalence that constitute and are articulated into structures of domination and resistance.

Such ideological struggles can only be read by examining the complex "ideological structuration" of the text and its insertion into concrete historical struggles. It is here that one must locate the most significant work that Hall accomplished and sponsored while at the Centre for Contemporary Cultural Studies. For example, Hall and Jefferson (1976) offer a theory of subcultures centering on the question of style as the articulation of an alternative ideology which offers its members a "magical" solution to the real contradictions of their social position. Similarly, the Centre's main contributions to media studies in the seventies can be understood in the context of Hall's developing theory of ideology. In particular, Hall's analytic separation of the moments of encoding and decoding (Hall et al. 1980) can be seen as one version of the struggle of articulation. In the studies around the *Nationwide* program (Brunsdon and Morley 1978, Morley 1980), the gap between the two moments becomes evident as the authors elucidate first the semiotic structures of the program and then the various ways in which audience fragments interpret the program. The particular signifying practices of the text (e.g., its modes of address, its modes of representation, the ways in which it frames various "ideological problematics") not only embody real historical choices (an "encoded" or "preferred" reading) but also become the active sites at which ideological struggles are waged. Of course, not only are different "decodings" possible, but such alternative readings are themselves inflected into different political formations and relations.

While Hall wants to argue that the ideology of a text is not guaranteed, no text is free of its encoded structures and its ideological history. Texts have "already appeared in some place—and are therefore already inscribed or placed by that earlier positioning. They will be inscribed in the particular social relations which produced them . . . The vast majority will already be organized within certain 'systems' of classification. Each practice, each placing, slides another layer of meaning across the frame" (1984b, 12). These "traces" of past struggles do not guarantee future articulations, but they do mark the ways in which the text has already been inflected. If we are to understand ideology as a contested terrain, we must not only recognize the struggle but also learn "to read the cultural signposts and traces which history has left behind"—as Gramsci says, 'without an inventory.' "

Furthermore, if we are to understand ideology as a contested terrain, we must recognize that ideological struggles are never wholly autonomous; they are themselves located within, articulated with, a broader field of economic, cultural, and political struggles. Thus Hall (1985b) does not totalize the claim of the ideological; he merely seeks to put it "on the agenda" of the Left's analyses of social power. He does not deny the importance of political economy or of the state (although many political economists would deny ideology its place or reduce it to one of simple domination and false consciousness), but he readily admits that he is still unable to theorize the complex articulations that exist between them. But ideology is not reducible to struggles located elsewhere; its importance cannot be dismissed by claiming that it is determined by the nonideological. Ideological practices have their own "relative autonomy" and they produce real effects in the social formation, even outside of their own (signifying) domain.

Hegemony. The concrete processes by which ideology enters into larger and more complex relations of power within the social formation define the point at which, most explicitly, Hall's theory attempts to understand its own historical conditions of existence. It is not only ideology that must be located within a broader context of struggle but Hall's arguments as well. His preference for "theorizing from the concrete" makes his work a response to historically specific conditions: the emergence of new forms of cultural power. Hall extends the parameters of "cultural studies," calling for us to look at

> the domain of cultural forms and activities as a constantly changing field . . . [to look] at the relations which constantly structure this field into dominant and subordinate formations . . . [to look] at the process by which these relations of dominance and subordination are articulated . . . [to place] at its centre the changing and uneven relations of force which define the field of culture—that is, the question of cultural struggle and its many forms . . . [to make our] main focus of attention . . . the relation between culture and questions of hegemony. (1981, 235)

Hall's work increasingly draws attention to the historical fact of "hegemonic politics" and the need to "cut into" the processes by which a dominant cultural order is consistently preferred, despite its articulation with structures of domination and oppression. For example, he has turned his attention to the "autonomy" of civil society (in the so-called democratic nations) as a problem. How is it that the very freedom of civil and cultural institutions from direct political intervention results in the rearticulation of the already dominant structures of meaning and power? How does the appeal to "professional codes" in the production of both news and entertainment consistently reinscribe "hegemonically preferred" meanings? How are people "subjected" to particular definitions and practices of "freedom"?

For Hall (1984c), the appearance of "hegemony" is tied to the incorporation of the great majority of people into broadly based relations of cultural consumption. Of course, this required both the incorporation of culture into the sphere of market relations and the application of modern industrial techniques to cultural production. This was and remains a limited form of cultural enfranchisement, for it left unchallenged the people's "expropriation from the processes of democratization of the means of cultural production." But it also had its real effects upon the social formation and empowered the population. Benjamin had observed that "The adjustment of reality to the masses and of the masses to reality is a process of unlimited scope, as much for thinking as for perception" (cited in Hall 1976). Hall echoes and elaborates this:

> Once the masses enter directly into the transformation of history, society and culture, it is not possible any longer to construct or appropriate the world as if reality issues in The World from the wholly individual person of the speaking, the uttering subject . . . We are, as historical subjects and as speakers, "spoken" by "the others." It is the end of a certain kind of Western innocence, as well as the birth-point of a new set of codes.

The appearance of "the masses" on the historical scene, especially as an agent in the scene of culture, displaces the field of cultural struggle from the expression of class conflict into a larger struggle between the people and the elite or ruling bloc. (This does not deny the continuing relevance of class contradictions but places them in relation to other contradictions: e.g., race, gender, age). As a result of this restructuring of the field of cultural relations, new forms and organizations of cultural politics emerged: this is Hall's reading (1986c) of the Gramscian notion of hegemony.

Hegemony is not a universally present struggle; it is a conjunctural politics opened up by the conditions of advanced capitalism, mass communication, and culture. Nor is it limited to the ideological struggle of the ruling-class block to win the consent of the masses to its definitions of reality, although it encompasses the processes by which such a consensus might be achieved. But it also depends upon the ability of the ruling bloc (an alliance of class fractions) to secure its economic domination and establish its political power. Hegemony need not depend upon consensus nor consent to particular ideological constructions. It is a matter of containment rather than compulsion or even incorporation. Hegemony defines the limits within which we can struggle, the field of "common sense" or "popular consciousness." It is the struggle to articulate the position of "leadership" within the social formation, the attempt by the ruling bloc to win for itself the position of leadership across the entire terrain of cultural and political life. Hegemony involves the mobilization of popular support, by a particular social bloc, for the broad range of its social projects. In this way, the people assent to a particular social order, to a particular system of power, to a particular articulation of chains of equivalence by which the interests of the ruling bloc come to define the leading positions of the people. It is a struggle over "the popular," a matter of the articulated relations, not only within civil society (which is itself more than culture) but between the state (as a condensed site of power), the economic sector, and civil society.

Hall (1980d) describes hegemony as the struggle between "popular" and "populist" articulations, where the latter points to structures that neutralize the opposition between the people and the power bloc. He has used this framework (1980d, 1988a, 1988c) to describe the unique configuration, emergence, and political successes of the "new right" and Thatcherism in Britian. However, it is important that we do not romanticize the "popular":

> Since the inception of commercial capitalism and the drawing of all relations into the net of market transactions, there has been little or no "pure" culture of the people—no wholly separate folk-realm of the authentic popular, where "the people" existed in their pure state, outside of the corrupting influences. The people have always had to make something out of the things the system was trying to make of them. (1984a, 19)

Nor can we locate the popular outside of the struggle for hegemony in the contemporary world. For hegemony is never securely achieved, if even momentarily. But it does describe a different form of social and political struggle, what Gramsci called a "war of positions" (as opposed to the more traditional war of maneuver) in which the sites and stakes of struggles over power are multiplied and dispersed throughout the social formation. Hall argues that the Left must enter into this complex set of struggles, across the entire range of social and cultural life, if it is to forge its own hegemonic politics, one dedicated to making a better life for everyone. Once again, Hall enjoins us to recognize that "people make history but in conditions not of their own making." This is Hall's model of practice, a model of our own practices, of our struggles to understand the relations, institutions, and texts that populate our communicative environment, and the processes that organize it. It is a model posed against the elitism that characterizes so much of contemporary scholarly and political practice, a model committed to respecting human beings, their lives, and their possibilities.

CULTURAL STUDIES AND THE POSTMODERN

Hall's dialectic involves the search for a middle ground that is never merely a "desired" synthesis or reconciliation of contradictions but the recognition and embodiment of struggle at every level. The tradition of cultural studies associated with the Birmingham School has been shaped by an almost continuous series of debates and challenges (Hall 1980c, Grossberg 1983, 1984b). On the one hand, it has constantly constituted itself by a critical engagement with other theoretical positions: with the humanism of the culturalists (e.g., Raymond Williams and E. P. Thompson), with the structural/functionalism of the structuralists (e.g., Althusser), with the antihumanism and textualism of deconstructionists and psychoanalytic discourse theory (e.g., Screen and certain versions of feminist theory). In each of these debates, cultural studies has moved onto the terrain in order to both learn and draw back from the differences. In each case, it has taken something from the other position, reshaped itself, its questions (empirical as well as theoretical), and its vocabularies. But it has refused to abandon the terrain of marxism and refused to succumb to the increasingly common pessimism of the Left. On the other hand, it has constituted itself by constantly anchoring its theoretical concerns in concrete historical events and political struggles. It has opened itself, however reluctantly at times, to the recognition that history constantly makes new demands upon us, presenting us with new configurations and new questions. One can simplify this history of "anchoring points": beginning with the New Left's concern with issues of imperialism, racism, and culture, continuing into questions of emerging forms of resistance, from "the margins" (in the form of subcultures) and from feminism, and arriving at the rise of the "new Right" and the simultaneous "collapse" of effective left opposition.

It is within these terms that we must consider the relationship between marxist cultural studies and postmodernism.[2] To speak metaphorically, the war of positions between them has only begun and the result will be not a hegemonic discourse, but a different theoretical position that has negotiated the space between them through an analysis of its own historical context. After all, both cultural studies and postmodern theory are concerned with the place of cultural practices in historical formations and political struggles. But marxists are often reluctant to acknowledge the historical differences that constitute everyday life in the contemporary world, and too often ignore the taunting playfulness and affective extremism (terrorism?) of postmodernists, while postmodernists are often too willing to retreat from the theoretical and critical ground that marxism has won with notions of articulation, hegemony, and struggle. Let me try, however briefly, to map some of the frontiers and struggles, and perhaps to make some suggestions about where the victories and defeats may lie. To begin with, we need to distinguish three discursive domains that are all, too commonly, named with the single master signifier "the postmodern": culture, theory, and history. Failing to recognize the difference has allowed some authors to slide from one domain to the other, as if one could confidently assume equivalences or correspondences. Of course, the distinction itself is strategic: one also needs to theorize the relations among the three domains.

The most commonly discussed, if also the least interesting, of these three domains of inquiry is that of cultural practice, for in fact, it takes us no further in our attempt to understand the contemporary social formation. Postmodern cultural texts (whether in architecture, literature, art, film, etc.) claim to be and in some respects are significantly different from previous aesthetic and communicative formations.[3] Many critics assert that such practices entail new cultural configurations, not only within particular texts but also across different intertextual fields. The question is, of course, how one describes that formal difference and locates its effects. In that sense, beginning with postmodern cultural texts seems to lead us right back into many of the undecidable theoretical problematics of cultural studies. For example, can we assume that a text's "postmodernism" is inscribed upon or encoded within it? What is its relation to its social and historical context? What are its politics? How is it inserted into and articulated with the everyday lives of those living within its cultural spaces, however one draws the boundaries? What is obvious is that such cultural practices are often defined by their quite explicit opposition to particular institutionalized definitions of modernism. Moreover they wear their opposition on their surfaces, letting it play with if not define their identity. They construct themselves out of the detritus of the past—not only of premodernist culture but of modernism as well—and the "ruins" of contemporary commercial culture. Does such a strategy represent a *radical* break in either culture or history? I think it unlikely (and certainly too easy a conclusion), but its powerful presence and popularity do suggest a series of questions that must be addressed about the possibilities of communication, opposition, elitism, and self-definition.

The second site at which cultural studies and postmodernism clash is that of theory itself, but the distance between the positions is not as great as it appears. They share a number of fundamental commitments. Both are anti-essentialist; that is, they accept that there are no guarantees of identity or effects outside of the determinations of particular contexts. Foucault's radical contextualism is built upon the same ground as Hall's conjuncturalism. (And it is significant that neither camp has quite figured out how to produce a convincing local analysis.) At the same time, both sides reject the deconstructionists' dismissal of all essences or identities (whether of contexts or elements), with its emphasis on polysemy and undecidability, arguing instead that such moments of identity and difference are both historically effective and contextually determined. To deny that a structure is necessary or universal is not to deny its concrete reality. Nor does it entail that there are no connections across contexts; neither position embraces an absolute nominalism since the question of the constitution of the relevant context or level of abstraction must itself be left open. Both positions are concerned, therefore, less with questions of origin and causality than with questions of effectivity, conditions of possibility, and overdetermination. Power is located precisely in the struggle to forge links, to direct the effective identity and relations of any practice, to articulate the existence, meanings, effects, and structures of practices that are not guaranteed in advance.

Thus, for example, neither position is content to simply dismantle the subject nor to see it as a simple fragmentary collection of determined subject-positions. Although both begin by problematizing the claims of a unified, stable, and self-determining subject, they also recognize the historical specificity and effectivity of such "subjects." Rather than merely dismantle these claims, they seek to account for them and to account as well for the possibilities of alternative constructions of the subject (and not merely for alternative subject-positions). In both camps, it apparently does matter who is acting/speaking and from where. Rather than a dispersed subject, they argue for what we might describe as a migratory or nomadic subject. This "posthumanistic" subject does not exist with a unified identity (even understood as an articulated hierarchical structure of its various subject-positionings) that somehow manifests itself in every practice. Rather it is a subject that is constantly remade, reshaped as a mobilely situated set of relations in a fluid context. The nomadic subject is amoebalike, struggling to win some space for itself in its local situation. The subject itself has become a site of struggle, an ongoing site of articulation with its own history, determinations, and effects.

Finally, both positions are also committed to the same epistemological and political strategy: the truth of a theory can only be defined by its ability to intervene into, to give us a different and perhaps better ability to come to grips with, the relations that constitute its context. If neither history nor texts speak their own truth, truth has to be won; and it is, consequently, inseparable from relations of power. Similarly, the viability of a political strategy can only be defined by its engagement with local struggles against particular relations of power and domination. This means that both positions are anti-elitist. Neither seeks to speak for the masses as a ventriloquist, but rather to make a space in which the voices of the masses can be heard. Neither seeks to define the appropriate sites of struggle, but rather to locate and assist those struggles that have already been opened up. And neither assumes that the masses are the passively manipulated, colonized zombies of the system, but rather the actively struggling site of a politics in, if not of, everyday life.

Nevertheless, there are significant theoretical differences between cultural studies and postmodernism. I want to argue for the former's theory of articulation and the latter's theory of "wild realism."[4] The failure of postmodern theory is not that it has no notion of macrostructures, but rather that it has no way of theorizing the relations between different levels of abstraction, between the microphysics of power and biopolitics (Foucault) or between the child in the bubble and the simulacrum (Baudrillard). Similarly, the failure of postmodern theory is not that it denies a reality behind the surfaces of everyday life, but rather that it always forgets that there are many surfaces to everyday life and that reality is produced within the relations among these surfaces. The factory (even in the third world) is as much a surface of our lives as is television. Because one does not frequently move across its terrain does not mean it is not having its effects. One must remember that not all surfaces are articulated or present or even effective in the same ways—that is precisely the site of the struggle over the real. In both instances, the lacuna in postmodernism is a theory of articulation.

On the other hand, the failure of cultural studies is not that it continues to hold to the importance of signifying and ideological practices, but rather that it always limits its sense of discursive effectivity to this plane. It fails to recognize that discourses may not only have contradictory effects within the ideological, but that those ideological effects may themselves be placed within complex networks of other sorts of effects. Consequently, the particular model of articulation falls back into a structuralism of empty spaces in which every place in the ideological web is equally weighted, equally charged, so to speak. The cultural field remains a product of oddly autonomous, indeterminate struggles, an amorphous field of equal differences and hence of equivalences. Surprisingly, in the end this seems to leave no space for the power of either the text itself or the historical actor to excite and incite historical struggles around particular discourses. While Hall argues that the audience cannot be seen as passive cultural dopes, he cannot elaborate its positivity. Neither aspect of the relation can be understood as merely a matter of the tendential structures that have, historically, already articulated a particular discourse or subject into powerful ideological positions. The critic, distanced from the effectivity of the popular, can decide neither where nor whether to struggle over any particular discourse. More importantly, the critic cannot understand why people have chosen a particular site of struggle or how to mobilize them around such a site.

The postmodernist's recognition of the multiple planes of effectivity—"wild realism"—allows the recognition that discursive fields are organized affectively ("mattering maps") as well as ideologically (Grossberg 1984c). Particular sites are differentially invested with energies and intensities that define the resources that can be mobilized into forms of popular struggle. Affect points to the (relatively autonomous) production of what is normally experienced as moods and emotions by an asignifying effectivity.[5] It refers to a dimension or plane of our lives that involves the enabling distribution of energies. While it is easy to conceptualize it as the originary (causal) libidinal economy postulated by psychoanalysis, one must avoid the temptation to go beyond its existence as a plane of effectivity. Moreover affect is not the Freudian notion of disruptive (or repressed) pulsions of pleasure breaking through the organized surfaces of power; rather it is an articulated plane whose organization defines its own relations of power and sites of struggle. And as such, like the ideological plane, it has its own principles that constrain the possibilities of struggle. And while it is true that the most powerfully visible moments of affective formations are often located in cultural activities (e.g., leisure, romance), affect is neither limited to nor isolatable within such relations. All affective relations are shaped by the materiality (and negativity) of everyday life. That is, we should not confuse affect with the positivity of enablement (e.g., pleasure and excitement), for it includes as well boredom and compulsion. Even the most obvious moments of pleasure are shaped to some extent by the continuing affectivity of particular institutions (e.g., home, work). Finally, we cannot ignore the interdeterminations between different levels of effects; thus the affective power of many cultural activities depends in part on the ideological articulations both of the activities in general (e.g., of leisure or fun) and of the specific activities in question.

Nevertheless, the recognition of an articulated plane of affect points to the existence of another politics, a politics of feeling . . . (good, bad, or indifferent), a politics that Benjamin had acknowledged. Again this is not to deny that such an affective politics is constantly being articulated to ideological, economic, and state politics, but it does not follow that it can be explained solely within the terms of such traditional political sites. Affective struggles cannot be conceptualized within the terms of theories of resistance, for their oppositional quality is constituted not in a negative dialectics, but by a project of or struggle over empowerment, an empowerment that energizes and connects specific social moments, practices, and subject-positions. Thus if we want to understand particular cultural practices, we need to ask how they empower their audiences and how the audiences empower the practices; that is, how the very materiality (including ideological) of cultural practices functions within an affective economy of everyday life. It is ironic that so much contemporary writing on popular culture offers accounts of affectively powerful texts that are always mired within what Benjamin called "organizations of pessimism." Hall himself has recognized (1984c) the need to theorize and describe the "sensibility of mass culture" but has, thus far, left the question unanswered. But without an answer, the enormous power of contemporary culture (especially the mass media) and the investment that we make in it cannot be adequately approached. I would suggest that this sensibility depends in fact on the particular historical relations between ideological and affective struggles, between resistance and empowerment, that surround the mass media and contemporary social struggles. It is here, in fact, in an understanding of "the popular" as an affective plane, that one can find any grounds for an "optimism of the will" today, any space to negotiate between utopianism and nihilism.

The third and perhaps most important domain of postmodern work involves the attempt to understand the specificity of the contemporary historical formation. This is also the most controversial and certainly the one most fraught with difficulties and dangers. Here postmodern irony and excess operate against themselves: a theory of the collapse of the distinction between elite and popular becomes a new elitism; a theory that denies innocent and totalized descriptions offers itself as an innocent and totalized description; a theory that denies the new in favor of bricolage not only offers itself as new, but announces that the absence of the new is a new situation; and a theory of the impossibility of metanarrative becomes its own metanarrative absence. More importantly, a theory that celebrates otherness fails to acknowledge the difference between experiences, real historical tendencies, and cultural discourses and meanings, as well as the complex relations that exist between them. Moreover even within the specific domains of experience and discourse, it fails to recognize the uneven and contradictory relations that exist within and between different sites of postmodern effects: history, subjectivity, values, reality, politics. I would agree with Hall that to read history as rupture, to see the present as the site of the apocalypse (the end of the old, the beginning of the new) is a powerful ideological moment. Echoing Hall, if reality was never as real as we have constructed it, it's not quite as unreal as we imagine it; if subjectivity was never as coherent as we imagine it, it's not quite as incoherent as we fantasize it; and if power was never as simple or monolithic as we fantasize it (reproducing itself, requiring giants and magical subjects to change it), it's not quite as dispersed and unchallengeable as we fear.

Thus I would argue that Baudrillard's theory of the simulacrum confuses the collapse of a particular ideology of the real for the collapse of reality; it confuses the collapse of a particular ideology of the social (articulated into public and private) with the end of the social. But that does not mean that it does not offer important insights into the changing ways in which the real is effective in the social formation and its organization of power. To the extent that Baudrillard's theory denies its own limits, it conflates the social formation with a particular set of effects, with the plane of simulation, rendering all of social reality the simple product of media causality. And in the end, that is no different than those who would reduce reality or desire or power to meaning. Contradicting itself, the position conflates ideology (in the form of the alibi or law of value) with the multiple and complex sites of power, enabling him to assume that only a refusal of any difference constitutes struggle. It conflates the multiple and fragmentary social positionings of the masses with a single configuration of or on the surface of the social body. The great burden of these reductions is placed upon the concept of implosion, as both indifference (in the masses who amusedly and in fascination live the media hype) and deterrence (as a control system), as both an ecstatic possibility and a catastrophic inevitability. But all of this says merely that Baudrillard, for all of the postmodern speed of his writing practice, fails to adequately theorize the sites of our postmodernity; he ends up being one of its most enjoyable (if horrifying, or perhaps, because horrifying) texts rather than its most reliable analyst.

The specificity of the contemporary social formation is more complex than simple descriptions of the simulacrum or late capitalism (commodification, bureaucratization, infotech, etc.) would suggest, although these are real events with real effects. Thus the problem is not with the postmodernists' descriptions as such but with the rather grandiose status they assign to their descriptions. The questions of postmodernity as a historical reality, whether experiential or tendential, have to be theorized within the context of the theory of articulation and wild realism, that is, within the spaces between cultural studies and postmodernism. This has two important consequences. First, from the perspective of cultural studies, it locates the critique of postmodernism in the project of inflecting such descriptions into a less global and more consistent context of theorizing. For example, we can reread Baudrillard's theory as a contribution to the analysis of the changing politics of representation in history. Baudrillard has described three planes of discursive effects that not only compete with and displace one another but that may be simultaneously operative and historically organized in any particular formation. Thus rather than making a global and ontological argument, Baudrillard's theory of the simulacrum marks the local articulations (and power relations) among three planes of discursive effectivity: representation, mediation, and modeling.

Second, from the perspective of postmodernism, it locates the critique of cultural studies in the project of detailing the determining displacements, gaps, and in some cases even ruptures that have become constitutive of our contemporary existence. There are powerful new historical determinations (e.g., the destructability and disposability of the planet; significant redistributions of wealth, population, and power; new structures of commodity production; new media of communication), ideological and affective experiences (e.g., the collapse of visions of the future and of transcendental values capable of giving shape and direction to our lives; an increasing sense of justified paranoia, terror, and boredom). Hall has already opened up these spaces by giving a central role to questions about the relation between the media and the masses (as it is defined in Benjamin's theory of history) and between leadership and the popular (in Gramsci's theory of hegemony). But they remain undeveloped, and one must assume that this is due, in part, to the difficulty of accounting for their effectivity within the traditional marxist categories of power.

The fact remains that such "postmodern events" appear to have an increasingly significant place in our everyday lives and that the discourses that anchor themselves in these events appear to have a powerful place in our cultural relations. Both postmodernism and cultural studies need to find ways of describing the complex contexts—the conjunctural formations—within which the possibilities of struggle are shaped, grasped, and enacted.

The Formation(s) of Cultural Studies:

An American in Birmingham

Any observer of the current academic scene in the United States will surely note that there is a cultural studies "boom" (Morris 1988d). As Allor (1987) notes, the term itself has become a cultural commodity, apparently free to circulate in the global economy of discourse, ideas, and cultural capital. Five years ago the term functioned largely as a proper name, referring primarily to a specifically British tradition, extending from the work of Raymond Williams and Richard Hoggart, through the contributions of the various members of the Centre for Contemporary Cultural Studies at the University of Birmingham, to the increasingly dispersed and institutionalized sites of its contemporary practitioners. Additionally—and especially within the field of communication—the term also referenced a uniquely American tradition rooted in the social pragmatism of the Chicago school of social thought. However, "cultural studies" is becoming one of the most ambiguous terms in contemporary theory as it is increasingly used to refer to the entire range of what previously had been thought of as "critical theory" (i.e., a range of competing theories of the relation of society and culture, of ideology and art, largely derived from "high literary theory" and anthropology, with communication and popular culture once again relegated to a secondary position).

While it is futile to protest against this appropriation of the term, it is important to point to a set of potential dangers: namely, that British cultural studies is reduced to a singular position or a linear history (thus ignoring its differences) or dispersed into a set of unrelated differences (thus ignoring its unity). The consequence is made all the more likely by the forms of the current interest in British cultural studies and the exigencies of its appearance in the United States. Understanding the "unity in difference" of this tradition requires us to recognize that it has always responded to the particular conditions of its intellectual, political, social, and historical contexts. The result is that within the tradition, theoretical positions are always provisional takes, meant to give us a better purchase on the world and always implicated within ongoing intellectual and political struggles. Any "position" is always engaged in and constituted by response to debates with other positions. Cultural studies has always been a contested terrain, and the contestation takes place both within and outside of the tradition itself. In fact, if cultural studies is seen as an open-ended and ongoing theoretical struggle to understand and intervene into the existing organizations of active domination and subordination within the formations of culture, then the boundaries of the tradition are themselves unstable and changing, sites of contestation and debate.

Failing to recognize the history and practice of this unity-in-difference threatens to dehistoricize intellectual practices and avoids the more difficult task of rearticulating the insights and practices of cultural studies into the specific contexts of our own work. If there is no single cultural studies position, we have to understand the projects, the commitments, and the vectors according to which it has continued to rearticulate itself, how it has constantly renegotiated its identity and repositioned itself within changing political and intellectual maps. Its history is a history of political engagements and theoretical debates in response to which alternative positions are constantly being taken into account and new positions offered. In this process, the very questions at the heart of cultural studies—its problematics—are constantly being reshaped and reinflected.

I want to begin this project by looking at some of the complexly structured differences that constitute the tradition of British cultural studies. Specifically, I will isolate one set of vectors that construct a specific formation around the biographical figure of Stuart Hall and the intellectual and political commitments of marxism. It is important to remember that this was not the only formation within the Centre (or within British cultural studies), but it does largely define the uniqueness of the Centre; other formations and lines of thought had other institutional sites in addition to their location within the Centre. However, we must remember that this formation itself has always been full of contradictions and antagonisms, defined individually and socially, intellectually and politically.

Not surprisingly, a version of the history of this formation within cultural studies has already been established and put into place. Within this narrative, cultural studies is constituted by two lines of determination. First, it has constantly emerged out of a series of debates with its theoretical "others," struggles within which cultural studies is often represented, in the end, as having taken the middle ground between theoretical extremes. Second, cultural studies has constantly rearticulated itself in direct response to overt historical events and demands. In this narrative, cultural studies is seen to offer a materialist theory of ideology and discourse. I want to argue not only that the narrative is too linear (and progressivist), that it ignores the continuing vitality and influence of earlier moments in the narrative, but also that it fails to account for the continuing challenge, from within the history of the formation, of competing definitions of the project of cultural studies. The contestation within cultural studies was not merely around competing theories of the politics of culture, or the relationship of culture to power, but also around differing theories of the nature of cultural and historical specificity. That is, within cultural studies, the question of its own problematic was itself constantly, if implicitly, called into question.

Despite these weaknesses, it is useful to begin by summarizing this taken-for-granted, "standard" history (Turner 1990). I will do this by presenting the two interrelated but analytically separable lines of determination (political and intellectual). Then I will offer a different, more contentious reading of this formation of cultural studies, a reading partly determined by my own history and situation (an American who studied at the Centre at a particular moment and who has maintained close ties with it), and partly determined by my own cultural and political contexts. I will no doubt continue to romanticize many aspects of the work of the Centre, but I do not mean to ignore its very real problems and failures. There were significant structured absences, questions that remain unaddressed, political struggles that remained "outside" of the cultural. Its ability to reflexively analyze its own practice was too often too limited. Forms of collective work were celebrated without analyzing the ways in which they could disempower as well as empower individuals and groups. Class and gender relations institutionalized within the academy remained sites of silence for too long and, despite a real concern for popular culture, the intellectual distanciation from the popular characteristic of the traditional intellectual remained in place for too long (Fry 1988). Nevertheless, I believe that the Centre (and the formation of cultural studies I am describing) is important not only intellectually, but also as a model of interdisciplinary, collective, and politically engaged research. Finally, I want at least to acknowledge the fact that this formation of cultural studies was produced in the social interactions of real individuals with their own agendas and biographies. A part of the history of the Centre—a part that I will not discuss here—involves the changing histories and relations of those working at the Centre and in cultural studies. Like C. Wright Mills, cultural studies has always embraced the passion of intellectual and political work (even if it rarely theorized passion in its objects of study). Such work is always determined partly by the very real—and, in the case of the Centre, enduring—relationships and communities (both positive and negative) that such work produces, even if only through imaginary and retrospective identifications. And the unity-in-difference of cultural studies is partly the result of very real social and emotional relationships.

A NORMATIVE HISTORY OF CULTURAL STUDIES: POLITICAL CONTEXTS

Cultural studies emerged in the 1950s at the intersection of a number of complex historical experiences. Sometimes the focus was on "the Americanization of Britain" and at others on the new forms that modernization was taking after the Second World War. Both descriptions pointed to the appearance of a "mass culture" made possible through the rationalization, capitalization, and technologization of the mass media. Within this new cultural space, for the first time, the vast majority of the population were incorporated into a common audience of cultural products. Of course, the concern for "mass culture" preexisted the Second World War. But the obviously central role of American culture and capital in these changes, their increasing reach into British society through popular cultural and communicative forms, seemed to make the threat they posed more substantial and specific. This threat was aimed neither at communities nor elites, but rather at class cultures and the possibilities of a democratic cultural formation.[1]

A second historical development was the emergence of the New Left—which counted among its members many of the founding figures of cultural studies—in response, at least in part, to the failure of the traditional marxist Left to confront, in both theoretical and political terms, the beginnings of late capitalism, the new forms of economic and political colonialism and imperialism, the existence of racism within the so-called democratic world, the place of culture and ideology in relations of power, and the effects of consumer capitalism upon the working classes and their cultures.

In the sixties other concerns impinged upon cultural studies, and while they did not totally displace the earlier concerns, they often gave them new inflections. Here again, one can point to two exemplary developments: first, the growing importance of the mass media, not only as forms of entertainment but, inseparably, as what Althusser called "ideological state apparatuses." There was, in fact, quite explicitly, a significant focus during the sixties (and through much of the seventies) on the more overt ideological functions of the media—in news and documentary programming—where one could see a direct connection to the political sphere. This narrowing of focus was contradicted to some extent by the second development that engaged cultural studies in the sixties: the emergence of various subcultures that seemed, in various ways, to resist at least some aspects of the dominant structures of power. Yet these subcultures were organized around nontraditional political issues, contradictions, and social positions, and struggled in the uncommon terrain of popular culture. Obviously the rise of various working-class youth cultures, and the sustained organization of a middle-class oppositional subculture, had an enormous impact on the work of cultural studies.

In the seventies, we might again identify two significant developments, both of which have had immediate and powerful effects on cultural studies. First, the renewed appearance of political and theoretical work around relations of gender and sexual difference. The response to feminism was immediate and sustained, if not always completely sympathetic or adequate. Nevertheless, I think it is fair to say that there is no cultural studies that is not "postfeminist," not in the sense of having moved beyond it, but rather in the sense of having opened itself to the radical critique and implications of feminist theory and politics. The second development was equally powerful, disturbing cultural studies' too easy identification and celebration of resistance (which rested upon a taken-for-granted analysis of domination and subordination). I am referring to the rise of the New Right as a powerful political and ideological force in Britain (as well as in other advanced capitalist democratic countries). Additionally, the fortunes of the neoconservatives seemed to be inversely related to the fragmentation, if not the apparent collapse, of organized opposition from the Left. As new political agencies and positions emerged on the Right, the traditional Left seemed incapable of offering coherent strategies and responses.

Finally, in the eighties, many of these problems continue to assert themselves, albeit in different and in some cases even more pressing forms. Moreover, there is a return of many of the more apocalyptic concerns that had emerged in the immediate postwar period (global threats to the future and epochal experiences of irrationality, terror, and meaninglessness), which reappear with great force both in popular media and intellectual discourses. Equally important is the increasing self-consciousness of our own insertion into the construction of domination in our relations to the production of intellectual work and students, and our complex relations to political differences at all levels of the social formation. And finally, the fact that the victory of the Right has been secured—apparently, at least enough to allow Thatcher to undermine significantly the social infrastructure of Britain—can be measured in the Left's apparent distance from the majority of the population (not only that between academics and their students) and the inability of the Left to secure new ground from which to organize opposition.

A NORMATIVE HISTORY OF CULTURAL STUDIES: THEORETICAL DEVELOPMENT

These political and historical concerns were organized by, responded to with, and mapped onto a series of theoretical debates and challenges. Sometimes these debates placed cultural studies on one side (e.g., when it firmly opposed what it saw as the abandoning of the materialist problematic by poststructuralist and psychoanalytic discourse theorists). More often, cultural studies places itself between the two extremes, as in Hall's description (1980c) of the need to locate the space between the dominant "two paradigms." In fact, cultural studies seems to slide, almost inevitably, from the former to the latter positioning (e.g., Hall [unpubl.] currently places cultural studies not in opposition to psychoanalysis but rather in between its extreme forms and those who would either deny its truth or water down its radical insights). Opposing alternative positions enables it to maintain its own identity and that of its specific problematic and commitments. But mediation allows it to take into account its own inadequacies and the insights that reinflect its problematic and commitments into new historical contexts. Thus one of the most common rhetorical figures in cultural studies is that which positions its intellectual antagonist as having rightly attempted to avoid one extreme position but having mistakenly gone "right through to the other extreme." Within these debates, which often took place within the Centre as well as between the Centre and other institutionalized sites of intellectual activity, we should not be surprised to find that each side necessarily misreads and misrepresents the other side in order to reconstitute its own position.[2]

The beginning of cultural studies is usually located in the debate between the socialist humanism of Williams, Thompson, and Hoggart (despite the significant political differences among them) and traditional marxist, literary, and historical approaches to contemporary life and politics. The former, including the original New Left group, challenged the economic reductionism of the marxists, arguing for the importance of the creative human actor, of human experience, and of the determining power of cultural production itself. They similarly rejected (to varying degrees) the elitism that was used to justify the erasure of working-class people and culture from the study of history. Such "culturalists," the first to attempt to define cultural studies, argued that culture was not only the site of struggle but its source and measure as well. Culture was the intersection of textuality and experience, and the task of criticism was to examine how the former represented and misrepresented the latter. They rejected both a theory of dominance (which denied the reality of cultural struggle) and a theory of reflection (which radically separates culture and society, reading society off the meanings of culture even as it was located outside of them).

But cultural studies emerges as a disciplinary formation and intellectual position in the confrontation (initially it was often silent) between this humanistic marxism (which Hall calls "culturalism") and the antihumanism of Althusser's structural marxism. The latter pointed to the former's reductionist assumption of a series of necessary correspondences between cultural forms, experience, and class position. Althusser challenged any appeal to either the subject or experience as the source or measure of history since neither existed outside the processes of historical (and specifically ideological) determination. At the same time, he recognized the power and relative autonomy of the cultural realm. By distancing the "real" as the determining moment of history (in either the first or last instance), Althusser gave renewed impetus to the project of defining the specificity of the cultural. It is out of this debate that the position many people identify with Birmingham cultural studies arises. It is a moment in which, to put it emblematically, Williams is "saved" by rereading him through Althusserean structuralism.

In the mid-seventies, this refined culturalism enters into very explicit (and often heated) debates, not with Althussereanism, but with a different appropriation of structural marxism. If cultural studies tempered Williams's humanism with structuralism (and in so doing, backed off from Althusser's radical antihumanism), it opposed those theories that took Althusser into the poststructuralist realm of the necessary lack of correspondence with a new reading of Gramsci, who served to define a different "middle ground." Such "discourse theories" read Althusser's theory of ideology, often in conjunction with Foucault's theory of power, through a Derridean explosion of both signification and subjectification. Moreover, culturalism opposed those who, often from within the Centre, attempted to link Althusser (and perhaps poststructuralism) with a Lacanian psychoanalysis which abandoned any notion of history in favor of a predefined psychoanalytic trajectory constantly traced out upon ideological practices. Both versions of "poststructural Althusser" ignored the materialist question of the role of ideology in the reproduction of the social formation in favor of what might be described as a discursive theory of social psychology. Cultural studies argued that such theories reduced the question of social identity and its political import to the predetermined repetition of textual and/or libidinal processes. Furthermore, such positions seemed incapable of theorizing even the possibility of resistance except through the production of radically alternative and avant-garde discursive forms. Such forms would either necessarily celebrate the infinite plurality of meaning and the endless fragmentation of the subject, or they would escape the political terrain entirely by appealing to the ultimate political undecidability of any text.

On the other hand, poststructural appropriations of Althusser argued that cultural studies' continued commitment to humanism (with its concomitant notions of essentialized class identities and experiences) made it impossible to theorize the production of subjectivity and subject-positions as a significant ideological effect that often contradicted the surface content of cultural forms. While cultural studies thought of ideology as a continuous process by which identities, organized at sites of social difference, were given meaning, it was unable to theorize the more fundamental nature of the process by which identities and social differences are themselves produced together as subject-positions. Thus it was not fortuitous that it would seek out and celebrate the sites of cultural resistance in the working classes; but at the same time, it was incapable of seeing that the forms of such resistances often reinscribed dominant relations of power—especially racism and sexism.

What emerged from this debate, according to the standard history, was a significantly different position, which can be seen as either a (re)reading of Gramsci (through Althusser) as a nonstructuralist antihumanist or, alternatively, as a rereading of Althusser (through Gramsci, who had of course been a source of Althusser's theorizing), without altogether following the poststructuralists, psychoanalysts, and discourse theorists out of the materialist problematic. This Gramscian position defined cultural studies as a nonreductionist marxism that was concerned with understanding specific historical contexts and formations, that assumed the lack of guarantees in history and the reality of struggles by which historical relationships are produced. Such a "conjuncturalist" theory refuses to assimilate all practices to culture and recognizes the real structuration of power according to relations of domination and subordination. It sees history as actively produced by individuals and social groups as they struggle to make the best they can out of their lives, under determinate conditions.

But this position is already entangled in yet another significant debate: its focus on historical and cultural specificity has led it into direct confrontation with the "postmodernist" theories of Baudrillard, Lyotard, Virillio, and others. While this moment has not yet been incorporated into this linear narrative, the debate between these two narrative opposites is already being constructed as the next chapter of the story. Thus it is already clear that the opposition of cultural studies to the extremism of much of postmodernist theorizing—to its radical critique of the very possibility of any structure, of any meaning, of any subject, and of any politics, and to its reinscription of a form of reductionism in which every text becomes a reflection of our non-contradictory existence within the postmodern condition—is resulting in yet another significant move.

CULTURAL STUDIES:
NARRATIVIZING A WAR OF POSITIONS

I do not want to argue against this history so much as to reread it in order to open it up to greater complexities. It is, as far as it goes, an accurate and important map of cultural studies' shifting position in relation to the larger field of materialist and structuralist theories of ideology and culture. Even more importantly, it allows us to see that the identity of any theoretical position within this larger terrain is constituted by a series of differences among the range of possible positions. Thus, to a limited extent, this narrative already suggests that cultural studies is constituted through a series of struggles around certain key concepts and critical strategies. For example, the meaning of "hegemony" within cultural studies cannot be taken for granted. There are significant, and in fact constitutive, differences between its appearance not only in Williams and Gramsci, but in the culturalist and the conjuncturalist positions of the Birmingham group. This normative narrative represents the history as a "war of maneuvers" in which a series of closed paradigms, each with its fixed set of assumptions, oppose each other. The narrative represents either a gradual and rational transformation through intellectual dialogue or a series of radically disjunctive and totalized paradigm shifts. In either case, the development of cultural studies appears to be linear, progressive, and internally directed. Cultural studies is portrayed as the continuing struggle to realize its own already defined, if imperfectly articulated, project (e.g., an anti-essentialist, antireductionist, anti-elitist cultural theory). Although not necessarily teleological, the narrative constructs a series of stages that did not have the necessary conceptual and reflexive tools to accomplish the project.

Moreover this narrative ignores the continuous debates within and between the variety of positions offered, not only over time but at any moment, within the Centre and cultural studies. It also ignores the ongoing labor of transformation that has operated on the complex and contradictory terrain of cultural studies. An alternative reading of that history would have to recognize that, within the discourses of cultural studies, theory proceeds discontinuously and often erratically, that it involves an ongoing struggle to rearrange and redefine the theoretical differences of the terrain itself in response to a particular set of historical questions.

Such a revisionist reading would begin with cultural studies as a historically articulated discursive formation, constantly redefining itself across a range of questions. Rather than assuming an essential and unified harmony, it would begin with diverse sets of conjoint positions in contention with each other at a variety of sites. Rather than offering a rational history of dialectical development, it would constantly destabilize the correspondences between conceptual differences and historical trajectories in order to describe a war of positions, operating over a range of theoretical and political sites. Cultural studies often moves onto terrain it will later have to abandon; and it often abandons some terrain it will later have to reoccupy. Cultural studies, like any critical project, has had its share of false starts which, however necessary, have often taken it down paths it has had to struggle to escape, forcing it at times to retrace its steps and at other times to leap onto paths it had barely imagined. Texts that were read at one point had to be read again; commitments that were articulated had to be reestablished at some moments and deconstructed at others.

If we begin to consider the discontinuities as well as the continuities in the various ways cultural studies has occupied and reshaped its own terrain, we need to identify some signposts for the various sites of struggle in this war of positions. Only then can we renarrativize the formation of cultural studies, not merely as one of intellectual influence and progress, but as a continuing struggle, on the one hand to define the specificity of *cultural struggle* and on the other hand to comprehend the specificity of the *historical context* of modernity and modernization within and against which contemporary cultural practices function. We might all acknowledge that cultural studies is concerned with describing and intervening in the ways "texts" and "discourses" are produced within, inserted into, and operate in the everyday lives of human beings and social formations, so as to reproduce, struggle against, and perhaps transform the existing structures of power. That is, if people make history but in conditions not of their own making, cultural studies explores the ways this is enacted within and through cultural practices and the place of these practices within specific historical formations. But this description—which underlies the standard narrative—fails to recognize that cultural studies has continuously problematized not only the meaning of "culture" and "society," but the historical articulations of the relationships between them.

I shall begin by identifying eight sites of what in contemporary political parlance might be called "low-intensity warfare," eight theoretical and political issues. They are not all specific to cultural studies but they do enable us to map out some of its directions and tendencies. For the sake of brevity, I will merely list the eight theoretical problematics. They are, I will assume, fairly self-explanatory (and if they are not, they will be explained as the shifts in position are charted): (1) epistemology and interpretation; (2) determination; (3) agency; (4) the structure of the social formation; (5) the structure of the cultural formation; (6) power; (7) the site of cultural struggle; and (8) the historical site of modernity (see Table 1). In what follows, I will not offer a complete and accurate description of any position (since these are available in other places); instead I want merely to show how the answers to these questions have changed, and often in ways that are neither necessary nor even necessarily consistent across the entire range.

On top of this "field of dispersion" I want to reinscribe a certain narrative structure of the development of cultural studies. While this revised trajectory will resemble the standard story (the war of maneuvers), it will allow that narrative to incorporate the fractured and uneven development implicit in the war of positions being fought out along the eight vectors I have listed. I will abstract from the ongoing battles across a wide range of conceptual and strategic differences five temporarily stable forms within the formation of cultural studies: (1) the literary humanism (of Hoggart and Williams); (2) the early eclectic effort to define a dialectical sociology; (3) the first distinctly "Centre position"; (4) a structural-conjuncturalist position; and (5) a postmodern-conjuncturalist position. Let me emphasize again the artificiality of my narrative. While these positions may be taken (for the sake of argument) as representing real stages in the history of the Centre or of cultural

Table 1 A Reference Map of Cultural Studies via Eight Theoretical Problematics

	Literary humanism	*Dialectical sociology*
Epistemology	intuitive empiricism	structural empiricism
Determination	atomic essentialism	dialectical essentialism
Agency	humanistic-aesthetic	social humanism
Social formation	class	class
Cultural formation	elite/masses	public/private
Power	legitimation/value	consent
Specificity of cultural struggle	culture/society as structure of feeling	ideology as worldview
Site of modernity	mass media	mass media

studies, or as interpretations of particular texts, they are actually abstractions out of the complex terrain of cultural studies meant to suggest something about the multiple sites and vectors along which the war of positions is constantly fought. Individual authors and works constantly moved around the terrain, often sliding back or forward along these idealized vectors. While I will make some effort to point to some of the disjunctions between the intellectual narrative and the real history of this particular formation of the Centre, I do not mean to offer a "true" historical account. These "positions" represent, at best, provisional efforts to occupy particular sites in specific ways and to connect them together into effective responses to the politics of the cultural and social context. Despite the apparent historicality of the narrative, they are offered as a map of the changing state of play in the field of forces that constitute cultural studies, and each of them continues to exist.

I will argue, first, that many of the commitments of cultural studies were defined by the effort to move against the "literary-humanistic pull" of Hoggart and his conceptualization of its project in opposition to mass communication theory. In this effort, cultural studies increasingly identified its object of study—communication—with a particular conceptual framework (a particular dialectical model of communication). It established a series of correspondences: between culture, ideology, communication, community, experience, and intersubjectivity. It is these assumed relationships that later, conjunc-

"Culturalism"	Structural-conjunctural	Postmodern-conjunctural
conventionalism	realism/contextualism	fabrication/apparatus
structural essentialism	articulation as specificity	articulation as effectivity
social humanism	social articulation	nomadic articulation
structure in dominance	fractured totality	fractured totality
center/margin	dominant/popular	sensibilities
incorporation/resistance	domination/subordination	empowerment/ disempowerment
ideology as experience	civil society	the popular
consumption	hegemony	the masses

turalist, positions would have to deconstruct. Second, I will argue that the moment of the formation of a "Centre position" depended upon a limited appropriation of structuralism into the continued framework of the struggle between a literary and sociological pull. This effort was embodied, figuratively and historically, in the constant return to the texts of Gramsci on the one hand and Althusser/Poulantzas on the other, each time rereading their positions in light of the effort to rearticulate the historical project of cultural studies.

A LITERARY HUMANISTIC VISION OF CULTURAL STUDIES

Richard Hoggart was the founder of both the Centre for Contemporary Cultural Studies and of cultural studies as an identifiable analytic/critical project. Through a series of lectures (1967, 1970) as well as the classic if oddly titled study, *The Uses of Literacy* (1957), he gave cultural studies its first intellectual shape. However great the distance that seems to have been traversed since that early moment, his influence is still strongly present. Hoggart extended and refined Leavis's notion of literary criticism. He argued that art, if read according to the specific practices of "close reading" that characterized literary criticism ("reading for tone"), revealed something about society that was unavailable in any other way: what he described as "the felt quality of life" and later as "a field of values." He explicitly located cultural studies in the line of critical concern that Raymond Williams (1958) had constructed as "the culture and society tradition." Its task was value analysis but its goal was value judgment. The question, defined with a decidedly literary pull, was not so much what people do with texts, but rather the relations between complex cultural texts and "the imaginative life" of their readers (1969, 18). Cultural studies was to explore the points at which the value-laden structures of society intersect and interact with the psychic life of individuals as represented in cultural texts (19). Although Hoggart's ultimate concern was always centered on the normative dimension of the structures of meaning, he argued forcefully for the complex multidimensionality of cultural existence. One could not understand the impact of cultural changes apart from the dense, sensuous, everyday life of the people: "Only here in art is life embodied, re-created, in all its dimensions—so that a particular moral choice is bound up with this time and that place, with that other person and those habits. Only here do we, at one and the same time, see ourselves densely and vulnerably; and also as creatures who think and dream outside the time-ridden texture of daily experience. This is, to borrow a nice phrase to describe the fusion, 'the real world of theology and horses' " (1970, 249).

Similarly, Raymond Williams (1965) had argued that any cultural text could only be understood in the context of the entire social formation, of the relations among all the elements in a whole way of life. And this totality was not reducible to a semantic abstraction divorced from the lived experience of individuals. Williams argued that the significance of any cultural text was always mediated by its relationship (which he assumed to be that of a structural homology) to the "structure of feeling." Hall's early (n.d.) model of the labor of cultural studies clearly demonstrates the distance between the Centre's project and that of the more socially based disciplines of communication studies: first, to obtain "as full a 'reading' of the material as is possible, using critical analysis both of content and structure, and of attitudes and assumptions, latent as well as manifest values." Second, "to consider its effect upon society, the nature of its appeal and popularity." And third, to "place" the material "in its social and cultural setting" and to interpret it, "as far as is possible, for its cultural meaning and significance."

At the same time, the Centre was seeking to find models of collective, interdisciplinary work that would enable them to carry out the project. Hoggart emphasized that the requirements of knowledge and competence would demand a methodology that was fractured across disciplines. Its model of interdisciplinary research was "divide and unite": literary studies on one side, sociologists and anthropologists on the other. They were to be brought together, to educate, enlighten, and help one another, but they remained separated; literary analysis was a difficult task that took a sophisticated education, and sociology was a discipline too far removed from it. Of course, the ultimate task was for the two disciplines to bring their insights together, to be able to offer new and important insights into the relationship between culture and society. Hall on the other hand focused on the need to work through and unite the three moments of cultural studies: "The analysis would not, of course, be split up into three separate phases: but it would not be complete until all three phases were carried through and related together" (n.d.).

Hoggart's position was built upon a number of commitments and assumptions. Epistemologically, it followed the path of Leavis's intuitive empiricism: close reading revealed the meaning of a text. This was obviously linked, through its strong literary pull (in its sense not only of method but of value as well), to a rather simple theory of determination, which might be described as "atomic essentialism." Both texts and cultures were self-identical and their relations could be read through an assumed necessary correspondence. Behind this correspondence was the (imaginative and creative) individual as the agency of history or at least of that province that was the concern of cultural studies. Moreover, behind the historical changes that *The Uses of Literacy* seemed to be tracing was a rather nostalgic sense of an "authentic" working-class experience. If its model of the social formation was that of class struggle, it was defined, especially in the specific terms of culture, in a decidedly nonmarxist way: the people caught between an artistic and a media elite. Power is necessarily expressed in terms of a struggle for legitimation and exposure, as the colonization of one way of life by the communicative "field of values" of a dominant elite rather than the expression and critique of a way of life by an artistic elite. And cultural struggle involved a war of legitimacy and cultural status. Finally, the specific site of modernity that concerned Hoggart was the mass media. *The Uses of Literacy* was taken to be a study in the ways in which the new cultural forms of mass media and Americanization were "colonizing" the working class. It was read "—such were the imperatives of the moment—essentially as a text about the mass media" (Centre 1969–71, 2). Consequently cultural studies was often framed as a literary-based alternative to the existing work on mass communication. "The notion that the Centre, in directing its attention to the critical study of 'contemporary culture' was, essentially, to be a Centre for the study of television, the mass media and popular arts . . . though never meeting our sense of the situation . . . nevertheless came, by default, to define us and our work" (2).

It was in this complex set of positions that the specificity of cultural studies was initially constituted: it studied the relationship between culture and society at a particular point of intersection, a point at which one had moved from texts and social structures to the whole way of life, to the structure of feeling. Here one was operating between the two realms or, perhaps more accurately, in their overlap. There was, however, even in its earliest stages, a certain dissatisfaction with the position and the way cultural studies was constructed within it. Thus at the same moment—in fact, as early as 1966—an alternative if undeveloped model of cultural studies was taking shape, one built upon a different reading of *The Uses of Literacy:* "Its graphic portrayal of the extremely complex ways in which the 'springs of action' of a subordinate class might be 'unbent' by a dominant culture intent, with the new means of communication at its disposal, of winning consent precisely in that class— the link, that is, indissoluable as it turned out, between the 'first' and the 'second' halves of *The Uses of Literacy*" (Centre 1969–71, 2). Furthermore, Hall was increasingly drawn to the project of locating this argument within a marxist theory of "mediations," a discursive image that was to increasingly dominate the work of the Centre and to displace the literary concerns of Hoggart: "Certainly, where the critic moves from the text 'in itself' to its relation to society and culture, the 'mediations' between the two need to be as clearly established as is possible, given the nature of the material studied and the complexity of relations which it is possible to discover" (Hall, n.d.).

THE FORMATION OF DIALECTICAL SOCIOLOGY

Historically speaking, the "second phase" of the Centre's work, which proceeded from the late sixties into the early seventies, often disappears. There are at least two significant reasons for this: First, on the surface, it is more difficult to describe because it often involved an eclectic and uncomfortable exploration of alternative positions and methods. Second, its texts are difficult to locate; they appeared in the Centre's working papers and later in its journal—which was and still is largely unavailable outside of England—and only some of this work has been reprinted subsequently in various collections. The result is that the different positions embodied within them have been glossed over as they are assimilated into later, more explicit positions. Yet it is a crucial period for, although many of its early theoretical formulations were soon abandoned, it did open up new spaces and shifted the grounds of cultural studies in ways that continue to be influential. It won important new positions even if, occasionally, it also gave up some positions that would have to be reappropriated later in different forms. Moreover it is during this phase that the Centre begins to explore truly collective forms of research; the first such effort was an attempt, in 1969, to read a short story, "Cure for Marriage," from a "woman's magazine."

Moving from questions of the actual history of the Centre, the position that emerged can be seen as a retheorization of the work of Raymond Williams. Two significant developments mark this early formation, and they roughly correspond to Williams's two major conceptualizations of culture: the structure of feeling (as the object of interpretation and the content of community) and the community of process (as the social process of community and communication). Thus, on the one hand, there was an attempt to find broader and more "scientifically" grounded or at least methodologically rigorous procedures for literary and cultural readings. Stylistic analysis, rhetoric, and semiotics/structuralism were all added onto the agenda of cultural studies as alternatives to the empiricism, elitism, and verbal bias of traditional literary studies. It was, in the final instance, semiotics and structuralism that had an enduring impact, not only methodologically but theoretically as well. On the other hand, reading in sociology and anthropology led the Centre increasingly into phenomenological sociology, not in its individualist forms but rather as a dialectical theory of intersubjectivity: "The question is . . . how subjective meanings and intentions come, under certain determinate conditions, to create and inform the 'structures' of social life? And how, in turn, the structures of social life shape and inform the interior spaces of individual consciousness" (Hall 1971, 98). By refusing to identify public and subjective meanings, cultural studies avoided the mechanism of traditional marxism; by refusing to identify situated social meanings and culture, it avoided the idealism of phenomenology and existential sociology. The question of cultural studies had to be understood dialectically: how people fill the void between inadequate collective representations and imperfect private meanings. "[B]y what 'mediations' do the subjective meanings of actors, who share a common social world, become expressed or 'objectivated' in cultural artifacts, in social gesture and interactions" (Centre 1966–67, 29). Intersubjectivity was the key mediating term between individual experiences and social structures. The problem for cultural studies was to find an adequate model of the processes of mediation by which "structures of meaning" came to move within the spaces of cultural texts, understood increasingly on a model of communication as the intersubjective construction of meaning (see, e.g., "The Social Eye of the Picture Post" [Hall 1972] and such early studies as *Paper Voices* [A. C. H. Smith 1975]). The focus on a theoretically constituted process of communication helped to dismantle the privileging of art, so common in Williams and Hoggart.

Despite the eclecticism of this period, the terrain of cultural studies was radically reorganized.[3] While much of the interpretive work was still based in an empiricist epistemology, it was increasingly a structural (or semiotic) empiricism, grounded in the reading of the structures and systems by which meanings are organized. It also moved beyond Hoggart's essentialism, which seemed to postulate a direct correspondence between culture and society. This first "Centre position" emphasized the necessary mediations between culture and society, the complex dialectic between the individual and society. That dialectic was given shape as the process of communication—an inherently "social form of Praxis" (Sartre)—as the relations between public and private meanings, or between personal and collective realities (the latter defined as "publicly routinised social existence").

Perhaps most importantly, this dialectical sociology took the emphasis away from the agency of the individual and increasingly located historical agency within the realm of intersubjective meaning, of the socially positioned subject. This does not mean that it abandoned a notion of an essentially creative human subject! But it did transform the structure of its humanism, increasingly defined less by the literary pull of Hoggart than by a "sociological" pull (Allor 1987). If the model of the social formation it offered continued to be defined as a class structure, that was given an increasingly marxist reading. But the cultural formation was significantly reenvisioned, not as a structure of the conflict between the people and the dominant elite, but as a processual totality produced through the ongoing processes and structures of social communication. Thus while it continued to locate modernity within the mass media (and to offer itself as an alternative to mass communication theory), it significantly rethought the site of cultural power and struggle. The specificity of cultural studies was located in the realm of intersubjective meaning (which mediated between culture and society) or, in what became the increasingly common term, ideology. The Centre, even in its earliest formations, argued against reflectionist and reductionist notions of ideology in favor of an effort to understand it as the construction of a consensual worldview: cultural power as consent, cultural struggle as the opposition of competing, sociologically locatable structures of meaning.

In this way, a cultural theory of communication was transformed into a communicational theory of culture which redirected the focus of cultural studies onto questions of shared meanings, participation within a community, and the ideological mediations between social position, the production of meaning, and experience. If culture was bifurcated into the relations between texts and lived reality, the former was defined by intersubjective meanings, the latter by socially determined experience. But this recognition of cultural complexity and competition (which in many ways reproduced aspects of Williams's work) did not, however, provide cultural studies with the grounds for theorizing the notion of struggle or even resistance. For it moved from a real recognition of complexity (or what Hall would later call difference) to notions of competing interests, overlapping structures of meaning, and negotiated compromises.

If this position as I have described it was dominated by the phenomenological reconceptualization of culture and communication, the increasing interest in semiotics and structuralism pointed in a radically different direction. For semiotics presented a different model of culture; in the work of Eco and Barthes, the Centre was drawn into a discourse that thought of communication as a formal process rather than a sociological one. The semiotic notions of encoding and decoding (Hall 1980b) as two points in a purely signifying structure increasingly forced cultural studies to recognize the implications of a concept of difference; it challenged the assumption of intersubjectivity (and the assumed existence of shared codes). An increasing attention to the texts of Marx (especially the *Grundrisse* and the "Notes on Method," in Hall 1974) and the beginnings of the Centre's efforts to read and argue with Althusser reinforced the possibility of a semiotic theory of culture which, by denying any unified consensus, would provide the theoretical grounds for the possibility of resistance.

THE CULTURALIST FORMATION

The position most commonly identified with the Centre emerged in the mid-seventies through the interaction of two fairly coherent and isolated bodies of work: the first focused on the study of youth subcultures; the second offered a model of media communication built upon the disjunction between encoding and decoding. It is important, however, to recognize the historical developments through which these researches were brought together into a theory of the complex relations between power and resistance. The theory of resistance in media developed from the purely semiotic theory of resistant decoding positionalities. While this formal theory had recognized that such positions were related to institutional and social determinants (drawing upon the work of Parkin [1971] and Mann [1973]), they remained abstract possibilities in the relations of power rather than interpretive positions. It was not until these positions were assigned sociological embodiments—that is, correlated with empirically identifiable audiences and social groups that could be characterized sociologically (Morley 1980)—that the Centre was able to argue that the working class had not been fully incorporated into the dominant culture. Subcultural theory, which is often taken as the primary example of the Centre's theory of resistance, actually began as part of the Centre's effort to define a phenomenological theory of society and culture. Using ethnography, this body of work opposed the "labeling theory" of the sociology of deviance with the argument that style was an ideological discourse (Willis 1978). It attempted to place the question of meaning—and the construction of deviant identities—into the broader context of specific social and cultural formations. The theory of resistance, so brilliantly articulated in the first chapter of *Resistance through Ritual* (Clarke et al., 1975), was, in fact, written after the actual work of the "subculture group." However, we must at least acknowledge the diversity that existed within each of these traditions: not only across different authors, but over time (as new ideas were engaged), positions differed (e.g., there are significant differences between the subcultural work of Clarke, Willis, Jefferson, and Hebdige).

It was Hall's article (1980b) "Two Paradigms" that partly helped to cement these two bodies of work into an apparently consistent theoretical space, located between Williams's culturalism and Althusser's structuralism. Hall's article can be read in fact as a retrospective effort to reinterpret the debate between humanism and structuralism from the perspective of a third, cultural studies position, which already saw itself as inhabiting the space between them. It was less a call than a self-representation. Hall argued that Williams's theory assumed a too harmonious and well-structured social totality in which everything fit together. While it allowed for resistance, located in the human subject, it had difficulty accounting for domination. And, most importantly, it explained ideology (and its mystificatory effects) by measuring it against reality understood experientially. Experience was available apart from ideology, and the struggle over ideology was then how those experiences were interpreted.

Structuralism, on the other hand, in the work of Althusser (and his followers) assumed a structure built upon difference, but the differences too easily became autonomous as the relations among the different levels were deferred into a mystical last instance that never came. While it explained domination (in its theory of social reproduction), it offered no space for resistance (not as a result of its antihumanism but in its failure to explore the connections between the socioeconomic and cultural relations of ideology—embodied in the gap between the two halves of the "ideological state apparatuses' " essay). And finally, structuralism explained experience as the product of ideology. There is no reality outside of ideology to which one can refer it—except of course for the possibility of a discourse (a science) that is not ideological. Ideology, then, is not false consciousness; rather it is a necessary mystification that represents "the way in which we live our imaginary relations to our real conditions of existence." The struggle is not over the interpretation of experiences but rather over the systems of representation that construct the experiences. Moreover, the most important (if not, in the end, the only) process by which ideology works is that of interpellation: ideological practices, by positioning the individual within discourse, define their subjectivity.

Thus what has often been taken as a theory of ideological resistance was, in many ways, an attempt to reinsert ideology into a broader, albeit historically specific cultural formation and that, in turn, into the real social, economic, and historical relations within which both subcultures and audiences were located. Following Hall's terms, I will begin by briefly suggesting where and how the Centre's position negotiated between culturalism and structuralism. The Centre maintained a basically humanistic conception of culture as "the way social categories and meanings mediate social processes between individuals and groups" (Centre 1972–74, 2): "We understand the word 'culture' to refer to that level at which social groups develop distinct patterns of life, and give *expressive form* to their social and material life-experience. Culture is the way, the forms, in which groups 'handle' the raw material of their social and material existence . . . The 'culture' of a group or class is the peculiar and distinctive 'way of life' . . . Culture is the distinctive shapes in which this material and social organisation of life expresses itself" (Clarke et al. 1975, 9).

And yet, while locating ideology within culture, they gave it a decidedly

Althusserean reading, recognizing that "men live, in ideology, an 'imaginary relation' to the real conditions of their existence" (Clarke et al. 1975, 33). Ideologies could serve as a form of resistance not because of some authentic "experience" behind it, but precisely because it offered "ways of expressing and realising in their culture their subordinate position and experiences" (12). Their experience is constructed as the dominant ideology's imaginary relations, and, at the same time, that very production of subordinate experiences opens up the possibility of expressions that resist the dominant ideology. The notion of consensus provided a common ground between the two positions: ideological domination (or "hegemony") "prescribes . . . the *limits* within which ideas and conflicts move and are resolved" (39). But the ideological construction of identity was rehumanized: ideology constructs identities by giving meanings to the various social differences and roles that are a part of our real conditions.

This view of the relationship between culture and ideology was itself located in a decidedly Althusserean image of the social formation within which cultures and ideologies are "relatively autonomous": "subcultures represent a necessary . . . but *inter-mediary* level of analysis. Any attempt to relate subcultures to the 'socio-cultural formation as a whole' must grasp its complex unity by way of these necessary differentiations" (Clarke et al. 1975, 15). Thus culture was "doubly articulated" (Centre 1972–74, 2), first, to its own specificity and second, to "the inextricable inter-connections of culture with social structures, historical trends, social relationships between groups and classes, institutions" (2). Not only did this position incorporate images of the structured complexity and historical specificity of social and cultural formations, it also emphasized the complex processes of overdetermination through which possibilities for resistance were enabled because the correspondences between the various levels of any formation were never guaranteed or predetermined. And yet at the same time that it appropriated "Althusserean" ways of talking about ideology and the social formation, its description of culture and experience remained decidedly humanistic, emphasizing their mediating role between social position and cultural interpretations, resources, and competencies.

It is this gap that defined the particular view the Centre took of the possibilities and forms of resistance. In both subcultural studies and encoding/decoding, a specific group was isolated, its identity defined by its place within an objective set of social relations. These real relations corresponded, on the one hand, to a social identity constructed by socially defined differences and, on the other hand, to a set of experiences. It was this identity that largely defined the site of ideological struggle, in the ways these differential experiences were themselves constructed within the ideological imaginary and hence experienced. That is, the identity of any group was doubly connected to experience, or rather the meaning of "experience" itself slides between two senses: that which is immediately and objectively determined by social position, and that which, through ideological interpretation, is how people live those relations. For example, when subculturalists talk about style as a "magical response" to the lived contradictions of a particular overdetermined social group, that contradiction is always ambiguously located in both the real relations and in lived experience. The style has to appear as a "magical" solution because it is, at least in the first instance, clearly within the lived (the imaginary) and has no necessary (and certainly no direct) connection to the real relations. It is a form of resistance precisely because the identity it constructs is "forbidden," outside the hegemonic limits of the dominant ideology. The connection between its resistance and its "responsiveness" to the lived contradictions, like that between the two senses of experience, depends upon the assumption of a structural correspondence—or homology—between the various levels of the subculture's existence. The contradictions acted out in a subcultural style are always determined elsewhere. Thus the correspondence between position, identity, and experience is not, at least theoretically, necessarily given (Althusser). Yet, in practice, whether homologies were understood as repeated commitments and images, structures of meaning, or signifying practices, they were always delivered in advance. The correspondence between the two levels of experience had to be assumed if experience was to effectively mediate between the larger terrains of culture and society.

The construction I have offered of this crucial moment in the formation of cultural studies focuses on the Centre's continued engagement with Althusser and the various post-Althusseans (Hall 1985a) through an increasing appropriation of Gramscian formulations. Cultural studies' concern for the specificity of ideological practices (operating within a hegemonic relation of consensus and incorporation) was explicitly opposed to the structuralist concern for the specificity of signifying practices. The Centre sought to study the *relative* autonomy of culture within historically specific social formations as an alternative to the structuralist tendency to give cultural practices an absolute autonomy and to ground them in universal textual and psychoanalytical processes. If, for structuralists, subjectivity is constitutive of ideology, cultural studies argued that ideology constitutes subjects. Rather than looking at

the problem of modernity into one of consumption itself: on the one hand, the new possibilities that consumption appeared to offer and, on the other, the rapidly increasing rate at which cultural practices and social groups were incorporated into the hegemonic formation. Finally, the Centre's position, despite its distinction between culture and ideology, continued and even furthered the identification of the problematic of cultural studies with that of ideology; ideology, however, was no longer referred directly to a coherent worldview but rather to the production of social identity and experience around real sociological differences.

But this view of the Centre's position, accurate as it may be, underplays the growing importance of Gramsci throughout this phase of the formation. Gramsci was continuously reread, first as a humanist, then as an alternative form of engaging with Althusser's theoreticism (in his theorizations of historical specificity, relative autonomy, and hegemony) and Poulantzas (on the state, class, and mode of production). His influence was felt not only in the broad theory of ideology and social formations, but in the emerging working groups on the state, race relations, and so on. The first real sign of the increasing pull of Gramsci was the collective work that led to the publication of *Policing the Crisis* (Hall et al. 1978), which, although still decidedly Althusserean in its view of ideology and the social formation, began to offer a different view of the relationship of culture to the historical conjuncture. While not yet able to theorize the conjuncture—*Policing the Crisis* began with the conjuncture already defined by the collapse of social democracy—it represented an important shift away from the communicational or transactional model of culture (defined either semiotically or intersubjectively) to a more historical and "structural" (not structuralist) theory:

> There are, we argue, clear historical and structural forces at work in this period, shaping, so to speak, from the outside, the immediate transactions on the ground between "muggers," potential muggers, their victims and their apprehenders. In many comparable studies, these larger and wider forces are merely noted and cited; their direct and indirect bearing on the phenomenon analysed is, however, left vague and abstract—part of "the background." In our case, we believe that these so-called "background issues" are, indeed, exactly the critical forces which *produce* "mugging" in the specific form in which it appears . . . It is to this shaping context, therefore, that we turn: attempting to make precise, without simplification or reduction, the other contradictory connections between

specific events of a criminal-and-control kind, and the historical conjuncture in which they appear." (185)

While *Policing* continued the focus on social identity through the construction of the meaning of social differences, it recognized that identity itself is structured in contradictions. As it began to move away from the subjective interpretations of texts and the experiential dimension of ideology, it placed a greater emphasis on popular languages and common sense, on the construction of a field of meanings and differences that is linked, on the one hand, to hegemonic projects and, on the other, to certain conditions of possibility. Although in many ways it remained with the cultural studies position that I have described, it represented an important vector pointing to other possibilities.

A STRUCTURAL-CONJUNCTURALIST FORMATION[4]

While the normative history of cultural studies sees Gramsci as offering a new and different way of occupying the middle ground, of limiting the tendencies of structuralism without falling back into humanism, I want to suggest that the (re)turn to Gramsci significantly rearticulated the commitments of cultural studies and shifted the very problematic that constituted its identity. Rather than occupying a middle ground, the position changes the rules of the game; it shifts the discourse of cultural studies in fundamental ways, opening it up to new questions of differences. Obviously, Gramsci's impact cannot be understood in isolation: there were historical and political pressures (both from within and from outside of the Centre), and there were other significant intellectual forces, including Foucault. Most especially, feminism challenged many of the intellectual and political assumptions of cultural studies. It offered, among other things, its own radical critique of essentialism and its own theory of difference even while it placed the problem of identity back onto the cultural studies agenda.

Perhaps the simplest way to present the radical implications of the theoretical shift into a "conjuncturalist" cultural studies is to describe the particular ways it responds to the eight questions that have, if only summarily, structured my presentation of earlier moments in this formation of cultural studies. "Conjuncturalism" can be seen as a model of "determinateness" which attempts to avoid the twin errors of essentialist theories of determination: necessary correspondences and necessary noncorrespondences. Both of these alternatives are reductionist: they assume that history is guaranteed, even if it is only its indifference or indeterminacy that is guaranteed. Conjuncturalism argues that while there are no necessary correspondences (relations), there are always real (effective) correspondences. The meaning, effects, and politics of particular social events, texts, practices, and structures (what we in fact mean by their "identity") are never guaranteed, either causally (by their origins, however deferred) or through inscription (as if they were self-determined). Thus while conjuncturalism follows the poststructuralist emphasis on difference and the need to deconstruct identity (so as to deny its essentiality and necessity), it follows feminist theory in arguing for the additional critical task of reconstructing the historical context within which the production of a particular identity has been accomplished. Only in this dual task can one understand both the reality of such productions and the possibilities for change. In conjuncturalism, the anti-essentialism of a theory of difference is not defined by its opposition to a theory of identity, but rather by its reinterpretation of the latter as a theory of specificity. The specificity of any conjuncture, at whatever level of abstraction, is always produced, determinate.

Its theory of agency can be condensed into the notion of "articulation" as an interpretation of Marx's statement that "people make history but in conditions not of their own making." The links that seem to give a particular text (or set of texts) a particular effective meaning, that connect it with a particular social group and political position, are forged by people operating within the limits of their real conditions and the historically articulated "tendential lines of force." Articulation refers to the ongoing construction of unstable (to varying degrees) relations between practices and structures. It involves the production of contexts, the ongoing effort by which particular practices are removed from and inserted into different structures of relationships, the construction of one set of relations out of another, the continuous struggle to reposition practices within a shifting field of forces. Yet neither the elements nor the context can be adequately described outside of the relations; neither can be taken to preexist the other. Texts are not added onto already existing contexts (intertexts); rather texts and contexts are articulated to each other, each inserted into the other, as it were. In fact, the difference between a text and its context, or a practice and a structure, is only a product of the level of abstraction at which one is operating and, often, the history of common sense (e.g., the fact that a narrative, or an author's name, or, at another level, the binding, is often taken to delimit a "text" is a deeply rooted part of our taken-for-granted assumptions).

A theory of articulation denies an essential human subject without giving up the active individual who is never entirely and simply "stitched" into its place in social organizations of power. Individuals and social groups can and do make history, not because of some essential creativity (or impulse to resistance), nor because they are determined by their historical, social, and cultural positions. Positions are won and lost, occupied and evacuated. There are always a multiplicity of positions, not only available but occupied, and a multiplicity of ways in which different meanings, experiences, powers, interests, and identities can be articulated together. The historical individual is itself the site of ongoing struggles and articulations. Still, this is always a socially defined individual, constituted by its location within already inscribed systems of difference. It begins with the givenness of sociological difference, around which articulations are organized. But perhaps its most important implication is its anti-elitism. It says that people are always active; we cannot predict or prejudge where their practices will operate in some way against particular historical tendencies. Nor can we predict, in those situations where there is a struggle between competing articulations, who will win or what such a victory will ultimately signify. While it is au courant to affirm that "people are not (cultural) dopes," its radical implications, both politically and analytically, are rarely taken seriously.

While conjuncturalism seems to describe the social formation, following Althusser as a "structure in dominance," it demands that the very concept, as well as any specific conjuncture, be historicized and therefore problematized. Not only does it reject that the structural totality is guaranteed, in either the first or last instances (as if somehow the economic always comes through for us), it also rejects the model of levels, each of whose specificity (relative autonomy) can be located outside of specific conjunctures. Of course, critics often do—and must—operate on different levels of abstraction, but specificity is always historically articulated. Furthermore, there are no guarantees concerning what levels, or even how many, are active in what ways, at any moment. Any level (e.g., the political, the ideological, the economic), to the extent that it is a useful concept, must be seen as both internally and externally articulated, full of differences and contradictions. Thus, rather than a totality in difference, we might talk instead about a fractured or articulated totality, in order to emphasize that how the totality breaks up—where its lines of fissure are, where it is stitched together, how its "teeth-gritting harmony" is constructed—is unpredictable in advance, never guaranteed, even though our theories might like it better the other way.

The conjuncturalist theory of the cultural formation significantly relocates both the problematic of cultural studies and the line between culture and society. Because it recognizes the complexity of the terrain of culture, models of elite/mass, public/private, and even center/margin are seen as specific historical—and politically inflected—descriptions. It is necessary then to turn to a more abstract description: dominant and popular, where the popular is always defined by and as its difference from, its subordination to, the dominant culture; this, in some sense, guarantees to the popular at least the possibility of resistance. But the abstractness of this structure is only a result of its decontextualized appearance here; specific relations will always demand a recognition of the different ways in which relations of dominant and popular cultures are constructed.

Conjuncturalism describes cultural relations within a discourse of power—a discourse of domination and subordination which sees people living in complex and changing networks of social relations. Consequently they are implicated, often in contradictory ways, in differential and hierarchical relations of power. Even at their most concrete, relations of power are always multiple and contradictory. Wherever people and practices are organized around particular contradictions, there are multiple, differential relations of power involved. State power, economic power, sexual and gender power, racial power, class power, national power, ethnic power, age power, and so on—all are potentially active at various points in the social formation as a "unity-in-difference," and, at any point, they may operate in different relations to each other as well. If there are no guarantees that the elimination of class domination and exploitation will eliminate sexual and gender domination and exploitation, there is also no guarantee that the latter will carry the former with it. A conjunctural theory of power is not claiming, however, that all such relations of power are equal, equally determining, or equally livable; these are questions that depend upon the analysis of the specific, concrete conjuncture. This theory of power has a number of consequences: First, the form of such cultural relations must always be analyzed conjuncturally; second, to be in either a dominant or subordinate position—whether at a specific historical site or within a more dispersed (but still articulated) social structure—involves a complex and determinate set of relations that are often contradictory not only internally but also in their relations with other social positions and structures; and third, both domination and subordination are always actively lived. And the active practice of living one's subordinate position need not always merely reproduce or even accept the dominant articulations of that positioning. Thus conjuncturalism makes explicit what remained implicit in earlier forms of cultural studies: that there are multiple forms of resistance as well as of power.

Before turning to how this conjuncturalist version of cultural studies understands the specificity of the cultural and of its historical conjuncture, let me (re)turn to the question of its epistemology and interpretive practice. Conjuncturalism eschews the conventionalism of culturalism in favor of a revised realism. Hall's reinvocation (1976) of Benjamin's image of the materialist—as a surgeon cutting into the real—as opposed to the empiricist—as a magician laying hands upon the surface—indicates a renewed effort to take seriously the constraint of historically and materially constituted realities (at least in the form of tendential forces, which are not the same as discursive "realisms"): There is a world that has to be made to mean! The fact that one can only make the real intelligible through ideological forms need not negate their difference, nor the effectivity of the real. Ideologies articulate real practices, positions, and relations; they do not invent them, nor do they render them irrelevant or undecidable. There is as well a particular interpretive strategy operating, one that is different from those by which the previously described form of cultural studies attempts to uncover practices of appropriation and resistance. The task is a contextualist one: not merely to try to identify the objective context into which a particular text is inserted, but to (re)construct the context—which can never be centered around any single text or practice—of a particular (e.g., ideological) field, in terms of how it is articulated, both internally and externally, into specific relations. That construction is always the site of contradiction and struggle. Interpretation involves mapping out the determinations that, *to varying degrees,* are actively producing the context, defining its specificity. But this can only be accomplished if the critic is constantly aware of the different "levels of abstraction"—the distances from the specific context one is interested in—on which determinations are operating. For example, Marx's description of the structure of capitalism in *Das Kapital* describes real historical determinations, but they are located at a high level of abstraction, far removed from the specificity of late capitalism in the 1980s. Within such a contextualist practice, the "depth" of the context is understood largely in epistemological terms. And consequently there always remains some distance between the political and the epistemological measures of completing theories and articulations.

We are now in a position to understand the "double articulation" of ideology as a way of moving beyond the methodological oppositions that structured previous forms of cultural studies—between encoding and decoding, or between a textualist-idealist problematic (its literary pull) and a social-materialist problematic (its sociological pull). Within conjuncturalism, the question of ideology is how a particular text articulates a specific signifier as part of common sense and the production of experience. Ideology, as discourse, first involves an internal articulation: what meaning is produced depends upon where and how particular discursive practices and forms are inserted into larger "intertextual" relations. Power is already operating here since struggles over how texts are interpreted can always be located within such competing articulations. Texts must not only be made to mean, but there are struggles over that production, struggles to achieve, maintain, and change the commonsense alignments and formations of discourse. Within the plane of signifying effects, other effects are produced and struggled over as well: particular subject-positions are offered, but these do not come in already-guaranteed relations to either signifying practices or particular structures of meaning. The ways in which meanings and subject-positions are linked is yet another site of articulation. Further, neither meaning nor subject-positions, once produced, guarantee how such an articulation will itself be articulated to other practices—in particular, to the real conditions of existence. If reality is not textual, it has to be "represented" as well as signified. Thus ideological struggles involve a second articulation, a second plane of effects, in which meanings are articulated to real social practices, relations, and conditions. Differences, which may be constructed elsewhere (e.g., in textual, psychoanalytic, or economic relations), are linked, through meanings, to social positions and to socially empowered systems of connotation. If such articulations are to be put into place, the connections have to be made apparent, real, natural, inevitable. Only in that way can they become "common sense," and only through that double articulation do ideological articulations come to constitute the ways we live our relations to the real (i.e., to produce experience). Difference, interpellation, connotation—wherever they are actively produced—are articulated together around the ideological production of representational effects. Cultural studies now looks at how it is that particular texts, practices, identities already appear to be interpreted, their politics predefined, while acknowledging that this appearance is always in part illusory because it is never guaranteed. People are always struggling against the preconstructed articulations (both internal and external, both signifying and representational), looking for the openings, the weak links, that allow them to bend texts and practices into their own lives. Of course, the points at which this double articulation is successful, at which an ideology is offered and

ticulations are taken up, and how. Moreover the struggle to construct hegemony is never a simple and singular one; it requires a national project that is articulated across the broad range of activities and institutions that make up civil society.

But I do not mean to argue that hegemony defines the specificity of cultural studies. For while there is a tendency to equate hegemony with the ongoing and omnipresent struggle for power within civil society, I want to follow Hall in restricting it to a description of a particular historically constructed structure of power. In that sense, hegemony defines not the specificity of cultural studies but rather a conjuncturalist conception of the locus of historical specificity. On this reading, it has been argued that Gramsci was concerned with the question of Italian hegemony because Italy had yet to achieve it (and the closest it had come was the moment of fascism). Hegemony is a historically emergent struggle for power called into existence by the appearance of the masses on the political and cultural scene of civil society. The masses are not identifiable with any of the usual divisions of power in society; they cut across class, gender, race, age, and so on. They are in fact only defined by their place within civil society and within the hegemonic struggle to win a position of leadership in the contemporary world of advanced capitalist, democratic societies.

A POSTMODERN CONJUNCTURALISM

Hegemony is one possible response to the historical context of modernity, to the broader historical conditions of the appearance of the masses as, in the first instance, a new form of cultural agency that is articulated into various political and economic positions. The close connection between the emergence of contemporary forms of mass cultural dissemination and the complex (re)articulation of historical agency (in which the masses are both the subject and object of the contemporary forms of power of late capitalism) is precisely the point at which a conjuncturalist form of cultural studies intersects with the postmodern turn (for cultural studies, it is a return) to the problematic of mass communication. Thus, to conclude my survey of the different forms within this specifically marxist formation, I want to point to the emergence of another position, one that is more difficult to define because it is a relatively recent and as yet unsystematized position, and because there are significant differences among its proponents (e.g., Hebdige [1987, 1988], and Chambers [1986] pull it back into the previous position, while Chambers simultaneously propels it into a postmodern position; McRobbie [1986] and

Morris [1988a, 1988b] link it in important ways to developments in feminism; while Grossberg [1988b] and Ross [1989] tend to emphasize its relation to the contemporary American political context). Consequently my attempt to present the commitments of this version of cultural studies will be more self-consciously an attempt to "fabricate" the position, following its own project of negating the epistemological concern: truth is itself an effect of power and history. The key difference between the two versions of conjuncturalism is that the postmodern form refuses to privilege difference, to assume its reality or effectivity. On this view, it is possible for differences not to make a difference; their existence (i.e., their effectivity) is itself the historical product of their articulation. Rather than confronting continuously self-reproducing discourses of otherness, postmodern cultural studies attempts to rearticulate the increasingly transnational context of (post)modernity.

As a model of interpretation, postmodern conjuncturalism emphasizes its own articulation of the conjuncture it analyzes; it cannot ignore its own reflexive position within it. Consequently the voice of the critic becomes determining (e.g., the emergence of first-person ethnographies in which the researcher, as a member of the culture, becomes his or her own native informant). We can draw upon Foucault's notion (1978b, 1979a) of "apparatuses" as heterogeneous ensembles of practices or events to describe the object of such postmodern cultural studies. Reality is not defined as a metaphysical or even a historical origin but rather as an interested mapping of the lines of concrete effects. Reality is not "outside" of any apparatus, merely represented within the discourses comprising it. This assumed difference between discourse and reality gives rise to the epistemological problem. But if reality is always articulated through our own fabrication of it, one cannot define the specificity (the difference) of any practice or conjuncture apart from its ongoing articulation within the history of our constructions. Reality is always a construction of and out of the complex intersections and interdeterminations among specific conjunctural effects. Reality in whatever form—as matter, as history, or as experience—is not a privileged referent but the ongoing (in Deleuze and Guattari's term, "rhizomatic" [1981]) production or articulation of apparatuses. And the only grounds for deciding, in Benjamin's terms, how deeply and precisely one has cut into the body of the real are political and historical.

This model of articulation as the production of the real implies a slightly different theory of determination as well. For the construction of an apparatus can never remain within, nor locate the specificity of a particular practice within, some small set of planes of effects. If reality is always constituted by the multiplicity of effects (e.g., the production and distribution of meanings, desires, representations, money, labor, capital, pleasures, moods, emotions, force), then one cannot, for very long, maintain any separation between the so-called levels of the social formation. Ideology (the double articulation of meaning and representational effects) is always in determinate relations with political and economic practices, but also with desiring-effects, mood-effects, and so on. These other planes of effects cannot be bracketed out, for they determine whether and how meanings and subject-positions are taken up, occupied, invested in, and possessed. There are no guarantees which practices are effectively determinate. For example, the commodification of discourse may have less of an effect on contemporary ideological struggles than other economic events and practices. While conjuncturalism continues to define culture (and discourse) through its articulation of meaning-effects (and secondarily, representational effects), discourse can, in particular apparatuses and to varying degrees, be articulated to other effects. In fact, its most powerful determinations within an apparatus may not even entail meanings or representations. Postmodern conjuncturalism opens up the fields of effects within which cultural studies operates. It does not begin by assuming that the question of the intersection of power and culture is defined by the ways in which texts articulate specific meanings and relations; instead it seeks to understand the text as and within a conjunctural assemblage determined by and determining its effectivity. That is, interpretation is always con-structural, (re-)producing the ways in which practices are positioned within and articulate a "unity-in-difference." This can be seen as a theoretical solution to a very real practical problem in contemporary cultural studies: What do you do when every event is potentially evidence, potentially determining, and, at the same time, changing too quickly to allow the comfortable leisure of academic criticism? It is also at least partially responsible for a new sense of inter-disciplinarity that is slowly emerging in cultural studies.

The theory of articulation and effectivity undermines as well our ability to assume the differences within which subjectivity and identity are constituted. It challenges, then, the sociological pull of cultural studies which has located the subject within multiple social differences and their ideological articulations. The subject—as actor, audience, communicator, or agent—is itself a construction, the articulated and articulating movement within and between apparatuses. In postmodern cultural studies, agency is always articulated through and depending upon specific effects. For example, the ideologically articulated subject has no necessary relationship to political agency. Such links have themselves to be constructed and taken up. Moreover the agent of articulation is always anonymous although articulation is carried out by real individuals and groups. This is merely to restate Marx's claim that while we make history, we are not in control of it. It is not merely a matter of unintended consequences, for that eliminates any question of agency; it is rather that practices are always actively contested, rearticulated, hijacked, detoured, and so on, that the relations between practices and effects do not follow preconstituted lines. Furthermore, as the above argument suggests, there is no necessary completeness of the subject that is required by the demands of agency: subjects can, in particular instances, be partial; on one level, the subject may be effective as a body (without consciousness) or even as a partial body; at another level, the complicitous subject may be defined in affective rather than ideological or material terms, and at still another level, whether, where, and how gendered identity is determinative within a particular apparatus (and not merely how that gender difference is articulated) is part of the active reality of the apparatus itself. This vision of "nomadic subjectivity" existing only within the movement of and between apparatuses rejects both the existential subject who has a single, unified identity and the deconstructed, permanently fragmented subject. Moreover it refuses to reduce the subject to either a psychoanalytic or a social-textual (ideological) production. The nomadic subject is constantly remade, reshaped as a mobile situated set of vectors in a fluid context. The subject remains the agent of articulation, the site of struggle within its own history, but the shape and effective nature of that subject is never guaranteed. The nomadic subject is amoebalike, struggling to win some space for itself in particular apparatuses (as historical formations). While its shape is always determined by its articulations, it always has an effective shape. Thus the possibilities of articulation depend in part on where and how the nomadic subject occupies its place(s) within a specific apparatus. Additionally it always inhabits numerous apparatuses simultaneously, which are themselves articulated to one another.

While the theory of the social formation remains the same in the two versions of conjuncturalism, their theories of power differ significantly. According to postmodern cultural studies, history is always the product of struggles that empower and disempower different practices and social positions in different ways. While the very articulation of relations and structures is the site of power, it is also the necessary shape of history. To deny structure is merely a utopian dream of anarchy. Power is real and operates at every level of our lives, located in the limited production and unequal distribution of capital, money, meanings, identities, desires, emotions, and so forth. It shapes relations; structures differences; draws boundaries; delimits complexity; reduces contradictions to claims of unity, coherence, and homogeneity; organizes the multiplicity of concrete practices and effects into identities, unities, hierarchies, and apparent necessities (which ideologies seek to predefine, by closure and naturalization, retroactively). At its most concrete, power is the enablement of particular practices within specific relations; power is always empowering (one need not actively use power to be in an empowered position) and disempowering. Thus the notion of empowerment suggests the complexity of the empowering effects operating within any conjuncture. A practice may have multiple and even contradictory effects not only within a single (e.g., ideological) register, but across a range of different registers as well. Thus a particular articulation can be both empowering and disempowering; people can win something and lose something. Power can only be analyzed in its specific, conjuncturally articulated forms. This model of power is opposed to the various versions of postmodern resistance: it refuses to celebrate any local resistance as if it were desirable in itself; it refuses to accept that only the oppressed can speak or struggle for themselves; it refuses to see the aim of resistance as the reflexive production of the self (as if all power were "technologies of the self"); and it refuses to valorize hyperconformity as radical resistance. Instead it argues that resistance is produced out of people's ongoing activities within specific conjunctures, activities that may be motivated by and directed toward very disparate effects. But resistance itself is never sufficient; it must be articulated into opposition that is effective and progressive within specific formations of power.

Finally, I want to consider the last three questions—the cultural formation, the specificity of cultural struggle, and the site of modernity—together, for they constitute a postmodern conjuncturalist conception of the specificity of cultural studies. Let me begin by returning to the notion of hegemony as a particular structuration of social power that operates within civil society to place an alliance of class fractions in the leading position. The masses then need not consent to the particular values and directions of those occupying the leading position: they must merely be articulated into the position of willing followers. A part of this articulation obviously involves ideological work on what Gramsci called "common sense." Sometimes this is accomplished through the work of formal ideological institutions (involved in the

and social power, but also mass communication theory and the various theories of postmodernity. Postmodern cultural studies returns to the questions that animated the original passion of cultural studies: What is the "modern" world? How do we locate ourselves as subjects within that world? How do our investments in that world provide the possibilities for regaining some sense of its possible futures?

The Circulation of Cultural Studies

Cultural studies is moving rapidly into the mainstream of contemporary intellectual and academic life in the United States. Within the discipline of communications, it seems that cultural studies is no longer merely tolerated as a marginal presence; it is courted and even empowered—within limited parameters—by the discipline's ruling blocs. It is one of the few intellectually marginal and politically oppositional positions to be legitimated and incorporated into the mainstream of this relatively young discipline. And this, to some extent, has made it problematic for those in other still marginalized positions, who see its success as an imperialistic attempt to represent them. At the same time, cultural studies has suddenly appeared in other disciplines, including sociology and literary studies, but with little sense of its radical challenge to these disciplinary traditions.

The fact that cultural studies increasingly, and in new ways, is being commodified and institutionalized raises a number of disturbing questions (Allor 1987, Morris 1988d). As a commodity, it has little identity of its own and is celebrated only for its mobility and its capacity to generate further surplus capital. As an institutional site, it is reinscribed into the academic and disciplinary protocols against which it has always struggled. I would like to address one consequence of the changing place of cultural studies: the more we talk about it, the less clear it is what we are talking about.[1] As cultural studies becomes something of an established position, it loses its specificity. As the term appears with increasing frequency, its relation to a specific British body of work disappears, and it becomes less clear what space we are supposed to be inhabiting.[2]

This dilemma is constructed from two sides. On the one hand, cultural studies has been hijacked by an alliance between the apparent demands of intellectual work (which requires that it be condensed into a position that can be defined and summarized), the exigencies of the distribution of its work (which have functionally erased its history, its internal differences, and its continuous reconstruction through ongoing debates), and its own successes as a politically committed and theoretically sophisticated body of work. This has meant that, too often, a specific exemplar of cultural studies—most commonly, a single position derived from somewhere in the work of the Centre for Contemporary Cultural Studies (whether defined in terms of theory, politics, or collective intellectual work)—is taken to be the defining position or model, the stable representation of the history and terrain of cultural studies. On the other hand, the assimilation of cultural studies into the broader universe of theories of cultural interpretation (e.g., the forums held on cultural studies at the 1988 meeting of the Modern Language Association) simply ends up substituting, metonymically, cultural studies for the more ambiguous notion of critical theory; the result is that cultural studies is entirely dispersed, left without any sense of how its intellectual and political history offers a different way of engaging questions of culture and power.

Those of us working in "cultural studies" find ourselves caught between the need to define and defend its specificity and the desire to refuse to close off the ongoing history of cultural studies by any such act of definition. This is, it must be said, a very real dilemma that cannot be solved by a simple assertion. It is not a question of "possessing" cultural studies but of asking why it is that the name has suddenly been taken up by people in different theoretical, political, and disciplinary positions. It is not a question of "policing" the boundaries but of recognizing that there is a history of intellectual and political practices that is worth struggling over. If there are real stakes in the struggle over namings, then the project of articulating "cultural studies" involves a refusal to relinquish the gains that a specific intellectual formation (with its own history, contradictions, uneven developments, conflicts, unities, and differences) brings to the study of culture.

THE FORMATION OF CULTURAL STUDIES

The power and attractiveness of cultural studies depends partly upon three features that often directly contradict the forms of its contemporary appropriation: First, it refuses to construct itself as a finished or singular theoretical position that can freely move across historical and political contexts. The history of cultural studies can be read as the continuous effort to reconstruct itself in the light of changing historical projects and intellectual resources. This does not mean, however, as some would have it, that there are no boundaries on that history, that every theory of culture, or even of culture and politics, represents a viable position within the field of cultural studies. It is not that cultural studies has no identity but rather that its identity is always contested, always multiple, always changing; cultural studies is a historically articulated "unity-in-difference."

Second, cultural studies refuses to define its own theoretical adequacy in academic or narrowly epistemological terms. Theory in cultural studies is measured by its relation to, its enablement of, strategic interventions into the specific practices, structures, and struggles characterizing its place in the contemporary world. Cultural studies is propelled by its desire to construct possibilities, both immediate and imaginary, out of its historical circumstances. It has no pretensions to totality or universality; it seeks only to give us a better understanding of where we are so that we can get somewhere else (some place, we hope, that is better—based on more just principles of equality and the distribution of wealth and power), so that we can have a little more control over the history that we are already making. This is not to say that it surrenders the epistemological question; rather it historicizes and politicizes it. A theory's ability to "cut into the real," to use Benjamin's metaphor, is measured by the political positions and trajectories theory enables in response to the concrete contexts of power it confronts. Just like people in everyday life, cultural studies begins to grapple with and analyze difficult political situations using the resources and experiences at hand; it draws upon and extends theories to enable it to break into experience in new ways. Thus cultural studies' development is not a series of epistemological ruptures or paradigm shifts (the rationalist illusion) but the ongoing attempt to measure old theories against the emergence of new historical articulations, new cultural events, changes in the tempo and texture of social life, new structures of social relationships and new subjectivities.

Cultural studies refuses to be driven by purely theoretical considerations; its agenda is always constructed by events and discourses that are located, in the first instance, outside of its own theoretical agenda. This anchor in history enables cultural studies to cope with the impossible complexity of its own historical context—a context in which our theories demand more of us than we can reasonably accomplish, in which everything is evidence and evidence is changing more rapidly than we can document.

Third, the form of its interdisciplinary character is built upon the recognition that much of what one requires to understand cultural practices and relations is not, in any obvious sense, cultural. Whatever the effects of cultural production, they are never autonomous facts to be located in, and compared with, other forms of social relationships. Culture exists in complex relations with other practices in the social formation, and these relations determine, enable, and constrain the possibilities of cultural practices. Cultural studies does not attempt to explain everything from the cultural point of view; rather it attempts to explain culture using whatever resources are intellectually and politically necessary and available, which is determined in part by the form and place of its institutionalization. Consequently cultural studies has always been a collective activity, although it is often produced by a single author and the forms of its collectivity have varied greatly and can never be defined in advance, outside of any specific historical and institutional context.

If there is no fixed definition of cultural studies, perhaps the terrain on which it operates can at least be identified: cultural studies is concerned with describing and intervening in the ways "texts" and "discourses" (i.e., cultural practices) are produced within, inserted into, and operate in the everyday life of human beings and social formations, so as to reproduce, struggle against, and perhaps transform the existing structures of power. That is, if people make history but in conditions not of their own making (Marx), cultural studies explores the ways this process is enacted within and through cultural practices, and the place of these practices within specific historical formations. But such statements are fraught with danger, for they suggest that the history of cultural studies, and the differences within it, can be represented as a continuous rephrasing of some original problematic. Cultural studies is then reducible to a particular theory of the relationship between culture and society or between culture and power, and the history of the formation is seen as the teleological or rational achievement of a more powerful and enlightening theory of the relationship.

I believe that we need to begin with the more troubling recognition that the very questions—the problematic—at the heart of cultural studies are constantly being reshaped and reinflected. Cultural studies is the ongoing effort to define its own local specificity. At any moment, the project of cultural studies involves locating "culture" by defining the specificity of both cultural struggle and the historical context within and against which such struggles are functioning. It is the historically constructed form, structure, and effectivity of the relationship itself as a terrain of power that defines the site of cultural studies' intervention. In other words, the point of cultural studies is that the relations between culture and society, or between culture and power, are always historically constituted. It follows, then, that cultural studies is not built upon a theory of the specificity of culture (usually defined in terms of signification, ideology, subjectivity, or community); rather cultural studies examines how specific practices are placed—and their productivity determined—between the social structures of power and the lived realities of everyday life. It is for this reason that current work on postmodernity intersects with cultural studies; it is not a matter of taking up postmodernism as a political and theoretical position but of engaging its description of the nature of contemporary cultural and historical life.

Obviously, any attempt to "define" cultural studies is immediately caught in a dilemma. There is not one cultural studies position, either synchronically or diachronically; there are always multiple, overlapping, changing projects, commitments, and vectors according to which it has continued to rearticulate itself. Cultural studies is constantly renegotiating its identity and repositioning itself within changing intellectual and political maps. Its identity—as well as the significance of any position or concept within cultural studies—can only be defined by an always incomplete history of political engagements and theoretical debates in response to which alternative positions are constantly being taken into account and new positions offered. But the history of cultural studies—the only place in which its specificity (as an emergent set of commitments and projects) can be found—is not a linear or progressive development. Cultural studies has always encompassed multiple positions, and it has always continuously engaged in debates, not only within these differences but also with positions that were never quite a part of cultural studies (although they sometimes were appropriated and rearticulated into it). Cultural studies has always proceeded discontinuously and erratically through a continuing struggle to rearrange and redefine the theoretical differences of the terrain itself in response to specific historical questions and events. Thus it has often moved onto terrain it will later have to abandon and abandoned terrain it will later have to reoccupy. It has had its share of false starts which have taken it down paths it has had to struggle to escape; it has at times been forced to retrace its own steps and even, occasionally, to leap onto paths it had scarcely imagined. In that sense, cultural studies involves constant theoretical work on already occupied—theoretically and politically—ground.

Thus practicing cultural studies is not simply a matter of taking up positions offered by various individuals or groups in the British tradition; such appropriations fail to recognize the complex ways in which these various efforts (e.g., the work of the Birmingham center, or Raymond Williams, or the *Screen* collective) were determined by their place within a specifically British topography and history. Nor is it a matter of erasing the specific formations, trajectories, and histories of the British tradition. Such a "fetishism of the local" would contradict cultural studies' commitment to explore the complex and changing relations between local contexts and larger (perhaps even global) vectors.

REARTICULATING CULTURAL STUDIES

The task confronting us is to work on already occupied ground, to rearticulate cultural studies into specific American contexts and, in the process, to transform cultural studies itself.[3] But this would seem to require some sense of the relevant ground, some map of the space we are to occupy and the ways we can take up places within it. I suggest that we can read the mobilities and stabilities of cultural studies, the various forms of its unity-in-difference,[4] as a continuing struggle to articulate a set of commitments that would both differentiate it from other theoretical positions and empower the places from which it seeks to intervene into a political space. I am not claiming that all of these commitments are unique to cultural studies, nor even that they "originate" within cultural studies. In fact, much of my description will reflect the radical way in which contemporary feminisms have transformed the social, intellectual, and political conditions of cultural studies. I offer my own take (motivated by my own context and project) on the "tendential lines of force" which have often propelled cultural studies, defined the concepts it has struggled around, and articulated it in ways and directions it could not have foreseen.

Materialism describes human reality in terms of material practices: what people do, how they transform the world. But it is less a matter of intentions than of effects, and it is less a matter of origins than of distribution (i.e., what practices are available to whom, and which are taken up). Materialism does not reduce the world to a collection of bodies, although it does recognize the reality of socially constructed biological bodies. It addresses the world of people in social, cultural, political, technological, and economic relations; it talks about people with ideas, desires, pleasures, and emotions, all of which are defined by the forms and organizations of practices that are available to transform these dimensions of reality. In that sense, ideas are real because they transform realities; they make a difference. But it is often less a matter of the content of ideas than the practices by which ideas are constructed and transformed and placed into the world.

Anti-essentialism describes a contingent history in which nothing is guaranteed in advance, in which no relationship (correspondence) is necessary, in which no identity is intrinsic. Such "essences" may be historically real, but they are not necessary. What we take for granted, the starting point of whatever story we tell, is always the end point of another story that has yet to be told. History is precisely the ongoing struggle to forge connections, to articulate practices together—linking this text to that meaning, this meaning to that experience, this experience to that political position, producing specific effects and thereby constructing the structures of social and historical life. Articulation describes this ongoing construction of one set of relations out of another: rearticulation always entails disarticulation. It is the continuous struggle to reposition practices within a shifting field of forces, to construct structures, moments in which things appear to be stitched into place, out of or on top of the differences.

I do not mean to suggest that the field is ever entirely open, that we are able to remake history at our whim. We are always constrained by a history we did not make, by the distribution of practices available to us, by the effective force of the multiple histories of articulation (leaving "traces without an inventory" that are often so tightly bound into place as to appear inevitable), by the multiple and often contradictory logics of those articulations that define the "tendential forces" of larger historical spaces. Thus the process of making history is always partly anonymous since we are never in control of the effects of our struggles. But it is carried out by the practices of real individuals and groups, consciously and unconsciously, through activity or inactivity, through victories—which may sometimes have disastrous consequences— or defeats.

It is in this sense that cultural studies is often described as antihumanistic; cultural studies does not deny real people, but it does place them in equally real and overdetermined historical realities. What they are, as individuals and human beings, is thus not intrinsic to them. Our practices produce our identity and our humanity, often behind our backs. In fact, the production of the individual as a social subject is a complex process by which different social positions are produced—there are no necessary correspondences among economic, political, ideological, and social subjects. Individuals must be won or interpellated into these positions or, if you prefer, they have to take them up in specific ways, and these positions can then be articulated to each other (as well as to other structures of meaning and practice) so that a certain cultural or ideological identification appears to pull its subjects into specific political positions. Antihumanism does not deny individuality, subjectivity, experience, or agency; it simply historicizes and politicizes them, their construction, and their relationships. If there is no essential human nature, we are always struggling to produce its boundaries, to constitute an effective (and hence real) human nature, but one that is different in different social formations. In other words, human nature is always real but never universal, singular, or fixed. It is in the history of struggles, of articulation, that history itself is given shape and direction, and that historically constituted relations of power are put into place.

Power operates at every level of human life; it is neither an abstract universal structure nor a subjective experience. It is both limiting and productive: producing differences, shaping relations, structuring identities and hierarchies, but also enabling practices and empowering social subjects. After all, every articulation provides the conditions of possibility for other articulations even as it structures and limits the field. At the level of social life, power involves the historical production of "economies"—the social production, distribution, and consumption—of different forms of value (e.g., capital, money, meanings, information, representations, identities, desires, emotions, pleasures).[5] It is the specific articulation of social subjects into these circuits of value, circuits that organize social possibilities and differences, that constructs the structured inequalities of social power. While there is no guarantee that different economies trace out the same lines of inequality, the inequalities are rarely random. On the contrary, they circulate around, and are articulated to, systems of social difference which are themselves historically constructed. Moreover different economies may operate in different ways; we cannot ignore the fact that sometimes the distribution of resources is strategically manipulated through conspiracies, intimidation, misrepresentation, and so forth. In these complex ways, the social formation is always organized into relations of domination and subordination. The struggle over power, then, involves the struggle to deconstruct and reconstruct correspondences between systems of the unequal distribution of resources and systems of social identities and differences.

Antireductionism claims that people and practices are always implicated, in contradictory ways, in hierarchical structures of power. It tells us to avoid assuming either too simple a beginning or too neat an ending to our story.

History is never all tied up into a single knot waiting to be unraveled. There is no single structure that stitches all of history into place, the patterns of which are indelibly sewn into the fabric of history. Consequently power cannot be reduced to any single dimension of value that can be assumed to be necessarily and always fundamental. Nor can power be reduced to any single social structure of difference. No single plane of disempowerment, suffering, or oppression has a guaranteed privileged relation to history.

The *conjuncture* defines cultural studies' methodological commitment to specificity. It dictates that we can only deal with, and from within, specific contexts, for it is only there that identities and relations exist effectively. The struggle to articulate a practice is the struggle to construct its context. Structures are real and effective only within a specific context, always defined at a particular level of abstraction. For example, the commodity is a necessary structure of capitalism. But having said that, we must recognize that it operates at such an abstract level—describing many centuries and many national contexts—that it tells us very little about more concrete contexts. If we remain at the high level of abstraction at which Marx wrote *Capital,* the effects of the commodity seem simple and direct. As we move to other levels, attempting to construct "the concrete," its effects are increasingly delayed, deferred, detoured, hybridized, and so forth. And the only way to arrive at its actual "local" effectivity is to recognize (a) how it is articulated by other relations and (b) its specific ability to produce effects—its reach or penetration into the social formation—across time and space. Thus the practice of cultural studies involves the attempt to construct the specificity of a conjuncture, the appropriateness of which is only given by the intellectual and political project at hand. This, then, is not merely a matter of acknowledging the context, of interpreting texts and taking the context into account. It involves the movement of cultural studies from an interpretive or transactional view to "a more historical and structural view" (Hall et al. 1978, 185).

The *popular* defines a necessary focus and commitment of cultural studies. As a political commitment, it is anti-elitist; it demands that we not separate ourselves entirely from the masses. We are, as it were, part of the people who are always trying to influence their own march through history. This does not assume that "the people" exists as a reified category always defined by some intrinsic property; "the people" is a historically constructed social category, a site of struggle articulated by specific interpellations (e.g., as nomadic subjects in media culture [Grossberg 1987a] and as the nation in hegemonic struggles [Hall 1988b]). Cultural studies recognizes that subordination is, after all, not the same as manipulation nor total subjection. People live their positions in complex, contradictory, and active ways; they reproduce and resist their subordination; they seek ways of transforming and improving their position according to their own imagined possibilities and resources; they live with, within, and against their subordination, attempting to make the best of what they are given, to win a bit more control over their lives, to extend themselves and their resources. This is not to say that they are always struggling, or that when they do it is always effective or victorious, or even that their victory will be progressive. To say that people are always empowered in some ways by their positions does not require us to equate empowerment with struggle, resistance, or opposition; it merely requires us to recognize the active complexity in which people live their lives. Nor does it require us to deny that sometimes people are manipulated, misled, misinformed, mystified; but we cannot take such passive positionings to be the totality or constitutive nature of the people. We need to recognize that subordination, empowerment, pleasure, resistance, and even struggle refer to complex sets of local effects and that the relations among them are never guaranteed in advance.

Only in this messy terrain can we begin to sort out how people recognize and transform themselves and their world within and through popular cultural practices. Thus we need to address how specific forms of popular culture, forms that may produce a variety of pleasures and that may empower their audiences in a variety of ways, are themselves struggled over and articulated to larger historically specific political projects. Hence "the popular" also defines a focus, for cultural studies' interventions will not succeed if it does not enter onto the terrain of people's own lives in order to offer them new possibilities, and to locate the ways in which "the people" are themselves constructed through their cultural practices. It is only by entering into the popular—popular languages, cultures, logics, emotions, experiences, moralities, desires, consciousnesses—that we can gain a better sense of the field of forces, that we can see where struggles are actualized and possible, that we can help articulate, nurture, and support them. It is in the popular that we can discover how subordination is lived and resisted, that we can understand the possibilities of subordination and resistance that are opened by and within the structures of domination and that point beyond these structures. It is the popular—as a field of culture and everyday life—that makes available to us the complex field of power in which people live their lives.

The popular—as both commitment and focus—forces us back into a strate-

Cultural Studies: What's in a Name?

(One More Time)

Defining cultural studies is a risky business. Lots of people are suddenly claiming to do cultural studies while others, nervous about its rather sudden success, are attacking it. Yet the fact is that few people working in cultural studies would agree on a definition, and that many who claim to "do" cultural studies might not recognize themselves in such a definition. This is often taken as evidence of the need to avoid offering one. It is sometimes assumed that such definitions, by attempting to police the boundaries, contradict the politics of cultural studies. In the end, the refusal to define it becomes the key to understanding what it is.[1]

But when the range of material being described as cultural studies is expanding exponentially, I believe that cultural studies can be and needs to be defined or delineated, that it is not so broad as to encompass any critical approach to culture nor so narrow as to be identified with a specific paradigm or tradition. This is not a matter of a proprietary definition, or of "the proper" form of cultural studies, but of holding on to the specificity of particular intellectual trajectories. In the past decade, cultural studies has appeared in a wide range of disciplines. And those disciplines—anthropology, sociology, history, literary criticism, women's studies, black and ethnic studies, and so on, in addition to communication and education—have put something into it, changing its shape and offering new versions of it. At the same time, cultural studies has appeared in a wide variety of national and ethnic contexts which have also brought different intellectual histories to the task of shaping their own visions of cultural studies. But cultural studies is not equivalent to critical or cultural theory.[2]

There are a wide variety of tropes that currently organize different discourses of culture: aesthetic discourses of discrimination; anthropological discourses of ritual and ways of life; social-psychological discourses of communication; and political discourses of the public sphere. There is also a range of problematics that intersect these tropes: community, ideology, hegemony, identity and subjectivity, the body, and formations of power. But this situation is not so different from other disciplines that similarly constitute themselves in relation to a particular object (e.g., culture) and then struggle to constitute that object.[3]

This paper is an intervention attempting to carve out a limited space for and of cultural studies. Despite my descriptive voice, my intentions are unabashedly prescriptive. Let me begin, then, by saying something about my understanding of and relation to cultural studies. I have sometimes been described as practicing or advocating British cultural studies in the United States. I prefer to think of myself as someone partly trained in British cultural studies, attempting to develop a cultural studies appropriate to fin de siècle America.[4] This is in fact the only way I know of to practice cultural studies: to constantly redefine it in response to changing geographical and historical, political, institutional, and intellectual conditions, to constantly make a home for it within a specific discipline even as it challenges the legitimacy of the existing disciplinization of intellectual work. I think of cultural studies as a particular way of contextualizing and politicizing intellectual practices. But cultural studies is not an intellectual panacea, nor even a new paradigm attempting to displace all competitors. It is not the only important body of political-intellectual work, nor the only approach committed to interdisciplinarity, intervention, and so on. It is a particular commitment to a particular style of intellectual work and to its importance both inside and outside of the academy. Unfortunately, cultural studies is too often being used merely as an excuse for disciplines to take on new, usually popular, cultural objects. Too many people in traditional disciplines seem to think that, when they start writing about television or rock music and so on, they are doing cultural studies. Cultural studies is not defined by a particular sort of text; in that sense, you can do cultural studies of almost anything. Nor can it be defined by a particular set of methods (although cultural studies does give any method its own particular inflection, and I am convinced that if cultural studies is to develop responsibly, we need to find ways to make our methods more rigorous; without this, cultural studies is too often condemned to repeating the same findings over and over).

I

Any discussion of cultural studies has to locate cultural studies in a variety of contexts in order to describe the forms of its success, the vectors of its dispersion and globalization, and the practices of its transformation, adaptation, and institutionalization. Yet I do believe that British cultural studies is a key point of identification even if, at the same time, I also believe it is a largely imaginary construction that often overlooks the enormous diversity and contestation within the series of intellectual projects that have given it some shape.[5] However, while I might argue that the link between cultural studies (as a somewhat dispersed intellectual discourse) and British cultural studies should not be ignored, it also cannot be essentialized as if it were the only way into the discourse, the only genealogy, of cultural studies. But the success of various figures and positions of British cultural studies as they followed the vectors of global cultural distribution certainly provided one of the conditions for the emergence of cultural studies as a global field of intellectual practice. Sometimes it enabled scholars and scholarly traditions to constitute and name themselves; other times, it helped them to place themselves in relation to other bodies of critical work.

There are lots of conditions—economic, sociogenerational, institutional, and cultural—that have contributed to the success of, and the excitement generated around, cultural studies. One could obviously write any number of different "cultural studies" of cultural studies itself, constructing them from a number of different narratives: the empowerment of the margins; the emergence of a hegemonic conservatism; the media-tization of culture and the globalization of capital; the theoretical excesses of "critical theory" (as the term was used in the United States); the failures of traditional "left" political institutions and movements; the crisis of the humanities (and the social sciences)—a partly self-produced crisis, not only of value but also of representation; and the changing nature of intellectual culture itself (e.g., in terms of its increasing mobility, commodification, professionalization, and alienation), the increasing "hybridization" (or postmodernization) not only of cultural practices but of populations and identities as well. None of these narratives offer a singular vision of a homogeneous, progressively developing field. Any story of cultural studies will be as discontinuous, uneven, fragmented, and contradictory as contemporary culture itself.

But any account of the success of cultural studies will also have to reflect on the specificity of cultural studies as an intellectual practice in and for the contemporary context. And, as I shall argue, it is precisely this articulation, this link between context and theory, that somehow defines the possibilities of cultural studies. For if cultural studies is nothing more than the latest name for any attempt to understand the relations of culture and power, then its success is probably little more than the result of its rapid commodification. Certainly cultural studies is, in the first instance, concerned with cultural practices, but only in the first instance, as its entrance into the context of the unequal relations of force and power. But the context itself cannot be separated from those cultural practices and the relations of power, because they articulate the unity and specificity of the context as a lived environment. As a result, cultural studies does not reduce culture to power, nor does it claim that particular relations of power are somehow inherent in, or intrinsic to, specific cultural texts, practices, or relations; rather it claims that the relationship, however contingent and historical it may be, is its focus. It treats culture, then, as more than either a text or a commodity. Moreover it tends to look at culture itself as the site of the production and struggle over power, where power is understood not necessarily in the form of domination, but always as an unequal relation of forces, in the interests of particular fractions of the population.

One can understand this, perhaps, by looking at the difference between the emergence of cultural studies in Britain and of a cultural theory of communication in the United States, both of which were intimately bound up with the particular historical and biographical conditions of its producers. One of the possible sources of an "American cultural studies" is the work of the Chicago school of social thought.[6] To oversimplify, the Chicago school emerged around the turn of the twentieth century, during a period of rapid modernization (connecting the various parts of the country together, and the country with the world), urbanization, and immigration; in a sense, it confronted the challenge of a kind of "multiculturalism." The central experience of the Chicago school, most literally embodied in John Dewey, was the move from (oppressive) New England towns to Chicago, where, ironically, they then mourned the disappearance of the community in America. The problem was to find a way to reconstitute community in the nation, in the form of the Great Community. The solution depended upon identifying culture with community and communication; the three terms were taken as equivalent processes. The solution was to foster and expand a common culture through communication. But this depended upon the assumption that power, that which prevented the process from working, was an extrinsic factor in the relationship, which had to and could be eliminated. Culture was entirely processual and existed somehow independently of power.

The British context of cultural studies was very different.[7] The question was not the historical loss of community for, as Raymond Williams would write later in his life, "There is more real community in the modern village that at any period in the remembered past" (1973b, 195). The context immediately after the Second World War did pose a significant social challenge, often understood as the impending threat of Americanization (which was not quite a crisis of multiculturalism, that would take another two decades to appear as such). But the terms within which the question of culture was posed were less those of a perceived social crisis than of a personal experience, immediate and deeply felt, of a distance between community and culture. That distance was the result of spatial and social mobility, as, for example, Raymond Williams and Richard Hoggart (and others, e.g., Doreen Massey) moved from, respectively, a Welsh farming village and working-class Leeds to Oxbridge. At Oxbridge, they found that the intellectual world denied not merely the quality but the very existence of a culture in the communities from which they had come. Williams described his own experience of this distance as "that border country so many of us have been living in: between custom and education, between work and ideas, between love of place and an experience of change," and he adds a bit further on, "between fellow-feeling and intelligence, between class and knowledge" (197 and 207). The distance between culture as community (labor, family, sentiment, etc.) and culture as knowledge defined the problem of living between cultures and the need for a lived or knowable community, the need to find "a position, convincingly experienced, from which community can begin to be known" (207). Culture then defined a problem of place and belonging or participation; it was the mediation between social position and experienced identity. Or, to put it in different terms, that distance was measured in the movement within the class structures of England; hence culture was not equated to community and communication, and it was not idealized.[8] At least, power was not seen as something external, eliminatable, a mere interruption of some idealized image of cultural processes. Instead they began with an assumed distance between community and culture, with the notion that power always fractures culture. Hence culture was always more than just a process, for it involved struggles between competing sets of practices and relations, and that sense of struggle meant that it was inevitably tied up with relations of power. This was, of course, partly the result of attempting to operate in the space between aesthetic and "vulgar marxist" responses to culture and cultural change. Increasingly, this placed British cultural studies "on the terrain" of marxism itself, even if it did not define cultural studies as marxist (Hall 1992a).

While locating cultural studies in its biographical or, perhaps more accu-

studies.[9] Raymond Williams traces this ambiguity back to the origins of modern European thought, where culture served both as a description of the changes resulting from modernization and a normative term by which those changes could be judged. And there is a second dimension of ambiguity that Williams identifies in the notion of culture: it is, on the one hand, a set of specialized practices (emphasized no doubt because of the literary roots of British cultural studies, roots that affirmed the fact that culture matters) and on the other, a whole way of life.

But the terms of this ambiguity—the very assumptions about the meaning of culture—provide the point from which forms of cultural studies more appropriate to the contemporary context may be articulated, even as the terms of this ambiguity are challenged by cultural studies' moves into an increasingly global and transdisciplinary context. One can identify at least four different trajectories challenging the dominant conceptions of culture. First, a number of critiques have challenged not only notions of national cultures and/or whole ways of life, but also the possibility of constructing a singular and limited space of a culture. Such notions of culture, it is argued, are the result of the articulation of culture to the colonizing and imperialistic structures of modern Europe. Second, critics have challenged not only nostalgic conceptions of community, but also the romantic-aesthetic-ethical conception of culture and criticism. Such notions of culture, it is argued, are the result of the articulation of culture to the disciplinizing and governmental strategies of modern European nation-states. Third, various writers have challenged not only the reduction of culture to the domain of meaning and representation, but also, more importantly, the invention and deployment of culture as (1) the necessary site of differences; (2) the necessary supplement of human existence (by which we compensate for a lack of biological instincts) that transforms the chaos of reality into the ordered sense of a human reality; (3) the necessary mediation by which culture is situated between the person and reality as the realm of experience and knowledge (and through which all reference to the real can be erased); and (4) the necessary historicity or temporality of human existence, both socially and individually. Such notions of culture, it is argued, are the result of the articulation of culture to the changing forms of intellectual and class power of modern Europe. And finally, scholars have begun to explore the ways in which culture functions in the production of "distinctions," thus undermining our ability to assume not only qualitative distinctions (between high and low) within the domain of culture, but also the existence of a self-contained category of cultural—creative, textual, signifying—practices such as literature or art outside of their institutional laws of regulation. Such distinctions, it is argued, are themselves the articulation of, and articulated to, specific structures of difference as relations of empowerment and disempowerment.

Such a series of challenges might at first seem to overwhelm the foundations of cultural studies, but this is exactly how cultural studies works. Because the field of culture is always changing, because in this fractured relationship marked by power culture is always contested and struggled over, precisely because of that, as Stuart Hall (1992c) says, it does matter in any particular context how cultural studies is defined. Or, to use Cornel West's terms (cited in Pfister 1991), cultural studies matters because it is about how to keep political work alive in an age of shrinking possibilities. Consequently it is necessary to repeat the fact that cultural studies is always open—not just with regard to disciplines, traditions, and genealogies; not just with regard to objects, methods, theories, and politics—because culture, power, and the relations between them are always changing. Thus, while it is the case that there is no single answer, for all places and all times, to the question, What is cultural studies?, it is still necessary to constantly define it because it does matter what it is and because not everything is cultural studies. The answer can only be given in, simultaneously, political and institutional terms, by questioning the conditions of possibility of cultural studies at any moment. But this does not mean that it is sufficient to describe it as a unity-in-difference; it is a network of political and discursive alliances, a discursive space constituted by certain trajectories which enables certain kinds of analyses and knowledges. And the construction of such a space requires precise and disciplined forms of work.

II

However, I have yet to offer a description of the specificity of cultural studies. I would propose that cultural studies, at any particular time and place, is constructed by articulating its *practice* into particular *projects* and *formations*. Cultural studies always and only exists in contextually specific theoretical and institutional *formations*. Such formations are always a response to a particular political project based on the available theoretical and historical resources. In that sense, in every particular instance, cultural studies has to be made up as it goes along. Thus cultural studies always reflects on and situates itself and its claims, limits its field, acknowledges its incompleteness.

If we cannot say much in the abstract about the formations of cultural studies, we can, I believe, say something about its *projects.* Cultural studies is interventionist in the sense that it attempts to use the best intellectual resources available to gain a better understanding of the relations of power (as the state of play or balance in a field of forces) in a particular context, believing that such knowledge will better enable people to change the context and hence the relations of power. Consequently its project is always political, always partisan, but its politics are always contextually defined. Moreover it seeks to understand not only the organizations of power but the possibilities of struggle, resistance, and change. It takes contestation for granted not as a reality in every instance, but as an assumption necessary for the existence of critical work and political opposition. I shall return to these issues in a moment.

While the ways this project is actualized depend on its context, we can further specify the nature of cultural studies by reflecting on its *practice,* since I think it is possible to describe cultural studies as a certain kind of intellectual practice, a certain style of doing intellectual work, a certain way of embodying the belief that what we do can actually matter. It is a way of inhabiting the position of scholar, teacher, and intellectual, a way of politicizing theory and theorizing politics. Of course, cultural studies is not the only such practice; it is not the only form of intellectual work attempting to bring politics and theory together, and many of the features or procedures that define the practice of cultural studies are shared with other forms of critical work. The only exception, the feature that I believe is unique to cultural studies, is what I shall identify as its radical contextualism. Moreover, it is, I believe, only cultural studies that exhibits all of these by attempting to enact a particular relationship between context, knowledge, and power. The features that, I want to argue, are constitutive of the practice of cultural studies are that it is disciplined; radically contextual (with three corollaries: it is anti-reductionist; its objects are discursive alliances; its method is articulation); theoretical; political; interdisciplinary; and self-reflective (about its theoretical, political, cultural, and institutional sites).[10]

i. First, just as cultural studies is neither monolithic nor pluralistic, so too it is neither authoritarian nor relativist, neither universalist nor particularist. While recognizing that knowledge and power are always inseparable, it refuses to give up either the search for an "objective truth" (always with a small "o" and a small "t") or the claim of the authority of knowledge. Or, perhaps more accurately, cultural studies seeks new forms and articulations of authority, built on the effectivities of knowledge (i.e., the possibilities opened up by particular knowledges) rather than the status of the producer.[11] It attempts to produce the best possible knowledge using the most sophisticated intellectual tools. To say that cultural studies is disciplined is to recognize that it does not deny the need for rigorous education, intellectual argument and analysis, and empirical research (built on rigorous methods); it does not deny the existence of traditions that need to be read and contemplated (even if it does refuse to construct them as a canon). Consider the following passage from Stuart Hall:

> Cultural studies' message is a message for academics and intellectuals but, fortunately, for many other people as well. In that sense I have tried to hold together in my own intellectual life, on the one hand the conviction and passion and the devotion to *objective* interpretation, to analysis, to *rigorous* analysis and understanding, to the passion to find out, and to the production of knowledge that we did not know before. But, on the other hand, I am convinced that no intellectual worth his or her salt and no university that wants to hold up its head in the face of the 21st century, can afford to turn dispassionate eyes away from the problem . . . understand what keeps making the lives we live and the societies we live in, profoundly and deeply antihumane. (1992c, 18; emphasis added)

There is, in this statement, a very real commitment to knowledge, to rigor, and to intellectual discipline, to knowing more than "the other side," as Gramsci put it. Of course, drawing on Foucault, Hall's rhetoric of needing to hold these two poles together appears to be the result of the institutional discourses of the contemporary academy which have produced the apparent rift between always articulated structures of power and knowledge. Cultural studies then can be described as a practice that attempts to maintain the discipline of authority in the face of relativism. Cultural studies, while it has no pretensions to totality or universality, does seek to give a better understanding of where "we" are so "we" can get somewhere else, hopefully somewhere better, leaving open the question of what is better and how one decides, as well as the question of who "we" are.

ii. Second, and most importantly, the practice of cultural studies is radically contextualist, and cultural studies might be described as a discipline of contextuality. Let me begin to explain and explore this by quoting from what is perhaps the classic work of British cultural studies: *Policing the Crisis,* a collective work that first predicted the rise of a new conservative hegemony: Thatcherism. However, *Policing the Crisis* starts off by investigating a specific empirical phenomenon in the 1970s: the appearance of an apparently new crime in England called mugging, and its discovery not only by the British press but by various state agencies as well. Not surprisingly, according to the press, mugging was a "black on white" crime. *Policing the Crisis* is largely an account of the social construction of this reality through an analysis of the practices of news production and their relations to institutions and structures of social control. This is how the authors described the object of their study—mugging: "There are, we argue, clear historical forces at work in this period, shaping so to speak, from the outside, the immediate transactions on the ground between 'muggers,' potential muggers, their victims, and their apprehenders. In many comparable studies, these larger and wider forces are merely noted and cited; their direct and indirect bearing on the phenomenon analysed is, however, left vague and abstract—part of 'the background.' In our case, we believe that these so-called 'background issues' are, indeed, exactly the critical forces which produce 'mugging' in the specific form in which it appears" (Hall et al. 1978, 185). That is, they argued that the very notion of mugging, its existence as a material and cultural form, could not be defined independently of its existence within the context. An event or practice (even a text) does not exist apart from the forces of the context that constitute it as what it is. Obviously, context is not merely background but the very conditions of possibility of something. It cannot be relegated to a series of footnotes or to an afterthought, to the first or last chapter. It is precisely what one is trying to analyze and it is the most difficult thing to construct. It is both the beginning and the end of cultural studies, although the two are not the same point.

The context of a particular research is not empirically given beforehand; it has to be defined by the project, by the political question that is at stake. The context can be as narrow as a neighborhood at a particular moment, or an urban region, or perhaps even some local high school that is having race problems, or it can be as broad as global capitalism after the cold war. To put it succinctly, for cultural studies context is everything and everything is contextual.

This contextualism affects every dimension of cultural studies. It affects the most fundamental concepts that define the discourse of cultural studies, which now cannot be defined outside the particular context or field of study and struggle: concepts of culture, cultural text, and cultural practice; concepts of power and the dimensions along which it is structured—race, gender, sex, class, ethnicity, generation, and so on; and even the form of the relationship between culture and power. The very relationships between culture and society are themselves contextually specific, the product of power, and hence they cannot be assumed to transcend particular contexts. Consequently the commonly held belief that cultural studies is necessarily a theory of ideology, of representation, identity, and subjectivity, or of communication (production-text-consumption) is mistaken.[12] While it is true that cultural studies, along with other critical discourses, has struggled to put these questions on the agenda, it has never asserted that those are the only effects that cultural practices can have or that they are always the relevant questions to be asked. There is no guarantee that, in a particular context, culture works as ideology. Too often, the task of cultural studies is assumed beforehand, independently of the context. To put it another way, the very questions cultural studies asks—its problematics—potentially change in every study. The problematic of one cultural studies investigation is not the same as that of another.

A number of consequences or corollaries follow from this radical contextualism. First, cultural studies is strongly antireductionist at all levels. It views cultural practices as the site of the intersection of many possible effects. It does not start by defining culture or its effects, or by assuming ahead of time the relevant dimensions within which to describe particular practices. Instead they are places where different things can and do happen, where different possibilities intersect (Frow and Morris 1993). Furthermore, cultural studies refuses to reduce reality to culture or to any single dimension or domain of existence: biology, economics, state politics, social and sexual relations, culture—all are a part of human reality. While cultural studies might be seen as a version of "the social construction of reality,"[13] it does not believe reality is entirely constructed by our social and cultural practices, for there are material realities that are being struggled over in various ways, that are being articulated, and that have real, measurable effects. Cultural studies believes that all the different forms of that reality, all the different kinds of practices that human beings are shaped by, have to be recognized. They cannot be reduced to one another. Hence cultural studies does not believe that culture can be explained in purely cultural terms, nor does it believe that everything is culture; rather it believes that culture can only be understood in terms of its relations to everything that is not culture. In this sense, cultural studies is always materialist.

Similarly, it sees power as complex and contradictory, as organized in complex ways, along multiple axes and dimensions that cannot be reduced to one another. One cannot explain gender or sexual relationships through economic and class relationships, nor can one explain economic and class relationships through gender and sexual relationships. If gender and sexual relationships are changed, there is no guarantee that class relationships will change (in a similar or comparable way), and if class relationships change, there is no guarantee that gender and sexual relationships will change (in a similar or comparable way). Power is, unfortunately, more complex than we might like. But to be optimistic, power is never able to totalize itself. There are always fissures and fault lines that may become the active sites of change. Power never quite accomplishes everything it might like to everywhere, and there is always the possibility of changing the structures and organization of power. Moreover, while power operates in institutions and in the state, it also operates where people live their lives, in what is sometimes called everyday life, and in the spaces where these fields intersect. Cultural studies is always interested in how power infiltrates, contaminates, limits, and empowers the possibilities that people have to live their lives in dignified and secure ways. For if one wants to change the relations of power, if one wants to move people, even a little bit, one must begin from where people are, from where and how they actually live their lives.

A second corollary of cultural studies' radical contextualism involves the definition of its object. Cultural studies is concerned with the role of cultural practices in the construction of the contexts of human life as milieus of power. In other words, it is concerned with how relations of force (effectivity) are organized into relations of power by the discursive practices that constitute the lived world as human. It starts with the assumption that particular cultural or discursive practices do not exist effectively (i.e., as effective) outside of relations, that they are themselves contextual. Thus, rather than practices, cultural studies always constitutes its object as an alliance, a set of relations among practices (not all of which need be textual, symbolic, signifying, or even discursive). Such alliances cannot be identified with texts, and certainly not with any particular genre of texts. More accurately, its object is the relations between cultural alliances and contexts, or contexts within contexts, always and already articulated to and by relations of power. An alliance is an event, always constituted with and constitutive of a larger context of relationships. For an alliance is always a set of practices dispersed across a delimited social space. Such relations or dispersions are, however, not random; they are defined by—and practices are located within—particular trajectories of which particular practices (or texts) are only moments (but not examples or synecdoches). Such trajectories, as well as the alliances they produce, are the product of work; it is an event, comparable perhaps to Mauss's total social phenomenon, which, as Frow and Morris (1993) describe it, is a point of intersection and negotiation of radically different kinds of determinations, of temporal and spatial, semiotic, and material vectors. Cultural studies then reconstitutes its object by mapping the relations or, more accurately, what I will describe shortly as the lines of articulation. That defines, in a sense, the continuing circularity of cultural studies' practice since it can only produce what it is to analyze through the practice of its analysis. The alliance as context is both a beginning and an end of sorts—but not an absolute end, since the analysis can and must continue, mapping the relations of and within contexts.

Radical contextualism also shapes the methodological practice of cultural studies as articulation. Articulation is a particular position in what has been, for many years, the major debate within contemporary cultural and political theory. Perhaps more accurately, articulation is a way of strategically avoiding this debate altogether. Let me lay out the terms of this argument. On the one hand, essentialism assumes that things are the way they are because they have to be that way. That is, relationships in history, the relationships that constitute history, are guaranteed, inevitable, intrinsic to the related elements. To be a woman is to have certain organs or experiences. To be black means to have certain experiences or perhaps to have come from Africa. A book has its own proper and correct meaning. The real—intrinsic and essential—interests of the working class define an inevitable relationship to socialism. The production or origin of something already defines its possibilities—so, for example, something made within a capitalist mode of production is inevitably a commodity and hence inevitably alienating and fetishized. Or, the ideology of a text produced by capitalists is necessarily capitalist. In essentialist positions, the answers are guaranteed and everything is sewn up in advance. Identities are fixed. Effects are determined before they are even produced, because all the important relations in history are necessary, that is, necessarily the way they are.

On the other hand, anti-essentialism says there are necessarily no relationships. Relations are an illusion; it is their very appearance that is the product of power, and hence the only response to a relation is to deconstruct it, to get rid of it, to deny it. A text has no meaning and there are no limits to what it can mean. Perhaps it means whatever a reader wants it to mean. Being a woman has no shared meaning; it does not entail any common experience. And hence, for example, it is difficult to know on what grounds one could organize a "women's movement." There are no relationships in history. Not only are origins (such as capitalist modes of production) not determining, they are themselves not real. The text does whatever it does. The working class has no common interests, and certainly no special relation to socialism (or the Left).

Both of these theoretical positions can be found everywhere in the discourses of cultural theory and criticism. But cultural studies takes neither of those positions; it operates in a different space, not exactly between them (Sedgwick 1990). It locates everything in relations but assumes that such relations, while always real, are never necessary. Power is both produced as, and produces contexts as, the set of "relations of a nonrelation," to echo Foucault. Articulation as a practice is politically—strategically—anti-essentialist, but it is also anti-anti-essentialist. It says there are relationships in history but they are not necessary. They did not have to be that way but, given that they are that way, they are real and they have real effects. A text does not have to mean what it seems to mean to 90 percent of the people who read it. But in fact it does mean that to 90 percent of the people who read it because the relationship between those words and that meaning has been produced. Those words, that text, have been articulated to that meaning. The working class does not have intrinsic and essential interests that it carries across contexts and over time, but at any moment it does have interests. Certain interests are articulated to and taken up by the working class. There is nothing essential about the relationship between labor and socialist parties; they certainly did not have to vote Labour or Democrat. It is not intrinsic to being a worker that one thinks the Labour Party or the Democrats represent one's interests—but for the past fifty years or so that relationship was real and effective. And now we can understand that Reagan and Thatcher did not dupe the working classes into misunderstanding their own interests but broke (disarticulated) the relationship and created (rearticulated) a new one. That is articulation: the making of a relationship out of a nonrelationship or, more often, the making of one relationship out of a different one. (This is, by the way, not the same as mutual constitution, as used in both phenomenology and poststructuralism.) It assumes that there are no necessary relations, but relations are real and have real effects.

Consequently cultural studies does not believe that you can understand the nature of culture and power by finding origins, by looking for some moment that guarantees the effects of culture. It rejects the notion that because a cultural text is produced as a commodity by capitalism you know ahead of time what its politics are. It rejects the notion that because a text is produced by a racist society you can know ahead of time what the effects of that text are. It rejects the notion that people have some authentic original experience that defines the truth against which power is an external mystifying divine force. Power is there for cultural studies from the very beginning. While it is nice to dream of eliminating power and ideology so that we can get back to some "true" experience as it existed before power reconstructed and misinterpreted it, that is not what power does nor how culture works. That's not how ideology operates. The most basic experiences one has, the things one believes most confidently because they are the most obvious, those are precisely what power and ideology have produced. That which one is sure cannot be doubted, that is what one must doubt, because that is what power is most concerned to produce. What one knows is there because one has seen it is precisely what ideology and culture are making one see. We see black and white. We see male and female. We see that these matter, that they make a difference. That is what we are being made to see. But if we could challenge and change these structures of perception and experience—by understanding the apparatuses of power that have produced these particular binarisms—we would not get back to some original untainted truth; there is no such thing. There is no experience to which we can appeal as some kind of original justification for the political visions that we have. We can only struggle between different articulations of reality to find one that is more humane for more (all) people.

For cultural studies, articulation is a model—not only of the social formations of power, but also of its own practice or method.[14] Articulation is the methodological face of a radically contextualist theory. It describes a nonlinear expansive practice of drawing lines, of mapping connections. Of course, different connections will have differing forces in particular contexts and these must be measured; not all connections are equal or equally important. Cultural studies is about understanding the possibilities for remaking contexts through cultural alliances and apparatuses, the very structures of which (and the relations between them) are the product of relations and struggles over power. Cultural studies attempts to construct political and contextual theories of the relations between cultural alliances and contexts,[15] as the milieus of the human relations of power. It is a theory of how contexts are made, unmade, and remade. This is precisely what cultural studies tries to intervene into. It is about the possibilities for remaking the context where context is always understood as a structure of power. But the very structure of the context is precisely where one must go to locate the power that is operating, since contexts do not exist independently of power.

Articulation calls for both deconstruction and reconstruction; it places the analyst-critic into the ongoing war of positions fought out through the various apparatuses and practices of articulation. Cultural studies offers an intellectually grounded practice for intervening into the becoming of contexts and power. It attempts, temporarily and locally, to place theory in between in order to enable people to act more strategically in ways that may change their context for the better. Of course, how temporarily and how locally are themselves defined by the project. Insofar as any locale is itself locatable within larger—and even global—contexts, cultural studies can only be advanced and served by the increasing polylogue now taking place along the trajectories of its global dissemination and the local invention of cultural studies. For such a polylogue is predicated on the recognition of the changing face of global relations: that we live in a polycentered world. Theories and problems may travel, but they travel as resources rather than answers and, in the end, the trajectory itself may be a more powerful force than either the departure or the arrival. For travel of any sort, of whatever bodies or practices, can never be entirely one way, and what travels is always remade by the complexities of the journey.

If a context can be understood as the relationships that have been made by the operation of power, in the interests of certain positions of power, the struggle to change the context involves the struggle to understand those relations, to locate those relations that can be disarticulated and to then struggle to rearticulate them. To use the most simple and in some sense the most powerful example, the civil rights movement's attempt to say that black is not evil, that black is beautiful, was an attempt to redefine a relationship, to rearticulate it into a different relationship. Cultural studies has to be multiple and changing because the contexts—and within them, the political stakes and potential or actual struggles—are always fluid, multiple, and contradictory. Cultural studies struggles within the space between, on the one hand, absolute containment, closure, complete and final understanding, total domination, and, on the other hand, absolute freedom and possibility, openness, open-endedness. It believes, with Marx, that people make history but in conditions not of their own making.

iii. I have already said a great deal, at least implicitly, about the next two (the third and fourth) features characterizing the practice of cultural studies. Cultural studies is always theoretical and political, but it is theoretical and political in specific—contextual—ways. Cultural studies' radical contextuality affects its theory and politics, which must be related not only to its historical context but to its institutional context as well.

Cultural studies is always theoretical. It is absolutely committed to the necessity of theoretical work, to what Karl Marx called the detour through theory. It does not assume that the context it is studying (and constituting) is available in some directly empirical way. Theory is necessary to gain an understanding of the context because the context itself has in part already been constructed by theory, or at least by cultural practices and alliances, which is not to say that the context is in any way reducible to those theoretical or cultural constructions. But its theory is always context-specific in two distinct ways. First, theory is always a response to specific questions and specific contexts; it is measured, its truth and validity judged, by its ability to give a better understanding of the context, to open up new, at least imagined, possibilities for changing that context. Cultural studies refuses to hold to one theory defined in advance. This is, again, not to say that it believes in letting the phenomenon speak for itself, but it does believe that the material and discursive context can speak back, as it were (if only as measured in political possibilities). Cultural studies treats theories as hypotheses and resources, to be fitted to, articulated with, its particular project. At the very least, this means that theory is contingent and that one cannot be too invested in particular theoretical paradigms. In a sense, cultural studies refuses to let theory let research off the hook. If one's theory tells one the answers in advance, because one's theory travels with one across any and every context, I do not think one is doing cultural studies. One may be doing interesting and important work, and one's answers may offer important truths.[16] But there is little possibility of surprise or discovery here. Theory and context are mutually constituted in cultural studies.

In that sense, you cannot take a theory in cultural studies—for example, subculture theory developed in 1970s Britain, or Hall's theory of Thatcherism as a hegemonic formation developed in the 1980s—and simply move it to a different context and apply it as if it could work there. Theory and context determine each other. And consequently, as I have suggested, its anti-essentialism is always contextual and political rather than epistemological (as in poststructuralism). Similarly cultural studies cannot be simply a theory of communication, and the model of encoding and decoding cannot be universalized, for it was, after all, a theoretical response to a specific context and a specific political question. Even the earliest statements of British cultural studies distance themselves from a communicational model of cultural studies. Here I might mention Raymond Williams's (1965) famous description of cultural studies as the study of all the relations between all the elements in a whole way of life. While this is admittedly a romantic ideal of totalization, it points, along with Williams's notion of a structure of feeling, to his radical commitment to contextualism: A text can only be understood by locating it within a structured set of contextual relations. Similarly, Richard Hoggart (1969) argued that cultural studies is not concerned with what people do with a text but with what relations the complex text has to the imaginative life of its readers.

The second way in which theory is contextual is that cultural studies is never driven by—its agenda is not dictated by—theory or by a particular theoretical position. It does not take its questions from theory or even from particular academic disciplines. It uses theories to "keep on theorizing," rigorously rearticulating them, strategically constructing theoretical formations in response to its particular projects and alternative formations. Cultural studies operates with a particular relationship between its theoretical work and the historical context in which it is working. It is in this sense that I describe cultural studies as interventionist; not in the sense that it intends to leave the realm of intellection and carry its practice to the streets. Rather it is interventionist insofar as it is not theory driven and theory is not its object of study. Where, then, do its specific research questions come from? Let me quote Stuart Hall again: "In thrusting onto the attention of scholarly reflection and critical analysis the hurly-burly of a rapidly changing, discordant and disorderly world, in insisting that academics sometimes attend the practical life where everyday social change exists out there, cultural studies tries, in its small way, to insist on what I want to call the vocation of the intellectual life. That is, cultural studies insists on the necessity to address the central, urgent and disturbing questions of a society and a culture in the most rigorous intellectual way we have available" (1992c, 11). Or, to quote Raymond Williams's description of the pedagogical project of cultural studies: it involves "taking the best we can in intellectual work and going with it in this very open way to confront people for whom it is not a way of life, for whom it is not in all probability a job, but for whom it is a matter of their own intellectual interest, their own understanding of the pressures on them, pressures of every kind, from the most personal to the most broadly political" (1989, 162).

In another context, Williams described the real power (in the classroom) as the power to ask the questions. Cultural studies begins by allowing the world outside the academy to ask the questions of us as intellectuals. Its questions then are derived from the researcher's own sense (admittedly, perhaps, commonsensical) of the context and the political questions and possibilities at stake. There is, I am aware, an apparent contradiction here, but I would prefer to see it as another example of the inevitable circularity of cultural studies: the "real" context is both constructed in the analysis and asks the questions before the analysis.[17] I am not claiming, in some naïve empiricism, that the context speaks for itself, but I am arguing that cultural studies starts by recognizing that the context is always already structured not only by relations of force and power, but also by voices of political hope and aspiration. If, as I have said, cultural studies must always begin where people are, then it must also begin with already constituted articulations of popular hope and disappointment in everyday life. This is not, of course, to say that the analysis should or will end up in the same place, or even using the same terms. Moreover, insofar as cultural studies is materialist, I think it does believe that there are real lines connecting such everyday politics (or their absence) to the real relations of forces (and contradictions) in specific social contexts.[18]

iv. It is obvious from everything I have said that cultural studies is politically driven, that it is committed to producing knowledge that both helps people understand that the world is changeable and that offers some direction for how to change it. But here too cultural studies is radically contextual in its vision of politics and political struggle. Cultural studies believes that politics is contextually specific. The sites, goals, and forms of struggle must be understood contextually. One cannot simply assume that because a certain kind of political struggle made sense in the 1980s, it will make sense in the 1990s. One cannot assume that because a certain kind of political struggle made sense in England, it will make sense in America.

But politics must also be understood theoretically. Cultural studies demands a certain distance from the existing constituencies of politics, if for no other reason than its commitment to the absolute necessity of theoretical intervention. It sees the need for a certain autonomy of intellectual work, and hence it cannot be said to produce organic intellectuals. For example, while it may be very reasonable to start with questions of identity in contemporary American politics, it does not follow that we must end up with some form of a politics of identity. We may, instead, chart a trajectory from a politics of identity and difference that leads, through an analysis of the geohistorical mechanisms by which relations have been constructed as differences and politics organized by identities, to a politics organized around singularity and otherness (see Agamben 1993). Cultural studies proposes that we take a flexible, somewhat pragmatic or strategic and often modest approach to political programs and possibilities. Such an approach denies the possibility of a totalizing politics (and hence of the saliency of political critiques based on the mere fact of the absence of some political issues or constituencies).

Since cultural studies believes that cultural practices have effects but that they are often difficult to find, it also believes that, as a cultural practice, it has effects but they too are difficult to identify. Further, it believes that one can always find possibilities for changing any context. In that sense cultural studies is motivated by a desire to maintain some ground for optimism in the face of the overwhelming and quite reasonable pessimism that confronts anyone looking at the contemporary world. Cultural studies critics are fond of quoting Gramsci: "pessimism of the intellect, optimism of the will." What's the point of being so pessimistic that you cannot find the will to begin to struggle? On the other hand, what's the point of being so optimistic that you cannot find a reason to struggle against the existing structures of power? Thus, while cultural studies often constructs "images of strength, courage, and the will to survive" (Bailey and Hall 1992a, 5) and even resist, in the face of overpowering hostility, while it is concerned with people's everyday lives, it does not erase that hostility or the systems of domination that produce it. Its belief that where there is power, there is resistance is not an assumption about agency but rather a corollary of its theory of power as always a relation between unequal forces. While it refuses to assume that people are, or to treat them as, cultural dopes, it does not assume that they are always in control, always resisting, always aware, always operating with an informed understanding of the context. This is a crucial misunderstanding, I think. If you assume people are so stupid, are such cultural dopes, that they have no idea of what is being done to them, what's the point of education or critical work? Moreover it's probably not the best way to try to organize political change—to start off by telling people that they're too stupid to understand what's hap-

footnotes to sources, usually theoretical, from outside the discipline; or alternatively, you do basically what you have been doing but you surround it with allusions or information from outside the discipline which, it is assumed, legitimates the argument. Cultural studies says that interdisciplinarity takes work. For example, Meaghan Morris (1992b) has criticized the widespread tendency among cultural critics to take a single source, such as David Harvey's widely discussed *The Condition of Postmodernity,* as an authoritative analysis of the global conditions of capitalism, as if Harvey's theories were uncontestably obvious or commonly accepted. It would be like one's deciding that one needed to know something about cultural studies; so one goes off and reads a few articles by someone (perhaps a colleague or someone that a colleague has told one about, or perhaps someone one has heard of), and then quotes that person as if his or her positions were the undisputed common sense of cultural studies. In fact, even a little reading in economics shows that there is even less agreement among economists than there is among cultural critics. If interdisciplinarity takes work, there is not one form that such work must take. It will often involve an individual or collective effort to, as it were, become an economist—not in the disciplinary terms of economics but within the interdisciplinary requirements of cultural studies. But there is, of course, a limit to the extent to which one can reinvent economics for cultural studies. And the question is as much one of deciding and coordinating what work has to be brought into cultural studies from other disciplines. This is, in a sense, no different from work within a discipline: one has to somehow decide what to let into one's own work. Once again, we have to recognize that cultural studies is not some magical panacea or salvation for the academy. In many ways, it is just like other disciplines (and it often exists within them). As Tony Bennett (1993) has pointed out, the current celebration of cultural studies' interdisciplinarity too often assumes that cultural studies is better than other disciplines or practices because it is somehow more totalizing, while they are merely partial. On the contrary, cultural studies is also partial; its difference lies perhaps in the fact that it recognizes its own partiality and hence constitutes it differently.

vi. This leads me to the final feature of the practice of cultural studies: it is self-reflective. This is the most difficult to define, for it is so dependent upon and integrated into the other features. But it is crucial because it instantiates the recognition that the analyst is also a participant in the very practices, formations, and contexts he or she is analyzing (another dimension of cul-

268

tural studies' circularity). This is not so much, I believe, a question of identity, or of a politics of location, but of reflecting on one's own relation to the various trajectories and dimensions, places and spaces, of the context one is exploring and mapping: theoretical, political, cultural, and institutional. As Frow and Morris describe it: "It is perhaps this 'self-situating' and *limiting* moment of analysis that most clearly distinguishes work in cultural studies from some other modes of analysis on which its practitioners may draw . . . cultural studies tends to incorporate into its object of study a critical account of its own motivating questions—and thus of the institutional framework and disciplinary rules by which its research imperatives are formed" (1993, xvii–xviii).

It is crucial to recognize the way in which Frow and Morris dissociate themselves from a psychological notion of self-reflection, for what is involved here is less a matter of a personal ethic, a psychological state, or a laundry list of subject-positions, than a matter of a form of discursive practice and an analysis of institutional conditions.

III

I am aware that my description of cultural studies may seem—and probably is—rather idealistic. While I am not sure that anyone has ever actually done what I have described, there are certainly scholars who have made the project comprehensible. But even the best writers in cultural studies have their problems, and I think they are serious problems and are only now beginning to be confronted. The first is simple to describe: Consider some of the statements I have quoted and made about how cultural studies addresses people, not only intellectuals and academics. Think of Raymond Williams's notion that cultural studies is a pedagogical project that we bring to people for whom these issues are real, personal, and immediate concerns. Cultural studies has not succeeded in doing that very well. Antonio Gramsci said that there are two functions of the political intellectual: the first is to know more than the other side; the second is to share that knowledge. Whatever one may think of the production of knowledge in cultural studies, it remains largely an academic discourse encircled by its theoretical vocabulary. I do not mean to suggest that we as academics and intellectuals should give up that vocabulary. It is necessary to what we do. I find it ironic that we expect car mechanics to have a technical vocabulary, we expect astronomers and physicists to have a technical vocabulary, but we do not expect people describing what is probably the most complex phenomenon we know of—human life—to have a technical

vocabulary. The problem is not the elitism of the vocabulary, for it is necessary for the production of certain kinds of knowledge, productions that are, in
a sense, always elitist. But production and distribution, however closely articulated, are not the same, and it is the second half of Gramsci's prescription
that has yet to be realized: to share that knowledge with people who want to
do something with it. That, it seems to me, is the problem facing cultural
studies—as well as many other forms of intellectual discourse. It is a problem
facing those of us in communications perhaps more profoundly than in any
other discipline, not only because communications is such an important political issue in the contemporary world, but also because we are the people
who most directly deal with the media by which communication and education have to be accomplished in the contemporary world. And this will no
doubt require reconstituting pedagogy in the face of such critical tasks as
cultural studies poses. However, it should also be clear that there is no necessary reason why those charged with communicating knowledge have to be
the same as those producing it; this is certainly one of the lessons that the
New Right has taught us. Perhaps we need to think about educating a generation of students who are more comfortable with both sides of the political
function; or perhaps we need to think about educating and training students
who consciously think of themselves as the translators of knowledge into the
public realm, as cultural workers in a variety of institutional sites. Is it not
peculiar that we have journalists trained to report science but none trained to
report social and cultural knowledge?

A second problem is more serious and difficult, and I touched on it earlier.
Recent work in postcolonial studies, and in certain traditions of cultural
studies, has begun to challenge some of the most fundamental concepts and
assumptions of cultural studies on the grounds that they are themselves implicated in particularly powerful structures and technologies of power.[19]
Many of the categories that we continue to use not only in cultural studies but
in cultural criticism more broadly—categories of the nation, culture, society,
race, gender, identity, institutions—were, not coincidentally, invented or significantly rearticulated at about the same time as the rise of modern society
and modern systems of power. Culture, as Raymond Williams points out, was
first used in a context outside of agriculture in the early eighteenth century,
with the rise of industrial society. As Paul Gilroy (1993) has argued, race itself
as a category was invented in the nineteenth century. To the extent that culture is always implicated in relations of power, cultural studies has to begin
to examine its own cultural categories. It has to question the concepts that

have founded its own critical practices. It must begin to ask to what extent we, as cultural studies analysts, are locked into the very systems of power that we are attempting to get out of because we use the cultural practices, categories, and concepts of that system of power. There is no easy way out of this dilemma, and I refuse to resign myself to it by saying that it is simply the fate of intellectuals. I think that is the lazy way. Instead what is demanded of us is that we begin to accept the possibility that we can rearticulate (which is not to say escape) our own social and cultural determinations, that we can begin to rearticulate our cultural and historical identities, that we can challenge our inherited philosophical common sense, in the name of the political struggles that must be carried on if we are to contribute as intellectuals to the creation of a better world in the face of the pressing challenges posed by the global conditions in which we are all living, albeit in different ways and places. We have to begin to describe and theorize the ways in which, in our present circumstances, culture often operates as both the site and the weapon of other—economic and political—struggles, even as these struggles appear to be always and already cultural. I believe cultural studies can be useful for this task; it will have to avoid the easy answer that once again simply puts the economic in the leading position as the machine of history in order to find a new and more sophisticated model of the contemporary articulations of cultural and economic practices.

I hope it is clear that my vision of cultural studies defines its task somewhat differently from others': the task of cultural studies is not to somehow map aesthetics onto the social or theory onto the textual. It is not about tracing the trajectory of desire and/or power or the inscription of the social in the text. It does not take theory as a metaphor for social or textual processes, nor does it take social or textual processes as metaphors of theory. Cultural studies is not about rediscovering what we already know—whether in the structures of domination or the possibilities of resistance—about the relations between the text and the subject or between the subject and the social. Cultural studies is not about communication, ideology, desire, or pleasure, although all these may enter into it. It is not about the ethnographic documentation of the local. Cultural studies is about mapping the deployment and effects of discursive practices and alliances within the context of specific social spaces and milieus. It is about the relations or articulations between (1) discursive alliances as the configurations of practices that define where and how people live specific practices and relations; (2) the practices and configurations of daily life (as the sites of specific forms of determinations, controls, structures of power, struggles, pleasures, etc.); and (3) the apparatuses of power that mobilize different practices and effects to organize the space of human life and the possibilities of alliances. And that means that cultural studies must avoid reducing power to the simple terms of domination, subordination, and resistance, and locating power only within culture and/or everyday life. It must struggle, in a sense, to escape culture—if it is to discover the powers of culture.

Toward a Genealogy of the State

of Cultural Studies

This is a significant moment, not only for the Left in the United States, but for cultural studies as well (although the problems facing cultural studies dwindle in comparison with the dystopian trajectories that seem to be leading us into the next millennium). Still, insofar as cultural studies purports to engage with such trajectories (and, in a certain way, a neoconservative articulation of cultural studies may be part of the mechanism constructing them), the question of the state of cultural studies is worth raising. In fact, cultural studies has never been in a more precarious and ambivalent position that it is now in the U.S. academy. In one sense it is certainly flourishing and prolifering throughout the academy, across space, institutions, and disciplines. In another sense, that very success has produced at least two conditions that threaten (which is not to say negate) its viability as a political and intellectual project.[1]

First, it has become so easily and broadly applied to a wide range of academic projects as to lose any sense of its own distinctive project. Now perhaps this is unavoidable and even necessary: when it rains, one seeks a good wide umbrella and, to continue the metaphor, progressive academics certainly need to come together not only to get in out of the rain but to ally their projects under a common banner. Cultural studies seems to be the umbrella of choice these days. But this also has serious dangers. Thus when Jan Radway was asked recently about "the growing prominence, indeed the hegemony, of cultural studies," she responded: "You'd think that some of us who have long been associated with cultural studies would be happy. But we're concerned by how easily it has been taken up and by the kind of research and writing that it increasingly seems to generate" (quoted in Winkler 1994). Part of the problem here is a question of representation. In what sense and where is cultural studies hegemonic? How broadly must we cast the net to make this claim seem as reasonable as it apparently does to the readers of the *Chronicle of Higher Education,* or *Lingua Franca,* or even the *Village Voice*?

Second, as the image of cultural studies as hegemonic has become commonsensical in at least some part of the media that cares about the academy, that image has become, paradoxically, extraordinarily narrow. Whether through the construction of celebrities or through attacks on particular scholars, what the media are producing is an especially truncated and static image of cultural studies. Nowhere is there the sense that part of what has made cultural studies so attractive for young progressive scholars is its sense of itself as an unstable and contested field of intellectual and political practices. That is, what cultural studies is or should be at any particular juncture (in any particular struggle) is part of what needs to be worked out. Instead the media identify cultural studies with a charismatic (and somewhat diverse) group of black intellectuals or with a particular "populist" position in the field of cultural studies (a position that is constantly in danger of sliding from the important recognition that the practice of consumption may have contradictory and even productive possibilities to a rather uncritical celebration of consumption) or with a particular issue that can easily be constructed as scandalous (e.g., the science wars).[2]

It is this dual construction of cultural studies by contradictory vectors of representation (one expanding it beyond recognition, one contracting it beyond redemption) that places cultural studies scholars in the untenable position Radway describes above. Personally I have nothing against the "umbrella" function of the term—as long as we don't get so many people under the umbrella that it offers no protection. In that sense, perhaps the simplest way to understand and defend this overly broad use of cultural studies is as a return to the empirical which yet refuses to give up the necessary advances of the theoretical. To put it another way, part of the success of cultural studies in the U.S. academy in the 1980s might be understood as a response against the excesses of high theory without simply allowing the pendulum to swing back to an antitheoretical empiricism (many of the critics of cultural studies speak from one or the other of these extremes). On the other hand, I would want to differentiate cultural studies in some narrower (and hopefully more productive) sense from just the attempt to combine theory with a concern for questions of the "local" and even of power. I would also want to distance it from all of the inflated claims occasionally made on its behalf: claims that would make cultural studies into the new organization (and hence salvation) for the humanities; claims that would build its counterdisciplinary impulses into a new totalizing discipline: and claims that somehow demand that cultural studies become the latest incarnation of the academic dream of an intellectual revolutionary agency: the practice of cultural studies as the life of the organic intellectual. On the contrary, I believe that cultural studies must remain more modest in its goals and self-representations.

Stuart Hall described the university (specifically the Centre for Contemporary Cultural Studies) as "the locus to which we [progressive intellectuals/educators/activists of the English New Left interested in questions of cultural change] *retreated* when that conversation in the open world could no longer be continued: it was politics by other means" (1990a, 12). This description plays into a common romanticization of the "marginality" (in Hall's terms) of cultural studies, and into a dangerous anti-academic critique of cultural studies. I want to argue, on the contrary, that the particular biographies of this generation of cultural studies scholars are less important than two other lessons of this history: first, that the questions of cultural studies are never generated within the academy (i.e., that cultural studies is always responding to "the dirty outside world") and second, that the move into the academy, the move to a "politics by other means," was itself constitutive of cultural studies at least in its British (and I would add U.S.) articulations. That is, cultural studies is a rigorous intellectual—even academic—practice that seeks to produce better knowledge of the political context of the world, knowledge that opens up new and hopefully progressive possibilities of struggle and transformation.

I am sure that using the example of British cultural studies here will raise the already hackneyed argument about its mythological status as an origin which erases the multiple histories and sites of cultural studies traditions. So let me be very clear about my use of it here. I do not want to argue that British cultural studies—even with all of its internal diversity and divisiveness—defines either the origin or the proper form of cultural studies. I do think it exemplifies certain aspects of my own sense of cultural studies and therefore it can serve an important educative function. I also think that at least certain fractions of British cultural studies played an important genealogical role in the current success of cultural studies, if not globally then certainly within the United States. At the very least it enabled some scholars and scholarly traditions to reconstitute and name themselves, and it helped them to place themselves in relation to other bodies of critical work. The move into the Centre for Contemporary Cultural Studies may have been a retreat from one possibility, but it was also a condition of possibility for a cultural studies that is both academic and, I might add, inevitably commodified. Thus, I would argue, the current (over)commodification of cultural studies is not an imposition of some external set of power relations on an otherwise pure political practice, but a specific articulation of the contradictory terrain on which cultural studies (in this genealogical trajectory) set out.

Hence the troubled state of cultural studies in the United States cannot simply be attributed to its institutionalization in the academy, nor to the fact of its agreeing in some sense to its own commodification. Rather we must look at the particular forms of both its institutionalization and its commodification. This suggests that we begin the impossible but necessary task of narrating the history—the formation, reception, articulation, distribution, and proliferation—of cultural studies in the United States. This is a daunting task, and here I only want to make some observations that might contribute to such a history.

We might begin by inquiring into the specific conditions, in the United States, of the rapid proliferation of cultural studies throughout the academy as the specific form of its success in the United States. Here again we could decide to focus on any number of different trajectories. For example, we might point out that it is the baby boomers (especially the second half) and the so-called Generation X (especially the first half) that have so passionately adopted cultural studies. These generations were not only the first in the world to be raised on the media but also the first to live in a context in which a commercial popular culture dominated the national culture, including that of an upwardly mobile petit bourgeoisie. Moreover both generations have been crucially shaped, albeit in different ways, by the apparent failures of the civil rights movement and the counterculture, and the lack of any credible alternative progressive presence on the political scene. They have also been shaped by the rise, since the election of Richard Nixon, of a new trajectory of conservatism, marked by the emergence of charismatic political and intellectual conservatives (and the absence of any such charismatic figures on the Left).

Paradoxically, the collapse of the Left and the fragmentation of its constituency into the multiplicity of identity politics also invigorated the political possibilities of the academic Left with the formation of all sorts of constituency-defined units—African American studies, women's studies, Chicano studies, gay and lesbian studies, and so on—displacing the interdisciplinary claims of American studies with a more politicized if also fractious practice. These constituency-defined approaches have helped to shape both particular discourses within cultural studies (e.g., black cultural studies) and particular ways of doing cultural studies in the United States (see Henderson 1996). This suggests a second trajectory: while the existence of these multiply overlapping intellectual and institutional formations provided a terrain within which cultural studies' commitment to "realpolitik" could find a sympathetic ear, at the same time cultural studies' lack of a preconstituted constituency, its explicit commitment to theory, and its rapid appropriation by university administrators in a time of shrinking budgets and competitive demands made it something to be distanced from if not resisted. (Moreover the fact that each of these areas provided something like a home for political intellectuals who identified with their particular constituencies allowed the perception to be created that cultural studies was largely the product of white male intellectuals.) Furthermore, because cultural studies appeared as an important force in the U.S. academy at a relatively late date (perhaps the mid-1980s) as compared with its appearance in other countries (Australia, Canada, and others), these constituency-oriented, politicized, and interdisciplinary endeavors were also bound to have a much greater claim and impact on cultural studies in the United States than in some other parts of the world.

The claim that cultural studies did not appear in any significant way in the United States until the mid-1980s points to yet another determining trajectory. For the claim is only true in the context of the taken-for-granted organization of power within the academy, not only around the disciplines but around particular disciplines as well. There are two conditions operating here: First, in the United States, cultural studies became visible only as something that operated within the existing disciplines, even as it claimed to disrupt and challenge the disciplinary structure. That is, unlike other interdisciplinary challenges, cultural studies has been only minimally successful in establishing a real interdisciplinary institutional presence. Rather it has operated within disciplines where it presents itself as a challenge to the discipline that provides the parameters of its practice. (For example, cultural studies in English has been used as a way to open the field to a broader range of texts without radically challenging most of the disciplinary assumptions. The same has been true across the curriculum.) But the second part of this trajectory involves the hierarchical status and power of the different disciplines in the U.S. academy. Thus the already taken-for-granted history of cultural studies in the United States begins with its appearance in the discipline of English literature (and, to a lesser extent, anthropology, and to an even lesser extent sociology and American studies). Apparently, cultural studies in the United States began only when it infiltrated such departments and was noticed by their professional organizations (the MLA and the AAA). I want to return to this point in a minute, because I think it is necessary to contest this particular disciplinizing history if we are to understand its current state.

However, the most important determinant of the peculiar form of cultural studies' success in the United States involves the economics of the academy, for the sheer size of the higher education systems defines it as a lucrative and attractive market—with competitions for commodities such as students and textbooks. In fact, unlike other nations, academic publishing—both texts and trade books—is a highly competitive and reasonably profitable market. In that context, cultural studies in the United States has been largely driven by the needs and actions of the publishing industry. Obviously, I cannot do justice to this trajectory in a few sentences, but it is worth pointing out that cultural studies has been more visible and successful as a marketing category for books than for professors. Publishers quite naturally have tried to incorporate older bodies of work (leftist politics, critical theory, film theory, and media criticism) into the new category of cultural studies; and they have attempted to link cultural studies with their already existing major markets in the largest disciplines of the humanities and social sciences. In publishing terms, cultural studies is everything from "high" theory to "low" or popular content, carefully and primarily articulated to the concerns of literature and anthropology. This link has been supplemented in the past five years by the overvisibility of issues of identity (especially around notions of race and ethnicity) in cultural studies, and of multiculturalism across the academy, which has enabled publishers simply to incorporate the concerns of the various constituency-oriented fields into their new "chic" category of cultural studies.

But these trajectories, even if developed further, would still not be adequate to construct a history of the reception and rearticulation of cultural studies in the United States, nor would they adequately explain its current state. In fact, one might have to begin with a very different sort of question, a more Foucauldian question: Why is it that a cultural studies project did not arise earlier in the United States? There have been, after all, numerous intellectual openings in the twentieth century that, in retrospect, clearly could have given rise to indigenous articulations of cultural studies (and that are now being rearticulated retrospectively to cultural studies). Among others one might think of certain traditions of Afro-Caribbean and African American criticism; progressivism (and its intellectual affiliations with the Chicago school of social thought); early research on media (such as Lippman's *Public Opinion* and the Payne studies); significant efforts at interdisciplinary and multimethodological studies of communication (Lazarfeld's attempt to link quantitative and critical studies at Columbia University or Schramm's later establishment of the Institute of Communications Research at the University of Illinois); the potential influence of Harold Innis (from Canada) or Kenneth Burke (both of whom did create, in their own work, a model for a cultural studies, but significantly, neither was taken up particularly in those terms in the United States); the mass culture debates of the 1940s and '50s; and, of course, the limited experimentation and temporary successes of American studies after the 1950s.

Many of these moments share something with the conditions canonically observed to mark the emergence of the British cultural studies tradition. Both Richard Hoggart's and Raymond Williams's early works are generally interpreted as interventions into a particular crisis of "English" national identity following the Second World War, a crisis embodied in the threat of "Americanization" and distributed in the materiality of American media and popular culture. Even Thompson's work, with its concerns for the origins and contributions of working-class culture, can be located in this crisis, for the crisis was, in part, a threat to the very existence of the working class (in its potential embourgeoisment) and its culture. However oversimplified this reading of the emergence of British cultural studies may be (ignoring, for example, the more varied interests of the New Left), it is still worth pointing out that U.S. intellectuals have confronted the problem of national identity and its relationship to culture and communication throughout the twentieth century (if not the entire history of the nation), and that many of the openings mentioned above are obviously analogous if not homologous to that which enabled the beginnings of British cultural studies. That is to say, if cultural studies arose in Britain in part as a response to a perceived need to reflect upon and study the relationship of culture to, on the one hand, communication (at least in the form of media culture) and, on the other, to the problem of national identity,[3] then it is somewhat surprising that a comparable tradition did not arise at least as early in the United States, where questions of culture, communication, and identity (involving issues of political representation, citizenship, technology, mobility, immigration, multiculturalism, etc.) have been central since at least the end of the nineteenth century. In fact, I cannot begin to offer a solution to this puzzle and do not intend to pursue this question except to suggest that insofar as the relation of power and culture was theorized at all in these various possible openings, power was assumed to be an external intervention into or imposition on the processes of culture. On the other side of the Atlantic, one of the theoretical conditions of the possibility of cultural studies was precisely the recognition that power operates within culture (and communication) itself.

However, I want to turn to a different trajectory and a different set of questions. For if, in fact, the specific nature of cultural studies as it developed in England depended on the fact that, as Perry Anderson (1968) has argued, the question of culture as a matter of normative and historical concern could only have been raised in the field of English literature (through the influence of F. R. Leavis and what Williams would call the "culture and society tradition"), the fact of the matter is that, in postwar America, the issue of culture, especially as it was expressed in the so-called mass culture debates (and journals such as the *Partisan Review*),[4] was often located in other fields, such as sociology, American studies, and education and, during the 1960s, was largely displaced into the field of communication. Perhaps this helps to explain why, historically and genealogically, the discipline of communication was the site of the first major opening for an obvious and explicit cultural studies project in the United States. It may be somewhat controversial to place the discipline of communications at the center of a discussion of cultural studies in the United States. In fact, not only has communication provided key resources for the construction of various indigenous cultural studies, but, equally important, along with the field of education communication studies was the first discipline to take up and provide a space in the United States academy for the developing work of British cultural studies. As early as the 1960s, James Carey was proposing something called "cultural studies" as part of an interdisciplinary project that would define "a cultural approach to communication."[5] And along with a small group of cultural historians and sociologists,[6] Carey was one of the first intellectuals to take seriously the work of Richard Hoggart, Raymond Williams, and the newly formed Centre for Contemporary Cultural Studies.[7] The field of communications has, over the decades, continued to provide a place, albeit not without resistance and initially often a minoritarian and marginal place, for emergent trends within the expanding field of cultural studies (e.g, popular culture, global culture, postmodernism). The fact that this history has itself been marginalized if not erased says a lot about the hierarchical organization of disciplinary power in the academy and the relation of the media to particular professional associations.[8]

I want to address three questions: Why was the field of communications open to cultural studies as early as the 1960s? What was the relationship of communications to the project of British cultural studies? And finally, how has the centrality of communications in the history of U.S. cultural studies affected cultural studies in the United States (i.e., in what ways has it determined the current state of cultural studies)? Again, I can only make some brief suggestions in each of these areas. The first question is perhaps the easiest to think about, partly because much of the work has already been done by others, including James Carey, Wick Rowland, and Ellen Wartella. The field of (mass) communications, while in its institutional infancy in the 1960s, already had a longer intellectual legacy. That legacy included an explicitly moral and political agenda defined by the Progressive movement, a sophisticated interpretive theoretical foundation defined by pragmatism and various idealist philosophers (including Cassirer, Burke, and Langer as well as various members of the Frankfurt school) and an unstated populism embodied in the constantly recurring notion of an active audience participating in a differentiated system of cultural texts (see Grossberg 1989a). In all of these precursors to the discipline, questions of communication were intimately tied to issues of culture and community, to the social nature of human reality, and to the political possibilities of utopian aspirations. However, under the pressures of the growing status of "science" and logical positivism, the emergence of psycholinguistics and information theory, the demands of propaganda research and the recurring public fears over new forms and technologies of communication, that legacy was largely submerged. The field of (mass) communications, into the 1970s, was largely quantitative and scientistic, seeking to find the statistically or experimentally verifiable effects determined by particular media and message variables. Its theoretical foundations were almost entirely located in neobehaviorist psychology and structural-functional sociology. The normative, theoretical, and populist impulses implicit in the study of communication were, to say the least, rendered suspect and invisible. While there was a vital and important (albeit marginal) counterposition defined by political economy, its framework was largely reductionist and economist. Cultural studies was appropriated and deployed as a countermeasure into this field of struggle; it was aimed primarily against this particular hegemonic paradigm but also against the vulgar political economy which defined the only available alternative at the time. Consequently the battle was largely fought on phenomenological grounds: meaning versus effects; interpretation versus quantification; consciousness versus behavior. Drawing upon its historical roots (as well as a specific appropriation of early British cultural studies) gave this emergent paradigm (best captured in Carey 1989) an authority that was largely unavailable to communications departments outside the United States.

At the same time, the fact that the intellectual roots of this alternative (and certainly at the time oppositional) paradigm did not define an explicit (or even, for that matter, implicit) theory of communication created a second feature that enabled the field to be open to cultural studies in a way that most other disciplines at the time could not be. The emergent "cultural approach to communication" was able to—in fact was forced to—operate with an ambiguity surrounding the concept of culture. While the various forms this ambiguity took at times resembled the polysemy Williams identified in the "culture and society tradition," they were not identical. I have argued elsewhere (Grossberg 1992) that this ambiguity is not only productive in cultural studies but is absolutely essential to it. Whatever form it takes—culture as text and process, as communication and Weltanschauung, as communication and elite practices; communication as problem and solution, as a representation of and for reality, as community and representation—the fact that such ambiguities seemed almost unavoidable in the attempt to formulate an oppositional paradigm distinguished discussions of culture in communication from those taking place in the 1970s in both English and anthropology. Finally, the almost total lack of self-reflective theoretical work in the field left a real and serious vacuum which made the project of cultural studies with its strong commitment to "the detour through theory" particularly attractive.[9]

The fact that the early work of British cultural studies was appropriated into this disciplinary struggle meant that the project of British cultural studies would inevitably be read as an alternative approach to the study of communication and media. There is in fact a certain historical rationale to this identification. Writing about the reception of Richard Hoggart's foundational book, *The Uses of Literacy,* Stuart Hall acknowledged that it was read "—such were the imperatives of the moment—essentially as a text about the mass media" (1969–70, 2). Consequently cultural studies was framed, both within and outside the Centre, as a literary-based alternative to the existing work on mass communication. Hall continued: "The notion that the Centre, in directing its attention to the critical study of 'contemporary culture' was, essentially, to be a centre for the study of television, the mass media and popular arts . . . though never meeting our sense of the situation . . . nevertheless came by default, to define us and our work." Of course, what Hall seems to be at least hinting at here is that this was, somehow, an inappropriate or inaccurate reading of the Centre's work, that cultural studies is a radically alternative practice to the very practice of constituting and interpreting the mass media and popular culture as objects of study.

Again, an adequate discussion of this issue would require more time and space than I can devote to it here. Certainly, the media and mass communication were among the major concerns of the Centre, and they saw themselves at least partially involved in a debate with the field of communication. But, at the very least, it never defined the totality of the interests at those of the Centre (even as they were trying to construct a collective understanding of cultural studies), nor did they ever equate culture with communication (or with texts, as I shall suggest later). Yet this simple equation has had profound effects on the development of cultural studies not only in the field of communication but in the U.S. academy more generally. For paradoxically, even while many of the disciplines that have recently "discovered" cultural studies have ignored its history in the discipline of communications, they have at the same time uncritically accepted a number of key slippages and assumptions about cultural studies that were the result of the particular appropriation of cultural studies within communications. In fact, in order for cultural studies to accomplish what those in communications intended for it, it had to compromise and reinvent itself in the image of communication. Cultural studies was reduced to a theory of communication by too quickly equating "culture" and "communication." Those who championed cultural studies— and I include myself here—whether intentionally or not, ended up reconstructing cultural studies itself as "communicational cultural studies."[10] This reduction can, in part, be explained by the fact that at least some people misread and then uncritically adopted Raymond Williams's and James Carey's apparent identifications of communication and culture. The result has been that the project of cultural studies has been submerged under a model of communication, rendering it an alternative paradigm of rather than a serious challenge to the existing forms of communication studies. And equally important, political struggles have been increasingly reduced to struggles over communication and culture which can be magically solved by the proliferation of communicative and cultural practices. I want to begin to look at the consequences of this too narrow vision of cultural studies, a vision that abandons what I think of as the radical project and practice of cultural studies.[11]

By equating culture and communication, communicational cultural studies conflates the general problematic of cultural studies,[12] with its instantiation as a question about the constitution and politics of textuality (i.e., about the nature of cultural and/or communicational practices). This itself has a number of important consequences. First, it installs the primacy of signification (with its logic of identity and difference) over power (with its logic of determination). It reduces the entire project of cultural studies to the admittedly important political and contextual struggle to put questions of ideology (signification, representation, and identity) on the agenda. As a result, the politics of culture becomes a question of meaning and identity (with an occasional nod to pleasure). Power (domination and subordination) is always hierarchical, understood on the model of either the oppressor and the oppressed or oppression and transgression. And following the idealist tradition of modern philosophy and social thought, "the real"—the material conditions of possibility and of effectivity, the material organization and consequences of life—disappears into culture, and social life is reduced to experience. All cultural studies has to worry about is culture!

Second, the conflation of the problematic of cultural studies (articulation) with the question of textuality legitimates the reification of Stuart Hall's encoding/decoding model (1980b). What was originally offered as a theoretical-semiotic solution to a particular contextually defined set of empirical problems has become instead *the* general model of cultural studies. At the same time, the sophistication of Hall's model was (and is) ignored so that it becomes little more than a recycling of the old, theoretically discredited, linear model of communication—sender-message-receiver—but the terms are changed (to hide the guilty): production-text-consumption. There are in fact two issues here: whether the way in which this model is used seriously distorts the power and originality of Hall's argument (as well as of Marx's analysis of the relations among these three moments of the cycle of production, see Hall 1974) and whether all of culture and cultural studies can be understood within this model.

The encoding/decoding model is generally used to frame a tripartite approach to the study of culture: the researcher is compelled to study the institutions and practices by which a particular text is produced, followed by a literary-critical analysis of the "encoded meaning" of the text, completed by an "ethnographic" study (usually in the form of interviews, questionnaires, or selected observational studies) of the uses to which different audiences put the text and/or the different ways in which they interpret it. Of course, very few studies actually do all three and even fewer ever get around to examining the articulated relationships between these three moments, or the relationship between this "cycle of textuality" and the questions of social and political effectivity. Particular studies may argue against the need for a consideration of the context of production (since intentions do not guarantee meanings). Or the analysis of the text itself may be considered unnecessary (since the intrinsic properties of the text do not guarantee meanings, thus granting specific audiences the full weight and power of determining the actual meanings). Or the ethnography may be jettisoned as either unnecessary (we already know that audiences are active) or complicitous (assuming the audience has so much power plays right into the hands of capitalism).

By taking the problem of culture to be in some way solved by dividing it into three separable moments, communicational cultural studies leaves the disciplinary practices and methodologies of political economic, literary, and anthropological studies largely in place. Cultural studies becomes reduced to the task of bridging the unbridgeable gap between the three disciplines. For the most part, research involves a hermeneutic project of uncovering a relationship, a structure of meaning, that already and necessarily exists. Whether embodied within the text or within the lives of some fraction of the audience, whether carried out through some form of textual interpretation or of ethnographic practice, communicational cultural studies attempts to open for critical scrutiny a dimension of human existence—meaning—that cannot be reduced to materiality but that bears some as yet undetermined relationship (representation, distortion, etc.) to this external reality. Communicational cultural studies is about the ways people make sense of the world and their lives, and the sense that is made for them. This dimension (of meaning) must be relatively autonomous of the real material and economic conditions of the world and people's lives. Consequently communicational cultural studies can never actually confront the question of effects, because it cannot theorize the relationship of meaning to anything else. It cannot even decide or explain when meaning (signification) becomes representation (ideology), for that involves its articulation to material practices and social relationships. Communicational cultural studies remains basically comfortable with the disciplinary boundaries of whatever field it is operating in, having largely too often abandoned the interdisciplinarity that is at the heart of cultural studies.

Its questions, its methods, and not surprisingly its answers as well remain firmly entrenched within the boundaries of culture and within the only slightly expanded boundaries of the discipline.

It is not that such questions—of production, textuality, and consumption—are irrelevant. On the contrary, they may well be crucial parts of the context within which cultural studies must locate specific cultural practices. But their identity and power cannot be identified apart from that context. The problem is that communicational cultural studies has prejudged the terms within which any context is to be analyzed and within which the effects of any practice are to be sought out and measured. Such a view fails to understand cultural studies' more radical attempt to locate specific cultural practices within their complexly determined and determining contexts. It reduces cultural studies to a concern with texts (no matter how intertextual) and/or audiences that can be identified and analyzed, at least initially, in isolation from their place within the material contexts of everyday life. In that sense, the study of producers, texts, and audiences merely provides some of the material with which cultural studies must grapple in its attempt to understand specific contextual relations of culture and power. And since such material does not directly reveal how it is located within the context, we cannot know in advance what knowledge they provide us with, what we know as a result of such studies. At the same time, it may well be the case that such material does not provide the most important determinations.

Communicational cultural studies, in the end, reduces culture to the symbolic representation of power and grants it a certain apparent autonomy. As a result, communicational cultural studies finds itself constantly rediscovering what it already knew: regarding domination, that particular cultural practices reproduce the structures of domination and subordination and that they reinscribe relations of identity, difference, and inequality; and regarding subordination, communicational cultural studies seems satisfied with finding the cracks in the processes of reproduction and reinscription. The assumption that people are active and capable of struggle and resistance becomes an apparent discovery. Domination and resistance are assumed to be understood in advance, to operate in always and everywhere the same ways. But the real questions remain unasked and unanswered: questions about the specific forms in which domination and subordination are organized, about the ways they operate, about how they are lived, mobilized, and empowered, that is, questions about the actual ways in which cultural practices are deployed in relations of power and how they themselves deploy power, questions about the actual effects of culture within specific contexts, questions about the relations of culture to practices of governance.

My claim is not that all work under the banner of cultural studies in the field of communication followed this particular trajectory into "communicational cultural studies" but rather that this has become the dominant trajectory and model of cultural studies in the field of (mass) communications. Moreover, while again I do not want to suggest that all work carried on under the banner of cultural studies in the United States fits this model, I do believe that it has become the dominant model and image of cultural studies. This largely explains the paradoxical state of cultural studies with which I began this paper. Of course, I am not claiming that the field of communications is somehow responsible for this trajectory, although I do believe that it has played a significant role and must take some responsibility. But other conditions and events have also had a part in this history: for example, the fact is that many academics in the United States were "introduced" to British cultural studies and to cultural studies through Richard Johnson's "What Is Cultural Studies Anyway?" Published in *Social Text* in Winter 1986–87, it was the first major defining piece from within British cultural studies that was easily and widely available to the U.S. academic audience. Johnson's essay presents a model of cultural studies that closely resembles the description of communicational cultural studies I have given above.[13] A fuller explanation of how this particular reading of cultural studies was put into place in the U.S. academy would have to re-turn to some of the conditions I discussed earlier.

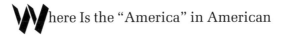

Where Is the "America" in American Cultural Studies?

I want to talk about the geography of cultural studies and about the politics of the increasingly common use of geographical adjectives to modify cultural studies. Let me make clear how I am using cultural studies, for I have come to realize and accept (if not happily) that there are two distinct uses of the term that have to be acknowledged. On the one hand, the term is applied to a large and varied body of progressive and critical work in the academy. Perhaps this is unavoidable and even necessary; and perhaps this is what Fred Jameson (1993) had in mind when he recently described cultural studies as "mass culture plus identity politics," although the umbrella is certainly broad enough to cover those who show not the slightest interest in mass culture. On the other hand, there is a narrower sense of cultural studies as a distinct set of intellectual and political practices (which I have characterized elsewhere; see Grossberg 1995). This more specific sense is not so narrow as to be identified with a particular school or national tradition or discipline; rather it is characterizable as an alliance or loose network or, to use Dwight Conquergood's felicitous term, a caravan. Over the years, my own work has been described as "British cultural studies in the United States" and as "American cultural studies." I would now reject both of these appellations, not only for my own work, but for my fellow travelers as well. And for the rest of this paper, it is the spatiality of the latter sense of cultural studies that I want to interrogate.

DIS-PLACING CULTURAL STUDIES

Let me begin by asking what is at stake in attempting to link cultural studies to particular geographical places—for the phrase "American cultural studies" can be used to mean many different things. First then, consider those articulations of cultural studies to geography to which I am fundamentally opposed: that there can and should be a "more American" or properly American version of cultural studies.[1] This seems to presuppose that there is some uniquely American experience, unique not only to America, but somehow constitutive of the Americanness of all Americans as well. This seems to fly in the face of current "deconstructions" of both national and regional identities where, as Ghassan Hage (1994) describes it, people struggle in and over the field of "national belonging." It also seems to presuppose that there is something wrong with the "strong European inflection"[2] of much of cultural studies, something that can only and must be rectified by building an American cultural studies upon the unique contributions of American theorists. Such assertions form a prescriptive call for the spatial specificity of American cultural studies, a specificity defined by the "being there" of America.

What then are my objections? First, they are political: I am in fact suspicious of this attempt to introduce a kind of identity politics (so typical of the United States) into the discourse about cultural studies itself. I cannot help but wonder what such a desire—to name our own discourse by placing it within the "local" space of our national affiliation—signals. I fear that such calls are too easily articulated into and participate in the revival of ethnicity that Stuart Hall calls "cultural fundamentalism." But at the same time, there is something strange about this project of self-nomination, for it is usually the subordinated, the minor-ity, that finds it necessary to name their own culture, to have their existence and worth recognized. Why would American academics want to do this? Is there some as-yet-unnamed threat? Are we engaged in a struggle within the global academic power bloc? I can't help but feel that there is something ironic about the U.S. academy's having to name itself as if it were beleaguered, as if it were in a subordinate position, or even as if, somehow, its domination were being challenged. Of course, there is another possibility: by naming and thus locating itself, American cultural studies relinquishes its claim to universality. But this simply denies both the power of the American academy in the global circulation of intellectual work and the diversity of cultural studies in the United States. Moreover such a claim would be disingenuous, since there is little ground for assuming that cultural studies is being defined globally through some universalization of American norms. It is more likely readable as analogous with a conservative backlash in which the dominant fractions name themselves as the oppressed.

Kuan-Hsing Chen has taken an even stronger position. He argues that such national nominations are the dominant form of "transnational global cultural studies," and that they are all (whether subordinate or dominant) "in complicity with economic neo-imperialism and the neocolonial politics of the nation-state structure." Instead he proposes to interrogate the "unchallenged epistemological boundary of the political nation-state, as a 'local context' of cultural analysis, without taking into account the increasingly uneven process of globalization . . . in effect reproducing the nation-state boundary as it is parallel to the hierarchically and unevenly structured global division of economic and political power" (1996, 40). Furthermore, he argues that regionalism is but "an upgraded ghost of nationalism," that it potentially remains part of an imperialist project grounded in nationalism. And the issue is not simply that the crucial question—Who is the articulating subject of any regionalism?—is rarely asked. For it goes deeper than that. To put it crudely, Chen might lead us to wonder whether calls for a (regionally bounded) American cultural studies are merely reproducing NAFTA within the discourse of cultural studies itself.

Second, my objections to such spatializations of cultural studies are theoretical, although I do not mean to separate politics and theory so easily (and in fact, my "theoretical" objections could be derived from what I have already said about the "geonationalist" presuppositions of such a project). The problem is not the attempt to articulate theory and geography, but the way it is done. For whatever the scale of the spatial identity that is offered in such calls, however one moves up and down the scale—from local to national to regional—such identifications assume that culture (in this case, critical discursive practices) is essentially linked to place, even while they reify the concept of place itself. Too often, discussions of American cultural studies represent places as if they were coherent, bounded, and settled, as if identities were always constituted through identifications with or against such fixed places. "Place" is made to act as a guarantee of cultural belongingness. When applied to our own work, this can only be described as a failure of our own critical distance. Or, to put it in a more active voice, we seem to have abandoned our own critical discourses in favor of our own deeply felt nationalisms. Daniels has pointed out that "National identities are coordinated, often largely defined, by 'legends and landscapes,' by stories of golden ages, enduring traditions, heroic deeds and dramatic destinies located in ancient or promised homelands" (cited in Hall 1995, 182). Calls for American cultural studies are similarly built upon such legends and landscapes, upon imaginations of golden ages and enduring traditions, and so forth.

Stuart Hall has argued that "the ways in which culture, place and identity are imagined and conceptualized are increasingly untenable in the light of the historical and contemporary evidence" (1995, 186). To put it simply, neither cultures nor theories necessarily depend on place. This is not to deny that cultural practices have a geography, that they are spatially articulated. Cultural practices are always in place or, more accurately, em-placed. But such relations cannot be understood as a matter of origins or identities. For places do not exist independently of the ways they are articulated and invested in. Consequently we need to reject the commonsense view of place and re-place it with what Doreen Massey (1991) has called a "global sense of place" that would "match community and security with the kind of openness that can stimulate a positive sense of challenge and contestation" (Robins 1991, 17). As Massey (1992) has described it: "spatial movement, interaction, influence and communication have become so extended, so fast and so available, that the borderlands and boundaries which once used to define places as distinct and in some degree separable from each other are so often crossed that the notion of place which was previously viable has to be rethought . . . The changing social organization of space has . . . disrupted our existing forms of, and concepts of, place" (1992, 83).

According to Massey (1994), we must begin to think of places as intersections of influence and movements, relations and forces, "stretched" over space. Or, echoing Hall and Gilroy, we must stop thinking in terms of roots and start thinking in terms of *routes.* This is the power of a theory of diaspora as more than (without denying) its historical referent, as an alternative framework for thinking about imagined communities, tradition, and culture. If places are constructed out of wider sets of forces and relations, and if identities exist in terms of interconnectedness rather than counterposition (Massey 1994; I would prefer to say that identities exist in the structural possibilities of mobility and stability) then we need a sense of place that is complex, permeable, and flexible. Certainly we cannot begin to understand the specificity of a place by looking at that place (or its history) in isolation.

Perhaps the strongest example we have of such a theoretical shift is Paul Gilroy's brilliant treatise, *The Black Atlantic* (1993), which is too often read only as an argument against the nation as the appropriate unit of analysis in cultural studies. While this is an important point—cultures cannot be equated to nations[3]— I want to foreground Gilroy's own more radical sense of the "Black Atlantic" as "a nontraditional tradition, an irreducibly modern, ex-centric, unstable and asymmetrical cultural ensemble that cannot be apprehended through the manichean logic of binary coding" (1993, 198). I would take it even further, as a fairly radical attempt to spatialize culture and history. For what Gilroy is analyzing is not merely the relations among places, but constitutive movements across a space. That is, space is no longer merely the empty gaps between places. It is not merely the Cartesian space of directionality; it has a dimensionality of its own that is constituted by the trajectories that move across it. It has a density and a thickness of its own that is productive as well as produced. Thus I take it that Gilroy is arguing that the space of the North Atlantic is already race-d, that the race-d movements of the various circulations (of communities, commodities, capital, and culture) are part of the constitutive being of the space of the North Atlantic. It follows that culture is inseparable not from place, but from a distribution and movement of space, a distribution and movement in space.

My third objection to the spatial nomination of cultural studies—to the project of prescribing an American cultural studies—is analytical. That is, it seems to me to fundamentally misunderstand the nature of cultural studies itself. I have argued many times that cultural studies is a radically contextual practice. However, it is important to emphasize that the context of cultural studies is always and only defined by its project, its question (which is always political), not by its place (although of course places may be implicated in different ways in different questions). Consequently its theory and analyses are always hybrid and strategic. Its theory is "cheap" in the sense that you use whatever works, whatever gives you a better understanding of the context so as to open up new political possibilities. Cultural studies is about trying to do something that has not been done before without knowing ahead of time what resources will work. Cultural studies is never about British or French or American theory; it is not about theory at all—although theory plays an absolutely necessary role in its analyses. It is not about high theory or theoretical debates; it is not about marking theoretical differences or staking out theoretical positions. It is about finding theoretical resources that allow you to redescribe the context that has posed a political challenge. The fact that the context may be part of the United States, or the United States itself, or even the region of the Americas does not guarantee that a theory that has been locally articulated will provide the best resources. As David Morley puts it, "The local is not to be considered as an indigenous source of cultural identity which remains authentic only insofar as it is unsullied by contact with [the other]" (1992, 282). The local cannot be separated from the global, and so any attempt to understand the local cannot close its eyes to the power (and the resources) of the global.

Cornel West has taken a similar position regarding cultural studies: "The traveling of [British] cultural studies to the U.S. must be met with a critical reception and by critical what I mean is an appropriation of the best: acknowledging where the blindnesses were, while discussing to what degree British cultural studies can be related to the U.S. context" (1992a, 693). But we need to unpack this in order to avoid two possible errors: first, the assumption that there is a single homogeneous body of work that is called British cultural studies; and second, that there is a U.S. context defined independently of particular political projects and struggles. Obviously, there are various assumptions and absences in various British authors. David Harvey is correct to point to Raymond Williams's "situatedness within the structures of feelings that were associated with working class support for the British empire" (1995, 74). This may help us understand a significant absence in Williams's work; it does not tell us whether that absence is constitutive of Williams's theoretical position—that is, whether the fact of empire is absent or necessarily erased in that theory. Nor does it tell us, in every instance, the pertinence of that absence.

Similarly many critics have argued that British cultural studies places too much weight on class (and hence locates itself too strongly in marxism) and not enough on race for it to be appropriate to the American context; in particular, the constitutive fact of the Middle Passage and slavery demands something other than the model of British cultural studies. There are many answers to this objection: First, it is simply not true to say that British cultural studies has ignored race over class, unless one takes a particular moment in its history as paradigmatic. Second, the commitment to marxism in British cultural studies was never about class per se but about a particular materialist practice and about a particular contextual politics. And finally, of course, if nothing else, recent American history should convince us of the absolute centrality of class articulations (cutting across other social differences) in American politics and culture. Again, the issue is not what the political question is—that must be taken as the starting point of any cultural studies project—but rather what theoretical resources can be mobilized to say something new and useful about the political context in relation to the question that is being posed.

None of this negates the need to understand diverse intellectual histories, including "our own," however that might be taken. But why should we privilege national identity and belongingness over ethnic or religious or racial identities as the content of "our own"? After all, West does not claim that such contributions, whether understood as American or as something else, can or should be taken to constitute their own cultural studies. This would be to fall into an "Americanism in the life of the mind . . . [an] atavistic patriotism in intellectual matters" (1992a, 694). Rather West's sense of the importance of such histories is precisely that they help us to understand the ongoing practice of theoretical criticism and appropriation. Pragmatism did not develop ex nihilo; it came out of an engagement with various European philosophies and it took place in the context of particular historical and political demands. In fact, West's broader view of the theoretical grounds of cultural studies seems to be: You go where you need to:

> If you're an Afro-American and you're a victim of the rule of capital, and a European Jewish figure who was born in the Catholic Rhineland, by the name of Karl Marx, provides certain analytic tools, then you go there. You can't find too many insightful formations in Marx about what it is to be black; you don't go to Marx for that. You go to Marx to keep track of the rule of capital, interlocking elites, political, banking, financial, that's one crucial source of your hybridity. You don't care where you get it from, you just want to get people off your back.
>
> If you want to know what it means to be black, to be African in Western civilizations and to deal with issues of identity, with bombardment of degrading images . . . For what it means to be politically marginalized, you go to a particular tradition that deals with that. (1992b, 330)

Perhaps part of that tradition is American, perhaps part is African, perhaps part is diasporic. You go where you need to. But one need not create an "American tradition" that enforces a singularity on the notion of Americanness, or which takes for granted the spatial articulation of discourse. Such constructions are not only politically suspect, they hide the political context in which they themselves had been called into existence, for such a move can only hide the fact that such a closure poses its own political problematic per se unless it is contextualized.

In fact, it seems to be that when one begins to talk about traditions of American thought, the interesting question is quite different.[4] For there have been, at least in North America, a number of possible openings for cultural studies, especially in the twentieth century, including a tradition of black criticism and thought; the Chicago school of social thought; a Canadian media theory extending from Innis (perhaps to McLuhan); the postwar mass culture debates; the work of Kenneth Burke, and so forth. While all of these have been influential, and have even influenced various trajectories of cultural studies, the interesting question is why none of these openings actually gave rise at the time to a viable practice and tradition of cultural studies. Recently some people have tried to suggest that such work was, in and of itself, cultural studies, and hence those who are reproducing it have been doing cultural studies all along. This seems to me nothing but self-delusion and self-promotion. The Chicago school perhaps created the intellectual conditions for a version of cultural studies (and perhaps some of its work should now be understood as cultural studies), but the traditions to which it has given rise (such as symbolic interactionism or pragmatism) are not cultural studies, any more than the rhetorical or literary-critical projects that have emerged out of the work of Kenneth Burke (whose own work may have some claim to cultural studies) are cultural studies.

What has been given up is precisely the sense of radical contextuality,[5] of developing the theoretical resources and the critical practices that would enable one to respond to the concrete challenges of a specific social and political context. And with that contextuality, the interdisciplinarity implicit in such openings has been sutured back into disciplinary matrices that permit one to study only that which is within their intellectual boundaries. This is not to say that such openings have, then, been entirely closed. On the contrary, in the work of James Carey and Cornel West, the possibilities opened by the Chicago school have been taken up precisely by being "hybridized"; similarly, in Canada, writers such as Jody Berland have taken up the challenge and the legacy of Innis. Such hybridizations of American discourses have produced important contributions to the discursive caravan of contemporary cultural studies. But these hybridizations were absolutely crucial: the contextuality and interdisciplinarity of cultural studies do not come cheaply. They demand—at least thus far—that cultural studies be built on a certain ambiguity, an undecidability, about culture: culture is both the representation of reality and the reality we live in; culture is both the creative and the mundane; culture is both the set of signifying practices and the whole way of life. Or, as I have put it elsewhere, cultural studies is built upon a conflicted and conflictual theory of culture.[6]

RE-PLACING CULTURAL STUDIES

Is there then no sense in which we might speak of an American or U.S. cultural studies? Of course there are a number of different ways in which it might be appropriate and perhaps even useful. First, there is a descriptive sense. One could describe what is done here and now under the sign of cultural studies, but one is likely to be struck by the truly enormous diversity of that work. In fact, even narrowing down the here and now to something smaller, like Champaign-Urbana, does not help much given the diversity of "Illinois cultural studies." Much of what might be included in either of these descriptions would even be unique in some ways, in a variety of ways, to the determinations of the American (or Illinois) context. We might even find that the diversity, the distribution of cultural studies practices, will vary across space. But does that mean that we should move, in some normative way, to a judgment about which of these ways, which determinations, which practices, constitute an "authentically" American (or Illinois) cultural studies?

Part of the problem is, of course, that the field and the name (cultural studies) are too contested at the moment to allow us to say much that is useful without staking out our own claim to the term. But even with such a claim, I think it is impossible to find any consistency or commonality in politics, theory, or methodology that might enable us to cut across the diversity to find the "truly American inheritance." I suppose, if pressed, one could say that, for the most part, work that claims the name of cultural studies in the United States is dominated by:

—the problem of identity (and, more specifically, it tends to walk a thin line between essentialism and anti-essentialism)

—the mantra of gender, sexuality, and race (the convergence of feminist, queer, and antiracist politics)

—high theory (especially literary poststructuralism, media postmodernism, and anthropological postcolonialism)

—a communicational model of culture (as encoding-decoding, or production and consumption)

—textual-interpretive methodologies, supplemented with a weak sense of ethnographic research

—the vague shadow of an apocalyptic postmodernism, whether celebratory or pessimistic

—an ambivalence about its orientation and relation to already existing political constituencies

—disciplinary definitions of intellectual problems, projects, and standards

However, there is a second and more interesting possibility for describing the geography of cultural studies and foregrounding the relations of (national) place and critical practices. Such a geography is interested in a relation not of origins, but of the conditions of possibility. That is, we can inquire into the conditions for the emergence and appropriation of cultural studies in particular (national) contexts, conditions that determine in some ways its particular shape and articulations, determine where and how it is inserted and toward what it is aimed, conditions that at least determine the strata and territories in which the struggle (to define cultural studies as a theoretical, political, and empirical project) is located.

Recently two volumes have appeared that claim to present and make sense of Australian cultural studies, and we might compare the two models to see what help they can give us. Graeme Turner's primary claim in *Nation, Culture, Text* (1993) seems to be that what characterizes and distinguishes Australian cultural studies is its hybridity: it "speaks explicitly from a local position while drawing on a range of theoretical influences." Obviously, I do not think this distinguishes any local versions of cultural studies. Frow and Morris, in *Australian Cultural Studies* (1993), take a very different tack, one more in line with what I have in mind. For if the object of analysis in cultural studies is always a "context" that is determined in the first instance by a political question already posed to the researcher, then there is some sense in which cultural studies is always geopolitically constituted and articulated. Interestingly, much of Frow and Morris's description of cultural studies as an intellectual practice—its theory of cultural practices as multidimensional and relational sites—is not place specific. Actually, this is not entirely true, for while Frow and Morris recognize that the hybridity of theory ("a kind of rigorous mixing") is a general feature, its particular Australian form has to be understood institutionally. Consider the following examples of the sorts of determinations they describe:

—where its "roots" (such experiences must be understood not as origin but as enabling conditions) might be traced, at least biographically, to the Workers Educational Association (and the teaching of specific individuals)

—where its social basis is partly academic, but also partly based in the constituency-oriented work of journalist-critics; this helps to explain the power of the model of the organic intellectual in Australian cultural studies

—where its social-historical models were often feminist bureaucrats who took the notion that "the personal is political" to be a demand for state resources

—where feminist historians were often the most important intellectual precursors

Frow and Morris use these specific conditions to provide partial explanations for particular intellectual appropriations in Australian cultural studies.

Thus, for example, Foucault was taken as a more institutionally anchored model of discourse and a microsociological mapping of power, and Baudrillard's concept of simulations was often used "to rethink the contradictions of colonialism and creativity in an import culture" (Eric Michaels, quoted in Frow and Morris 1993, xxvii).

On the other hand, Frow and Morris point to the economic internationalism implicit in Australia's position in global relations (and the subsequent "geo-economic insistence on location" [1993, xii]) to account for the intense and explicit discourse of nation-formation in Australia and Australian cultural studies. This, they claim, helps to explain why doctrinal disputes (between competing theories of culture, for example) "have not long remained the focus of debate." Rather the most interesting work "examines the political conflicts at stake . . . articulates the historical struggles occurring in the gaps between competing narrative programs [i.e., particular moments of cultural practice] and the complex social experiences these aspire to organize" (xii). They go on to argue, perhaps most importantly, that "*In this context* it is not simply a conceit of cultural studies to claim that people can contest and transform the meanings circulated by the culture industries of a media society. On the contrary, the fact that people actually do this is a *given* of contemporary politics, and one determinant of the social context in which cultural studies is practiced" (xiv; emphasis added). Finally, they claim that this social and institutional context helps to explain the emphasis on policy and industries, rather than text-audience relations per se: "Australian cultural studies has not only been a *response* to the political and social movements of the past three decades (this much can be said of cultural studies as a project in general) but has also derived many of its themes, its research priorities, its polemics and, in some ways, its theoretical emphases and privileged working methods, from an *engagement* with these movements—and the 'worldly historical frames' in which they operate" (xv). Yet even so, there is a reluctance, at least on the part of Meaghan Morris, to reify this nationalist nomination of cultural studies work. As she put it to me recently, talking about "Australian cultural studies" is largely "a matter of publishing our books." But understanding this statement requires us to think about the nature of the contemporary circulation of scholarly discourses, in which the United States is "the only Western English-language market that can afford an ex-nominated national mode of address."

The trajectory of this circulation (which has determined the ways cultural studies is being globalized) has been determined in large part by the changing context of the economics of publishing in the 1980s. Recently Meaghan and I met with a sympathetic publisher to propose a book series that would address the question of how cultural studies *should* be globalized by publishing concrete examples of cultural studies from distinct national and regional traditions of cultural studies other than those that have emerged from within North Atlantic academic communities. We argued that the flow of such work into the international discourse has been severely limited because publishers are often nervous about studies of cultural forms or events that are distinct to specific marginal or non-Western societies. Thus they commonly impose two requirements that undermine much of the power of these distinct articulations of cultural studies: either examples must be chosen from "Western" culture (often disguised as "global") or from events that would be both familiar and significant to Western readers, or the examples must be so totally submerged below the theoretical argument as to be rendered invisible. Insofar as such work operates at the purely theoretical level, it is, of course, acceptable to Western readers, or at least that's what publishers seem to assume. While Western writers are allowed to address Western audiences on the assumption that this defines the "global" audience, non-Western authors are told that they must address Western audiences as well. One of the most important ways this has manifested itself is the current domination of "postcolonial" and diasporic theories and authors over indigenous voices.

The publisher's response was edifying. Basically he said that we were using the wrong frame of reference since the relevant dichotomy was no longer "the West and the rest," but the United States and everything else. That is, according to the bottom line in publishing, the United States is the only academic market large enough to sustain a serious academic publishing effort in cultural studies. Thus even the British—for all the claims that they dominate cultural studies—must take into account the demands of an American audience. Understood in this light, Morris's view of "Australian cultural studies" as a marketing category is not as cynical as it might sound at first, for the category attempts, in the first instance, to create a market within Australia for Australian work. The existence of such a market could of course be used to persuade publishers to support Australian work. Whether the strategy has worked is a different question.

If we take our lead from Frow and Morris, rather than approaching the question of American essentiality, either experientially or in terms of a uniquely American cultural studies tradition, we might ask about the conditions that are shaping the reception of cultural studies in the United States. Here we can point to a number of active determinations:

—the key role of communication and education in the initial reception of cultural studies, counterbalanced by the increasing domination of literary and anthropological studies

—the key role of public universities in the formation of cultural studies, counterbalanced by their relative lack of prestige

—the capitalization of the academy and of academic publishing, but in a way that has not challenged their relative isolation from the American public

—a particular set of crises facing the humanities: one the result of particular routes of high theory and other self-indulgences; another the result of the rise of the New Right

—the reassertion of multiple forms and sites of racism and sexism, calling forth an increasingly fragmented and fragmenting form of popular identity politics

—the expansion of a capitalized media culture and the shrinking of an already meager space of public intellectual life

—the dominance of the baby boomers in university faculties (and the specific conditions of their political experiences in the 1960s)

—the real distance between cultural studies and other political interdisciplinary projects (African American studies, women's studies, etc.)

—the Left's traditional suspicions of mass culture, counterbalanced by a long-standing popular anti-intellectualism

—the professionalization of the university and the social strength of disciplinary boundaries, especially insofar as these are represented by such organizations as the Modern Language Association

—the estrangement of the intelligentsia from the government bureaucracy

We can even talk about the American contributions to the discursive resources of contemporary cultural studies, including a particular identity-based version of critical race theory, an anthropological postcolonialism (institutionally rooted in and yet based on a critique of area studies), pragmatism, performance theory, and so forth. But are Americans the only ones able to use such contributions? Obviously not. Is there anything necessarily American about them? Obviously not. We can talk about the particular political tendencies of cultural studies in the United States, and we can talk as well about the tendencies toward particular critical practices (e.g., radically separating political economy and cultural studies). But again, these are more likely to be accounted for institutionally than by any essentially American identity or any essentially American intellectual tradition.

CONCLUSION

Some time ago, a close friend asked me how a generation born after the Second World War could develop a cultural studies appropriate to contemporary America by beginning with British cultural studies. My inclination at the time was to say that it could not, even while acknowledging that British cultural studies had provided me (and others) with the best starting point I could find. But today I would challenge the very notion of "British cultural studies" as anything other than a marketing category which, like any nationalist appeal, covers over differences within an imagined unity. I would also defend its influence as both a model of "cheap theory, expensive politics," and as a perfectly appropriate—but certainly not the only—starting place. I would, like Cornel West, argue that the key question is not where you begin but what you do with the resources you find there, how you inflect them into specific contextual politics and institutional histories in order to end up somewhere else.

However, it seems to me that my friend was asking—and I was answering— the wrong question, for there are more important issues to be discussed. How should cultural studies be globalized (given that it is already happening)? How does one do cultural studies in the current spatial conditions of global economic and cultural relations, conditions in which we are implicated, at the very least, by the circulation of our bodies and our work as commodities through the circuits of global culture and capitalism, conditions in which, as Meaghan Morris puts it, "European-American culture can no longer experience itself as the sole subject of capitalism or as co-extensive with it" (1990a)? How can the dialogue already taking place in cultural studies be enhanced and empowered? Where and how is it appropriate to do cultural studies about the United States? from within the United States? in a global context?

In this way, the geography of cultural studies opens up the need for cultural studies to rethink its own implicit geography. It brings us back to the question of space and of the relationship between places and spaces and the local and the global. We have to begin to confront, both theoretically and politically, what David Harvey describes as "the acute problems of political identity depending upon the spatial range across which political thought and action [are] constrained as possible" (1995, 82). For we are necessarily involved in "the battle between different levels of abstraction, between distinctively understood particularities of places and the necessary abstractions required to take those understandings into a wider realm, the fight to transform militant particularism into something more substantial on the world stage of capitalism" (85). The issue is how we begin to "negotiate between and link across different spatial scales of social theorizing and political action" (93). Rather than thinking about the proper places of ideas, and the proper ideas for places, we need to begin to think about the ways in which ideas are articulated spatially, and spaces articulated theoretically. Is it enough, as contemporary geographers would have it, to think of the local and the global as flexible and strategic relations? Is it enough to follow Neil Smith's argument (1992) that contemporary events (his example is Tiananmen Square) can be local, regional, national, and global? Is it enough to think about the different ways in which events can be local, or regional, or national, or global?

It seems to me that this is the challenge posed to American cultural studies, speaking as it does from one of the centers of power in an increasingly dense space. What we need are better analyses and better strategies that might be articulated to a progressive politics, one that would speak into and from contemporary America. What we need is to understand how the politics of commitment, alliance, and agency are already being rearticulated in a very real struggle with very high stakes both for the United States and the world. And to develop that, I am willing to practice any kind of cultural studies I can find that may have a chance of succeeding. In that struggle, like so many other things that are absolutely necessary for survival and success, theory is cheap; its space is rather obvious and its places numerous. And like so many things necessary to transform the conditions of survival, politics (and the politically strategic articulation of theory) is costly; and unfortunately its space is rather circumscribed and its places are rare. That is, cultural studies is not about theory; it is about getting a better understanding of what's going on—the only political/academic question worth asking—especially in a context in which appeals to the possibility of a humane existence are apparently ineffective. It is, as Foucault knew all along, about the complex relationships between knowledge and power.

3 SUBJECTS, AUDIENCES,

AND IDENTITIES

Wandering Audiences, Nomadic Critics

Stuart Hall (1986b, 60) once described the purpose of theory as helping us get a bit further down the road. This is an apt metaphor, not only for the politics of theory as it intersects the real world of historical forces and everyday life, but also for the theory of politics, for our own ongoing intellectual work. The fruitless arguments between those who see such work as a continuous dialogue and those who see it as a discontinuous series of wars are better replaced with an image of work—whether the work of everyday life or the work of intellectuals—as travel (transformation) and of travel as work (commutation). This allows us to see the complexity of intellectual alliances and disputes: sometimes people travel with you, or near you, or against you; sometimes they help you, or distract you, or interrupt you, or redirect you; sometimes we take a wrong turn, or a detour, or a dead end; sometimes we are "hijacked" (Hall 1988c) by another position and sometimes we are the "hijackers." The image suggests the inevitability (and, indeed, the pleasurable and enabling possibilities) of different and temporary alliances, built upon different grounds, along different dimensions, with different intensities, as we move in different directions, without ever knowing precisely where we are heading. The following comments, then, are meant to serve as a signpost for an intersection of trajectories available to cultural studies; they chronicle my thoughts at the present moment in an ongoing, collective effort[1] to think through (disentangle, criticize, and reconstruct) the problems of, and possibilities for, studying the contemporary cultural formations.

But the language of travel is polymorphous, and we must take seriously Meaghan Morris's warning (1988a) that specific vocabularies of travel are never innocent, that they are always implicated in and articulated to larger structures of ideological, cultural, and political relations. Morris analyzes the political implications of two trajectories of contemporary cultural criticism

built on different images of travel: I shall describe these as the poststructuralist and the urban-culturalist.[2] After briefly summarizing her criticisms, I shall
offer a parallel critique of an ethnographic model of cultural studies before
turning to Morris's and my collective efforts to articulate a fourth trajectory.
Finally, I want to consider Janice Radway's important and original efforts to
rethink the practice of ethnography in "Reception Study: Ethnography and
the Problems of Dispersed Audiences and Nomadic Subjects." I shall suggest
that the position she takes up is located at a crossroads, that it is pulled in
different directions at the same time, that it attempts to traverse simultaneously a number of different roads. To put it simply, Radway treats ethnography both too generously (giving it credit for having always sought to accomplish her project) and too vaguely (defining it by the presence of the
researcher in an empirical field, while bracketing the theoretical baggage of
its hermeneutical project). Her project is, I suggest, more radical than she
allows, for it involves the rearticulation of ethnography into both the historical field of contemporary mass-mediated culture and the theoretical field of
"postmodern" anti-essentialism.

The poststructuralist critic is like the tour guide, reflective and reflexive,
who always finds the familiar already strange. The tour guide distances himself from the tourist—it makes no difference whether the tourist is the everyday actor or the "totalizing Seer"—who is looking for the Truth. The tourist
operates within the metaphysics of Presence, traveling from one home to
another, from an imaginary origin to an imaginary destination, seeking to
(re)discover an authenticity that never exists. The tourist "hopes to 'ambush'
the site [i.e., to discover its authentic presence and meaning], but he is always
already ambushed by the marker-site relation. The trap is unavoidable; and,
in one sense, it is the inevitability of the 'ambush' that is . . . always already
present" (Morris 1988a, 10). In fact, the tourist unwittingly sets his own trap
because the work of his travels actively produces the very social differences
he seeks to comprehend and ultimately erase. The tourist produces society as
a "figural displacement" (14). The only strategy available to the theorist as a
tour guide, who knows that the authentic is always and already contaminated
by the inauthentic, is to "render impertinent any opposition" (15), to deconstruct any moment of authenticity and/or social difference, since "every
institutionalization of the voyage is already ambushed; it is already an alibi."
Morris argues that such a critical strategy erases the politics of culture in favor
of an endlessly reflexive politics of criticism. The "other" disappears in the
deconstruction, while specific social differences and relations of power are

reinscribed as the unavoidable a priori of the poststructural voyage. That is, deconstruction is never complete and its choice of where to begin (and hence of what always remains as its "excess") is never innocent.

Counterposed to the poststructuralist tour guide, the "urban-culturalist" critic[3] is like a detective constantly seeking to make the familiar strange or, better, traveling through the realms of the familiar searching for signs of (clues to) the strange. The detective looks for the signs of the "criminal" (the marginal, the resistant, productivity) in the places of the "normal" (the every-day, the dominant, consumption). Morris describes it as an "informal [popu-list] equivalent of traditional socialist realism" (1988a, 31). It is an extension of subcultural theory that takes particular cultural relations—"the emblem-atic street experience of un- and under-employed males in European or Amer-ican cities (or what then becomes its echoes everywhere)" (33)—as the image of "real" or "proper" popular culture and, by extension, of contemporary (postmodern) existence.

Cultural criticism is consequently structured by two interrelated bina-risms. The first assumes a constitutive difference between mainstream (domi-nant) culture and marginal (popular) culture. The result is that the politics of any cultural practice is defined not intrinsically, but by its articulation into a dichotomous version of the social formation, as if British culture, for exam-ple, could be described simply in terms of the opposition between an austere Thatcherism and a playful street style. The question addressed to any cul-tural practice is Which side are you on? and the answer is always determined, ahead of time, by the social location of cultural consumers. The same "post-modern" practices located in trendy business establishments are inevitably articulated to Thatcherism, but when they appear as street fashion they are understood as articulating some form, however mute and ineffective, of re-sistance.[4] As Morris (1988a, 33) argues, "the complex 'immediate mishmash of the everyday,'" within which the relations between "the (global) 'machin-ery of capital' and (local) cultural machinations" are articulated, is collapsed into a predefined topography of cultural and political binary difference. The second binarism reproduces a similar constitutive difference at the level of intellectual work: the official intellectual, marked by an absolute hostility to, and absence of, popular culture, is positioned across and against the radical intellectual, who champions the possibilities of popular culture. Not only do these binarisms assume that there is a single problem of theory (e.g., "strong" versus "weak" thought) which is "the same everywhere" but, more impor-tantly, they structure the world into a very simple narrative of good versus bad. This is, according to Morris, "an odd outcome from what starts out . . . as an affirmation of the priority of complex social experience over totalizing theoretical activity . . . The real mystery in this case is why, if the metaphysical adventure *is* over, the streetwise intellectual should begin his practice so strictly positioned in a constitutive opposition to 'the Other' " (32). According to Morris, the real challenge is to face "the difficulties that follow once criticism of popular culture is already based on complex experience of *taste* rather than distaste, of involvement rather than distance, so that a strategic 'siding' for or against the 'popular' becomes a quite pointless manoeuvre" (34). This suggests a quite different conception of the cultural terrain, what Williams (1965) described as the complex relations within a "whole way of life," structured by shifting, interrelated formations of practices and investments (or ways of "taking up" practices). Thus, rather than isolating something called "popular culture" and identifying various "structures of taste," we need to talk about the differentially distributed intensities articulated to specific practices and formations. Popularity is less a matter of different cultural practices than a form of articulation and effectivity.

Within the third trajectory of cultural criticism, the ethnographer can be conceptualized as a tourist traveling to an alien world of the native. The tourist is constantly seeking to make the strange familiar by bringing it home in the form of travel notes, photographs, postcards, and souvenirs. These travel momentos guarantee the tourist's identity as a traveler who has encountered authentically foreign sites, attractions, and people in the purposeful movement through space known as a trip. Ethnography is thus more than simply fieldwork; it involves the interpretive project of locating the other within a hermeneutic dialogue, within a relationship of identity and difference in which, as I shall suggest, otherness is already denied. Ethnography is built upon a model of communication, interaction, and intersubjectivity[5] through which it seeks to (re)produce an imaginary negotiation between different systems of meaning which will enable the ethnographer to understand another culture "from the native's point of view." Ethnography seeks to understand the structures of experience that define the reality of another's way of being in the world. Even the more sophisticated contemporary efforts to rethink the practices of ethnographic research and its relations to structures of power consistently reproduce this hermeneutic foundation: "Ethnography is actively situated between powerful systems of meaning . . . [It] decodes and recodes, telling the ground of collective order and diversity, inclusion and exclusion" (Clifford 1986, 2). Consequently the native is always inscribed into "the productive encounter of self and other" (107), "a mutually constitutive relation of difference" in which "ethnography's narrative . . . presupposes, and always refers to, an abstract plane of similarity" (101). One cannot help but wonder for whom the ethnography is productive and whether its constitution can ever be truly "mutual."

For Tyler, "a postmodern ethnography is a cooperatively evolved text . . . intended to evoke in the minds of both reader and writer an emergent fantasy of a possible world of common sense reality" (1986, 125). If ethnography is a way of coping with our anxiety of the other, it quickly assuages this anxiety by appropriating the other into its own hermeneutic dialectic of difference. This always brings the question back not to the material reality of cultural practices, but to the subjective experiences of a predefined "community" whose empirical location is identified by a set of subject-positions and experiences. Ethnography asserts the universality and innocence of a mutually available, intersubjectively (interactively) constituted experience. While it is not my intention to deny the "reality" or effectivity of experience, I do question its status—its place and effectivity within the material relations of social life and power. One needs to ask what we know when we know how someone experiences material relations. And its privileged position within ethnography—the product of the identification of culture with certain notions of communication and semiotic constitution—is even more problematic. If, as Althusser and others have argued, experience is ideologically produced, then "experience"[6] itself has to be located within the determining discursive and material conditions of its own production. People live different ideological positions in different ways (partly through different secondary interpretations), to different degrees, with differing investments and intensities, not only because people live in different contradictions and multiple subject-positions, and not only because ideological effects are always traversed by other sorts of investments, but also because subject-ion is always broader than the interpellation of an experiencing/knowing subject. Bodies are disciplined along with minds! Uncovering experiences does not tell us how particular experiences are effective, how they are articulated by and into the terrain of everyday life.

Recent work in ethnography has attempted to rethink this hermeneutical model by invoking various tenets of poststructuralism. Perhaps the most widely discussed example of this turn to poststructuralism in ethnography is the collection of essays, *Writing Culture* (Clifford and Marcus 1986). The various efforts in this volume to recognize the real relations of power implicated in the ethnographic relationship do so only by displacing the question back into the ethnographer's home, as a question of his[7] constitutive power within the (imaginary) communicative circuit. These essays are less concerned with the ethnographer in the field, confronting an other, than with the ethnographer within the security of his academic community, inscribing the other into discourse. In this sense, the politics of reality are reduced to the epistemology of writing at home. At best, such revisionist attempts call for a writing practice in which the other is empowered to speak, to tell its own story; but this simply displaces the disempowerment of the other to another level. For, as Spivak (1988) has argued, even these revisionist writing practices ignore the very real conditions of impossibility that prevent the other from speaking, conditions that are material as well as discursive. This is not to claim that the other cannot ever speak, but rather that discourse is enabled only within certain forms, at particular institutional and material sites. As Valaskakis (1988) suggests, the "subaltern" speak from within their own places, but different conditions of (im)possibility operate as they move into the colonized spaces of "international" economic, political, and cultural practices.

This is also the case with more radical efforts to use poststructuralism to critique the hermeneutic foundations of ethnography in which the encounter is constructed as a "clash of worlds," a dialogue between self and other, between the familiar and the strange. For example, Paul Smith condemns this practice as a "metaparanoid" projection "that wishes to maintain its rights on a reality which it will not yet recognize as its own offspring or production" (1988). Smith wants to deconstruct "the self-other distinction, even as it almost daily becomes more reflective": "The 'subject' in these practices, as in paranoia, is an interpreter, unable and/or unwilling to recognize the condition of its own interpretations as constructs, fictions, imaginary narratives. Such a 'subject' not only constructs the order of reality in which it wants to live, but also has to defend itself against the otherness of that very world" (Smith 1978, 97). But the consequence of this radical reflexivity is the reproduction of what Morris calls the "indifferent producer of social reality as differentiation" (1988a, 14). Smith deconstructs the other into the productivity of the ethnographer's subjectivity, a subjectivity that can, in turn, be deconstructed into the productivity of discourses. In this deconstructive move, the very facticity of the other is erased, dissolved into the ethnographer's semiotic constructions. But again, as Spivak has argued, "The ones talking about the critique of the subject are the ones who have had the luxury of a subject. The much publicized critique of the Sovereign subject thus actually inaugurates a subject" (1988, 272). And even though Crapanzano argues that there can be "no understanding of the native from the native's point of view," instead of seeking an alternative, materialist ethnography, he argues that "There is only the constructed understanding of the constructed native's constructed point of view" (1986, 74). Thus in both these strategic critiques of ethnography, the moment of otherness—the materiality of social and cultural practices and networks—is always displaced into its interpellation into, and construction within, a system of textual, signifying differences. And through this displacement the other is always further disempowered.[8]

A reconception of ethnography must begin by recognizing precisely that there is a "reality," an otherness that is not merely its mark of difference within our signifying systems. As Probyn (1989) states, "Ethnography requires its share of bodies," bodies that are not only biological organisms but also social and material organizations. Probyn calls for an epistemological (and political) critique of the ontological assumption that the other is produced as other (i.e., outside of our discourses) from within our discourses. We need to criticize the practice that identifies material otherness with semiotic difference, that always begins and ends by reinscribing the other into the constitutive semiotic relations of identity and difference, located within a communicative economy. Such a critique opens up a materialist ethnography and reconstructs the image of the tourist. In the hermeneutic tradition, the tourist seeks the pleasure of the authentic because, somehow, in comprehending its difference, he or she can reconstruct its "sameness" and thus his or her own authenticity. In a materialist ethnography, the tourist seeks the pleasures of proximities and distances, escaping, however impossibly, from the social power of his or her own economy of difference. The tourist becomes a "nomad" who, with complex cultural and social histories and memories, discovers the possibility of a terrain that is not mapped by the differences between authenticity and inauthenticity, between the same and the different, between (a singular) self and (a singular different) other. On this terrain, both the nomad and the ethnographer confront the anxiety of facing our own otherness.

Such a materialist ethnographer takes on the task of mapping an empirical field of the effectivity of practices rather than assuming that the specificity of cultural practice is always and already defined by its productivity within an economy of signification as difference. This a priori assumption of cultural specificity flattens the place of cultural practices in everyday life to a level of abstraction in which subjects exist only in relation to discourses (while yet always existing outside of any particular discourse), and discourses function only in relation to the production of difference (meaning) and identity (subjectivity). We should bear in mind Morley's observation that "The notion of decoding may well blur together a number of different processes that would be better addressed separately" (1981, 5). The notion of decoding suggests that reading a text involves a single act that is always and everywhere the same. Morley argues that it would be better understood as a set of processes. Additionally, Morris cautions us to avoid "any move to predetermine the kind—and the tempo—of spatial (reading, walking) practices deemed 'appropriate' to particular places. A written text . . . may be spatially practised in ways, in directions, and at velocities as various as any street" (1988a, 37). Perhaps what we need is to "make talk walk" (McRobbie 1982a).

Instead of starting with notions of difference as constitutive negation, the fourth trajectory—what I have been calling materialist—of cultural studies begins with what Foucault describes as the "positivity" of otherness, with the prospective and retrospective conditions of possibility and enablement. Rather than collapsing everything into texts, this position proposes to disperse texts into everything, into the broad range of effects. It recognizes that any practice has multiple effects and that the identity of a practice is only the articulated site of the intersection of lines of effects. Moreover effects are always inter-effective, always on the way to and from other effects. Thus one can never guarantee which effects are pertinent in a specific context. Cultural effects may or may not depend upon semiotic "content," meaning, or claims of representation. For example, the most powerful effects of video games may be determined less by ideological dimensions than by certain forms of embodiment, by the way in which the player controls/produces the sounds and lights that engulf, produce, and define a "rhythmic body." Thus the task of cultural criticism is less that of interpreting texts and audiences than of describing vectors, distances and densities, intersections and interruptions, and the nomadic wandering (whether of people in everyday life or as cultural critics) through this unequally and unstably organized field of tendential forces and struggles. To describe a practice is to consider its place within this dispersed field and how it occupies that space in relation to structures existing at different levels of abstraction.

The nomadic cultural critic finds that the strange is always and already familiar. Cultural practices engender and articulate the temporal and spatial structures of everyday life, the possibilities for mobility and placement (location). It is in this sense that Morris and I use the term "billboards" to describe the multiple effectivity of cultural practices. Billboards are neither authentic nor inauthentic; their function cannot be predefined, nor are they distributed according to some logic of the "proper" organization of space or the "proper" use of place. They follow what Morris calls a "logic of the next." And they perform, provoke, and enable a variety of different activities: they open a space for many different discourses and practices, both serious and playful, both institutional and guerrilla. We stop or turn near them, we adjust our speed, our mood, our desires, we get on and off roads, we "live near them, photograph them, picnic and read books beside them, deface them, or even . . . shoot at them" (Morris 1988a, 42). Billboards mark "strategic installations"—"a fixed address for temporary lodgment"—and the lines that connect and reshape them in a constant movement of "place-invention." They manifest complex appeals that draw us down certain roads, open and close alternative routes, and enable us to be located in a variety of different ways at different sites and intersections where we can rest, or engage in other activities, or move on in different directions. Billboards then construct "homes," not necessarily as sites of domesticity (that is, after all, only one way of stopping, only one of our many addresses) nor even as sites of comfort. Because the effects of billboards are always articulated, the availability and "comfort" of different constructed "homes" or addresses are themselves differentially distributed and articulated. And, of course, not all roads and not all billboards are equally available to everyone traveling within the broader social spaces. Not all roads intersect, and some roads have very limited access from specific social points. Access may even be granted only in one direction (e.g., the complex relations between forms of African American culture and the predominantly white mainstream). Thus Bourdieu (1984) has argued that it is not sufficient to describe the unequal distribution of both cultural and economic capital; one must also recognize the differential availability of the different life trajectories by which one might acquire such resources. Billboards are the signposts not only of various vectors that define the travels and work of everyday life, but also of the effectivity of power within everyday life.

This suggests a very different model of the subject of cultural practices: neither the tourist looking for authenticity, the native looking for a home, nor the subculturalist looking for pleasure (and always finding resistance). While such a nomadic or materialist model rejects a single unified subject that somehow exists in the same way in every practice, it also rejects the notion of a fractured and multiple subject—as if discrete, isolatable subject-positions

and distastes (although our travelogues are always contaminated by them), or our own sense of some imaginary boundary that divides a mythic (and always dominant) mainstream from a magical (and always resisting or reflexive) marginality, or our own notion of an assumed gulf between our intellectual self and our popular-media self. I repeat: we are reshaped by the stories we tell, stories that are always at least partly purposive and partly reconstructive. These stories offer a record of roads taken and a few not taken, of successes and failures, of sites we stopped at as well as some we saw from a distance, some we passed by too quickly and some that we missed entirely but heard about along the way, and sometimes even of other people's travels, whether real or only possible. The cultural critic constructs a record, always partly imaginary, that re-marks the densities and distances within which our travels are constituted.

Let me now, finally, turn to Radway's article (1988) in order to suggest that the method it proposes is rather unstably situated at a number of intersections among the four trajectories described above. Nevertheless its significance extends well beyond its concrete proposals. Radway's argument brings us back to questions of ethnographic practice in the field as inseparable from, but not reducible to, its inscription at some later point in the tourist's home world. But, most importantly, it opens the possibility of inserting ethnography into the "everywhere-mediated world." In so doing, Radway argues that both the questions and our resources have been transformed by epistemological, political, and historical circumstances. Thus Radway rejects the traditional model of ethnographic media research which looks at the relationship between singular texts or genres and locatable audiences. The notion of a "media text" is, for her, in fact impossible, not merely because the media are a prime example of "intertextuality gone mad," not merely because any generic category is always the prior construction of academic (disciplinary) and economic interests, and not merely because of the fragmentary structure of any text's multiple presentations. It is also the case that, quite simply, we cannot recuperate the text as an object of study for very practical reasons: First, it is never merely an objective text but is always, simultaneously, multiply contextualized and intersected by other practices; second, we cannot collect media texts, at least not enough of them, and moreover we are never able to know ahead of time which are the right ones, the ones we need to tape and collect. Additionally, the audience of the mass media is never available to us. Again, it is not merely a matter of the radical overdetermination of the individual audience member or group—what Barthes (1981) described as the "impossible science of the individual"—but, more to the point, we can never confidently identify interpretive communities. Media audiences are shifting constellations, located within varying multiple discourses that are never entirely outside of the media discourse themselves.

Nor is it enough simply to acknowledge intertextuality and multiple subjectivity, for Radway claims that

> No matter how extensive the effort to dissolve the boundaries of the textual object or the audience, most recent studies of reception, including my own, continue to begin with the "factual" existence of a particular kind of text which is understood to be received by some set of individuals. Such studies perpetuate, then, the notion of a circuit neatly bounded and therefore identifiable, locatable, and open to observation. (1988, 363)

In the light of these comments, Radway proposes a different notion of audiences that are "never assembled fixedly on a site or even in an easily identifiable space." She wonders, then, "can ethnography . . . manage to capture the fluid, destabilized, ever-shifting nature of subjectivity produced through the articulation of discourses and their fragments?" (368). But this, she recognizes, entails a new "object of analysis, one more difficult to analyze because it can't be so easily pinned down—that is, the endlessly shifting, ever-evolving kaleidoscope of daily life and the way in which the media are integrated and implicated within it" (366). Thus a new project for ethnography emerges:

> Instead of segmenting a social formation automatically by construing it precisely as a set of audiences for specific media and/or genres, I have been wondering whether it might not be more fruitful to start with the habits and practices of everyday life as they are actively, discontinuously, even contradictorily pieced together by historical subjects themselves as they move nomadically via disparate associations and relations through day-to-day existence. (366)

This is clearly an attempt to formulate a research agenda within that fourth trajectory I identified earlier, one that would "theorize the dispersed, anonymous, unpredictable nature of the use of mass-produced, mass-mediated cultural forms," and one that would study the "ever-shifting kaleidoscope of cultural circulation, production and consumption" (361). In this project, the ethnographer would begin with "an expedition through the already inhabited, already elaborated built-up cultural terrain" (373).

But Radway takes a detour, arguing that the problem is not with the ethnographic method itself but rather in the fact that "the ethnographic method has been applied in an extremely limited fashion" (367). This results from "the commonsense understanding of the process of communication" (360) as a circuit of exchange in which the moment of enunciation is privileged as productive and determining. This denies the engendering power of the moment of reception so that the audience is empowered only to refuse to enter into the circuit. Radway then turns to the urban-culturalist strategy of focusing on the productivity of consumption as articulation in order to empower the agent of consumption. Consequently, it is "historical subjects" who "articulate their cultural universe" and "articulately produce subjectivity." Like the culturalist, Radway's project returns to the assumption that it is always the subject who constructs reality.[12]

Alternatively, a materialist or nomadic model argues that reality is constructed by the "anonymous" travels of people within the historically articulated social spaces, places, and structures of practices. To describe this process as "anonymous" is not to deny that people make history but to emphasize that they do it in conditions not of their own making. Consequently they are not in control of the multiple and often unintended consequences of their actions. Talking about articulation within the field of contemporary culture allows us to recognize that nomadic subjects are always empowered and disempowered, shaped and reshaped, by the effectivities of the practices (trajectories, apparatuses, etc.) within which their agency is itself located. Thus a materialist theory of articulation proposes studying not people but practices. For example, even within the plane of ideology, a theory of articulation involves looking neither for the intrinsic meaning of a text nor for people's interpretations/uses of it. Instead it directs us to look at how a place or contradictory places are made for the text in the wider field of forces. Such a theory does not eliminate people's agency, their ability to struggle, or even their effective desire to resist (although it has to distinguish not only between struggle and resistance but between different forms of resistance). It does, however, refuse to reconstruct a model of history and the social formation predicated on the privileged effectivity of individual agency.

The distance Radway assumes between the subject and any singular cultural practice reestablishes a model of communication. The subject, no longer nomadic but a fragmented and unstable social position, is outside of the particular practice, able to articulate it. Here effectivity is reappropriated and reduced to "use." The subject remains the causal agent who engages with an external practice. The audience is reconstituted as outside of any specific cultural region, determined elsewhere, so that it can consume, appropriate, or articulate the specific region from which it was initially excluded. Alternatively, if the nomadic subject never comes to any media event without already belonging to the whole field of interlocking media events and contexts, then the audience is always and already within the region, articulated by the very practices and contexts it articulates.

Radway's continued commitment to a communication model, albeit one weighted in favor of the consumer, reconstitutes the audience as a "single heterogeneous community," which, however problematic, is still locatable within the spatial site of the ethnographic field. Continuing to rely upon a communicative economy reconstructs an implicit distance between the ethnographer and the community. Consequently instead of starting with the "point of view we share with others in our everywhere-mediated society," we must once again construct our map by first reconciling our "distant point of view" with "the inhabitant's point of view," a reconciliation that seems to entail leaving "our own world" behind. This reproduction of the difference between Us and Them, between the self and the other, has important consequences, for it leads Radway back to a conception of the cultural field predicated on the inevitable distance and hostility between legitimate and popular culture, where the latter is always produced by people in opposition to the former. Further, this view of the other as a "distant" or "alien" world ignores the fact that—insofar as we are talking about the media world of culture—we are already part of it. By saying this I do not mean to deny that there are social differences, that our access to various media forms and various forms of cultural capital is never equal. But I do want to question our ability to decide ahead of time the pertinence of such differences within the study of the effectivity of cultural practices. For within the domain of contemporary cultural practices the other is never any more exotic or strange than we are. Insofar as otherness is effective in the field of media culture, the nomadic subject is always other to itself.

In the end, the return to a communication economy almost inevitably forces Radway back into a hermeneutic model of ethnography as "a written account of a lengthy *social interaction* between a scholar and a distant culture" (my italics). The empirical field of articulations (the everyday, the "tapestry of social life") is transformed into the interpretive field of experience. Thus she concludes her paper by wondering whether it is possible "to preserve the gains secured by the distance and abstraction of intellectual work and yet continue to respect the particularities and concreteness of *subjective experience* in such a way that the distance between them can continually be negotiated and renegotiated" (1988, 373; my italics). The distances (otherness) within our social and cultural realities are reconstructed into the differences of "the worlds of words." The ethnographer has once again become a tourist seeking to make the strange familiar by locating it within the world of his or her own discourses. And now the tourist has become a detective, seeking to find the moments in which the natives are empowered as constructing their own social reality. While this is, in itself, an interesting reinflection of ethnography, it is a long way from the project Radway identifies at the beginning.

While it is important to recognize the specific power of intellectual practices, they cannot be separated from our existence as nomadic subjects in everyday life. We have the resources to articulate social trajectories and travels; we have access not only to vocabularies, but to sites of production and distribution. But this does not guarantee the stories we tell or their effects; our discourses are, after all, constrained and empowered to appear at specific sites. We can recognize, with Radway, the limitations of our work— that every map has its own angle of projection. And we can refuse to narrativize our travelogue in ways that locate it back into dichotomies of true/false, accurate/distorted, complete/partial, useful/useless. We can recognize, with Morris, the power of our own tastes and find ways of distancing them (e.g., by moving the discussion to a higher level of abstraction). It is, after all, not our function to tell people what are the "proper" cultural tastes or political positions. Politics is always derived from everyday life, and not from theory. But if politics enters theory "from below," intellectuals can seek to articulate directions and alliances through which it can move. Intellectuals do not construct reality any more than do everyday subjects. Cultural critics are cotravelers and, within the limited possibilities available to us at any moment, we have our role to play, a role that is unnecessarily further circumscribed by our voluntary self-exclusion from the everyday world of media life.

The Context of Audiences and

the Politics of Difference

Two of the most common terms in contemporary communication and cultural theory—"contexts" and "audiences"—are also among the most difficult
to pin down, and they are often used rather unreflectively (Slack 1989). Of the
two, "context" is the more troublesome. It appears in many different guises,
with different imports, in different theories: situatedness, specificity, local-
ism, difference, conjuncturalism, and so on. The very concept of "a theory
of contexts" seems, at first, to be paradoxical, for the concept itself argues
against the possibility of a normative theory, one that is fixed and transport-
able across national, political, and historical boundaries. If theory is itself an
active response to local conditions, it cannot exist outside of or "above" those
conditions. And yet it is only with those same theoretical tools that we are
able to construct the very context to which theory responds. In some sense,
the task of theorizing is always to find or create the tools—both theoretical
and methodological—that are appropriate to the particular questions and
contexts we confront from within. How is one to take seriously the injunction
to locate theory, culture, criticism, and politics in their contexts? What are the
implications of recognizing that the issues and problems that communications researchers face are never given to them apart from their historical
context? Does it matter that, as researchers, we are always directed toward
those historically articulated questions that seem to demand an immediate
answer?

If our theories are contextually located and determined, then the current fascination with the concept of the active audience can itself become
the starting point for inquiry. I have suggested elsewhere (Grossberg 1988a,
1988b) that there are good theoretical and historical/empirical arguments
against the current turn to audience research in cultural and communication
studies. Here I want to consider the political contexts and consequences of

this turn, and to suggest at least that the politics of the contemporary deployments of "the audience" are themselves problematic. I hope it will be clear that I am not saying that we should not study real people doing real things, but simply that the fact that there is an active audience does not guarantee that it is the appropriate way to ground theory or the appropriate place to focus research. We take too much for granted when we start talking about "active audiences," as if it guarantees something about the theoretical, empirical, or political inflections of our research, as if one can assume that the relevant political sites to which the active audience is articulated (e.g., citizenship, nation) are somehow there in advance. The fervor with which the active audience has been embraced suggests not only that it is often thought of as a recent discovery, but also that it somehow provides a necessary escape from something; what it allows us to escape from in different contexts is precisely the question that I want to raise. It is not merely a question of whether the audience(s) exists, or even who it is at any moment. Rather it is a question of where the audience is, when it is, how it is, for whom it is; it is a question of what conditions enable the discourse to suddenly be heard in powerful, central ways, to what ends, and with what effects. To suggest a simple example: Why does so much current research re-place the audience into the domestic context and the family as the scene of consumption and social life and the site of research? One cannot help but notice that discourses of the family and domestic relations play an important role in a variety of national political struggles and that, to a large extent, such discourses are articulated to the Right in these struggles.

TALKING ABOUT CONTEXTS

But first, what are the consequences of a commitment to context? In fact, the radical implications of contextualism have rarely been embraced because of five common misinterpretations when we try to contextualize our own theories as well as the practices we are studying. Each of these limits the practice and effects of contextualization by reestablishing a definition of the *proper* forms and places of both research and politics. First, too often the context is treated as a background, as something that can be taken for granted. While we may spend a great deal of time problematizing our description of the focus of our study, we assume the description of the background is unproblematically given—if only for the purposes of our study. Consequently we rarely examine how the two—focus and background—are mutually constitutive. Second, too often the context is fetishized as "the local," as an atomized fragment that can be isolated from *its* taken-for-granted background. By disarticulating the context of our focus from even larger contexts, the context becomes a new object of study with the researcher once again located outside it. This merely constructs a more abstract empiricism, one that some Foucauldians seem to embrace.

Third, the "call to context," which is so closely related to an attack on notions of universal essences and identities, is often taken to mean that there are no effective essences or identities. That is, it is assumed that anti-essentialism entails that every identity or moment of unity and stability is deconstructable and, for both theoretical and political reasons, should be deconstructed. To give an example, the attack on a specific image of subjectivity (as unified and intentional) is taken so far that we are unable to reconstitute a theory of agency, of how and where people *do* make history under conditions not of their own making.

Fourth, too often, the recognition of the contextuality of our own perspective is taken to imply that the researcher's task is to examine and deconstruct his or her own position within the context. The result is often that historical reality is displaced in favor of an autoreflexivity that not only privileges the researcher's perspective, but his or her social position as well. And at the same time, it renders the researcher unable to do anything other than "confess" his or her own limitations.

Fifth, contextualism is often taken as a call for what Roland Barthes (1981) called "the impossible science of the individual." This assumes a corporatist or accumulation model of contexts in which we simply try to add all of the pieces that overdetermine the particular individuality or specificity of our object of study. But, of course, it constantly confronts the fact we can never gather together all the pieces that determine the totality, and, if we could, we could never locate all the determining relationships that exist among them.

Without offering my own "theory of contexts," I want to briefly state my own take on each of these five points. First, the task of cultural analysts is to (re)construct, through their own intellectual labor, the context they are studying and how they are located in it. That is, the "local," like the "concrete" in Marx, is the end, not the beginning, of research. It is, in fact, the most difficult "thing" to get hold of. Second, the context is constituted not only by the "horizontal" relations among practices, but also by the "vertical" articulations between practices and tendencies operating across different levels of abstraction. For example, the community always partly involves the rearticulation of national discourses into local conditions. Rather than thinking of the community as the negation of the nation, the community is constructed precisely by locating national discourses into other relationships that define it as both national and local at any moment. Such vertical or hierarchical articulations constitute the reality of structures constantly transcending the local, although they only exist in their local effectivities. There are always different levels of structures—where levels are defined precisely by the effective spatial, temporal, and social reach of different practices across contexts—that have to be taken into account. And the local is merely our own reconstruction of a level of abstraction adequate to specific empirical and political projects. For example, those who would argue that the state (or the individual) is merely an abstraction that does not have its own real effects ignore the multidimensional articulation of contexts. Or, to use a different example, the commodity is an abstract concept with an enormous purchase: it is a necessary aspect of the description of the economic conditions of many countries, over at least four centuries. But for just that reason it does not tell us much about the articulation of the commodity in any particular conjuncture and it does not, by itself, provide a particularly powerful political intervention.

Third, we need to construct a theory of agency in light of contemporary critiques of a particular historical model of agency. As a result of these critiques, we can no longer equate agency with subjectivity. But this need not be taken to deny that people make history, nor that they are engaged in real practices. Of course, they do it in conditions not of their own making, and, I would add, they do it in such a way that history is often made "behind their backs." The active production of history is neither the product of a simple interaction of intentions, nor the outcome of a single set of conspiracies. Once we have disarticulated agency and subjectivity, we can begin to think about forms of agency as those historically specific "apparatuses" of practices that, in any conjuncture, are the active site of the production of history. We can examine not only the differential access that people have to these forms of agency, but also the different ways they are placed in different apparatuses.

Fourth, intellectuals cannot be satisfied with deconstructing their own position according to a "diagnostics of discourse" (Gouldner 1976), which reduces the content of every intellectual and political statement to the social position of the author, and which often results in an endlessly reflexive self-absorption. Rather we must, through our own labor, construct a place for ourselves (and others) within our descriptions of the context, places from which we (and they) can speak with a certain intellectual, moral, and political authority.

Fifth, a radically contextualist theory of cultural analysis would begin to approach a "science of singularity" (Certeau 1984) which, at best, finds the questions—but not the answers—in the interpretation of texts and of people's experience of them. Traditional models of communication and culture assume that the relationship between culture and its historical context is an external one that can only be described through the accumulation of transactional, homologous, or mediated relationships. Culture is, in these models, always determined elsewhere in the last instance. The binary difference between meaning (assigned to culture) and reality (assigned to history)—or the collapse of the two into a single dimension—raises the impossible task of reconstructing the lines of correspondence between quasi-independent domains. All of the popular media are located in an economy of signs and ideology, in the circuit of communication, in which the specificity of communication as the ideological penetration of real historical processes can only be conceptualized in the contradictory space of the conscious (representation) and unconscious (fantasy, desire, pleasure) manifestations of the universal register of culture: signification. The model of the circuit of communication has largely determined the shifts of emphasis within cultural and communication theory; research moves from one cluster to another: text, effects, audience-activities, audience-experience, industry. At best there have been repeated calls to find models that can put the Humpty Dumpty of communication back together again, always made with the best of intentions and always, I think, doomed to failure.

A science of singularity, by attempting to realize Marx's concept of the concrete, implies a different model of cultural analysis, one that attempts to map out the lines that distribute, place, and connect cultural practices and social individuals. It is concerned with the differential access that social groups have to specific clusters of practices and specific forms of agency. It looks at how the material deployment of cultural practices constructs the space within which people live their lives, at how everyday life is articulated by and with the specific forms and formations of cultural practices. By describing the circulation of cultural practices, it seeks to understand the various ways culture can empower and disempower specific groups and practices.[1] The lines of this circulation constitute a "structured mobility" that defines the spaces and places of everyday life. In other words, culture is constantly enacting and enabling specific forms of movement (change) and stability (identity). The latter provide the possible sites of individuals' investments, sites at which "selves" are constructed; the former defines the vectors by which people can move between and connect such investments. The aim is to describe how particular cultural contexts enable and empower specific forms of agency and action.

A GENEALOGY OF THE ACTIVE AUDIENCE

Let me now return to the question of the audience. I am not concerned here with questions about the theoretical adequacy or empirical efficacy of competing definitions of the audience. Rather I am concerned with the political significance and effectivity of the appearance of the notion of the active audience at specific moments. Why, at a particular conjuncture, might one use the audience to argue against strong media effects? How and where is the concept of the active audience situated so as to function as a crucial limit on what we at least intuitively fear to be the profound effects of the media on contemporary people and society? Such questions cannot be answered merely by offering a critique of audience theories, for if such appeals to the power of the audience are often too easy, the critiques are equally easy. For there is no real audience waiting out there to be constructed; in fact, the "audience" is not only a theoretical abstraction but, at the present moment, a rather chaotic one (not unlike Marx's sense about the concept of population). Nor is it merely a matter of pluralizing the concept—audiences—as if they all shared in some common and singular essence. The very category changes as it moves across social, political, and historical space. The concept is itself filled with difference, existing at multiple levels of abstraction, within different strategies, for different reasons; each specification of the concept finds a different unity amidst the differences.

At its most abstract level, we can only say that the concept of the audience serves to limit the autonomy of both the text and the subject in specific ways. The fact that there must be such specific ways in which audiences function serves to distinguish them from both the more general category of cultural relations and the more specific category of the public. The concept of the audience does describe a relationship, one that is both produced and productive, a relationship that is itself constitutive of the existence of communication as a social practice. Thus every theory of the audience is both a theory about a particular form of relationship (e.g., causality, functionality, homology, literacy, competency, identification, investment, articulation) and a particular form of effectivity (usually these are limited to the simple dichotomy of comprehension or interpretation and use). Of course, there is no reason why the latter list cannot or should not be expanded to include patterns of engagement and attention, productions of time and space, organizations of choices and priorities, determinations of perspectives (i.e., how the text is taken up) and investments, constructions of identifications, agreements, and responses, and so on. After all, the audience is not merely the site of meanings, beliefs, and attitudes, but also of commodity choices, social relations, experiences, pleasures, behaviors, agencies, bodies, and more. In fact, what we may conclude is that the concept of the audience is so unstructured that we would be better off starting from the fact that the concept has been constructed and invoked, in different forms, in different contexts, for different purposes.

The current turn to the audience is a re-turn that depends in part on the erasure of selected moments in the history of communications research, of cultural criticism, and of the relations between them *in the United States.* (My comments are only concerned with the context of the United States; I do not intend them to be taken as a general critique, for I assume that the concept of the audience has been deployed in different discursive roles and with different political agendas in other national contexts.) Basically my argument is quite simple: The fact that audiences are active does not necessarily imply that that is where we should begin our research or ground our theories, any more than the fact that texts produce meanings demands an immediate textual analysis. The issues circulating around the study of culture and communication are too important to be left to the imaginary protocols of academic interest. Because they have real and often immediate consequences, we must also take into account the possibilities of articulating such notions as the active audience to historically specific political projects and positions.

To recover something of that history that has been erased, we cannot focus on the content of the concept. Instead, following Foucault's notion of genealogy (1980c), we must focus on the appearance of the concept. Such a genealogy would elucidate the fact that the concept of an active audience has appeared, at particular places and times, both historically and discursively, in particular ways. It would reconstruct the conditions that enabled the concept to appear, and that put the concept into place, with a certain power to enable other discursive relations at other places. In other words, a genealogy of the audience is concerned with how the repeated but discontinuous assumption of the active audience as a focus in media and cultural research is itself articulated to larger historical and political questions.

The valorization of the study of active audiences in America can be located in a larger history of the nation's long crisis of self-representations; in varying ways, the issue of the audience has been articulated to the struggle for a national identity (geographically, culturally, and politically) at moments of what Robert Park called "social disorganization" (1967). Because the United States had no tradition on which to build its own sense of identity, communication as process, technology and content has always taken the central place. From the very founding of the constitutional democracy, the vision of the nation was connected to the possibility of imagining a democracy that saw itself as continental and that could not, at least at that moment, imagine the limits of its own population (Carey, 1989b). It was to be a nation whose currency was made possible not by proximity and tradition, but by transportation and communication. Seen from a slightly different perspective, the complex and ambiguous processes of building both communities, and a nation out of them, while avoiding the authority and authoritarianism implicit in both structures, has always remained a constitutive structure of American cultural life and thought.

In the twentieth century, there have been at least three moments when this cultural vector—the crisis of American self-representation—has been articulated with the concept of an active audience, moments at which the active audience is both "discovered" and valorized. It is not the same audience at each moment, nor is the audience put into play at the same place or in the same way. What I am interested in is how, at each moment, the active audience is historically connected to specific political agendas, how it is articulated into larger cultural struggles, around questions of national self-representation and crisis. The first moment, in the early twentieth century, is the period of progressivism and pragmatism, and of the now erased history of audience research in the 1920s and '30s (see Wartella and Reeves 1987). The second moment is dominated by the cultural debates of the 1940s and '50s, in which the postwar anti-Stalinist liberals were key advocates of the active audience (giving rise to liberal communication theories such as "mediated effects" and "uses and gratifications"). And the final moment is the contemporary one, built around theories of difference and, too often, the fetishism of specificity. Each of these periods—the '20s, the '50s, and the '80s—for its own complex reasons and in its own complex ways, marks a moment when, almost literally, "all that is solid melts into air," when there is a sense that everything is changing so rapidly as to be incomprehensible. Each marks a moment when old ways of being and belonging were becoming problematic, demanding an active search for new forms of individual and national identity and new forms of social, cultural, and political life. Moreover in each of these periods, there is an explicit attempt to shed European traditions, canons, and categories on the grounds that America could only understand its own identity and history in uniquely American terms. It had to find new categories and theories that would allow it to make sense of, to reimagine, its own experiences (e.g., Turner's "frontier hypothesis" in the '20s) and accomplishments. Finally, at each of these moments, communication itself becomes the focus of a widespread and heated public debate in which it is both demonized and sacralized.

AUDIENCES AND THE POLITICS OF NATIONAL IDENTITY[2]

It is not my intention here to provide anything like an adequate analysis of the first two historical conjunctures to which I have alluded, nor will I attempt to demonstrate the specific ways in which the audience was articulated within these contexts. Since my primary interest is in making an argument about the current context of the concept of the audience, I wish to use these earlier moments only to provide examples of such articulations, examples that contrast rather sharply with the contemporary conjuncture. Following Rowland (1982), I want to point to the connection between the emergence of an early conception of an active audience in the 1920s and '30s and the progressive era of social reform of the first two decades of the twentieth century. That is, I want to at least suggest that, in this context, the active audience was articulated out of, and into, the political agenda of progressivism. The period between 1890 and 1939, when progressivism was at its height, saw the birth of many reformist movements, including populism, nativism, various ethnic movements, women's suffrage, temperance, the grange movement, the Know-Nothings, propaganda analysis, and more. As Carey (1989b) argues, what made the Progressive movement not only unique but enormously influential was its explicit struggle over the relations between national identity, community, democracy, communication, and science. John Dewey, for example, envisioned a newspaper, *The Thought News,* which would use the possibilities of the new social sciences to represent the nation to its people, in a popular statistical discourse, as an alternative to other forms of traditional self-representation (a vision that has finally been realized in *USA Today* and Cable News Network). The progressivists sought to reconcile the importance of local identity in America with their increasing valorization of national identity and Americanness over the local. Thus their often romantic celebration of community life was always counterbalanced by their critique of small-town communities (e.g., in Masters's *Spoon River Anthology*, Lewis's *Main Street,* and Veblen's sociological descriptions of small-town mentality). Progressivism in all its diversity—its muckraking tradition, its cultural reformers, its economic antiplutocrats, and its anticorruption (which often meant anti-working-class) political reformers—continuously placed itself and its positions into a national political arena; its struggles were defended in the name of the nation and of democracy (against what it saw as elitist conceptions of democracy: e.g., Lippmann's *Public Opinion*), with communication as its greatest weapon. As Carey (1989b) writes, "The consistent strategy of the early progressive intellectuals was to tack back and forth between the great society brought about by industry and mass communication and the local as a site of community, politics and character formation." Eventually the desire to reconcile "the identity forming habitat of community" and "the national life of the modern period" was transformed into a "common desire" that united the various wings of progressivism: "a desire to escape the merely local, an enthusiasm for everything that was distant and remote, a love of the national over the provincial." It is in the space between these two desires, the space between two competing definitions of America, in the local and the national, that progressivism was articulated to the need for an active conception of the audience.

And it is in this context that we find not only increasing concerns about, and research on, the impact of the new mass media, but also the apparent assumption of the need to focus that research on the audience and on the active nature of the audience. This research, framed in the reformist spirit of progressivism, was concerned with the impact of the new national media on the local populations of American communities. As early as 1929, Alice Mitchell's research on children and movies (see Wartella and Reeves 1987), like the later Mass Observations studies in England, focused not merely on identifying the audience for movies, but also on how they used movies. And in the 1930s, the Payne studies, which are sometimes seen as the precursor to contemporary communication studies, similarly assumed that the audience was actively and differentially implicated in the process of communication (again see Wartella and Reeves 1987). Already in these studies, however, one can see the weakening articulations that tied the conception of the active audience to progressivism or, perhaps more accurately, one can see the gradual transformation of progressivist goals into more conservative (censorship and moralist) reformist agendas. This tradition of research disappears rather abruptly as a result of a number of developments: the political collapse of progressivism (partly a result of the uncomfortable relations between progressives and the various communist positions: e.g., John Dewey, Upton Sinclair, and Lincoln Steffens) and the intellectual defeat of the Chicago school of social thought; the approach of war and the turn within communications research to questions generated out of the need to "train" soldiers; and the increasing presence of another cultural and discursive context for the debate about communication and national identity.

Following Brookeman (1984) and especially Ross (1989), we can see that this emergent context was closely linked with the history of the communist Left in the United States between the world wars. During the 1930s, there was a particularly lively debate among the various fractions of the Left on issues of politics and culture: the progressive ethnographic spirit of a self-represented, classless, intellectual avant-garde (e.g., Agee and Evans), which viewed the population as a foreign other to be respectfully studied; those who argued for the creation of an alternative "proletarian culture" (at least potentially through the new media); the Popular Front's commitment to national cohesion and consensus in the face of fascism, which led them to reject the elitism of modernism in favor of a common mass culture (often derided as petit bourgeois); and a Trotskyist, anti-Stalinist defense of modernism against the "drift toward totalitarianism" (MacDonald, cited in Brookeman 1984, 47). As various writers moved into and through these positions, the debates increasingly intersected the more conservative, antidemocratic discourses attacking mass culture itself (e.g., the exchanges between Clement Greenberg and Dwight MacDonald in 1939) as a disease to be contained (Ross 1989).

What emerged in the late 1940s, and continued through the 1950s and '60s, was a new realignment of cultural intellectuals in response to the cold war and the growing presence of electronically distributed mass culture. As Paul Lazarsfeld, one of the founding figures of contemporary communication theory, acknowledged, "In this country we attained a peak of discussion about mass culture between 1935 and 1955." This discussion helped to shape the postwar "age of consensus" (at least that is how the emerging dominant liberal traditions rewrote their own place in American history), which marked, according to the *Partisan Review* in 1952, the end of the alienation of the intellectual and the beginning of a new cultural authority for intellectuals. The "cold war liberals" equated communism, totalitarianism, and mass culture and identified them as the greatest threats to America, to the American national identity. They argued that the very sense of what it means to be American was challenged, externally by communism and internally by mass culture. The result was that these critics had to argue that these "European" systems were not at home in the United States, that they did not accurately describe what did exist in America, nor did they reflect the experience of American culture and politics. The history of the nation had to be rewritten (e.g., in the works of Boorstin, Hofstadter, Schlesinger, and Riesman) in such a way that these threatening possibilities could not have taken root in American soil.

The problems of European society were the result of their inability to accommodate difference, which made them vulnerable to forms of political and cultural authoritarianism. But America had always taken difference for granted. Thus the real threat to America, and the reasons these foreign systems had to be undermined at all cost, was that these authoritarian systems would erase difference and establish uniformity. The American identity was put into place by denying that there could be a single identity. As Schlesinger wrote, "The only answer to mass culture lies in the affirmation of America, not as a uniform society but as a various and pluralistic society, made up of many groups with diverse interests" (cited in Ross 1989, 55). Of course, this embracing of difference did not include any acknowledgment of the inequalities that were mapped out along the systems of difference.

In the context of such a vision of America, it becomes crucial to argue—or assume—that the American audience was actually a series of large audiences, differentiated by taste and class. As early as 1952, David Riesman declared that "We need to know how individuals and groups interpret the commodities and endow them with meaning" (cited in Ross 1989, 53). Even Dwight MacDonald could allow mass culture based "on the recent discovery since 1945 that there is not One Big Audience but rather, a number of smaller, more specialised audiences. The mass audience is divisible . . . and the more it is divided, the better" (cited in Brookeman 1984, 53). Notice that Riesman has already assumed the active nature of interpretation, an assumption he went on to make explicit: "They fight back, by refusing to understand, by selective interpretation and by apathy" (cited in Ross 1989, 53). Similarly Henry Rabassiere confidently declared in 1957 that "there is no conformist material that cannot be turned into conformist outcries" (cited in Ross 1989, 53), and critics like Robert Warshow (in *The Immediate Experience,* 1974) were devoted to finding the oppositional currents in various popular forms, including westerns, gangster films, and even soap operas. The affirmation of difference, located in the diverse tastes of the cultural audience (as well as different political interest groups), was crucial to constituting a definition of America as different from the conflict-ridden structures of European societies. Tastes and interests could harmoniously coexist and even create a consensual society, unlike the strife-ridden class cultures of Europe. American pluralism meant that the imposed uniformity of both totalitarianism and a certain kind of mass culture were and would remain foreign to American soil as long as its cultural intellectuals remained ever-vigilant.

If difference was the true mark of the American identity, the enemy of America was anything that attempted to erase difference. The liberal guardians of the American identity had to continuously attack the erasure of cultural and social (class understood in terms of consumption) difference. In cultural terms, the pejorative sense of mass culture was transferred to what was increasingly conceptualized as mid-cult or middlebrow culture, the culture of the petit bourgeoisie. This "mass culture of the educated class" was seen as the legacy of Stalinism (and of the Popular Front) in its refusal to legitimate the markers of taste hierarchies and in its denial of the naturally harmonious range of differences constitutive of the American audience. To quote MacDonald again, "Let the masses have their mass cult, let the few who care about good writing, painting . . . have their high Culture, and don't fuzz up the distinction with Midcult" (cited in Brookeman 1984, 53). The enemy, that which negates America's unique identity, is not mass culture but that culture which does not allow for and respect the different tastes and uses of audiences. It's all right to have high culture, and low culture, but it is not all right to have high culture for the lower tastes (e.g., Shakespeare for the masses) or low culture for the high (e.g., sentimentality posing as art).

So the liberals found that to define and defend America, they had to assume or, even better, discover that the specificity of America depended on the difference within and activity of American audiences. Thus while the culture of America may have appeared to be a mass culture, the fact that the nation could not be constructed as a uniform audience for that culture protected America from the possibility of a nation that could be made to act as a singular—that is, totalitarian—whole. Equally important, those audiences could not be passive or totally pliable, for that would still place them at the bidding of the media. The active audience had to be affirmed, studied, valorized as if it had just been discovered. Of course, the source, form, and content of their obstinacy and activity was still determined elsewhere so that cultural diversity could always be taken to already demonstrate a prior social and political diversity. All of this was absolutely crucial in order to protect the American claim to its own uniqueness and to protect itself from the threat of (the European categories of) fascism and communism. Yet given the terms of the liberal consensus (e.g., the "end of ideology") it is easy to see why, when this position gets institutionalized as a theory of communication, especially in "uses and gratifications theory," the terms of activity are transformed. The audiences become demographically defined individuals rather than socially and politically positioned groups, and the activity itself is drained of any ideological import: interpretation and resistance are replaced by uses and gratifications.

THE AUDIENCE AND THE POLITICS
OF DIFFERENCE

The progressives in the 1920s struggled to find ways of valorizing the national over the local and concomitantly opened the door to a conception of the active audience. The liberals in the 1950s valorized the local in order to defend the national and the nation and quite explicitly placed the active audience at the center of American culture. I want now to suggest that contemporary theorists increasingly valorize the local, in the form of a theory of difference, in place of the nation. The question is: What are the politics of the current fetishism of difference? What are the possible results of locating the active audience—however we might conceptualize it—in the context of a theory of difference? And, given the range of such articulations, what are the implications for understanding the power and effectivity of the popular media and for struggling against them?

To begin, it is helpful to consider the different uses or contexts of "difference" in contemporary theory. Drawing on Barrett (1987), we can identify three senses of difference. First, it refers to the pluralistic diversity of situations. This ethnographic context of difference assumes that situations determine experience, and that different social positions (geographic, national, economic, gender, sexual, racial, etc.) constitute the local as always and inevitably other. Consequently not only is experience privileged, but the specificity of each position guarantees it an experiential authenticity and a political value. In many ways, this ethnographic difference is a continuation of the liberal tradition except for its important recognition of the ways power works in and around such differences. The second context of difference refers to the problematic construction of identities and subjectivities. Here difference is located within identity itself; the subject is seen as internally fractured, and any appeal to subjectivity must be answered by a continuous call for deconstruction. Such a theory, in attempting to deconstruct a particular definition of liberal humanism, ends up rendering any possibility of agency, any form of politically effective humanism, impossible. It tends to elevate power to the point where the active making of history, and the real possibility of historically effective resistance, disappears. The third context of difference refers to the heterogeneity of discourses. Here difference is not located in the space between situations or within subjectivity but rather in the space between discourses and "the world," where knowledges are constituted. This third theory offers an epistemological challenge to the traditions of Western thought or, perhaps more accurately, it challenges the epistemological basis of the traditions of Western thought. It renders the grand metanarratives of Western civilization problematic. Barrett argues, correctly I think, that this epistemological difference tends to erase all but the most simple appearances of power. It too easily becomes a relativistic position within which all knowledges are equally implicated in relations of power, in which all hierarchies and all structures are equally culpable and in need of deconstruction.

While I think that much of contemporary audience research conflates these three senses of difference, it may be useful to treat them separately in order to look at their political articulation. The question I want to pose is: What are the consequences of valorizing audience activity in the context of each of these three theories of difference? All of them are predicated on the assumption that difference is an expression of an anti-essentialist argument that refuses, at various levels and at various places, notions of a universal and stable identity, be it for human beings, for the subject, or for knowledge. Each of them, in different ways, contributes to a "diagnostics of discourse" in which one's social position always and already determines one's right and ability to address any specific social problem. The result is that any disagreement about a particular struggle is traced back to the social differences between the speakers (and the social "illnesses" these differences produce) rather than projected forward into an analysis of the historical adequacy and political efficacy of the alternatives.

The consequences of locating audiences in an ethnographic theory of difference are the easiest to identify, for they have been widely discussed. In fact, such a model can be traced back to the "decoding" and subcultures researches in the 1970s, in which social differences, social position, and social experience were assumed to be equivalent and to determine one's relation to the media.[3] That is, where one stood in a system of binary distinctions (often demographically defined) was assumed to locate one's social position, which, in turn, was taken to determine the context of experience (or everyday life) into which any message was appropriated and from which any interpretation was constructed. But I am less interested in the inadequacies of this model of the audience than in how it has been politically articulated. For it has helped to shape what is perhaps the dominant political strategy of the various post-1960s struggles, including many feminist and antiracist movements.

The result of fetishizing differences as autonomous identities is that, when carried to its logical conclusion, diversity is reified into fragmentation rather than appropriated as a historical resource. As a theory of audiences, it implies that every audience is different, and hence one can only study various fractions ad infinitum. If the possibility of generalization is admitted, it can only be possible because the audience's activity is determined by common social differences (e.g., we study and write about "the female audience"). In some of its current (so-called) postmodern versions, every activity of an audience is an authentic expression of their subordinate social position and experience and as such must be celebrated as some form of resistance.

Such a politics of difference is "a troubling, volatile politics in which each group justifies itself, its sense of worth and its pursuit of power, through difference alone . . . groups are forced to assert their entitlement and vie for power based on the single quality that makes them different from one another" (Steele 1989, 49 and 52). Recently some feminists have offered the most sustained critique of what has come to be called "identity politics"—"a politics steeped in identity and personal experience" (M. L. Adams 1989, 24).[4] Identity politics begins by identifying the common "difference" of an oppressed group and assuming that this corresponds to a common structure of experience and oppression. The flip side is, of course, that it entails a celebration of the active possibilities of this common identity. It assumes a hierarchy rather than a structured interconnectedness of oppression. Based on the "authenticity" of their own experience, identity politics claims that moral and political superiority is determined solely by the singular position of subordination. Consequently it often results in a "politics of guilt" (Parmar 1989). Political struggle is replaced too easily by the ongoing analysis of one's own oppression and experience or, only slightly better, by a politics in which the only site of struggle is the local (difference) constitution of one's experience.

In more traditional feminist terms, identity politics derives from the argument that the personal (i.e., experience, determined by social difference) is political. But it ignores the fact that "the political cannot be reduced to the personal" (Parmar 1989, 59). That is, it assumes that politics is determined by identity and consequently ignores the most obvious lesson of contemporary political history: that the politics of any social position is not guaranteed in advance. There is no necessary reason why anyone inhabiting a particular experiential field or located in a particular social position has to adhere to particular political agendas and interests; if they do not, we simply assume that they are suffering from false consciousness and that their experience has not yet become authentic. As June Jordan puts it, "People have to begin to understand that just because somebody is a woman or somebody is black does not mean that he or she and I should have the same politics. We should try to measure each on the basis of what we do for each other rather than on the basis of who we are" (cited in Parmar 1989, 29). On the other hand, the critique of identity politics has to tread softly, for, in the current political climate, it can easily be articulated to the Right's attack on the legitimacy of such struggles as "special interests."

The second context in which the audience is articulated to difference identifies politics with epistemology, in the sense that the only relevant political question is that of the formation of the subject through the textual production of subject-positions. By locating difference within the subject itself, it continuously offers the same attack on any claim of either a unified, self-possessed subject or an authentic experience. While it may seem paradoxical at first glance, the political implications of this poststructural context of difference are actually quite similar to those of the ethnographic articulation of difference. The paradox is due, of course, to the fact that the former challenges everything the latter privileges: identity, experience, authenticity. But because both start with the question of the individual as the marker of social differences, their options are quite limited.

There are two different ways in which the audience can be articulated into the context of poststructuralist difference. For, like the ethnographic version of difference, the poststructuralist view can either find its own measure of authenticity to celebrate, or it can turn back upon itself. In the first instance, certain media practices are privileged by virtue of their refusal to construct a singular humanistic subject or, alternatively, audiences are celebrated for their ability to locate subject-positions for themselves that explicitly refuse, and at least implicitly challenge, the position of the essentialized humanistic

subject, which, it is assumed, any text produced from positions of domination must offer. Such a politics merely conflates the problem of historical and
political agency with the epistemological question of the constitution of subjectivity. Moreover it fails to adequately account for the relationship between
ideologically offered subject-positions and the ways people are able to and
actually do take them up and live them.

By rendering all of experience suspect, it is ultimately incapable of addressing real people on the terrain where they live: the real fears, needs,
desires, aspirations, hopes, struggles, and problems which, for most of us,
constitute the limits within which we can imagine our own political positions. It ignores the contribution and empowering possibilities of such "essential moments of identity," for, as Spivak has argued, "The ones talking
about the critique of the subject are the ones who have had the luxury of a
subject" (1988, 272). If politics is merely a matter of the subject-positions
offered to us, it is difficult to see how we can escape the reduction of politics
to the plane of text/subject relations, and it is even more difficult to see how
we can find a measure of political empowerment and betterment. At best,
such a politics seeks to identify subject-positions from which the oppressed
might be empowered to speak. But again, as Spivak (1988) has argued, it is not
merely a matter of identifying the differential access people have to various
speaking positions; it is also necessary to identify the conditions that have
made it impossible for certain people to take up such positions and to speak
particular sorts of discourses.

In the second instance of the poststructuralist articulation of the audience,
the audience becomes merely the occasion for an analysis of the discursive
and epistemological production of reality through a reflexive deconstruction
of the researcher's own subjectivity. Here, "the much publicised critique of
the subject actually inaugurates a subject" (Spivak 1988, 272). Relations of
power in the real world, relations in which different audiences are implicated in different ways, are simply erased in favor of a self-critique of the
researcher's own position of power. Perhaps more accurately, the ways in
which the researcher is already inserted into various subject-positions is
metonymically substituted for the reality of the audience's relations. Since
any attempt to produce knowledge or understanding that is not totally reflexive must already locate the researcher in a humanistically constituted hierarchical relationship. the only viable form of political analysis is deconstruction and the only real object of political analysis is the researcher's
historically determined and fragmented subjectivity. The result is that the

real world of politics disappears into the constitution of subjective identities, and the relationships of people to both the media and structural relations of power are always reduced to the inevitable failure of the researchers to transcend the limits of their historical subjectivity. The distance between the researcher and audience, their otherness, is dissolved into the otherness of the researcher, his or her distance from himself or herself. But once we acknowledge the material reality of forms of disempowerment (as above), we must reject the conclusion of the poststructuralist theory of difference which denies any real need for, or effectivity of, practices of representation. For in the face of the real historical determinations of relations of domination and subordination, political struggle would seem to demand that we take seriously the question of political representation in the modern world. For those who are unable to enter into discourse directly, part of the political responsibility of those empowered to speak may precisely demand that they speak for—represent—others.

But it is the third context in which the audience is articulated to difference that is the most common and, I believe, the most dangerous; in many ways, it both grounds and surrounds the first two. It begins and ends with the assumption that the cultural critic cannot address the problematic effects of the media in contemporary history because the critic has no privileged ability to represent reality. Here contextualism becomes identified with a crisis of representation in both the political and epistemological senses: We cannot represent the world, others (e.g., audiences), or even ourselves within discourse. And if we cannot speak of such things with any authority, we also cannot speak for them. At this point, this position sometimes begins to reproduce the consequences of the ethnographic model, for the only way in which the critic can approach the reality of the media's effects is by erasing himself or herself in favor of the uncritical reproduction of the audience. In other words, the researcher can merely re-inscribe the audience's own sense of their place within and relationship to media practices. At other times, it recreates itself along the lines of poststructuralism, dissolving critical analysis into self-reflexivity.

In this context, difference is equated with a relativism that is articulated, on the one hand, to a specific and I believe inadequate form of political practice and, on the other hand, to a broader social crisis of authority. It begins as an intellectual argument that renders the authority of any knowledge suspect, since all knowledge is historically determined and implicated in relations of power. While such a moment of intellectual suspicion is necessary, it goes too far when it assumes that the only useful response to knowledge claims is either the constant deconstruction of all authority and knowledge or the celebration of a radical and relativist pluralism. For the fact of contextual determination does not render all knowledge claims false (i.e., it need not entail relativism), and the fact that specific discourses are articulated into relations of power does not mean that these relations are necessary or guaranteed. Nor does it mean that all knowledges are equally bad—and to be opposed—for even if they are implicated with particular structures of power, there is no reason to assume that all structures of power are equally bad. Such an assumption would, of course, entail the futility of political struggle and the end of history.

But even more importantly, this "intellectual's" crisis of representation and relativism, which has resulted from a certain theoretical trajectory, is frequently projected onto the real world. The result is that it is equated with a very differently constituted crisis of authority, a very real historical context of political struggle. Radway (Radway and Grossberg, unpublished) has described it as the "post Vietnam, post Watergate, post Three Mile Island" context in which the traditions of moral, political, and even intellectual authority which had been empowered by the postwar consensus and continued into the seventies, have collapsed. But even the intellectual component of this conjunctural crisis is not the same as the relativism constituted through the theory of difference. While the conjunctural crisis has been overdetermined, it is at least partly the result of the fact that, during the postwar years, liberal cultural critics renounced their own critical authority as well as their cultural alienation (Ross 1989). By giving American society a "clean bill of health," they largely ceded their authority to a scientific establishment that secured its position through its articulation to the state apparatuses, the military establishment, and the institutions of commerce. Increasingly there is a deep-seated public anxiety that America's power (moral, political, economic, etc.) is on the wane and that none of the traditional authorities is capable of protecting Americans from the many forces—natural and social—that threaten them. In this historical crisis, the intellectual stands ambiguously poised. On the one hand, he or she is at home in that crisis of culture, a part of the very audience of that crisis. And on the other hand, he or she is unable to speak to or for that audience, unable to find a position from which he or she could speak of or to "us" (i.e., a nation) with any authority.

The current arguments about the decline of the public intellectual in America tell us something about the significance of the articulation between the theoretical crisis of representation and the historical crisis of authority. Both vectors address a struggle to redefine cultural authority. But while the former defines it as the struggle to reestablish the political role of the intellectual in the face of difference, the latter defines it as the need to construct politically inflected positions and statements of authority, to relocate the right of the Left to claim such authority. The contemporary crisis of authority is, after all, another statement about the identity of America and about the need to rearticulate the intellectual's relation to the political fragmentation and unity of the nation. The intellectual's crisis is a reflexive and, in the end, self-indulgent struggle of intellectuals against the context of pessimism which they have largely created for themselves; it avoids precisely the questions constituting the real historical struggles that need to be organized around and within the conjunctural crisis of authority. The crisis of relativism enables critics to avoid confronting the crisis of authority and, for example, the very real and often deleterious power of the contemporary media at the level of national and international existence. For, at these levels, the decline of the public intellectual is actually a metaphorical gloss for the increasing presence (even as popular figures) of neoconservative intellectuals and the threatening implications of the power of a popular neoconservatism. The New Right has precisely and, in this instance I believe quite intentionally, used the lived crisis of authority—often blaming it on the Left's intellectual crisis—as the occasion for their own efforts to set in place new authorities: new positions, new criteria, and new statements. The Right has established a new critical elite that speak to and of specifically cultural values, that speak to and about the nation, and that have apparently succeeded in establishing their own authority from within the popular discourses of which they speak.

This struggle for the "natural" and "national" authority of conservative discourses is, I believe, potentially more significant than the New Right's struggle to achieve political control of the state. It entails the creation of a cultural hegemony through the articulation of positions from which only the Right is able to speak of, and for, the nation. Insofar as the Left continues to locate the audience in a context of difference, and to valorize the local, it cannot even enter into the struggle. For the Right need not offer a singular national identity (although at any moment, and in different discourses, such identities may be offered); rather it need only negotiate a popular national discourse that can be lived locally, that is, that speaks into and of the lived conditions of people's lives. The Right articulates the national to the local by increasingly valorizing the national in defense of the local. In that way, it can also turn its own discourse around and articulate the local out of the national, thus using the local to valorize the national. This discursive strategy, however unconscious and incompletely realized, establishes their claim to political and moral authority as already given in the position from which they speak; for it is a matter of how popular discourses are differentially invested in and taken up: for example, the current attacks on rock and roll do not aim to erase the music, only the differences within rock that enable and justify the investments fans make in it. Or consider the complex ways in which the discourses of the family are placed in the service of a neoconservative reconstruction of the American experience; here again, it is not a matter of the accuracy of the content of the representations of family life, or even of the audience's interpretations or experiences. Rather it is a question of how the discourses of the family are located in the lives of individuals, communities, and the nation, of how they are taken up, invested in, and placed into the spaces between the local and the national. In the end, the authority of the discourses of the family reconstitutes the taken-for-granted hierarchical demands of power.

CONCLUSION

The mistake of the current re-turn to notions of the active audience is that it confuses the contextuality of culture and cultural analysis with an abstract theory of contexts as difference. The practice of contemporary cultural criticism has to take into account the historical context of our lives not only as intellectuals, but also as members of the cultural audience. And it must confront not only the very real and often dire political conditions of the United States, but also the important place of the media in the current reconstruction of those conditions. We need to examine the conditions of possibility of our own discourses and authority as we speak to the audience of the media about the effects of the media. Those conditions include the environmental crisis, the changing international and economic climates, the limited successes of the New Right, and the greater power of a popular conservative sensibility that is reinvigorating and reorganizing the major sites of popular discourse and political activity. We need, then, not a theory of audiences, but a theory of the organization and possibilities of agency at specific sites in everyday life. We need not the fetishism of differences, but a theory of articulation and circulation that will enable us to see how unity is constantly and effectively created out of difference. We need not the denial of strong media effects, but the careful consideration of how and where the media are effective, and how their effectivity is produced. We need not to challenge all

Cultural Studies in/and

New Worlds

I begin with a rather obvious observation: Cultural studies is going through changes. But I also want to emphasize that this is not a "crisis," for cultural studies has always been changing. That is part of what makes it so attractive: cultural studies is always remaking itself as it responds to a world that is always being remade. This is possible, even necessary, precisely because it matters to cultural studies itself that this field always remain open, one with competing questions, projects, and positions. Cultural studies is always more than one thing, but its openness should not be construed as pluralism. Its openness should rather be considered as the necessary condition for its own commitments to "go on theorizing" in the face of changing historical demands.[1]

But certainly the present moment in cultural studies is not exactly like previous ones; and there is no reason to think that it should be. One reason it is not the same is that cultural studies has to deal with its own "success," a transformation not so much of its status as of its place. Prior to this "success," cultural studies could be conceived of as a minoritarian critical practice that existed in a number of different places and traditions, both intellectually and nationally. The lines that connected these places, the degrees of familiarity and influence, were highly varied and often relatively invisible.[2]

So what has success transformed? Perhaps it can be described as the degree of cultural studies' dispersion: that is, the proliferation of its speaking positions (defining where and by whom it is spoken), across ethnicities and nationalities, across traditions and disciplines. But more, I would suggest that the grid of lines connecting these positions is changing—the density, intensity, and visibility of the lines themselves.

And this raises a significant question: How should cultural studies travel? How should it locate itself in the relations between its local speaking positions and the increasingly dense and intense lines connecting these positions? Certainly cultural studies has become something of a global intellectual commodity. We may not like this, at least in principle, but it need not necessarily negate cultural studies' "use value," to use a rather simple image.

Perhaps more dangerously, cultural studies has become something of a global fantasy, so that the more we talk about it, the less clear it is what we are talking about. There is a danger that cultural studies then becomes an idealized but empty vision of a politically and/or theoretically informed intellectual practice. It remains empty because its status as a fantasy relieves us of the obligation of recognizing that it also matters to the field itself that not everything is cultural studies, that the field is not entirely open. In other words, it does matter what cultural studies is in any specific context. The fact is that cultural studies takes work, work that must partly be directed to remaking cultural studies, in response to its context, even as it is responding to that context (see Hall 1992a).

It may be useful at this point to offer at least some preliminary description of the terrain, if only in terms of the struggle over how the signifier of cultural studies is being deployed. British cultural studies is not the only space of cultural studies, but it has recently provided a common vocabulary and iconography for diverse traditions to come together. Of course, even if we acknowledge the diversity of positions that come together in "British cultural studies," we are, in the words of John Clarke (personal conversation), still only acknowledging "the diversity that won." I am aware that policing the frontiers of cultural studies is a dangerous endeavor: still, as "cultural studies" as a description of a certain body of work becomes increasingly content-free, we will increasingly need to ask, What is being lost? What specific bodies of work have no name?

If it matters how cultural studies is defined contextually, I would argue that it is less a question of theoretical positions than of critical practices. Cultural studies is obviously a set of approaches that attempt to understand and intervene into the relations of culture and power, but the particular relationship between theory and context in cultural studies is equally important. Cultural studies neither applies theory as if answers could be known in advance, nor is it empiricism without theory. Cultural studies is committed to the detour through theory even though it is not theory-driven: it is driven by its own sense of history and politics. Furthermore, cultural studies is committed to contestation, both as a fact of reality (although not necessarily in every instant) and as a strategic practice for itself.

Finally, and perhaps most importantly, cultural studies is radically contextual. Culture itself cannot be defined autonomously apart from the context any more than theory can. This contextuality can be described at three levels. First, the concept of "culture" in cultural studies is caught between community (social formations), totality (the whole way of life), and aesthetics (representational practice), to use the more common notions. I have argued elsewhere (Grossberg 1992) that, as a result, cultural studies always operates within the ambiguous space of "culture," refusing to give it a singular definition and refusing, at the same time, to reduce reality to its cultural representations. Second, the very significance not only of culture but of the relationship between culture and power depends upon the particular space into which cultural studies imagines itself to intervene. Third, the cultural "text" is neither a microcosmic representation of, nor the embodiment of a meaning related to, some social other (whether a totality or a specific set of relations). It is a place at which a multiplicity of forces (determinations and effects) are articulated. As Morris (1988a) argues, such practices have to be seen as places where different things can and do happen, where different possibilities of use and effects intersect. In other words, a cultural practice is itself a complex and conflictual place that cannot be separated from the context of its articulation. It can have no existence or identity outside of that context. For this reason, cultural studies is never merely a practice of textual interpretation and/or audience ethnography.[3]

At the same time, I want to separate myself from another strategy that closes off the terrain of cultural studies by identifying it with a particular speaking position. Tony Bennett (1993) calls this a "charismatic closure." Such a move assumes that the speaking position of cultural studies is identical to the speaker's biographical one (thus demanding "proof" of the speaker's actual political commitment). At the same time, a charismatic closure demands a *particular* political commitment by equating the speaking position of cultural studies with the abstract position of the subordinate. Consequently the biographical identity of the speaker becomes a measure of the acceptability of his or her version of cultural studies. (This obviously echoes the "political correctness debates.")[4]

Too much of the contemporary discussion about cultural studies is trapped in the fruitless opposition between the global and the local. The former tends to see cultural studies as "traveling theory" and consequently often fetishizes and reifies theory. The latter tends to emphasize local exigencies and political demands and often ends up substituting "political necessity" for theoretical work. It underestimates the values of the lines linking the various sites of cultural studies. Both positions fail to take seriously Stuart Hall's admonition that "theory is always a [necessary] detour on the way to something more important" (Hall 1991a, 42). If the relation between the global and the local is itself an articulated one, with each existing in and constituting the other, cultural studies needs to map the lines connecting them. Only then can it begin to challenge some of these relations and offer new possibilities. This work has already begun, but I want to suggest that it has not gone far enough.

For those like myself, who are positioned somewhere within the space opened up by British cultural studies or for whom it is a touchstone of sorts, this rearticulation of cultural studies has involved a questioning of the complicity of its own intellectual frameworks (culture/society, relative autonomy, ideology) and practices (a hermeneutics of understanding) with "the modern,"[5] with modern institutions and technologies of power. This is the moment of the "post-" in cultural studies—I would rather not refer to it as "postmodern"[6]—a moment that problematizes its place within broader discursive spaces, a moment that recognizes that its own conditions of possibilities also articulate both its limits and its complicitous silences. It is too easy to reduce these complicities to some singular criticism such as Eurocentrism, as if concepts were intrinsically spatially placed or all worked in the same way (for example, universalization) to claim power. But it is also too easy to explain the moment of the "post-" as if it were simply "the return" of the voices repressed by Eurocentric discourses.

For the most part, the attempt to disarticulate cultural studies from "the modern" has focused on the concept of culture and the practice of cultural interpretation (e.g., Hunter 1988, Bennett 1990, Miller 1993, and Viswanathan 1991). These authors have identified a paradox in the way "culture" is used in cultural studies: culture is both autonomous from and deeply implicated in social and historical processes. This division has to be both maintained and reconciled. Culture's autonomy must be maintained as the domain of aesthetic value or social cultivation if it is to serve a normative function as a technology of power. Only in this way can culture remain apparently untainted by its constitutive role in, for example, imperialism. These authors propose that we change our conception of culture from the field in which power is symbolized to a set of practices that apply power. In their terms, culture "civilizes" the population by altering their behavior.

Simultaneously, but from a different trajectory—one involving the effort to reconsider questions of race and ethnicity—cultural studies has moved from a practice of critical interpretation to one of articulation, from the attempt to uncover a relation that necessarily exists (for example, between a text, a meaning, and a political position) to the project of looking at the continuous production of relations that are never guaranteed in advance. This leads cultural studies to reinterpret its interventionism and contextualism so that it sees both history and its own practice as the struggle to produce one context out of another, one set of relations out of another. Articulation transforms cultural studies from a model of communication (production-text-consumption; encoding-decoding) to a theory of contexts.[7]

Both of these moves within cultural studies are predicated on recognizing one of the constitutive features of "the modern": that it fragments the social formation into a number of isolated realms—whether Rousseau's "society sui generis" or the invention of civil society and culture, always separated from economics and politics—each with its own history and its own temporality. But I want to turn to another constitutive feature of "the modern," one that points to a different possible trajectory for cultural studies' rearticulation.

THE MODERN, TIME, AND SPACE

"The modern" is always defined, positioned, in relation to an other. Each is finally conceivable only in terms of the apparently undefinable rupture separating them. In its own terms, "the modern" implies an alienation from some imaginary past or future (for example, the traditional), which is in fact the projection of a position and a measure from which "the modern" can both describe and judge itself. This temporal displacement, as Raymond Williams suggested, is precisely what constituted the notion of culture as an autonomous realm.

A number of authors, including Wolf (1982) and Amin (1989), have offered a different interpretation of this displacement.[8] Amin, for example, refuses to identify Eurocentrism with provincialism or ethnocentrism or even the claim of Europe to have the right to represent others. Instead he locates the specificity of Eurocentrism as a certain prejudice or mythology necessary for Europe to reconcile its supposed superiority with its universalist ambitions. Europe constructed its exceptionality not on the basis that "the modern" (or capitalism—although the two are not quite identical) was born there, but rather that it could not have been born elsewhere. This mythology is based on two conflicting assumptions according to Amin: the first is that internal factors peculiar to each society are decisive for their evolution. Thus Europe located its claim to uniqueness in its Christian faith and its supposed Greek ancestry. It is important to notice that this assumption identifies history with the notion of an isolatable, autonomous culture, closed off from its outside, from its others.

The second assumption underlying Eurocentrism is that the Western model of "the modern" (or capitalism) can be generalized. In fact, the European imagination assumed that the only imaginable future was the progressive Europeanization of the world. This universalization, embodied in a rhetoric of homogenization—they would become like us—legitimated a project of world conquest and colonial violence. Of course, this universality was never actually descriptive; it was distributive and normative or, in Amin's terms, polarizing. As Stuart Hall (1992b) describes it, it organized the world into "the west and the rest." The conjunction of these two conflicting assumptions— one that defined the local conditions of possibility of the modern, the other that proposed to universalize the modern and ignore local conditions—instituted and legitimated the unequal distribution of both power and value across space. And this inequality was produced both inside of and outside of every nation-space colonized by capitalism.

On this reading, we might argue that Eurocentrism—and the technologies of power of the modern—temporalizes space and rearticulates the other into the different. This opens a problematic that could only be solved by the search for or construction of a self-enclosed, isolated identity. And for just this reason, Amin rejects any politics in which modernization is treated as Westernization and opposed by the search for an alternative cultural identity. But I am getting ahead of myself. I need first to say something about time and space in "the modern." My argument is that by temporalizing reality and human existence, "the modern" effectively erased space.[9]

In fact, modernism has often been described as embodying a temporalizing logic and a specific temporality. Modern time is linear, irreversible, and unrepeatable: change, the transitory, the immanent replaced the Kantian transcendental ideal (giving rise to the paradox of a relativism that must be resisted). Even the modernist avant-garde, which offered itself as the adversary of "the modern," was caught in this specific sense of time. Because these artists assumed that the present was by definition unprepared for their art, its worth could only be recognized in the future and the only contemporary proof of its validity was its shock effect (giving rise to the paradox of an aesthetic that demands experiment and compels repetition).

In more philosophical terms, according to Young (1990),[10] Hegel is the key philosophical figure. Hegel simultaneously (1) viewed space as a product and residue of historical time; (2) fetishized a particular space—the nation-state; and (3) idealized historical time as History. The great philosophers who followed Hegel—Marx, Bergson, Husserl—all sought to restore the immanence of time in response to Hegel's idealization of time. But consequently they all failed to challenge the identification of space with reification, false consciousness, and the distortion of time. (As Meaghan Morris [1992b] has pointed out, this privileging of time continues in such celebrated works as David Harvey's *The Condition of Postmodernity* [1989].) If Hegel defined History as the continuity and coherence of time, as a historical totality, Sartre asked how there can be such a totalization without a totalizer. Or, in other words, What is the relation of individual practice to this totality?

But it was not until Lévi-Strauss and Foucault that the real question was raised: Is History, historicity, historical consciousness, essential to human existence? Or is it a construct imposed upon differential histories across space? If the answer to the latter is yes, this suggests what Foucault calls "a transformation of history into a totally different form" (cited in Young 1990, 61). And this has radical implications for how we think of power. For example, metaphors like the "survival" or "reproduction" of capitalism over time as defining images of power would have to be rethought; but of course, this is exactly what Foucault has attempted to do.

This would also obviously require a rearticulation of the concept of space in "the modern," a reconsideration not only of where it was excluded, but where and how it was included as well. This is not for me a question of the changing structures of history, as it is for John Berger: "Prophesy now involves a geographical rather than a historical projection. It is space not time that hides consequences from us" (cited in Soja 1989, 22). Even Foucault has at times treated space as a historical issue, as in his description of the present age as "an epoch of space. We are in the epoch of simultaneity; we are in the epoch of juxtaposition, the epoch of the near and the far, of the side by side, of the dispersed . . . Time probably appears to us only as one of the various distributive operations that are possible for the elements that are spread out in space" (1986, 22–23).

Such strategies merely privilege time once again and reproduce the structure of "the modern" in arguments about the "postmodern." Nor is it a question that can be entirely addressed at the level of critical social theory or philosophical anthropology. Such theories assert the mutability of history, its social production, against the claim of a necessary and universal History. One can imagine theories that assert the mutability or social production of geographies of space against the assumption of a necessary and universal—what shall we call it?—Geography (whether on the model of world-system or center-periphery or any other). That is, such theories assert that human beings make space but in conditions not of their own making, to echo Marx. They would see space, following Lefebvre (1991), as both the presupposition or medium and the outcome or embodiment of human life.

I do not want to deny the need for such work, as in the new critical geographers,[11] but it does not go far enough. They often leave temporality as the precondition of spatiality, so that, for example, Soja (1989) can still identify sequence with time and simultaneity with space. They often reduce the relation of space and power to an instrumental one, as if power merely manipulates space. And they often take spatial figures or images to be metaphorical rather than real (for example, Rosi Braidotti's otherwise brilliant analysis [1991] of feminism and philosophy).

CULTURAL STUDIES AND DIFFERENCE

I began the discussion of temporality by suggesting that the modern always constitutes itself in difference. Thus difference is itself one of its constitutive logics. The logic of difference offers a particular interpretation of the relation between identity and modernity, an interpretation that, by its very logic, denies the possibility of any alternative that might escape its logic (the logic of the modern). Since the modern constitutes its own identity by differentiating itself from an other (usually tradition as a temporal other or spatial others transformed into temporal others), identity is always constituted out of difference. The modern makes identities into social constructions. And thus a countermodern politics has to contest the particular relations of identity and difference that have been constructed by, offered in, and taken up in the modern. Here we have no choice but to start with questions of difference and to explore the nature of difference and its relation to identity. This is certainly the dominant response in cultural studies. But the real question is, To what end? If difference is irrevocable, then modernity is inescapable. It may seem somewhat ironic that just as we discover that not only particular identities but identity itself is socially constructed, we organize political struggle within the category of identity, around particular socially constructed identities.

But there is, of course, an alternative understanding of the relation of the modern and identity which suggests that the modern transforms all relations of identity into relations of difference. Thus the modern constitutes not identity out of difference but difference out of identity. The modern never constitutes itself as an identity (different from others) but as a difference (always different from itself—across time and space). In this sense, the fundamental structures of modernity are always productions of difference. Here the problem is to avoid starting with questions of difference; a countermodern politics has to elude the logic of difference and to (re)capture the possibility of a politics of otherness. If the first interpretation condemns itself (and every possible counterstrategy) to remaining within the modern; the second attempts to escape the determining boundaries of the modern by seeing the first interpretation as itself a historical product of modern power.

Let me attempt to clarify the relation between theories of difference and what I will call theories of otherness. The former is certainly dominant in contemporary theories and is built upon a very strong notion of difference, derived largely from structuralist and poststructuralist theory: that the identity or meaning of a term depends entirely (except perhaps for a necessary but indeterminate excess) on its relation to, its difference from, other terms. In fact, theories of difference take difference itself as given, as the economy out of which identities are produced. Theories of otherness, on the other hand, assume that difference is itself a historically produced economy, imposed in modern structures of power on the real. Difference as much as identity is an effect of power. While such theories obviously accept a weak notion of difference (a is not b or c or d), they do not see such differences as fundamentally constitutive. Rather they begin with a strong sense of otherness that recognizes that the other exists, in its own place, as what it is, independently of any *specific* relations. But what it is need not be defined in transcendental or essential terms; what it is can be defined by its particular (contextual) power to affect and be affected. That is, such views of otherness grant to each term an unspecified, but specifiable, positivity. After all, modern thought is not just binary but a particular kind of binary-producing machine, where binaries become constitutive differences in which the other is defined by its negativity. As Deleuze and Guattari put it, "how to think about fragments whose sole relationship is sheer difference—fragments that are related to one another only in that each of them is different—without having recourse to any sort of original totality (not even one that has been lost), or to a subsequent totality that may not yet have come about" (1987, 42).

In more philosophical terms, these alternatives can be located within the argument between Derrida and Foucault: for example, around their differing readings of Descartes (Derrida 1978, Foucault 1979b). Derrida argues that Descartes's exclusion of madness from reason itself constituted the possibility and identity of reason. The relation between reason and madness is, then, an originary structure of difference, in the sense that, once again, difference always exists at the center of identity. And in that sense, for Derrida Descartes is still alive since any conception of reason must produce and negate madness. For Foucault, on the other hand, Descartes's exclusion of madness was a philosophical representation of a real historical event; the exclusion was material and spatial as much as discursive. While this exclusion was necessary to establish the status of reason and to naturalize the identification of reason and subjectivity, it is not itself constitutive either of reason or of madness. Each of these terms has its own positivity or exteriority which can and does affect the other. In that sense, for Foucault Descartes is irrelevant today. It is not coincidental, of course, that Derrida argues that philosophy can never escape the logocentrism that, I would argue, is constitutive of modernity. Foucault, on the other hand, often writes as if he had already done so.

Much of the contemporary work on identity can be seen as a struggle taking place in the space between Derrida and Foucault. Thus, for example, Laclau and Mouffe's influential work (1985), which has contributed significantly to the theoretical frameworks with which cultural studies has approached questions of identity, can be seen as an attempt to bring Foucault and Derrida together (with a lot of Gramsci). But what has really happened is that Laclau and Mouffe have reread Foucault as if he were Derrida. Foucault's notion of the regularity of dispersion becomes an ensemble of differential positions; the rarity of discourse becomes exteriority as an excess found in the surplus of meaning. And Foucault's concern with subjectivization becomes the centrality of the production of subjects as the basis of the chain of discourse which produces both temporary fixity and the excess that destabilizes it.

Similarly, Edward Said claims to have based much of his work in *Orientalism* (1978) on Foucault. As numerous commentators have pointed out, however, the notion of "Orientalism" is intentionally ambiguous in a way that makes it quite difficult to actually pin down Said's theoretical position. At times, Said seems to suggest that Orientalism is a mode of representation by which we distinguish ourselves from others; but again, as numerous critics have pointed out, this is insufficient, for it would seem to condemn any attempt to represent an other. At another point, Said describes Orientalism as "a style of thought based on an ontological and epistemological distinction," but he fails to consider the political history of the relationship between epistemology and ontology. Is it that any ontological distinction is an act of power, or is it that when such ontological distinctions are defined by and placed in the service of knowledge—that is, when epistemology is equated with or supersedes ontology—Orientalism emerges? Of course, Said actually does begin to sound like Foucault when he connects specific discourses and their distribution to the institutions of colonialism itself. Here in fact we can see the crucial ambiguity in Said's thesis, an ambiguity that has itself defined the field of identity theories. To put it rather too simply, the question is, Does "the Oriental" exist apart from Orientalism? While many interpreters have responded in the negative, they have failed to distinguish a number of possible explanations. One possible interpretation of the existence of the Orient is tautological: since the Orient and the Oriental are constructions of colonial discourses, they cannot exist outside of those discourses. The Orient as an object of knowledge is the product of colonial relations of power. But is it so simple? Because, as numerous critics have pointed out, if this is the case, then all knowledge—and the construction of any object of knowledge—must itself be condemned as appropriative and oppressive. Is it not the articulation of knowledge into particular geo-economic and political relations that reconfigures curiosity into power?

There are at least three different positions on the existence of the Oriental that can be laid out along a continuum: the first sees it as pure excess or supplement, as the negativity at the heart of the Occident's own self-understanding. On this view, if it weren't the Orient that the West created, it would have had to have been somewhere else (and obviously, it was other places as well). The second position places the Orient and the Occident in an unequal relation of constitutive difference; they each are necessary to the self-definition of the other. Each defines itself by marking itself as different from the other. But like any theory of constitution, there is a necessary uncertainty at the center, for the fact is that each must exist independently of the relationship in order to be appropriated into the relation, and each must therefore, in some sense, have its own positivity. But this positivity is itself never specified, for it is always deferred, always irrelevant to the constitutive relation itself. The third position would seem to have actually been Said's: that Orientalism involves actual material processes of colonization, travel, exploitation, and domination. That is, people traveled to places and cultures that already existed. The Oriental, as it were, existed independently of the Orientalist. The act of power comes not in creating something from nothing, but in reducing something to nothing (to pure semantic and differential terms)—in negating the positivity of the Arab world with all of its diversity, for example, to nothing but a singular constitutive other, to the different. Thus it is precisely the articulation of difference on top of otherness that becomes the material site of discursive power and that is, I would argue, a fundamental logic of the formations of modern power.

I have already suggested that the modern itself is constituted by the logic of difference through which the modern is constructed as an "adversarial space" living in "an anxiety of contamination by its other" (Huyssen 1986, vii). This logic of difference, in which the other is defined by its negativity, has, as Nietzsche pointed out, only the possibility of a politics of "ressentiment." But increasingly such theories have begun to come under attack: "There is nothing remotely groovy about difference and diversity as political problems . . . The management of diversity and difference through the bureaucratic mantra of race, class and gender encouraged the divisive rhetoric of being more marginal, more oppressed" (Mercer 1992b, 33). And despite the intentions of antimodernist critics, celebrations of difference do not give up the totalizing speaking voice of the modern; instead "it becomes the master of differing, offering a unified theory of difference" (Wark 1992, 436). The alternative is to begin to construct a theory of otherness that is not essentialist, a theory of positivity based on notions of effectivity, belonging, and, as Paul Gilroy (1993) describes it, "the changing same."

CULTURAL STUDIES AND THE SPACE OF POWER

As cultural studies moves into different sites—"new" worlds, to speak ironically, worlds that have been irretrievably reconstructed by the violence of the various forms of modern power, including those of colonialism, imperialism, racism, sexism, disciplinization, and normalization—it too will have to be irretrievably reconstructed in some fundamental ways. It will have to rethink its articulations of culture and power. I want to propose two related trajectories of such a rearticulation. First, cultural studies must move from a temporal to a spatial logic of power, and second, it must move from a structural to a machinic theory of power.

To begin to try to think of power spatially does not mean that we erase history but that we see it as singular events or "becomings" (in the terms of Deleuze and Guattari [1987]) rather than as continuity or reproduction. It also requires that we recognize that on certain maps, where a map is a geography of becomings, the places marked as history, time, and reproduction can be invested with a great deal of intensity or even power. History, then, becomes inseparable from memory, not as a dis-placed "popular memory," but precisely as "placed time," as a geography of temporalities (Hay, 1993).

But the project of mapping the spaces of power will inevitably raise different and other questions: questions about mobilities rather than change, about lines of intensities rather than identities. Spatial power is a matter of orientations and directions, of entries and exits, rather than of beginnings and ends. Let me emphasize here that by describing this as a spatial logic, I do not mean only that we need to look at the organization of space in literal or material terms as the site of power, or that we need to look at the nontextual existences of culture.[12] Rather culture itself must be understood spatially before it is seen hermeneutically. To say that space is material does not mean that it is reducible to material space. To look at different spatial organizations and the different technologies that produce them is to consider the vectors, intensities, and maps of space as regimes of power rather than simply structures of relationality. But such regimes are often defined as well by structures of what we might call "the spatial imaginary" (Wark 1994).

Similarly, thinking of power machinically requires a significant shift in the questions we ask: as Deleuze and Guattari put it, "the question . . . is not whether the status of women, or those on the bottom, is better or worse, but the type of organization from which that status results" (1987, 210). This suggests that we give up a view of the critical project that merely constantly rediscovers what we already know: that structures of domination and subordination are reproduced, that representations of difference and inequality are reinscribed. But we must also give up our willingness to be satisfied with finding the cracks in the processes of reproduction and reinscription, with discovering that people are indeed active and capable of struggle and even resistance. In this sense, I would propose that cultural studies needs to move beyond models of oppression, both the "colonial model" of the oppressor and the oppressed and the "transgression model" of oppression and resistance, and toward a model of articulation or "transformative practice" (Cameron McCarthy, personal conversation). Both models of oppression seem not only inappropriate to the contemporary relations of power but also incapable of creating alliances because they cannot tell us how to interpellate fractions of the "empowered" into the struggle for change in something other than a masochistic (guilt-ridden) way.

I am suggesting that cultural studies explore the concrete ways in which different machines—or, in Foucault's terms, apparatuses—produce the specific spaces, configurations, and circulations of power.[13] These spaces, configurations, and circulations constitute not only the specific conjuncture or social formation but also the relations between the local and the global. In this regard, I would argue that we need (and the project is being carried out by others more capable) to rethink not only the history of capitalism but the very nature of capitalism—in spatial terms. If I can offer a very small and simple piece of this puzzle as an example, we might begin to understand Taylorism—a crucial aspect of the fordist articulation of capitalism—as an apparatus that quite precisely and intentionally temporalized the space of the production of surplus value. And on the other hand, many of the strategies that have been discussed as "postfordist" (for example, subcontracting, the construction of what Castells [1989] calls "informational" or "dual cities," the spatial redistribution of labor and wealth) are all part of a set of apparatuses that is reorganizing the spatial distribution of capital and respatializing the time of production. In fact, any analysis of contemporary capitalism should recognize that there is a struggle over the spatial distribution of different articulations of capitalism itself. The goal seems to be an increasingly rapid but controlled flow of capital, people, and commodities in order to remonetarize capitalism through the creation of a globally circulating debt.

IDENTITY AND DIFFERENCE[14]

Rather than continuing in this vein, however, I want to turn my attention to some themes that may have a more immediate and obvious relevance (although they are not by that fact more important) to the questions facing an international cultural studies. I want to try to consider, perhaps even demonstrate, the significance of the move away from models of difference and to a spatial and machinic model of power by considering one of the central concerns in cultural studies: the problem of identity. Within cultural studies, investigations of the constitution and politics of identity are often predicated on a distinction, nicely articulated by Hall (1990b), between two forms of struggle over—two models of the production of—identities. It is important to recognize that Hall offers this not as a theoretical distinction, although it certainly can be mapped onto the dispute between essentialists and anti-essentialists, but as a historical and strategic distinction. The first model assumes that there is some intrinsic and essential content to any identity which is defined by either a common origin or a common structure of experience or both. Struggling against existing constructions of a particular identity takes the form of contesting negative images with positive ones, and of trying to discover the "authentic" and "original" content of the identity. Basically, the struggle over representations of identity here takes the form of offering one fully constituted, separate, and distinct identity in place of another.

The second model emphasizes the impossibility of such fully constituted, separate, and distinct identities. It denies the existence of authentic and originary identities based in a universally shared origin or experience. Identities are always relational and incomplete, in process. Any identity depends upon its difference from, its negation of, some other term, even as the identity of the latter term depends upon its difference from, its negation of, the former. As Hall puts it: "Identity is a structured representation which only achieves its positive through the narrow eye of the negative. It has to go through the eye of the needle of the other before it can construct itself" (1991a, 21). Identity is always a temporary and unstable effect of relations that define identities by marking differences. Thus the emphasis here is on the multiplicity of identities and differences rather than on a singular identity and on the connections or articulations between the fragments or differences. The fact of multiple identities gives rise to the necessity of what Kobena Mercer has called "the mantra of race, class and gender" (1992b, 34): "The challenge is to be able to theorize more than one difference at once" (1992a, 425). This suggests a much more difficult politics, because the sides are not given in advance, nor in neat divisions. As Michele Wallace says, echoing June Jordan, "The thing that needs to be said—women are not to be trusted just because they're women, anymore than blacks are to be trusted because they're black, or gays because they're gay and so on" (1994, 185). Here struggles over identity no longer involve questions of adequacy or distortion, but of the politics of representation itself. That is, politics involves questioning how identities are produced and taken up through practices of representation. Obviously influenced by Derrida, such a position sees identity as an entirely cultural, even an entirely linguistic, construction. While this model certainly suggests that the identity of one term cannot be explored or challenged without a simultaneous investigation of the second term, this is rarely the case in practice. Most work in cultural studies is concerned with investigating and challenging the construction of subaltern, marginalized, or dominated identities, although some recent work has begun to explore dominant identities as social constructions. Rarely, however, are the two ever studied together, as the theory would seem to dictate, as mutually constitutive.

It is obviously this second model that defines work around identity in cultural studies, but I do not mean to suggest that this model defines a singular theoretical position or vocabulary. On the contrary, there are a number of different, overlapping, intersecting, and sometimes even competing figures which, taken together, define the space within which cultural studies has theorized the problem of identity. Often they function together to define specific theories. Interestingly, these figures construct a continuum of images of spatiality, although, as I will suggest, they are for the most part structures of temporality. All of these figures can be seen as models of articulation or, in more spatial terms, as figures of borders. And all of them are predicated on a principle of difference or negativity. They all operate in a Derridean space of textuality in which the difference between a place and a position is erased. Moreover, because all of them ground identity, in one way or another, in language and signification, they can all be read as grounding identity in the temporality of consciousness or what Homi Bhabha calls the "temporal nonsynchronicity of signification" (1991, 58). I will describe these figures as *différance,* fragmentation, hybridity, border, and diaspora.

The figure of *différance* describes a particular constitutive relation of negativity in which the subordinate term (the marginalized other or subaltern) is a necessary and internal force of destabilization existing within the identity of the dominant term. The subaltern here is itself constitutive of, and necessary for, the dominant term. The instability of any dominant identity—since it must always and already incorporate its negation—is the result of the very nature of language and signification. The subaltern represents an inherent ambiguity or instability at the center of any formation of language (or identity) which constantly undermines language's power to define a unified stable identity. We can identify two variants of this figure: notions of the "supplement" locate the other outside of the field of subjectivity, as it were, as pure excess; notions of "negativity" locate the other within the field of subjectivity as a constitutive exotic other. In the former, the subaltern constitutes the boundaries of the very possibility of subjectivity; in the latter, the subaltern may be granted an incomprehensible subjectivity. There are numerous examples of these two variants of the figure of *différance* in contemporary theories of identity. For example, Lyotard (1990) sees "the jews" as that which European culture cannot identify because its exclusion, its unnameability, is itself constitutive of European identity. Similarly, Bhabha's notion (1994) of mimicry as an intentional misappropriation of the dominant discourse locates the power of the subaltern in a kind of textual insurrection in which the subaltern is defined only by its internal negation of the colonizer. Certeau's attempt (1984) to define subordinate populations only by their lack of a place that would entitle them to their own practices or strategies similarly ends up defining the subaltern as pure *différance*. Finally, there is a common reading of Said's *Orientalism* (1978) in which the dominant power necessarily constructs its other as a repressed and desired difference.

The figure of *fragmentation* emphasizes the multiplicity of identities and of positions within any apparent identity. It thus sees a particular concrete or lived identity as "a kind of disassembled and reassembled unity." Identities are thus always contradictory, made up out of partial fragments. Theories of fragmentation can focus on the fragmentation of either individual identities or of the social categories (of difference) within which individuals are placed, or some combination of the two. Further, such fragmentations can be seen as either historical or constitutive. This is perhaps the most powerful image, certainly in British cultural studies, with echoes in Hebdige's notion of "cut 'n' mix" and Gilroy's notion of syncretism. Donna Haraway also seems to offer such a figure in the image of a cyborg as "a potent subjectivity synthesized from the fusion of outsider identities" (1991, 174). Or, from David Bailey and Stuart Hall: "Identities can, therefore, be contradictory and are always situational . . . In short, we are all involved in a series of political games around fractured or decentered identities . . . since black signifies a range of experiences, the act of representation becomes not just about de-centering the subject but actually exploring the kaleidoscopic conditions of blackness" (1992b, 21).

The figure of *hybridity* is more difficult to characterize, for it is often used synonymously with a number of other figures. Nevertheless I will use it to describe three different images of *border* existences, of subaltern identities as existing between two competing identities. Images of a *"third space"* (as in Bhabha) see subaltern identities as unique third terms literally defining an "in-between" place inhabited by the subaltern. Images of *liminality* collapse the geography of the third space into the border itself; the subaltern lives, as it were, on the border. In both of these variants of hybridity, the subaltern is neither one nor the other but is defined by its location in a unique spatial condition that constitutes it as different from either alternative. Neither colonizer nor precolonial subject, the postcolonial subject exists as a unique hybrid that may, by definition, constitute the other two as well. Closely related to these two figures of hybridity is that of the *"border-crossing,"* marking an image of betweenness that does not construct a place or condition of its own other than the mobility, uncertainty, and multiplicity of the fact of the constant border-crossing itself. Often, these three versions of hybridity are conflated in various ways, as in Gloria Anzaldúa's description of the Atzlán: "A borderland is a vague and undetermined place created by the emotional residue of an unnatural boundary . . . People who inhabit both realities . . . are forced to live in the interface between the two" (1987, 37).

Finally, the figure of *diaspora* is closely related to that of border-crossing, but it is often given a more diachronic inflection. This figure has become increasingly visible through the work of anthropologists such as James Clifford and Smadar Lavie, cultural critics such as Paul Gilroy, and various postcolonial theorists. As Jim Clifford describes it, "The term 'diaspora' is a signifier not simply of transnationality and movement, but of political struggles to define the local—I would prefer to call it place—as a distinctive community, in historical contexts of displacement" (1994, 308). That is, diaspora emphasizes the historically spatial fluidity and intentionality of identity, its articulation to structures of historical movements (whether forced or chosen, necessary or desired). Diaspora links identity to spatial location and identifications, to "histories of alternate cosmopolitanisms and diasporic networks" (327). While this figure offers significantly new possibilities for a cultural politics that avoids many of the logics of the modern—by rooting identity in structures of affiliations and ways of belonging—it is, too often, drawn back into the modern. Identity is ultimately returned to history, and the subaltern's place is subsumed within a history of movements and an experience of oppression that privileges particular exemplars as the "proper" figures of identity.

Such theories—built on the range of diverse figures described above—have recently come under attack (e.g., Parry 1987, O'Hanlon 1988): for ignoring the fragmentary and conflictual nature of the discourses of power (different at different places and spaces, of course); for ignoring the heterogeneity of power and apparently reducing it to discourses of representation and ignoring its material realities; for ignoring the positivity of the subaltern—as the possessor of other knowledges and traditions and as having their own history in which there are power relations defined within the ranks of the subordinated. And one might add yet another problem concerning the status of the marginal or subordinate in these figures. On what grounds do we assume that a privileged or even different structure of subjectivity belongs to the subaltern? And if, as Hall suggests, the marginal has become central, is it not descriptive of the contemporary subject? The other side of the question is,

Can one form of subordination become the model of all structural domination? Insofar as we have now created a figure of the subaltern, have we not developed another universalizing theory, providing answers to any local struggle before we have even begun, since we know we will always find the production of the other as different?[15]

But these various turns to difference are predicated on an even more central and particularly difficult set of questions that have arisen out of the philosophical inheritance of "the modern." Many people date the beginning of modern philosophy with the Cartesian problematic of the relations between the individual and reality, understood as the epistemological problematic of truth. Descartes of course solved it by postulating a self-reflective consciousness. Kant identified this consciousness with the mediating position of experience (giving birth on the one hand to phenomenology and on the other to structuralism).[16]

This privileging of consciousness (or in romanticism, of imagination) as the space of the mediation of opposition depended upon an identification of subjectivity with temporality. Only in this way was consciousness capable of totalizing and transcending chaos: the unity of the subject depended upon the unity of time, an assumption that continues at least through Heidegger (if not Derrida). In political terms, this traditional set of assumptions gives rise to what O'Hanlon (1988) calls "the virile figure of the subject-agent." In other words, the modern "humanistic" individual is predicated on the articulation or assumed identification of three distinct events: (1) the subject as a unified source of knowledge and experience; (2) the agent as a position of activity; and (3) the self as the bearer of a social identity.

If "maps of identification and belonging" define how and where individuals and groups are located in the world, the articulation of these three different aspects of our maps of identification and belonging into a singular and presumably coherent figure inevitably gave rise to a paradox. This paradox, however, only became painfully visible when anti-essentialist arguments were successfully mounted against any claim to the unity of both the subject and the self and critical arguments were successfully mounted to demonstrate the social construction of both the subject and the self. The paradox is simple: How can the individual be both cause and effect, both subject and subjected? Or, in other words, how does one locate agency? This problem has animated the large body of contemporary political and theoretical work on the production of subordinate identities and the possibilities of resistance, whether in the name of the subaltern, feminism, antiracism, postcolonialism, or the new ethnicities. I do not intend to rehearse the positions and debates that have made such work so exciting and so important in both theoretical and political terms. Instead I want to identify three dominant strategies operating in this field. But I emphasize that I am isolating these out of their discursive contexts to construct something like "ideal types." Often a single author will use more than one and this need not necessarily result in a contradictory or paradoxical position.

Let me now briefly describe the three dominant strategies: The first assumes that interpellation is never entirely successful, that there is always an excess or residue that is not interpellated by any particular ideological text. Such positions tend to emphasize the multiplicity of interpellations and the complex and even contradictory relations that may exist between the different subject-positions. If the individual as a subject is overdetermined, then he or she transcends any single ideology. This argument is closely connected to a number of theories of identity that see the subject as fundamentally fragmented. However, I do not see how the assumption of multiple interpellations solves the paradox of agency, since it must assume that, somehow, agency is the product of the contradiction or gaps between the different subject-positions.

The second strategy attempts to locate agency in another—usually ontological and often repressed—realm of human existence. The domain of agency is thus independent of and transcends the realm of subjectivity. Whether agency is located in the unconscious or some other manifestation of a privileged "will," such as Mead's "creative I," such theories end up reifying an essentialist notion of agency that denies the possibility that agency or at least the forms of agency are themselves produced. Moreover such theories often assume that agency is required only to explain or allow the possibility of resistance; there is little attempt to describe the agency of domination.

The final strategy disconnects interpellation and identity, usually arguing that identity involves the articulation of interpellated subject-positions into ideologically produced systems of meaning. These articulations are themselves determined by a number of different social forces that operate differentially within different social domains. Thus cultural identities determine the meaning and experience of various subject-positions. Like the first strategy, this one too assumes that agency must be located in the space between various identities, but it begins with a gap between subject-positions and identity. Moreover it fractures the notion of identity across the various social domains, so that agency depends on the articulation of the various moments of identity across domains. For example, it may result from the articulation of a subordinated economic subject to a politically oppositional identity. But in the end, this merely delays and displaces the question into the practice of articulation itself.

IDENTITY AND SPACE

I do not wish to underestimate the importance of the theoretical and political work represented by these discourses. And yet I want to place them in the context of my own frustrations. I do not mean to reject the concept of identity or its political importance in certain political struggles; but I do reject the subsumption of identity within a logic of difference, and the assumption that such structures of identity necessarily belong to particular subject groups. And I believe it is important to ask whether every struggle over power can or should be organized around issues of identity. At the very least, it may be necessary to rearticulate the category of identity and its place in cultural studies and politics. Debates about multiculturalism, for example, too quickly assume a necessary relation between identity (ethnicity) and culture. I would argue instead that the question of the desirability of a multicultural society is a normative one (to what extent can a society continue to exist without a common—albeit constantly rearticulated and negotiated—culture), while the fact that the United States is (and has been) a multiethnic society with a wide range of cultural practices cannot be ignored.

After all, if, as I believe, cultural studies is to be judged by whether and how it opens up new possibilities and enables new political strategies, then something is wrong. It may be that such work has constrained our possibilities as much as it has advanced them. This seems especially true in the context of contemporary events and trends in the United States. Let me point to two examples. At the broader level, any critical perspective has to begin by acknowledging our apparent inability to comprehend, to say nothing about challenging, the power of the new conservatism and the increasingly conservative tone of American life. At the more specific level, and in some ways even more disturbing, I would point to the 1992 violence in Los Angeles (I refuse to call it either a riot or an uprising). In Los Angeles, it seems that the lessons of anti-essentialism disappeared, assuming we believe that they ever took hold. The fact of the matter is that when people actually took to the streets, all of their anger, their disappointment, and their antagonism came out in the most essential of terms. And for all of the struggle and suffering to which this event gave witness, we know that little or nothing is likely to change for the urban populations of the United States.[17]

It seems to me that, in part, we have become so fascinated with theory that we have forgotten a fundamental lesson: that people cannot be successfully changed or moved politically if one begins by telling them that their deepest beliefs and investments are mistaken. Or, to put it another way, we must begin where people already are if we want to move them to somewhere else. This does not mean that we accept the commonsense grounds of the often ineffective forms of contemporary struggle. It does mean that we have to find a theoretical project that will enable us to do two things: first, to draw the lines that make the local and the global always inseparable; and second, to rearticulate the forms and sites of people's antagonisms and hopes.

It is this project that has led me to seek a different way of looking at identity, alterity, and agency—spatially and machinically. Let me begin then by looking at the three different machinic productions involved. First, there is the production of subjectivity or, in other words, of a phenomenological field. I would argue that insofar as everyone experiences the world, subjectivity is a universal, if unequally distributed, value. But everyone has subjectivity in the sense that everyone exists at the center of their own phenomenological field; consequently they have access to some experience, to some knowledge about themselves and the world. And to a certain extent, as Althusser argued, subjectivity "authorizes" experience. Such a notion of experience, however, is not ontological. Subjectivity is a machinally produced value rather than a prediscursive or preterritorial reality.[18]

But of course, subjectivity in this sense is abstract, and it must be articulated to and within a second "differentiating machine," a machine that discursively (or ideologically) produces differentially valued subject-positions (through a discursive interpellation), which, when articulated to maps of meaning, produce what we more commonly call identities. Thus, although everyone exists within what we might call the "strata" of subjectivity, they are also located at particular positions within the strata, each of which enables and constrains the possibilities of experience, but even more, of representing and legitimating those representations. In this sense, we can agree with the various positions described above that the subject exists only after the inscription of historical difference. As Lefebvre says, the subject "can never be caught red-handed, because it is made up after the event" (1984, 92).

However, because people take up their different identities in different ways and do not always internalize or live the discursive interpellation, we need yet another machine, a machine in which the individuality is constructed as a vector through an affective interpellation. This third machinic production is more difficult to describe. It involves a more explicit spatial territorialization—an organization of places and spaces—and it requires a notion of affective investment. To explain, let me begin with some quotations, first two from Stuart Hall:

> By ethnicity, we mean the astonishing return to the political agenda of all those points of attachment which give the individual some sense of place and position in the world, whether these be in relation to particular communities, localities, territorialities, languages, religions, or cultures. (1989, 33)

> ... the recreation, the reconstruction of imaginary knowable places in the face of the global postmodern which has, as it were, destroyed the identities of specific places ... So one understands the moment when people reach for these groundings ... and the reach for those groundings is what I call ethnicity. (1991a, 35–36)

Rudolfo Anaya and Francisco Lomeli describe Aztlán as the simultaneously historical and imaginary place within which Chicanos and Chicanas increasingly come to place their ethnicity:

> The element of identity is but a fragment of the totality that permits the experiencing of origins as a comfort zone which enhances our development. Aztlán localizes this process in a particular milieu in relation to a complex network of historical events and happenings. In other words, through Aztlán we come to better understand psychological time (identity), regional makeup (place), and evolution (historical time). Without any one of these ingredients, we would be contemporary displaced nomads, suffering the diaspora in our own land, and at the mercy of other social forces. Aztlán allows us to come full circle with our communal background as well as to maintain ourselves as fully integrated individuals. (1989)

Here we turn our attention to the relations of spaces, places, things, and people. But this is not meant as a return to a Cartesian dualism in which we separate psychology from the material world. Rather we must raise the question of psychology in new and, perhaps, sometimes disconcerting ways. I want to describe a territorializing machine that distributes subjectivity and subject-positions in space. A territorializing machine diagrams lines of mobility and placement; it defines or maps the possibilities of where and how people can stop and *place* themselves. Such places are temporary points of belonging and identification, of orientation and installation, of investment and empowerment. Such places create temporary addresses or homes. But as Meaghan Morris (1992a) points out, such places or homes do not preexist the lines of mobility, the space. They are not origins. They are the product of an effort to organize a limited space, as Deleuze and Guattari describe it (1987, 311). They define forms of empowerment or agency, ways of going on and going out. Around such places, maps of meaning, of desire, and of pleasure can be articulated.

A territorializing machine attempts to map the sorts of places people can occupy and how they can occupy them. It maps how much room people have to move, and where and how they can move. A territorializing machine produces lines of specific vectors, intensities, and densities that differentially enable and enact specific forms of mobility and stability, specific lines of investment (or anchoring) and flight. It maps the ways in which people live the always limited freedom to stop in and move through a field of force.

Within the structured mobility of such machinic operations, as O'Hanlon has observed, "the subaltern is not a social category but a statement of power" (1988, 207). And power and resistance are defined by the spatial relations of places and spaces and the distribution of people and practices within them. In that sense, marginalization is neither an identity nor a spatial position but a vector or distribution defining access, mobility, and the possibilities of investment and agency. Turning to O'Hanlon once again: "The subaltern is rendered marginal in quite a different way—in part through his inability, in his poverty, his lack of leisure and his inarticulacy, to participate to any significant degree in the public institutions of civil society, with all the particular kinds of power which they confer, but most of all, and least visibly, through his consequently weaker ability to articulate civil society's self-sustaining myth" (221).

It is within the machinic operation of territorialization that agency is constructed and its possibilities distributed. Particular places define specific forms of agency and empower specific populations. In this sense, we can inquire into the conditions of possibility of agency, for agency—the ability to make history, as it were—is not intrinsic either to subjectivity or to subjects. It is not an ontological principle that distinguishes humans from other sorts of beings. Agency is defined by the articulations of subject-positions into specific places (sites of investment) and spaces (fields of activity) on socially constructed territorialities. Agency is the empowerment enabled at particular sites and along particular vectors. Thus when we speak of the agent of articulation, we need to distinguish between the fact that people do things that have effects, often while they are struggling to change their circumstances or even history, and the existence of agents—places and vectors—that make history. Agency points to the existence of particular formations of practices as places on social maps, where such places are at least potentially involved in the making of history. Agency as a site is, of course, only realized if specific investments are enabled and articulated.[19]

A number of consequences follow from this: First, resistance cannot be explained by an abstract metaphysical (or philosophical anthropological) principle, or by an appeal to the return of the repressed, or by the fact of contradictory interpellations and subject-positions. It can only be explained as the concrete overdetermined articulation of fractions of the population to particular sites of agency. Second, we need to radically rethink our assumptions about the nature, possibility, and effectivity of alliances. Too often we get captured by the assumed equivalence of subject and agent, resulting in such bizarre debates as the place of "men in feminism." A more fruitful approach, especially in the context of the resurgence of racism, sexism, and homophobia in the United States, might be to reconsider the civil rights movement as a model in which affect and agency were successfully articulated to morality and politics.

The question of agency, then, is how access and investment are distributed within a particular structured mobility. And this suggests that political identity is not the same as subject-positions or cultural identities. We need a different conception of political identity and of politics: a politics of commitment, of affect, of identification and belonging. Here we might, once more, return to Stuart Hall: "Political identity often requires the need to make conscious commitments. Thus it may be necessary to momentarily abandon the multiplicity of cultural identities for more simple ones around which political lines have been drawn. You need all the folks together, under one hat, carrying one banner, saying we are this, for the purpose of this fight, we are all the same, just black and just here" (cited in Grossberg 1992, 380).

Hall's proposal, albeit too voluntaristic and individualistic for my tastes, nevertheless seems to me to take the diaspora literally, to see the subaltern in spatial, affective, and machinic terms. And it sees agency and ethnicity as a struggle over the articulation of places and investments. It is a matter of what I (following Rebecca Goldstein) have called mattering maps, which define where and how one can and does invest, and where and how one is em- powered, made into an agent. Here, as Deleuze and Guattari say (1987, 316), the proper name is not the mark of a subject, but the constituting mark of an abode.

TOWARD A CONCRETE POLITICS OF SPACE

In concluding, I have two possible vectors before me. One leads me to the abstract theoretical question of how we map the space of power, remembering that we are interested in how that space is produced. I have offered something like a model of triangulation which suggests that any such space is produced by the simultaneous operation of three types of machines, three active orga- nizations of power: an abstract or stratifying machine of value; a coding- decoding machine of differentiation; and a territorializing-deterritorializing machine of distribution. Not only are these three machines or structurations of power complexly articulated, but each is itself multiple and internally articulated. The three machines operate on each other but not in any temporal sequence. Moreover the whole operation, as well as the operation of each machine, is a site of contestation. Hence the relations between them are not guaranteed, nor is any one equivalent to, for example, capitalism, patriarchy, racism, or colonialism. Each is articulated by specific relations, although one assemblage (for example, capitalism) may deploy others (for example, rac- ism, patriarchy). This means that any analysis of the machinic production of power must always be conjunctural. A map of the conjunctural operation of such a machinic complex describes what Foucault calls a "diagram" (Deleuze 1988).

It may be helpful to say a little more about each of these machines in the abstract. The first—*abstract*—machine produces value (axioms) by what De- leuze and Guattari (1987) describe as a double articulation or "acts of cap- ture" (connective synthesis). It produces strata by bringing together two planes: the plane of content and the plane of expression. It is, therefore, a machine of production or positivity. The second—*coding*—machine estab- lishes (inscribes via a disjunctive synthesis) relations within the strata (on each plane) or between "milieus." It is a differentiating machine of subjectiv- ization and normalization that, through negativity and exchange, produces a striated space marked by dimensionality (lines of extension). The third—

territorializing—machine establishes (anchors via a conjunctive synthesis) relations between strata, between expression and content. It is a distributive machine of alterity that produces a smooth space marked by intension (vectors or lines of intensity) and the possibility of nonextensional relations (voyage in place). Alterity then becomes a distribution of places and spaces where each place is not only the site of expressivity but also of multiple vectors (hybridity) and agency. The problem with Deleuze and Guattari's theory of the politics of the diagram is that they equate the politics of becoming in the three moments of the diagram: becoming body-without-organs; becoming different (for example, woman; and by the way, it is only at this level that real women are not erased); and becoming minor (other).

The second vector leads me back to the new conservatism of the United States (see Grossberg 1992) and to Los Angeles, about which I want to say a few words in conclusion. When thinking about Los Angeles, I am reminded of Mike Davis's critique (1985) of Fred Jameson's "reading" of Portman's Bonaventura Hotel as a postmodern text—a classic interpretation and a classic part of Jameson's analysis of the postmodern. Davis, rather than reading the hotel as a text with its own aesthetic, points instead to the "savagery of its insertion into the surrounding city" (112) and identifies it as part of a larger project to "polarize [the city] into radically antagonistic spaces" (113). It is an outpost, part of the fortifications, of the newly emerging "Fortress America" which is arising in the midst of the dual or multiple cities of global capitalism.

The question is how we can rearticulate the antagonisms that erupted between African Americans, Latinos, and Koreans, antagonisms that seem to be based on assumptions of essential identities. The traditional answer—that we must use education to overcome cultural relativism—not only assumes that the problem is one of understanding and communication (probably a mistaken assumption), but it also seems to preclude the possibility of effective alliances as much as does the antagonism itself.

I offer the following suggestion only as a possibility and only in the briefest terms since, as I must acknowledge, I have not yet done the research necessary to make my analysis concrete at the local level, nor have I gotten very far in my efforts to make the connections between Los Angeles and regional, national, and global political and economic developments. I want to suggest that the antagonisms can be displaced from questions of identity to the more sympathetic question of the relations among the different maps of territorialized marginality that have come to define postwar U.S. urban space. This space cannot even be described as a dual city in which two different maps (two different populations, two different economies, two different structured mobilities) coexist; it is a complex and overlapping system of spatial empowerment and disempowerment, of mobility and placement, of openness and closure. It is a polyspatial city.

In particular, I think we can identify four different modes of spatial existence, four different territorializing maps or structured mobilities existing within the common space of the city: (1) a population that is increasingly demobilized, with no access to any places of agency (and which is, of course, largely black); (2) a highly mobile diasporic population but also with almost no access to places of agency (largely Latino);[20] (3) a population with a highly constrained but nevertheless extensive line of mobility. The Korean population, like the Jews before them, find that they must work in South Central Los Angeles but that they are free to live elsewhere (although certainly not anywhere: their mobility is also constrained by racism). Moreover, like the Jews, the Koreans come with their own economic and cultural capital which allows them to establish alternative places and institutions of agency and empowerment (such as communal and interfamilial "banks").[21]

If we can understand the antagonisms that exist among these groups as a matter not of identities but of the conflicts constructed among these different spatial configurations, can we begin to rearticulate them into a common opposition to the fourth spatial map? This fourth map describes the increasingly "fortresslike" organization of significant fractions of the white (but not entirely) and wealthy (how far down into the middle class does this map extend?) dominant populations. Yet it is a fortress that, through a variety of technologies and capital flows, allows for an extraordinary degree of mobility. And more than anything, I think, it is this apparent paradox that defines the existence of domination in urban centers like Los Angeles.

Regarding political strategies, I believe we should not eliminate any possibility to begin with. After all, political strategies must themselves be conjuncturally determined. In spatial terms, a social movement can be understood as a territorializing map that attempts to reorganize space and to create new places. A social movement must be seen as an affective alliance that does not merely bring together multiple interests but finds affective investments that unite them "under one banner." But this can only be accomplished if we strategically consider the proper level of abstraction at which a political struggle must operate.

CONCLUSION

Recently a number of authors have challenged the particular confluence of logics that have defined modern theories of identity. Ahmad (1992), for example, argues that there is often a rather easy slide from an "absence of belonging" to an "excess of belonging" predicated on the assumption of migrancy as an ontological and epistemological condition. Similarly, Dhareshwar warns against the desire for "an identity that fully coheres with the narrative force of theory," which takes the figures of a theoretical system as the "storyline" for narrative identity: "for example, 'decentered subjectivity' as postmodern reality, dissemination as 'immigritude' (my word for the whole narrative of displacement which has become a normative experience in metropolitan politics of cultural description)" (1989, 142–43). I would argue that, insofar as the various theories of identity remain grounded in modern logics of difference, individuality, and temporality, the radical implications of the increasingly spatial language of such theories remains unrealized and unrealizable. With Dhareshwar, I wonder whether we need to raise "the possibility and necessity of an entirely different theoretical practice" (146).

I am interested in the implications of the alternative logics of otherness, production, and spatiality for a theory of human agency and historical change. In particular, for the moment, I am interested in the possibilities of political identities and alliances. My discussion of agency—and its difference from either subjectivity or "identity" (self)—would seem to suggest the need for a radical rethinking of political identity (and the possibilities of collective agency). It seems to suggest the concept of a belonging without identity, a notion of what might be called *singularity* as the basis for an alternative politics, a politics based on what Giorgio Agamben (1993) has called "the coming community." This project is political at its core, for as Young says, this quest for the singular can "be related to the project of constructing a form of knowledge that respects the other without absorbing it into the same" (1990, 11), or, I might add, the different. As Dhareshwar points out, "the fetishization and relentless celebration of 'difference' and 'otherness' [used here to describe a poststructuralist appropriation of Said's thesis] has displaced any discussion of political identity" (1990, 235).

Agamben describes singularity as a mode of existence that is neither universal (i.e., conceptual) nor particular (i.e., individual). He takes as an example of such a mode of existence the existence of the example qua example itself, for the example exists both inside and outside of the class it exemplifies. The example exists "by the indifference of the common and the proper, of the genus and the species, of the essential and the accidental. [It] is the thing with all its properties none of which, however, constitutes difference. In-difference with respect to properties is what individuates and dissemi-nates singularities" (1993, 19). Moreover the status of the example is not accomplished once and for all; it is a line of becoming, "a shuttling between the common and the singular" (20). In other words, the example is defined not by an appeal to a common universal property—an identity—but by its appropriation of belonging (to the class, in this instance) itself. The example belongs to the set that exists alongside of it, and hence it is defined by its substitutability, since it always already belongs in the place of the other. This is "an unconditioned substitutability, without either representation or possi-ble description" (24–25), an absolutely unrepresentable community. This community, that on which the example borders, is an empty and indetermi-nate totality, an external space of possibilities. Thus a singularity can be defined as "a being whose community is mediated not by any condition of belonging . . . nor by the simple absence of conditions . . . but by belonging itself" (85). To put all this in simpler terms, Agamben is arguing that the example functions as an example not by virtue of some common property it shares with all the other possible members of the set, but rather by virtue of its metonymical (understood both literally and spatially) relation to the set it-self. Any term can become an example of the set because what is at stake is the very claim of belonging to the set.

Agamben turns this to politics by considering the events—the alliance—of Tiananmen Square: "Because if instead of continuing to search for a proper identity in the already improper and senseless form of individuality, humans were to succeed in belonging to this impropriety as such, in making of the proper being—thus not an identity and an individual property but a sin-gularity without identity, a common and absolutely exposed singularity . . . then they would for the first time enter into a community without presup-positions and without subjects" (1993, 65). Consider how one would de-scribe the common identity of those who gathered in Tiananmen Square and, whether intentionally or not, came to define and embody a community of opposition not only to the Chinese state, but to the state machine itself. In fact, there is no common identity, no property that defines them apart from the fact that they were there, together, in that place. It was the fact of belong-ing that constituted their belonging together. Such a singularity operates as a "transport machine" following a logic of involvement, a logic of the next (rather than of the proper). It refuses to take any instance as a synecdochal image of the whole. It is only at the intersection of the various lines at the concrete place of belonging that we can identify the different processes of "individuation carried out through groups and people," new modes of individuation and even subjectivization with no identity. Such a community would be based only on the exteriority, the exposure, of the singularity of belonging.

In this sense, we might also reconsider the civil rights movement as a machine of mobilization whose product was a singular belonging rather than a structure of membership. A politics of singularity would need to define places people can belong to or, even more fundamentally, places people can find their way to. Hall and Held describe this as the problem of citizenship: "the diverse communities to which we belong, the complex interplay of identity and identification and the differentiated ways in which people participate in social life" (cited in Giroux 1994, 31). Similarly, Mercer describes "what was important" about the politics of race of the 1980s as the result of the fact "that we actively constructed an elective community of belonging through a variety of practices" (1992b, 33). Perhaps Hall and Mercer would assent to the argument that, in specific contexts, identity can become a marker of people's abiding in such a singular community, where the community defines an abode marking people's ways of belonging within the structured mobilities of contemporary life. That would be an identity worth struggling to create.

I do not know if such a model can help to open up new possibilities. But it seems to me that this is the only justification for the privileged position of political intellectuals and for the labor of cultural studies. What I do know is that finally the answer will only be available as we open up the lines that are making cultural studies into a global as well as a local endeavor. For that reason, perhaps the answers to the questions I am raising about the United States can only come from those who are caught up in its lines of power, but who also define its exterior whether from within or from outside its spaces.

Bringing It All Back Home: Pedagogy

and Cultural Studies

EDUCATION AND THE EMERGENCE
OF CULTURAL STUDIES

In this chapter I want to acknowledge, and try to contribute to, one of the most pressing, promising, and paradoxical sites of cultural studies to have emerged recently: education. I describe it as paradoxical because, despite a strong connection between cultural studies and education at the former's beginnings, the concern for education has apparently had only a limited impact until recently.

Contrary to popular wisdom, which locates the origins of cultural studies in universities and in the production of a series of academic texts, Raymond Williams offers a different version, based in pedagogy and a common interest in a "democratic culture":

> In the late 40s, people were doing courses in the visual arts, in music, in town planning and the nature of community, the nature of settlement, in film, in press, in advertising, in radio; courses which if they had not taken place in that notably unprivileged sector of education [adult education] would have been acknowledged much earlier. (1989, 154)

And here is Stuart Hall's redescription of the traditionally acknowledged founding figures of cultural studies:

> We thus came from a tradition entirely marginal to the centers of English academic life, and our engagement in the questions of cultural change . . . were first reckoned within the dirty outside world. The Centre for Contemporary Cultural Studies was the locus to which we *retreated* when that conversation in the open world could no longer be continued: it

was politics by other means. Some of us—me, especially—had always planned never to return to the university, indeed, never to darken its doors again. But, then, one always has to make pragmatic adjustments to where real work, important work, can be done. (1990a, 12)

All of the founding figures of cultural studies (including Richard Hoggart, Raymond Williams, E. P. Thompson, and Stuart Hall) started their careers, and their intellectual projects, in the field of education, outside the university, in extramural departments and adult working-class courses. It was in such adult education classes that Raymond Williams first started to look at the idea of culture. Such pedagogical contexts, which existed outside the formal educational institutions of the state, served people (primarily women and the working class) who were deprived of any opportunities for, indeed actively "blocked from," any higher education. What these students brought to the classes, according to Williams, was a very real desire to discuss what they read "in a context to which they brought their own situation, their own experience" (1989, 152).

Williams argues that some of this same energy that characterized his extramural students reappeared in the 1960s, when students confronted the various disciplines in relation to their own situations and experiences, forcing their teachers to acknowledge the fact that specific disciplines might have been inadequate to address the questions that students were raising. But Williams also suggests that this energy of the 1960s "lacks to this day that crucial process of interchange and encounter between the people offering the intellectual disciplines and those using them" (1989, 157). Here Williams points to a crucial element, often lacking in many so-called democratic pedagogies: "the more basic right to define the questions . . . regardless of disciplinary boundaries" (157).

But even beyond the occasion of the emergence of cultural studies, education has played an important role in Williams's understanding of cultural studies. Starting with a common assumption of cultural studies—that the development of any cultural practice, including cultural studies itself, must be related "to the very precise formations and social institutions in which [the] consequences happened and had to happen" (Williams 1989, 161)— Williams concludes that we must ask what the role of cultural studies can be in a particular "educational conjuncture."[1] He argues that it "must be more than just a resented interruption from what is otherwise taught." It must offer "a persuasive, reasoned and practical proposal" (161). And he concludes, "If this is thought through now, if we fight for it, even if we fail we shall have done something to justify ourselves before the future. But I don't think we need fail at all; I think that the results will be uneven and scattered, but this is where the challenge is" (162).

Given this challenge, the relative absence of education in the body of texts that have come to constitute (British) cultural studies, especially in the United States, becomes ironic at best. There is in fact very little explicit work published in either the "Occasional Papers" or the more formal *Working Papers* published by the Centre for Contemporary Cultural Studies during the 1970s.[2] In the mid-70s, an Education Working Group was established which, in 1981, published *Unpopular Education: Schooling and Social Democracy in England since 1944* (Education Group 1981). This work attempted to "understand the ways in which educational politics have been constructed in England during the post second world war period" (8). And, not surprisingly, it shared the model of incorporation and resistance that dominated the Centre and cultural studies during the 1970s.

Another line of work, with more visibility in both the "Occasional Papers" and the *Working Papers*, involved the "transition from school to work."[3] This research, which connected as much to the Centre's interest in youth culture as to an interest in education, gave rise to one of the most influential books to come out of the Centre: Paul Willis's *Learning to Labour: How Working Class Kids Get Working Class Jobs* (1977).

The 1980s saw more activity from Centre members (and ex-members) in researching education, although this work was neither widely distributed nor apparently centrally recognized in contemporary discussions of cultural studies, especially outside of Britain.[4] This work continued the interest in the relations between state politics and educational policy, an interest that found its most sophisticated expression in the re-forming of the Education Working Group in the 1980s and the publication of *Education Ltd: Schooling, Training and the New Right in England since 1979* (Education Group II 1990), which examines the transformation of public education under Thatcherism.

Of course, the Centre in Birmingham was not the only site where cultural studies and other important, albeit often scattered work on education was done. Here one has to mention the Ideology and Consciousness Collective, which, besides the journal *Ideology and Consciousness* (later *I & C*), published an important collection entitled *Changing the Subject: Psychology, Social Regulation and Subjectivity* (Henriques et al. 1984). Additionally, one has to acknowledge the important, largely theoretical work organized by and around the journal *Screen Education* and the Society for Education in Film and Television (SEFT).

Finally, one more thing needs to be said about the place of education in cultural studies, a point that is often ignored but is actually crucial to the history of the reception of cultural studies in the United States: the discipline of education was, as early as the 1970s, one of the only places to give cultural studies a home of sorts (communication was the other). I say "of sorts" because while scholars like Michael Apple and Henry Giroux read, taught, and talked about some of the British work, I do not think that they were yet quite moved to locate themselves within the cultural studies project or to identify cultural studies with their own project of a critical pedagogy.

IN DEFENSE OF CULTURAL STUDIES

While the current boom in cultural studies has opened up new and exciting possibilities, it is I believe necessary to approach every claim to cultural studies with a certain skepticism. Williams's distinction between a project and a formation can be helpful here: "the relation between a project and a formation is always decisive; and . . . the emphasis of Cultural Studies is precisely that it engages with both . . . We have to look at what kind of formation it was from which the project of Cultural Studies developed, and then the changes of formation that produced different definitions of that project . . . what is happening each time is that a formation in a given general relationship to its society is taking what you could otherwise trace as a project with certain continuities, and in fact altering it, not necessarily for the better. There have been as many reversions as there have been advances" (1989, 151, 155). In other words, not every formation of cultural studies remains faithful to the project, and not every project is possible within a specific formation. While the space of cultural studies is and must remain open to new projects and formations, new articulations and configurations, it is important to remember that in any specific place, it does matter what shape cultural studies takes, how it is defined. And consequently, not everything is—or need be—cultural studies. The insertion is important because cultural studies does not claim to hold any privileged position; it has never presented itself as the only important or valid sort of intellectual work that can be or should be done.

It is thus necessary to say something about the trajectory (the relation of project and formation) of cultural studies, and to go beyond the obvious claim that it encompasses a number of attempts to understand and intervene into the relations of culture and power. What distinguishes cultural studies, I would argue, is its radical contextualism. In this sense, I agree with Manthia Diawara's critique: "Unfortunately a good deal of U.S. cultural studies that invokes the Birmingham tradition disengages theory from its space of application. The perspectives of the Birmingham school cannot simply be lifted and applied to the U.S. . . . the anti-essentialism of this cultural studies has become an essentialism of its own kind: the reification of discourse . . . This abstract discourse belies the fact that they have been more influenced by certain strains of post-structuralism than by recent developments in the black studies strand of cultural studies" (1992, 7). Thus David Bailey and Stuart Hall locate the important work in 1980s British cultural studies on race, ethnicity, and black cultural politics in "a period of rapid and turbulent change which encompassed several paradigm shifts in both theory and practice and was marked by a powerful synergy between race, politics and representation." They emphasize that "no single position can ever be secure in its correctness. Different strategies [and, I might add, theories] are right in different locations and at different moments" (1992a, 4–5).[5]

At the same time, the contextuality of theory in cultural studies also leads me to disagree with any effort to reduce cultural studies to a single theoretical insight, such as Patrick Brantlinger's decontextualized claim that the "main lesson of cultural studies" is that "in order to understand ourselves, the discourses of the Other—of all the others—is that which we most urgently need to know" (cited in Pfister 1991, 207). While this is of course a crucial lesson of cultural studies (as well as of other political interventions, including feminist theory), Brantlinger writes as if the "recognition and respect for difference" were sufficient to produce "an authentically democratic mass culture unifying people."

The very concept of culture itself is contextual or at least polysemic. It is caught between social formations, everyday life, and representational practices (or, to use more common terms, between community, a whole way of life, and maps of meaning). Here we can take notice of a certain irony. On the one hand, some critics (such as Diawara) argue that cultural studies, at least in one of its strains, is often marked by a propensity to reduce culture to textuality. Yet on the other hand, other critics agree with Ellen Rooney's characterization: "The resistance to textuality is announced as an effort to maintain a proper space for political action 'outside the text' but its actual effect is to depoliticize the very signifying practices which enable us to engage in any kind of politically motivated intellectual work whatsoever" (1990, 24). Obviously I do not agree with Rooney's argument, based in a feminist poststructuralism, that cultural studies depoliticizes discourse, but I do agree that cultural studies refuses to reduce culture, or the politics of culture, to questions of textuality. Cultural studies assumes a reality that is constantly reworked by and only made available through cultural practices.[6] In some cultural studies work, this has led to a rejection of the model of critical practice as a hermeneutic or interpretive act of theoretical self-reflection. Echoing Hebdige (1993), critical practice becomes a "witness" of the effects of reality, culture, and critical work on each other.[7] In effect, cultural studies denies the apparent autonomy of culture which is often reinforced by theories of textuality. It argues that cultural practices are not only the sites and the stakes of struggle, but the weapons as well. In other words, cultural practices not only represent power, they also deploy it.

As I have already suggested, politics—its sites, goals, and forms of struggle—are contextually defined in cultural studies. Here I want to consider one of the common, and I believe mistaken, criticisms of cultural studies. For example, Alan O'Connor writes that "cultural studies in the U.S. is being sponsored by scholars who rarely have any connection to existing political and cultural movements and are somewhat surprised that this might be possible" (1989, 407). Even more strongly, Ellen Rooney asserts that "Cultural studies in the U.S. has a political problem insofar as its relationship to a specifically political struggle outside the university is at best contested. Practically speaking, women's studies has an enormous advantage over . . . cultural studies . . . its students offer a politically conscious constituency before they enter the field . . . I want to stress the theoretical importance of the political activities of women's studies students outside the university" (1990, 20). I certainly do not want to reject the model of intellectual politics suggested here. And while I agree that the origins of women's, black, and ethnic studies programs can be traced to oppositional social movements (in part located outside the university), I also agree with Mohanty that the origins of such programs were often "a defensive political move: the state institutionalization of a discourse of reform in response to the civil rights movement" (1994, 110). That is, for Mohanty, such programs must also be seen as part of a process of the "management" of race and difference.[8]

Cultural studies, however, offers a different model of intellectual politics: neither the organic intellectual, who has an already existing relation to an already existing constituency, nor the specific intellectual, who can only construct local and temporary constituencies based entirely on his or her expertise. Cultural studies attempts at least to construct a more flexible, more pragmatic, more modest, and more contextual model of the political function of the intellectual, connecting to, constructing, and reconstructing its conjunctural constituency. Cultural studies thinks constituencies are made, not given in advance, as if the relationship of social identity and politics was already inscribed on the walls of our social experiences. This is how Raymond Williams described the pedagogical responsibility of cultural studies: "taking the best we can in intellectual work and going with it in this very open way to confront people for whom it is not a way of life, for whom it is not in all probability a job, but for whom it is a matter of their own intellectual interest, their own understanding of the pressures on them, pressures of every kind, from the most personal to the most broadly political" (1989, 162). Or to quote Stuart Hall again:

> The work that cultural studies has to do is to mobilize everything that it can find in terms of intellectual resources in order to understand what keeps making the lives we live, and the societies we live in, profoundly and deeply anti-humane . . . Cultural studies' message is a message for academics and intellectuals but, fortunately, for many other people as well. In that sense I have tried to hold together in my own intellectual life, on the one hand, the conviction and passion and the devotion to . . . rigorous analysis and understanding, to the passion to find out, and to the production of knowledge that we did not know before. But, on the other hand, I am convinced that no intellectual worth his or her salt, and no university that wants to hold up its head in the face of the twenty-first century, can afford to turn dispassionate eyes away from the problems . . . that beset our world. (1992c, 17–18)

The question of cultural studies is not so much whom we are speaking to (audience) or even for (representation), but whom we are speaking against. And consequently the resources we need, the strategies we adopt, and the politics we attempt to define must always take into account the particular context in which we are struggling. As Bailey and Hall argue, "It is perfectly possible that what is politically progressive and opens up new discursive opportunities in the 1970s and 1980s can become a form of closure—and have a repressive value—by the time it is installed as the dominant genre . . . It will run out of steam; it will become a style; people will use it not because it opens up anything but because they are being spoken by it, and at that point, you need another shift" (1992b, 15).

THE SPACE OF EDUCATION

No one can doubt that not only the institutions and practices of education but the very concept of education have come under intense scrutiny and even attack in recent years. Most visibly, of course, this has been the result of education's being caught between the conflicting demands and critiques of two opposed discourses. On the one side, there is a discourse of multiculturalism and liberation which calls for a democratic culture based on an acceptance of social difference and which is usually predicated on a theory of identity and representation. On the other side, there is a discourse of conservatism based on canonical notions of general education and a desire to impose what it cannot justify—the existence of an illusory common culture. From this imaginary place it has launched an attack, largely through the media, by articulating an identity between three distinct strands of work on the Left: the critique of the canon, the renewed power of theory, and the interest in radical pedagogy. These debates may be, as Michael Denning has argued, "skirmishes over the forms and ownership of cultural capital, a war of interclass position" (1992, 33). Or they may be the current forms in which the contradictions in the very idea of a democratic and universal education are being played out (involving questions of appropriateness—of subjects and objects—as well as of normative standards and aims).

But as Paul Willis has recently suggested,

> The field of education is likely to come under even more intense pressure. It will be further marginalized in most people's experience by common [read "popular" or "everyday"] culture. In so far as educational practices are still predicated on traditional liberal humanist lines and on the assumed superiority of high art, they will become almost totally irrelevant to the real energies and interests of most young people and have no part of their identity formation. Common culture will, increasingly, undertake in its own ways, the roles that education has vacated.
>
> Insofar as education/training becomes ever more subordinated to technical instrumentalism and to the "needs" of industry, it will be seen as a necessary evil to be tolerated in order to obtain access to the wage in

order to obtain access to leisure and consumption and their cultural energies. . . .

. . . We need an altogether new approach in education. (1990, 147)

Without intending to sound too paranoid, it seems fair to say that education is surrounded on all sides: from the Left, by the concerns of multiculturalism and radical pedagogy; from the Right, by the demand for a reinstantiation of general education, which Denning describes as "a key part of middlebrow culture" (1992, 41), using the mass media and culture industries to distribute a packaged translation of the classical curriculum; from the top, by the increasing economic and technological rationality imposed on educational institutions; and from below, by the microapparatuses and macroalliances of popular culture.

In this context, the recent conjunction of cultural studies and educational theory has produced a wide range of questions, positions, and practices; it has provoked some of the most interesting explorations and some of the most troubling speculations. And it has expanded our understanding of education, so that, at its most problematic, education becomes identified with culture itself, leaving open the task that it be rearticulated, respecified. Compare, for example, two views. First, Roger Simon defines pedagogy as "a term which signals the practical synthesis of the questions 'what should be taught and why' with considerations as to how that teaching should take place" (1994, 130). This rather narrow view contrasts sharply with Willis's claim that "Making (not receiving) messages and meanings in your own context and from materials you have appropriated is, in essence, a form of education in the broadest sense. It is the specifically developmental part of symbolic work, an education about 'the self' and its relation to the world and to others in it. Where everyday symbolic work differs from what is normally thought of as 'education' is that it 'culturally produces' from its own chosen symbolic resources" (1990, 137).

What we actually have here is not the equation of education and culture, an equation that would erase the specificity of schooling altogether, but a space that extends from the pedagogy of culture to the culture of pedagogy. At one extreme, we can locate Michael Dyson's concern with Michael Jordan as a public pedagogue, as a "figure of . . . authority whose career educates us" (1994, 119). Or Roger Simon's attempt to understand the pedagogy of a particular T-shirt as part of a larger process, which includes schooling, of the production of popular memory, "a pedagogy of historical re-formation" that elucidates the "different educative forms of reciprocal relations between the present and the past" (1994).

At the other extreme, cultural practices have to be located in the institutional and technological conditions that regulate specific fields. Here we can locate an even broader range of projects: Ava Collins's (1994) attempt to bring popular culture into the classroom while respecting its existence in a discursive space outside the academy, by finding systems of evaluation inherent within popular texts themselves; David Trend's (1994) arguments for media education as the teaching of skills or literacies that value difference; Carol Becker's original effort to think about both the possibilities of educating the audience of art about its often mystifying and discomforting effects, and the need to educate young art students to understand the effects of their work in relation to particular audiences; or Henry Giroux's (1994) trenchant investigations into how particular forms of authority are secured through the organization of the curriculum at all levels of schooling.

In the space between these extremes, we move from the important issue of the relation between teachers and students to questions about the relation of the classroom to the outside world. Here we can consider (from Giroux and McLaren 1994) bell hooks's important argument that an empowering pedagogy must reconsider (and admit) the place of passion, energy, and eros (which is not merely sexual) in the classroom. Hooks calls for a pedagogy in which teachers openly care about and even love not only their subject matter, but their subjects (students) as well. David Trend similarly proposes the educational relation as a model for other relationships, while both Chandra Mohanty and Nancy Fraser seem to call for the school to become the agent or site (respectively) of a "public culture of dissent." All of these are attempts to elucidate the often taken-for-granted assumption that education should lead our students to live their lives differently.

In the space between the extremes described above, in the new space of educational discourse, the very concept of pedagogy has been exploded and multiplied. No longer satisfied with a pedagogy of knowledge, we now must consider the possibilities of a pedagogy of voices (Mohanty) and of liberation (McLaren), a pedagogy of place (Giroux), of desire, style, and presence (Dyson), of desiring machines (McLaren). The taken-for-granted site of pedagogy has opened up, and what we have begun to explore are the pedagogies of border intellectuals (Giroux, JanMohammed) and the possibilities of postmodern pedagogies.

Yet for all of the excitement that this new space produces, I think we must take seriously the possibility that something is also being lost. It is not just that our confidence that we know what the question of pedagogy or education is about has been rendered uncertain. It is that having given up the assumption that we know in advance the relationship between education and culture, we have still to do the work necessary to theorize and politicize that relationship. I do not want to suggest that the current intersection of cultural studies and educational theory represents some kind of failure. On the contrary, I want to point to an apparent irony: that precisely by approaching the apparent equivalence of education and culture, we are actually moving closer to their differentiation, a differentiation that takes us beyond the commonsensical notion of education as the production and dissemination of knowledge.

THE POLITICS OF EDUCATION

Finally, I want to consider some of the implications of cultural studies for questions of pedagogy. If we take seriously Michael Denning's statement that "it is necessary that we begin to imagine cultural studies not simply as the critique of the disciplines [or, I might add, as simply another discipline] but as an alternative to the humanities themselves, a reformation of general education" (1992, 41), then there are consequences, not only in terms of our objects of study and our aims, but also in terms of our practice. Cultural studies requires us to consider not only pedagogy as a cultural practice, but the pedagogy of cultural practices. There is a double articulation here, which must always be located in the specific historical conjuncture and institutional context in which the articulations are both enabled and constrained.

It is possible to identify three models of a progressive pedagogical practice. The first, a hierarchical practice, assumes that the teacher already understands the truth to be imparted to the student. Of course, sometimes such a practice is quite appropriate and can truly contribute to emancipatory struggles. But the problems with such a practice become more apparent when the teacher assumes that he or she understands the real meanings of particular texts and practices, the real relations of power embodied within them, and the real interests of the different social groups brought together in the classroom or in the broader society. Then it is the teacher who draws the line between the good, the bad, and the ugly, between the politically correct and the politically incorrect.

The second, a dialogic practice, aims to allow the silenced to speak; only when absolutely necessary does it claim to speak for them. But this assumes that they are not already speaking simply because we, the teachers, do not hear them, perhaps because they are not speaking the right languages or not saying what we would demand of them. Moreover such a practice fails to see that there are often real material and social conditions that have dis-enabled people from speaking at particular places, in particular ways, at particular moments.

The third, a praxical pedagogy, attempts to offer people the skills that would enable them to understand and intervene into their own history. Hopefully, such skills would enable them to move beyond the realm of discursive struggles to challenge the institutional relations to power by connecting themselves with "the broader struggles of communities to democratize and reconstruct the public sphere" (Fraser 1994). The problem with this practice is not only that it assumes that people are not already trying to intervene into their own history but, more importantly, that it assumes that the teacher already understands the right skills that would enable emancipatory and transformative action, as if such skills were themselves not contextually determined. In my opinion, this is the problem with identifying an emancipatory pedagogy with the practice of reading texts in order to develop interpretive skills for the analysis of the construction of difference. To put it another way, such a pedagogy only gets half of cultural studies' practice right. It does grasp the fact that "theory is only a detour on the way to something more important" (Hall 1991a, 42), but it fails to see that its political stakes as well must be context-specific. There are no universal skills we can offer independent of the context into which we want to intervene and, more importantly, into which our students want to intervene.

It seems to me that all three of these pedagogical strategies avoid the really difficult question: not of the elitism that all three continue to deploy but of the possibility of an "earned elitism." It is too easy to say that the task of becoming critical is not something we can give to or perform for our students. But this does not mean that we as teachers can give up the need to construct positions of authority for ourselves, as teachers. We need to locate places from which we can construct and disseminate knowledge in relation to the materiality of power, conflict, and oppression. It is here, then, that we can return to the question of the specificity of the pedagogical in terms of "the politics and ethics of criticism" (Bailey and Hall 1992b, 21). Recognizing that pedagogies are themselves always institutionalized, placed, as it were, we must look into the social relations of discourse, into the ethics of enunciation and of the different possible enunciative positions, the places of authority we construct for ourselves and our students.

Here it may be useful to turn to a different formation of cultural studies, particularly strong in Australia, that sees particular cultural practices and formations as technologies of power, apparatuses that deploy power in organizing the relations between people, practices, and things.[9] In particular, the "technology of the humanities"—which was put into place as the modern formation of literary education and critical reading, and which also positioned the teacher as the intellectual and moral model (supposedly lived out in his or her ability to reconcile the contradictions of social existence, such as reason versus the will)—is, Ian Hunter (1988) argues, a central part of the machinery of modern power. It is part of a larger system of disciplinization that produces the "civil-ized" student, or what Toby Miller (1993) has called the "well-tempered" or "well-tuned" subject. Unfortunately, this machinery is often reproduced in contemporary instantiations of cultural studies and even critical pedagogy. We can glean some further evidence of the too common complicity of pedagogical practices, even radical ones, with contemporary forms of power if we recognize that the distance such practices often assume or demand (from the text at least) is really a demand for disinvestment, an indifference, a "refusal to invest oneself and take things seriously." This sense of difference is, of course, precisely what Pierre Bourdieu (1984) has described as the dominant aesthetic sensibility.

I want to suggest here the possibility of a fourth model of pedagogy, a pedagogy of articulation and risk. Such a practice, while refusing the traditional forms of intellectual authority, would not abandon all claims to authority. Refusing to assume ahead of time that it knows the appropriate knowledge, language, or skills, it is a contextual practice that is willing to take the risk of making connections, drawing lines, mapping articulations, between different domains, discourses, and practices, to see what will work, both theoretically and politically. It employs the rhizomatic "methods" of Deleuze and Guattari, "the freaky method of experiment and collage" (Mercer 1992b, 37). Kobena Mercer describes such a practice as one that seeks not to "save the world" but, more modestly, to "multipl[y] connections between things that have [apparently] nothing to do with each other . . . rhizomatic thinking invites research for routes out of the common predicaments we share here and now" (38–39). Mercer sees this method as somehow more appropriate to the stakes of contemporary cultural and pedagogical struggles: it "speaks to the conditions of exile and displacement . . . to conditions of homelessness and restlessness in terms of a renewed commitment to theory that is motivated by the desire to displace established orthodoxies; to keep on moving, from soul to soul, from station to station, on the dark side of the political imaginary. Diaspora is a domain of dissemination and dispersal, where seeds are scattered along diverse vectors and trajectories" (39).

This is an affective pedagogy, a pedagogy of possibilities (but every possibility has to risk failure) and of agency. It refuses to assume that either theory or politics, theoretical or political correctness, can be known in advance. It is a pedagogy that aims not to predefine its outcome (even in terms of some imagined value of emancipation or democracy) but to empower its students to begin to reconstruct their world in new ways, and to rearticulate their future in unimagined and perhaps even unimaginable ways. It is a pedagogy that demands of students not that they conform to some image of political liberation nor even that they resist, but simply that they gain some understanding of their own involvement in the world and in the making of their own future. Consequently it neither starts with nor works within a set of texts but rather with the formations of the popular, the cartographies of taste, stability, and mobility, within which students are located. It does not take for granted the context of specific cultural practices nor the terms within which they produce effects. It is a pedagogy that draws unexpected maps of the possibilities of and constraints on agency as it intersects with both everyday life and the social formation.[10]

Of course, such a pedagogy does not deny that the teacher must take responsibility for the production of knowledge in the classroom. But now the teacher is no longer expected to provide an ethical model of authority, but rather what Cameron McCarthy (in conversation) has called a model of thoughtfulness. This is obviously riskier, both pedagogically and politically. It offers a risky politics of risk, a politics of contextuality that attempts to offer new positions and forms of authority. (In that sense, it is as much a reconfiguration of the first practice described above as anything else.) It is also a practice that, I believe, constantly traverses the line between teaching and research, allowing them to rearticulate one another, opening knowledge up to new questions, spoken from elsewhere. It is here that our critical and pedagogical practice is inevitably transformed from a reflective and distant relation to both the subjects and objects of our authority, to an active and passionate articulation. Such a pedagogy, however, can only be a politicizing engagement in the last instance, for it must leave the field of articulations as open as possible. And it is here as well that we will always encounter the limits of our claim to authority, at just the moment when the claim is legitimated.

This leads me to the question of our political intervention as teachers, of the aims or possibilities of pedagogy. I will approach this in terms of two final issues: the place of the popular in education, and the articulation of a political vision in education. If political struggles are won and lost in the space between people's everyday lives and the material production and distribution of values and power, in the space where people and groups are articulated, both ideologically and affectively, to social identities, cultural practices, and political projects, then it is here that pedagogy must operate. The task of a politically engaged pedagogy is, after all, never to convince a predefined subject—whether empty or full, whether essential or fragmented—to adopt a new position. Rather the task is to win an already positioned, already invested individual or group to a different set of places, a different organization of the space of possibilities.

If there are no guarantees in history, there can be no secure knowledge that predefines people's interests or the parameters of a progressive politics. If people are neither totally unaware nor totally passive in the face of their own interests, needs, and subordinations, they are not waiting to be told where and how to struggle. To repeat what I said earlier, people are not cultural dopes. After all, if they were, how could we teach them (other than through manipulation as grotesque as that which we claim to be struggling against)? But this is not to say that we must simply accept or celebrate where people are, their common sense, their sense of who they are, for that is precisely what the struggle over culture is about. On the other hand, if people are not being "duped," if their positions are not sometimes being articulated "behind their backs," there would be no need to teach them, to make them aware of their existence as both a stake and a possible agent in the struggle. Moreover we must recognize that as teachers we are not separated from "the people," and our authority, while it may be temporarily and contextually legitimated, is always institutionally and discursively located. I might sum this up by saying that we must give up the too easy model of domination and resistance, built on a logic of either/or.

Cultural studies starts where people are, but it does not assume that either they or we know the answers in advance. It is perhaps not surprising to hear echoes of Williams in Mostern's statement that "the critical pedagogue is always someone who teaches from where the student is at, rather than from where the teacher is at. This does not mean that the teacher denies his or her pedagogical intention or specific expertise, but merely that s/he respects the myriad expertise of the students that s/he does not share" (1994, 256).

Such a pedagogy must go against the all too common tendency on the Left to propose alternative media or cultural practices to replace those in which students are already invested, inventing marginal and populist counterdiscourses. Instead I would argue that the critical pedagogue must listen for the "stutterings," the unexpected dialects and misspeakings, the unpredicted articulations, within the hegemonic culture, which are capable of producing a minor and popular remapping (Deleuze and Guattari 1987), which may enable the mobilization of people's memories, fantasies, and desires, and redirect their investments in politics and the other.

Keeping this in mind, I think it is possible to see that the elitism of so much critical work is not defined by its theory or even by its esoteric vocabulary. People are uninterested, not because they can't do the work (in most cases, the so-called jargon is in the dictionary) but because they don't see any reason to; they don't care about the questions we ask. The elitism of the intellectuals comes not merely from our assumption that we already know the answers but, even more, from our assumption that we already know the questions. It would, however, be too easy to assume that we simply need to ask our students what the questions are. We need to use our authority, mobilized through a pedagogy of risk and experimentation, to discover what the questions can be in the everyday lives of our students and what political possibilities such questions open up. We have to be willing to enter the terrain of everyday life, the terrain of dispersed others, in order to make sense of the realities of their (our) lives. Only then can we prise open already existing contradictions, "thereby renovating and making critical an already existing activity" (Gramsci 1971, 331).

But then it also follows that we cannot tell our students what ethics or politics—obviously the two are intimately connected although not identical—to embrace. Again, we must connect to the ethics and politics they already embrace and then struggle to rearticulate them to a different position (without necessarily knowing in advance that we will be successful, or even what that different position will actually be). At the same time, we must collectively articulate a common affective vision of a shared political future based on a politics of practice (what people do, what they invest in, where they belong) rather than on a politics of identity. This must go beyond the mere invocation of an ideal such as democracy; we must invoke and bear witness to the concrete meanings of such political values, and to the concrete possibilities of human life.[11]

If we are to imagine a different, a better future, we need to consider the

otes

INTRODUCTION: "BIRMINGHAM" IN AMERICA?

I would like to thank my wonderful friend Ellen Wartella for many conversations about these issues, and for many of the ideas which appear here. This introduction draws on a number of essays not collected here.

1   Much of the following section is based on Grossberg 1995a.

2   See the discussion of Sean Nixon's work in McRobbie 1996.

3   This paragraph is largely a paraphrase of arguments made to me by John Clarke in his comments on an early draft of Grossberg 1995.

4   For example, in my own work (Grossberg 1992) I have argued that while capitalism does not explain either the emergence or the affectivity of particular cultural formations, it is the case that the formations are currently being rearticulated to and by (i.e., being deployed in the service of) particular contradictions and struggles of contemporary capitalism.

5   Angela McRobbie has described the marketplace as the "collision place of capitalist commerce with popular desires" (1996, 243) and as "an expansive popular system" (245).

6   For an elaboration of the place of economics in cultural studies, see McRobbie 1996 and Clarke 1991.

7   Of course, this is a crucial problem with broad implications. Does one need such a position in order to define and mobilize political opposition? Must such a position equate the political and the ethical? How is one to respond to a postmodern relativism that would seem to undermine not only the possibility of such a position, but the possibility of politics itself? What is the relation between ethical and political positions, especially in the context of the United States, where ethics tends to dominate politics even in political discourses?

8   Of course, in that light, Kantianism has to be seen as the crystallization in philosophy of developments that were taking place in other institutions and discourses as well.

9   My own work draws upon a line of philosophy that can be traced back to the premodern philosophy of Spinoza. However, Spinoza's has to be contextualized as part of a regional history of the Mediterranean/Middle East, which includes Jewish (e.g., Maimonides) and Arab (Ibn Sina) thinkers. See Alcalay 1993.

10 There is an obvious if implicit reference to Marx here. And after all, Marx as much as Deleuze and Guattari (or Spinoza) can be read as a critique of Kantian modernism. But

Marx's critique of Kant was limited: while he made the space of culture into the site of power, he could not problematize that space. He could not recognize that the production of this space itself (in the logic of mediation) was a product/production of power. At the same time, he obviously could neither account for nor escape the privileging of temporality and history. At the same time, I do not see my position as "postmarxist" except in the weakest sense: I am trying to take account of the limitations of marxism as articulated by Marx, produced by the articulation of the apparatuses of modernity and a particular formation of capitalism.

11   Obviously this would seem to raise serious epistemological issues—about how we know, how we constitute the object (event) and the subject. I am reluctant to take these issues up, partly because I think the priority of epistemology is a function of the logic of modern thought.

12   I am aware of a certain rhetorical excess here. While it would certainly be reasonable to refer here to a logic of space-time rather than simply space, there are at least two reasons to favor the latter strategy. First, because of the central place of temporality in modernity, space-time is likely to quickly become time, or at least, and this is the second reason, the relation between space and time is likely to be conceptualized dimensionally, thus enabling space and time to be radically separated and opening the possibility of a re-privileging of time.

13   I use the example in an attempt to undermine the claim of the exemplary.

14   Massumi also argues that an adequate theory of affect requires a distinction, within the real, between the actual and the virtual (as incipiencies and tendencies). While I agree with him, I do not want to take up this question in the present context.

15   In other words, the struggle over distributing texts into categories like "serious" versus "popular" is a struggle to control their effects. Articulating certain texts as popular enables them to operate within particular regimes of affect (e.g., the effects of the popular are often written on the body). Similarly to articulate texts as "serious" is to disallow such effects, while enabling the discourse to operate in other affective registers. This leaves open the question of how such enablement is itself produced: Is it, for example, a matter of discipline by which the individual regulates his or her own responses?

INTERPRETING THE "CRISIS" OF CULTURE IN COMMUNICATION THEORY

1   The term "crisis" may be inappropriate to describe this idea, as Professor Richard Grabau of Purdue has pointed out to me, since the "crisis of culture" is too long-term and, in fact, seems to have become normal. Perhaps the notion would be better captured as "the threat of culture which is also a threat to culture." I will, however, use the term because of its long-standing presence within the literature.

2   This typology is derived from Grossberg 1979a, where I attempted to construct a typology of philosophies of meaning and language.

3   The works of Daniel Bell, Edward Shils, and David M. White provide good examples of the liberal response to mass society.

4   This separates Dewey as well as Gerbner (1972) from mainstream communication research.

5   My own inclination would be to argue that each of the six views is broader than the previous ones and each attempts to incorporate and account for previous ones as limited cases.

THE IDEOLOGY OF COMMUNICATION: POSTSTRUCTURALISM AND THE LIMITS OF COMMUNICATION

An early version of this paper was presented at a conference on Communication Theory from Eastern and Western Perspectives, the East-West Center, Communication Institute, Honolulu, Hawaii, December 1980.

1   Such images of communication are most obviously determining in the range of linear or transmission views of communication. An objective view is obvious in Berlo 1960. A subjective view operates in Mortenson 1972.

2   Structural images of communication can be seen in, for example, Hawes 1973 and Nofsinger 1975. An interactional view is operative in the recent interest in symbolic interaction theory: see, for example, Faules and Alexander 1978.

3   The vocabulary of a phenomenological view is obvious in O'Keefe, Delia, and O'Keefe 1983 and Deetz 1973. The hermeneutic view is apparent in Hawes 1977 and Apel 1972.

4   For a discussion of the later works of Heidegger, see Poggeler 1975. For an overview of poststructuralism, see Coward and Ellis 1977 and Wahl 1979.

5   On the notion of a genealogy, see, for example, Foucault 1977a, 1978a, 1980a. On the question of the Real, see Deleuze and Guattari 1977.

EXPERIENCE, SIGNIFICATION, AND REALITY: THE BOUNDARIES OF CULTURAL SEMIOTICS

I would like to thank Charles Stivale and Martin Allor for their invaluable assistance in the preparation of this paper.

1   This description of poststructuralism is not intended to correspond to the thought of any single author; it is a composite. Thus while the concept of "positionality" cannot be found in Derrida, I think it is not therefore a misrepresentation. (I might describe this as the American appropriation/construction of poststructuralism.)

2   These criticisms of Derrida are all based on his early writings, but I think they apply for the most part to his more recent work as well.

3   I would like to thank Paul St. Pierre for his help in understanding Kristeva. Note that all translations of Kristeva 1974a are taken from White 1977.

4   The best introduction of Deleuze and Guattari is Charles Stivale 1981. Also, the translations used from Guattari (1979a and b) were done by Stivale.

5   For a presentation of his definition of signifying practices, see Foucault 1972. The notion of nondiscursive events is important: for example, starvation is nondiscursive but discursified by news reporting.

6   On the question of whether the "apparatus" is taken as a totality, see Foucault 1980a, 197.

7   "Biopolitics" may be taken as a name of the largest rhizome that Foucault has yet constructed. See Foucault 1978a, 135–59.

8   The model, both in terms of ideological analysis and political action, seems to be that of

the Autonomia movement in Italy. See the special issue of *Semiotexte* (no. 9, 1980) devoted to Italy: "Autonomia: Post-Political Politics."

STRATEGIES OF MARXIST CULTURAL INTERPRETATION

1   I use the term "function" broadly to encompass any theory of the relationship between discourse and practice. Thus it includes theories of meaning, effects, and functions (understood in a narrower "functionalist" sense).

2   These positions have developed in response to historical conditions and events, as well as through theoretical arguments. The positions or strategies presented here could be described in different frameworks, although the results would be, to differing degrees, not entirely equivalent. For example, Ellen Wartella (in conversation) has suggested that the distinction between classical, hermeneutic, and discursive approaches can be seen in terms of the problem of the audience. Classical approaches tend to ignore the audience or assume that it is passive; hermeneutic approaches assume an active audience; and discursive approaches attempt to insert the audience into the very structures of cultural textuality. Similarly, Martin Allor (in conversation) has suggested that the three approaches can be distinguished on the basis of their differing views of determination: as a simple causal process, as a process of defining constraints and exerting pressures, or as "overdetermination" (see Slack 1984). I could also have chosen to make the distinctions on the basis of competing theories of ideology.

3   Of course, in the last analysis, a text must be evaluated in the different contexts within which it functions. Thus one must acknowledge that Dorfman and Mattelart's work has an important place not only in the development of a marxist interpretation of popular culture, but also within the concrete political struggles of the Latin American Left against the power of the United States. And despite what I take to be its methodological weaknesses, the analysis is still an insightful critique of Disney's texts.

4   The problems with Adorno's critique are obvious. Adorno, like other modernists, sees art as a transcendental, autonomous activity capable of utopian criticism. His definition of art, however, is derived from a particular historical moment which is then generalized into a universal measure. Thus the "standardization" of popular music is defined by comparison to the harmonic and structural complexity of the "canon." He ignores other normative measures—such as rhythmic complexity, timbre, texture, and so on—which may give different aesthetic conclusions. Further, he ignores the conventionality of all cultural forms—based in the specificity of signifying practices—which would make the question of individuality and creativity a problematic matter of degree and local judgment.

5   I am not concerned here with the historical and theoretical adequacy of the economic theory that such positions use to describe specific media contexts. Obviously, such considerations should form an important part of the ongoing development and elaboration of the various "economisms."

6   One other comparison may be useful. While certain poststructuralist theories (like various humanisms) such as *Screen*'s tend to assume that some correspondences are necessary, others tend to assume that there are necessarily no correspondences. Hall's position rejects both "necessary correspondence" and "necessary non-correspondence" in

favor of "no necessary correspondence or non-correspondence" (a "Marxism without guarantees"). Foucault makes the question an empirical one in each instance. Thus there may be events that are, for all practical purposes, inserted into necessary correspondences. For example, a practice already embedded within an apparatus may be articulated in already defined ways. Note that there are significant methodological similarities between Foucault and the work of the "Annales" school of history (Braudel 1981).

7   Such alliances, motivated and shaped by the political contexts of both the discipline of communications research and the recent state-formation, would require a critique of the various political practices that have become associated with the interpretive strategies presented here. For such alliances must avoid reproducing, at either the structural or practical level, the very forms of power they seek to challenge.

HISTORY, POLITICS, AND POSTMODERNISM: STUART HALL AND CULTURAL STUDIES

1   For a more complete biography of Stuart Hall, see my entry in Gorman 1985.

2   There is an ongoing debate about the relationship between poststructuralism (as a theoretical and cultural practice) and postmodernism. My own assumption is that the former represents the last stages of the modernist epistemological problematic: the relationship between the subject and the forms of mediation, in which the problem of reality is constantly displaced. Postmodernism on the other hand moves from epistemology to history, from subjectivity to a recovery of the real, from mediation and universality to effectivity and contextuality. The conflation of these positions has serious consequences for the analysis of both cultural practices and historical context. It often leads one back into the politics of codes and communications, of the construction and deconstruction of boundaries, despite what may be interesting and insightful analyses of the postmodern context of contemporary life.

3   Postmodern cultural practices are often characterized as denying totality, coherence, closure, depth (both expressive and representational), meaning, teleology, narrativity, history, freedom, creativity, and hierarchy; and as celebrating discontinuity, fragmentation, rupture, materiality, surfaces, language as intervention, diversity, chance, contextuality, egalitarianism, pastiche, heterogeneity without norms, quotations without quotation marks, parodies without originals.

4   Postmodernism's lack of a theory of articulation results in the "flatness" (albeit defined by a multiplicity of vectors and planes) of its analysis of contextual effectivity. In neither postmodernism nor cultural studies is articulation ever complete. In cultural studies, no articulation is either complete or final; no term is ever finally sewn up. This is the condition of possibility of its dialectic of struggle. In postmodernism not every element is articulated or stitched into the fabric of any particular larger structure. This is a crucial part of its analysis of contemporaneity. Speaking metaphorically, a theory of articulation augments vertical complexity while a theory of wild realism augments horizontal complexity.

5   Theorizing the concept of affect involves deconstructing the opposition between the rational and the irrational in order to undercut not only the assumed irrationality of

desire, but also the assumed rationality of signification and ideology. Current theories of ideology, rooted in structuralism, have too easily abandoned the insights embodied in notions of "the structure of feeling" (Williams) and "the texture of lived experience" (Hoggart). (I am grateful to John Clarke for his observations on this point.)

THE FORMATION(S) OF CULTURAL STUDIES: AN AMERICAN IN BIRMINGHAM

A number of people read an earlier draft and provided valuable comments. I would like to thank Stuart Hall, Martin Allor, Jennifer Daryl Slack, James Hay, Elspeth Probyn, Jon Crane, Julian Halliday, and Charles Acland. For an overview of the Centre's work, see Hall et al. 1980.

1   There is of course a history, yet to be written, of the postwar American response to mass culture which has its own similarities and differences to the British response. See Ross 1989.

2   See, for example, Coward 1977 and Chambers et al. 1978.

3   See Grossberg 1988b for a more detailed analysis of the historical conditions and theoretical logic of this system of identifications.

4   For a discussion of Hall's Gramscian position, see the special issue of the *Journal of Communication Inquiry* 10 (Summer 1986) (expanded as Morley and Chen 1996). See also Hall 1988c. Hall (1987) explicitly addresses questions of identity and subjectivity.

THE CIRCULATION OF CULTURAL STUDIES

1   This essay represents my latest effort to think through the specificity of cultural studies; however, it is in many ways better represented as the latest take in an ongoing polylogue, my own statement of a truly collective effort. Thus I am indebted to many people, and I apologize for not having attempted to document their individual contributions, ideas, and phrases. I can only acknowledge their great help and contribution to this essay: Martin Allor, James Hay, Meaghan Morris, Janice Radway, Andrew Ross, Jennifer Daryl Slack, and Ellen Wartella. In addition, I acknowledge a very real debt to Tony Bennett, John Clarke, and Stuart Hall.

2   Hall 1980c and Johnson 1986–87 are the "standard" descriptions of cultural studies.

3   See Grossberg 1988b for a critique of the British tradition in the service of an effort to define an American practice of cultural studies responding to the specific political context constructed by the rise of the New Right. Part of the labor of this transformation involves reading one history into another: cultural studies in the United States has to locate itself within the trajectories of the American Left, including the various urban, immigrant, labor, and agrarian-populist formations, the culturalism of the New Left, the various feminist struggles, and the different intellectually inspired projects of *Monthly Review, Cultural Correspondence, Social Text,* and so on. It would have to recognize the specific conjunctural limits of the American Left: the United States never formed an integrated and institutionalized Left that could occupy a place in common sense. I am grateful to Jody Berland for this point.

4   For histories of cultural studies, see Grossberg 1989b and my earlier, flawed effort (Grossberg 1983).

5   Certainly, within the British tradition, cultural studies focused on a limited set of these values—specifically meaning, representation, and identity. It is the articulation of these three economies that Hall describes as ideology.

CULTURAL STUDIES: WHAT'S IN A NAME?
(ONE MORE TIME)

An earlier version of this paper was delivered as the B. Aubrey Fisher Memorial Lecture at the University of Utah in October 1993. It was published by the Department of Communication as "Cultural Studies: What's in a Name?" I would like to thank the Department of Communication at the University of Utah and especially Len Hawes for the invitation and the honor. I would also like to thank Tony Bennett, Cameron McCarthy, Carol Stabile, John Clarke, and Ellen Wartella for their comments and criticisms of that version.

1   I want to emphasize that the name "cultural studies" applies to works and not people. Not everything that someone identified with cultural studies writes must necessarily be cultural studies. This confusion of individuals with work is all too common, and the result is that experiences are substituted for practices, and ethics for politics. This is dangerously close to "political correctness." The real questions, however, are (1) whether and how one can generalize from the experience of the individuals involved to the structural conditions of the institution, and (2) what such experiences have to do with the constitutions of a field of intellectual practice.

2   While cultural studies has been influenced by many of these positions, including structuralism, poststructuralism, certain traditions in feminism, marxism, and postmodernism, it cannot be identified with any one of them or with the field of theory in general. Such theories travel as resources rather than answers, and they are rearticulated by their appropriation into particular projects in the course of their travels.

3   In this I would like to argue that the situation of cultural studies is somewhat akin to that of phenomenology. Since intellectuals are always studying phenomena, it might be fairly argued that we are all doing phenomenology. But that loses the specificity of the practice of phenomenology, a specificity that yet leaves a great deal of latitude for disagreement and difference.

4   Speaking as I do from within the U.S. academy, I am aware of the difficulty of trying to describe cultural studies in terms general enough to have some relevance to those in very different institutional and geographical conditions.

5   There is not, and never has been, a singular thing called British cultural studies. There never even was a thing called *the* position of the Centre for Contemporary Cultural Studies at Birmingham, which is often mythically and sometimes nostalgically seen as the location of the origin of British cultural studies. Even at the Centre there were always different and sometimes competing, powerfully invested, positions and projects. The differences were both theoretical and political, and they often led to highly charged, emotionally difficult debates. Consequently even the best histories of the Centre, or of British cultural studies, that have been written manage at best to describe what John Clarke has called "the diversity that won." There are always voices that were part of the discussion that have been excluded (or that excluded themselves) or erased.

6   The Chicago school has had an enormous impact on a wide range of disciplines and perspectives in North America. We need at the very least to distinguish its influence on social theory—particularly as the source of symbolic interactionism—from its continuing presence as one of the early articulations of pragmatism (visible in the work of such diverse writers as Richard Rorty and Cornel West). In a more complete analysis of the Chicago school's theory of culture, one would also need to distinguish and compare the work of John Dewey, the philosopher, and sociologists such as Robert Park.

7   Bill Schwarz has described the geographical determinations of British cultural studies, connecting the fact that it was "decentred and mis-placed" from the "metropolitan culture of imperial Britain" to its "structural ambiguity." See Schwarz 1994.

8   This is not entirely accurate, since in Williams's earlier theoretical writings there is certainly an image of an idealized culture that depends upon the projection of a time when culture and community would be equivalent. In fact, the rhetoric of *The Long Revolution* is remarkably similar to that of John Dewey at times. However, this idealized image ("the community of process") was never assumed to be the reality and was always juxtaposed to another, less ideal concept (the structure of feeling, the community of culture). Moreover, the development of British cultural studies depended as well on the work of E. P. Thompson, and in particular on Thompson's critique (1961) of Williams.

9   Thus, for example, James Carey creates a cultural studies by bringing together the Chicago school and the work of Harold Innis. Similarly, an anthropological cultural studies emerges when the anthropological model of culture is critiqued by, and juxtaposed with, emergent notions of culture in postcolonial studies.

10 Following Tony Bennett, I want to emphasize that I am trying to describe a set of procedures that can be empirically discriminated, and not a set of biographical or psychological characteristics of the intellectuals practicing them. Bennett has argued that this distinction results from a choice between Foucault and Gramsci as different bodies and styles of theory and politics. Alternatively, I see it as a decision about how Foucault is to be brought into and allowed to reconfigure cultural studies. Or in other words, which Foucault, what part of Foucault, is central to the projects of cultural studies? Foucault, after all, might himself be described as a founder of a discourse: Does one read Foucault as a theorist of knowledge/power? effectivity, the body, and the critique of ideology? genealogies? archaeologies? discipline? governmentality? the constitution and care of the self? the micropolitics, mechanisms, and apparatuses of power? My own reading emphasizes questions of effectivity and of the particular deployments of power, that is, the organizations and machineries producing particular unequal relations of force and power. See Tony Bennett 1992b.

11 Tony Bennett (1993) has criticized the way in which the commitment to discipline is often contradicted in practice by a "specific political technology of the intellectual" which he describes as "charismatic authority and closure," often constructed by the apparatuses of cultural studies. Such a technology conflates intellectual work and biography, so that one's ideas are read and judged through one's life, and one's life is read and judged as the embodiment of one's ideas. For Bennett, this is the result of the moral-aesthetic tradition out of which British cultural studies arose. Obviously, the existence of such a technology in the United States cannot be assigned to the same history, as

education always functioned in more pragmatic and political terms. While such authoritative voices may be useful in particular contexts, for certain ends, they are not, Bennett argues, particularly useful in defining the intellectual enterprise of cultural studies.

12   Here I am obviously distancing myself from Richard Johnson's "What Is Cultural Studies Anyway?" (1986–87), which defines cultural studies by articulating a model of culture as communication (sender-message-receiver) to Marx's model of the cycle of production (production-distribution-consumption). Johnson would make cultural studies into a combination of political economy, textual analysis, and ethnographic audience studies, although how this is to be accomplished remains something of a mystery. I am also distancing myself from, for example, Brantlinger (1990).

13   Actually I would argue that the assumption of the social construction of reality defines the continuing modernist basis of cultural studies. Consequently if we are to find a form of cultural studies appropriate to its contemporary global situation, we must renounce this assumption in order to articulate a different—spatial—form of materialism.

14   Cultural studies' methods vary widely. Sometimes articulation is the only way to describe what the critic is doing. More often, however, the method is derived from another disciplinary methodology—ethnography, textual analysis, survey research—but the way it is enacted and interpreted changes significantly as a result of the commitment to articulation.

15   For cultural studies, the context might be better thought of as specific bits of daily life, positioned between culture (as a specific body of practices) and social forces/institutions/apparatuses.

16   I think this describes the work of such important critics as Fred Jameson, discovering once again the class struggle (or the third world struggling against the colonizers), as well as a large number of identity critics discovering once again, apparently to their surprise, that the latest Hollywood production is sexist and racist.

17   I am aware that I am also leaving unremarked the issue of who, if anyone, can claim to "speak for the context."

18   The question of the "empirical" reality of contexts and power cannot be addressed here. I believe it can only be answered by a serious reconsideration of the foundations of contemporary cultural theory and of the relations between ontology and epistemology. See Deleuze 1988.

19   Viswanathan (1991) argues that there is a serious problem with the notion of culture as it is used in cultural studies and, in particular, in the work of Raymond Williams. She challenges the notion of English culture (and, by extension, of any national culture) and argues that, in fact, significant aspects of the English culture of the nineteenth and twentieth centuries were actually developed by the colonial regime in India (as forms of regulation and control) and then exported back to England (also as forms of regulation and control). For example, pedagogical practices that Williams assumes to have been constructed in the English educational system were actually developed as strategic weapons in the struggle to "civilize the colonial masses" and were then brought back to England in order to civilize the working masses. Eventually they worked their way up into the middle class, where they were not only normalized but nationalized as well. What became English culture was not English, but part of a global colonial culture that

Williams has erased. The very complexity and contextuality that cultural studies is supposedly committed to has been ignored.

TOWARD A GENEALOGY OF THE STATE
OF CULTURAL STUDIES

1 I will not speak here about its existence in other parts of the world, for the two issues, while connected, are not the same.

2 Here the media repeat the injustice they did to poststructuralism in the United States by so quickly and totally identifying it with a few individuals associated with Yale deconstructionism and with a particular reading of Derrida.

3 This can be seen as a rearticulation of the founding question of social theory—namely, the relationship between modernity, modernism, and modernization—although the transformation of the question is at least as significant as its continuity. Both versions are concerned with the problem of historical change and continuity, but they have radically different conceptions of the forces and forms of history.

4 See Ross 1989, ch. 2.

5 Significantly, like the development of British cultural studies much of the initial motivation and rhetoric of this project came from wider public discourses outside of the academy. See Carey 1995.

6 For example, Jim Kaufman, Hayden White, and Loren Baritz at the University of Rochester.

7 After having studied at the Centre (on the advice of those Rochester historians), and returned to the United States, I asked Stuart Hall where to continue my graduate career in cultural studies in the United States. The only answer he could give me was to go to the University of Illinois to work with Jim Carey. In fact, he either neglected to tell me or did not realize that Carey was a professor of communications. Moreover, insofar as the current boom can be traced back to any significant events, they would seem to be the presence of Stuart Hall at the Marxism and the Interpretation of Culture Teaching Institute and of Hall and other cultural studies scholars at the conference that followed, at the University of Illinois in 1983, Stuart Hall's keynote address at the International Communication Association meeting of 1985 and the Cultural Studies conference at the University of Illinois in 1990. It is important to note that in all of these events, including the two conferences (and teaching institute) at the University of Illinois, the discipline of communication was the dominant if not the determinant field.

8 It is, I would guess, more the result of the insularity of such disciplines than of any intentional misrepresentation.

9 Interestingly, the first major site within the professional organizations of the discipline of communication (the International Communications Association) was an interest group (later a division) formed by a coalition of people interested in cultural studies with those interested in the philosophy of communication. At the same time, the particular way in which cultural studies was appropriated (see discussion to follow) enabled the field to ignore most of the theoretical complexity and diversity and struggle that was part of British cultural studies.

10 This argument is taken from Grossberg 1993b.

11   Such a claim is not meant as a criticism of those working within the discourses of communications study, for in one way or another, in the contemporary academy, we all do. Rather it is meant as a call for a more reflective and critical contextualization of the power of our own discourses as communications scholars. My claim, or at least my hope, is that a more radical understanding of the possibilities of cultural studies, even as it is located within the discipline of communications, can contribute to such a project as well as to a better understanding of the imbrication of communicative and cultural practices in the material organization and deployment of power in the contemporary world.

12   However this might be defined (e.g., in its simplest form, the relationship between culture and society), what is really at stake here is the problem of determination or articulation between different domains of practices.

13   Although the *Journal of Communication Inquiry* special issue on Stuart Hall (which included a number of his most important articles) was published in the summer of 1986, the journal was not well known and was poorly distributed. Interestingly, I think it is true to say what while Johnson's article is frequently cited with some authority in the United States, it is rarely cited as a definitive statement of cultural studies in the U.K.

WHERE IS THE "AMERICA" IN AMERICAN CULTURAL STUDIES?

1   I am intentionally leaving the phrase "American" ambiguous, for it can refer both to the United States and to the broader geographical formation of the Americas. This ambiguity is often operating in calls for an American cultural studies. And the objections I raise, it seems to me, apply equally to either option. However, for the most part, I will intentionally misuse the phrase to refer to cultural studies in the United States. Hopefully, the context will clarify each instance of the phrase.

2   I am quoting from the invitation to the conference at which this paper was originally given. However, I do not mean to single out the conference organizers, for I believe this sense of intellectual geography is widely shared.

3   This is obviously part of a much larger critique not only of the equation of culture and nation, but of the very category of the nation itself.

4   I am explicitly avoiding the question of Latin American traditions here, for that poses very different and interesting challenges.

5   Although pragmatism attempted to define a philosophy of radical contextualism, I do not think its practice succeeded, since it reinscribed the same concrete processes at every level, and at every site, of existence.

6   In fact, I think this has to do with the modernist foundations of cultural studies and of the concept of culture.

WANDERING AUDIENCES, NOMADIC CRITICS

1   This paper represents a collective journey with Janice Radway and Meaghan Morris, the former carried out through manuscripts and the telephone, the latter through articles and the post. I also need to thank Anne Balsamo, Elspeth Probyn, Gail Valaskakis, and Jennifer Daryl Slack for their invaluable comments and their infinite patience.

2 I shall not attempt to reproduce the rich and insightful analysis Morris offers. Moreover I have not only changed the descriptive names to fit my own argument, I have also generalized her readings of specific texts to the interpretations of general positions. It is important to note that the use of the masculine pronoun in Morris's analysis of the poststructuralist and urban-culturalist positions (and my summary of her work) is intentional, since her argument is precisely that the structure of the argument always ends up coding both the everyday subject and the critic as masculine.

3 This form of urban-culturalism can be seen as a Gramscian position, articulated through Barthes's distinction between pleasure and *jouissance*.

4 See Hebdige 1987 for a clear example of this binarism.

5 For a critique of these "magical terms," see Henriques et al. 1984.

6 Note the ambiguity of the term "experience": it refers both to the way in which any social position is lived and to the interpretations of that lived position.

7 The gendering of the ethnographer in Clifford and Marcus (1986) is decidedly male! See Clifford 1986 for an attempt to describe the absence of feminist ethnographers in the collection on the grounds that there is little interesting writing produced by them.

8 For other efforts to rethink ethnography, see Walkerdine 1986 and Morley 1986. Walkerdine seems to fall into the same problem as the poststructuralists, largely erasing the other in favor of her own autobiography.

9 See Henriques et al 1984, 204. This theory of the subject is at least partly derived from the work of Deleuze and Guattari, who view the subject in terms of residual qualities, intensities (not internalities), and tertiary productions. Even in Foucault, the subject becomes one moment of discourse which, while often foregrounded in his researches, is not privileged. See Grossberg 1982a.

10 I am grateful to Joanna Maclay, who provided this term.

11 Morris, citing Certeau, describes the relation of place and space as follows: "A *place* delimits a field; it is ruled by the law of the 'proper,' by an orderly contiguity of elements in the location it defines . . . A *space* is not a substance of a space but the product of its transformation. It exists only in relation to vectors of direction, velocities, and time variables. Space 'occurs'; composed of intersections of mobile elements, it is *actuated* by the ensemble of movements deployed within it . . . 'space is a *practised place*' " (1988a, 37).

12 One might also critically examine Bennett and Woollacott's theory (1987) of reading formations, and Corrigan and Willis's efforts (1980) to semioticize the cultural capital of any audience's decoding. These projects merely reify a new displaced text and fetishize a new audience.

THE CONTEXT OF AUDIENCES AND
THE POLITICS OF DIFFERENCE

A version of this paper was originally delivered (at least on video) at the 1989 meeting of the Australian Communication Association. I would like to thank Ros Petelin for her patience and encouragement. I would also like to thank Meaghan Morris and Janice Radway for their many generous hours of conversation and criticism.

1 I find it interesting that two of the most recent and strongest calls for such models of

cultural circulation have come from countries in which critics have to face the challenge of the enormity of national space, populations, and social and cultural differences. See Morris 1988a and Grossberg 1988b.

2   I want to thank, and emphasize my debt in this section to the work of James Carey, Ellen Wartella, and Andrew Ross. All I have done is inadequately summarize and slightly misrepresent their arguments.

3   Actually I think that the work of the Centre for Contemporary Cultural Studies through the seventies involves a constant tension between a liberal theory of the active audience and an ethnographic theory of difference.

4   It is important to remember that this debate has been taking place for a long time within feminist and antiracist struggles. See, for example, Segal 1987 and Gilroy 1987.

CULTURAL STUDIES IN/AND NEW WORLDS

This paper, and the ongoing work it represents, would not be possible without the help of Meaghan Morris. It attempts to extend the argument of my book (*We Gotta Get Out of This Place* [1992]). This paper was first presented at the Trajectories: Toward an Internationalist Cultural Studies conference, Taipei, Taiwan, July 1992. I am grateful to Kuan-Hsing Chen for having invited me. I also want to thank May Joseph, Cameron McCarthy, James Hay, and the students in my graduate seminar (spring 1992) for all their help. Finally, I would like to acknowledge the fact that this revised paper reflects many of the discussions and comments of the various participants in the Trajectories conference. It is, therefore, in a very real sense, part of a collective and ongoing project.

1   Cultural studies is never purist in the sense that it can be identified with a single theoretical figure or position. Cultural studies tends to use theorists, to bring them together critically and pragmatically, in order to offer its own positions. Thus cultural studies has been influenced by a wide range of texts, although not all of them need to be construed as themselves cultural studies.

2   An interesting but unanswered question involves the conditions of possibility of cultural studies in different places: Why is it, for example, largely absent in France? Here we might talk about the power of a certain cultural elitism, the organization of intellectual formations (which placed the study of culture in philosophy, semiotics, and history), the dominant model of the political intellectual (existentialism), the major sources of marginality (North Africa), the economics of publication (making translation from English not necessarily profitable), and so forth.

As far as the United States is concerned, we might distinguish the conditions of its success (and the particular form of that success) from the conditions of its rapid proliferation, since obviously I do not think these are equivalent. Regarding the former, I might point to the so-called mass-culture debates (and the fact that they were eventually displaced from English to communications and education departments, the latter being the original places where cultural studies was taken up in the United States), the "commitment" to democratic education, the importance of questions of culture and communication (in terms of community and technology, multiculturalism, mobility, and a national identity that was never fixed). Regarding the conditions of its proliferation I would point to the economics of the academy (its size as a market determines not only the competition for students but the organization of academic publishing and the fact that cultural studies here is largely publishing driven), the rise of a generation raised on media and politics, the lack of charismatic intellectual figures, and the existence of multiple overlapping intellectual formations (African American studies, women's studies, and so forth). It would also be interesting to locate cultural studies in the context of the history of discourses of culture in American society and politics, including (1) a discourse of the technological sublime; (2) a discourse of the landscape and the land (the pioneer versus the family; the repression of history as the site of the genocidal founding act; the gender-coding of the land); (3) the discourses of state and state policy (and its relation to the "empty" identity of the nation except in relation to itself as an "other" or temporary external enemies). See Berland 1992.

3   For the best description of the specificity of cultural studies, see the introduction to Frow and Morris 1993. See also the introduction to Grossberg 1992 for a discussion of the specific disciplinary and historical articulation of the specificity of cultural studies.

4   We must be particularly careful here since every knowledge-project has its own conditions of "being in the true." Every such project sets up its own rhetorical, constitutive, political, and theoretical demands that define the legitimacy (the very possibility of truth) of a statement. We need to be critical of such conditions, especially with regard to how they authorize only particular subjects (both speaking subjects and subjects of discourse) and exclude others. At the same time, we need to recognize that the simple existence of such conditions and exclusions is not, in itself, a sufficient critique, since it is a fact of all knowledge production.

5   I do not mean to suggest that "the modern" is a singular or homogeneous structure.

6   I am reluctant to use "postmodern" here, not only because it constructs a homogeneous "before," but also because it too often assumes a necessary relation between cultural forms and their effects. Moreover it tends to reduce the multiple levels of cultural effectivity to questions of aesthetics and economics/history.

7   For a discussion of articulation, see Grossberg 1992 and Centre for Contemporary Cultural Studies 1982.

8   In the following discussion, I will deal only with Amin's arguments.

9   I want to privilege space not merely because it has been left off the agenda, but because it has been "intentionally" left off the agenda. But I do not mean to close off the possibility of, and even the necessity for, reintroducing a temporal or historical dimension (albeit one radically rearticulated). There is an important difference between criticizing an argument for not having addressed a specific issue (every argument ignores some important issues) and claiming that it does not have the theoretical and political space to address it.

10   Much of the following argument is taken from Young (1990).

11   The best example of a critical geography is Soja (1989). A more promising path might be found in the distributive maps of Bourdieu (1984).

12   As Foucault says, "A whole history remains to be written of spaces—which would at the same time be the history of powers (both of these terms in the plural)—from the great strategies of geopolitics to the little tactics of the habitat" (cited in Soja 1989, 21).

13   I leave open here the question of the relationship between articulation and rhizomatics.

14   I have incorporated sections of Grossberg (1996b) into this essay.

15   I am also aware of the potential charge that, as a white middle-class man, I am attempting to undermine a concept that has proved to be empowering for various subaltern populations. I can only plead that I am not trying to undermine political empowerment and struggle, but to find more powerful theoretical tools that may open up more effective forms and sites of struggle.

16   This points to another "modern" logic that I will not discuss here: what might be called the semanticization of reality or, in other words, the reduction of the real to meaning. It is only on this basis that the modern can assert its most fundamental proposition: that reality is socially constructed.

17   Obviously a fuller discussion would need to recognize historical and economic determinations. It would need to explore how class distinctions operated (after all, not the entire black population was involved), and the operation of the changing economic context (in which the contradiction between the forces and relations of production is itself being rearticulated: Is it that the forces are becoming socialized while the relations are becoming privatized?). It would also need to consider the specific circumstances that defined the condition of emergence of this particular event. (I want to thank Mark Reid for reminding me of this.)

      But the question remains: Was the violence aimed at a specific people understood in terms of a subject-identity? If that is true, then education should help to overcome the implicit cultural relativism that underlies such misunderstandings. But if the violence is defined by and aimed at the role that various people play in the lives of black people, we need to ask how that role is to be defined. My answer is, obviously, spatially. And if this is the case, then education would quickly be made irrelevant, for new surface features would quickly be found to justify the antagonism. In this sense, local racisms are increasingly a matter of place rather than of race or even ethnicity as it is commonly used.

18   In Deleuzean terms, subjectivity is the content of the body as expression, produced as a folding of the outside upon itself to create a stratum of the inside.

19   It is here that we can understand Foucault's distinction between different machines of power—societies of sovereignty and disciplinary societies—as different ways in which agency is itself constituted. In the former, agency is constructed on the materiality of the body; in the latter, through vision (surveillance) and structure (normalization). In disciplinary societies, the individual is placed into a mass space and monitored. Life is organized through enclosed environments (and capitalism is defined by processes of concentration and production). I might add a third category here—societies of disciplined mobilization—in which agency is organized through the control of mobility (and capitalism is defined by dispersion and futures/services).

20   Here one would also need to consider the effects of the high number of illegal immigrants who, in fact, often have greater access to limited work than the black population. Also one would have to consider the empowering identification with another culture and another place.

21   Here we would need to look at the different conditions and diagrams of other Asian populations—Japanese, Vietnamese, and Chinese—who have arrived in California in various movements, at various moments.

BRINGING IT ALL BACK HOME:
PEDAGOGY AND CULTURAL STUDIES

This paper is a revision of my inaugural lecture of the Waterbury Forum for Education and Cultural Studies at Pennsylvania State University. I want to thank Henry Giroux for inviting me to give the lecture and for his generous support and insightful comments.

1   In *Politics and Letters* (1979, 78–83), Williams offers us a very specific example of such contextual thinking (particularly relevant to contemporary debates) drawn from his own extramural teaching. In the period between the two world wars, when he was teaching, there was a particularly heated split between the National Council of Labour Colleges (defending consciously affiliated socialist workers' education) and the Worker's Education Association (which argued that a distinct class affiliation "had to be mediated by a kind of education that made no presumptions," that explored all positions rather than teaching only the party line). While the former risked subordinating education to party politics, the latter risked incorporation, by accepting the academic standards of the universities to which its classes were attached. Here is Williams's personal response to this conflict: "I agreed that it would have been wholly wrong in class not to declare your position; and equally that you made no assumption at the beginning of the class that you shared anything else than an interest in the subject." He describes the danger of "teaching declining into a propaganda exercise." However, he quickly adds that "in fact increasingly through the 50s the dangers were the opposite."

2   There is, however, one noteworthy exception: In *Working Papers* 10 (1977), Dan Finn, Neil Grant, and Richard Johnson authored "Social Democracy, Education and the Crisis." This paper was revised and published in 1978 as an "Occasional Paper." These three authors, together with Steven Baron and Michael Green, published *Unpopular Education* in 1981. Other occasional papers include Marilyn Moos, "Government Youth Training Policy and Its Impact on Further Education" (1979); Brian Doyle, "Some Uses of English: Denys Thompson and the Development of English in Secondary Schools" (1981); James Avis, "Curriculum Innovation in F.E.: A Case Study" (1983); and Mariette Calre, "Ideologies of Adult Literacy" (1985).

3   Although this literature is absent from *Working Papers,* the "Occasional Papers" include the following, all by Paul Willis: "Transition from School to Work Bibliography" (1973); "The Main Reality: Transition School/Work: SSRC Report" (1975); "How Working Class Kids Get Working Class Jobs" (1975). Also relevant is Janice Winship, "Women and Work Bibliography" (1978).

4   See, for example, Finn 1987 and Bates et al. 1984.

5   Diawara's binary division of the terrain (abstract poststructuralism versus black cultural studies) is, however, inadequate, and his celebration of "the black studies strand of cultural studies" fails to acknowledge that much of this work not only also follows poststructuralism in its "fetishism of difference" (a term I borrow from Keya Ganguly), but also often underestimates the necessary contextuality of theory and of its political possibilities. As much as some writers looking at questions of, for example, popular culture and hegemony fail to adequately contextualize their work, the same may be said of a certain proportion of those working in "black cultural studies." Some of this latter

group, in fact, not only fail to recognize the gap between theories of difference and hybridity, they also ignore the contextual specificity of such notions as hybridity, fragmentation, and otherness.

6   This is the site of a significant theoretical debate within cultural studies, over two readings, as it were, of Foucault's notion of the positivity of discourse. On the one hand, there are those (generally following Ernesto Laclau) who see the outside, the real, as a constitutive and indeterminate other. On the other hand, there are those (generally following Deleuze and Guattari) who argue that the real is a contingent and effective configuration of material effects. A second dimension of this dispute concerns the theory of hegemony, which, according to Laclau, involves the organization of the social into a struggle between "the people" and the power bloc, a difference that is then mapped onto the cultural terrain as well. Deleuzeans tend to reject this binary model. See Grossberg 1992.

7   For a critique of interpretive practices, see Bennett 1990.

8   But, as Mohanty points out, this is not the fault of these intellectual and political formations themselves: "the process of the individualization of histories of dominance is . . . characteristic of educational institutions and processes in general." Such programs then must often set themselves to fight against what Henry Giroux has called a pedagogy of normative pluralism: where race and gender are treated in terms of personal or individual experiences, where individuals are treated as representatives of cultural groups, and whatever legitimation is offered to traditionally subordinated groups "takes place purely at an attitudinal, interpersonal level rather than in terms of a fundamental challenge to hegemonic knowledge and history" (Mohanty 1994, 151).

9   See, e.g., Bennett 1992; the important work of the journal *Culture and Policy;* and the debate "Culture, Policy and Beyond" in *Meanjin* 51.3 (Spring 1992).

10 See Grossberg 1992 for a more elaborate description of one approach to such a pedagogical project.

11 Consequently I think it take more work than we have often been willing to perform to define the real stakes of our pedagogical strategies. We cannot take for granted the affective and ideological resonances that appeals to values like "democracy" will have for our students. In the abstract, "democracy" is a useful basis for a critique of existing political relations, but it often remains vague and unspecified. While I don't want to deny the importance of an "educated and participatory democracy," I am uneasy about the wholesale adoption of "self-management" as a model for all of life, and of "collective decision making" as a solution to all problems. We need to rethink not only the meaning of democracy and the possibilities of its relocation from the domain of the state to that of culture, but even more, we need to think about whether democracy is sufficient by itself, or whether there are in fact limits that have to be thought through in its relation to questions of liberty, justice, and other forms of equality. After all, even Laclau and Mouffe, the leading advocates of "democracy" as a central principle of struggle, suggest that "no hegemonic project can be based exclusively on a democratic logic, but must also consist of a set of proposals for the positive organization of the social" (1985, 189).

eferences

Adams, Mary Louise. 1989. There's no place like home: On the place of identity in feminist politics. *Feminist Review*, no. 31: 22–33.

Adams, Parveen. 1978. Representation and sexuality. *M/F* 1: 65–82.

Adorno, T. 1941. On popular music. *Studies in Philosophy and Social Science* 9: 17–48.

Agamben, Giorgio. 1993. *The coming community*. Trans. Michael Hardt. Minneapolis: University of Minnesota Press.

Ahmad, Aijaz. 1992. *In theory: Classes, nations, literatures*. London: Verso.

Albig, William. 1939. *Public opinion*. New York: McGraw Hill.

Alcalay, Ammiel. 1993. *After Jews and Arabs: Remaking Levantine culture*. Minneapolis: University of Minnesota Press.

Allor, Martin. 1984. Cinema, culture and the social formation: Ideology and critical practice. Ph.D. University of Illinois, Urbana.

———. 1987. Projective readings: Cultural studies from here. *Canadian Journal of Political and Social Theory* 11: 134–37.

Althusser, Louis. 1970. *For Marx*. Trans. Ben Brewster. New York: Vintage.

———. 1971. Ideology and ideological state apparatuses. In *Lenin and philosophy and other essays*. Trans. Ben Brewster. New York: Monthly Review Press.

Amin, Samir. 1989. *Eurocentrism*. New York: Monthly Review Press.

Anaya, Rudolfo A., and Francisco Lomeli, eds. 1989. *Aztlán: Essays on the Chicano homeland*. Albuquerque: Academia/El Norte Publications.

Anderson, Perry. 1968. Components of the national culture. *New Left Review* 50: 3–57.

Anzaldúa, Gloria. 1987. *Borderlands/La frontera: The new mestiza*. San Francisco: Spinsters/Aunt Lute.

Apel, Karl-Otto. 1972. The a priori of communication and the foundation of the humanities. *Man and World* 5: 30–37.

Aronowitz, Stanley. 1981. *The crisis in historical materialism: Class, politics and culture in marxist theory*. South Hadley: Bergin.

Bailey, David, and Stuart Hall. 1992a. Critical decade: An introduction. In *Critical decade*. Ed. David Bailey and Stuart Hall. *Ten-8* 2(3): 4–7.

———. 1992b. The vertigo of displacement: Shifts within black documentary practices. *Critical decade*. Ed. David Bailey and Stuart Hall. *Ten-8* 2(3): 15–23.

———, eds. 1992. *Critical decade: Black British photography in the 80s. Ten-8* 2(3).

Bakhtin, Mikhail. 1981. *The dialogic imagination.* Trans. C. Emerson and M. Holquist. Austin: University of Texas Press.

Barrett, Michele. 1987. The concept of difference. *Feminist Review,* no. 26: 29–42.

Barthes, Roland. 1972. *Mythologies.* Trans. Annette Lavers. New York: Hill and Wang.

——. 1974. *S/Z: An essay.* Trans. Richard Miller. New York: Hill and Wang.

——. 1975. *The pleasure of the text.* Trans. Richard Miller. New York: Hill and Wang.

——. 1978. *A lover's discourse: Fragments.* Trans. Richard Howard. New York: Hill and Wang.

——. 1981. *Camera lucida: Reflections on photography.* Trans. Richard Howard. New York: Hill and Wang.

Bates, Inge, John Clarke, Philip Cohen, Dan Finn, Robert Moore, and Paul Willis. 1984. *Schooling for the dole? The new vocationalism.* London: Macmillan.

Baudrillard, Jean. 1978. Requiem for the media. In *Language, sexuality and subversion.* Ed. Paul Foss and Meaghan Morris. Darlington: Feral Publications. 83–96.

——. 1980. Forgetting Foucault. *Humanities in Society* 3: 87–111.

——. 1983. *Simulations.* Trans. P. Foss, P. Patton, and P. Beitchman. New York: Semiotexte.

Belman, Lary. 1977. John Dewey's concept of communication. *Journal of Communication* 27: 29–37.

Benjamin, Walter. 1968. *Illuminations.* Ed. Hannah Arendt. New York: Harcourt, Brace and World.

Bennett, Tony. 1990. *Outside literature.* London: Routledge.

——. 1992a. Putting policy into cultural studies. In *Cultural studies.* Ed. Lawrence Grossberg, Cary Nelson, and Paula Treichler. New York: Routledge. 23–34.

——. 1992b. Useful culture. *Cultural Studies* 6: 395–408.

——. 1992c. Coming out of English. Paper presented at Trajectories: Toward an Internationalist Cultural Studies conference. Taipei, Taiwan. July 1992.

——. 1993. Being "in the true" of cultural studies. *Southern Review* 26: 217–38.

Bennett, Tony, and Janet Woollacott. 1987. *Bond and beyond: The political career of a popular hero.* New York: Methuen.

Berger, John. 1972. *Ways of seeing.* London: BBC and Penguin.

Berland, Jody. 1992. Cultural studies and Canadian communications theory: Critical problematics. Paper presented at Trajectories: Toward an Internationalist Cultural Studies conference. Taipei, Taiwan. July 1992.

Berlo, David. 1960. *The process of communication.* New York: Holt.

Bhabha, Homi K. 1992. Postcolonial authority and postmodern guilt. In *Cultural studies.* Ed. Lawrence Grossberg, Cary Nelson, and Paula Treichler. New York: Routledge. 56–66.

——. 1994. *The location of culture.* London: Routledge.

Blum, Alan. 1961. Popular culture and the image of the Gesellschaft. *Studies in Public Communication* 3: 145–58.

Bourdieu, Pierre. 1980. The aristocracy of culture. *Media, Culture, Society* 2: 225–54.

——. 1984. *Distinction: A social critique of the judgement of taste.* Trans. R. Nice. Cambridge: Harvard University Press.

Bradley, David. n.d. The cultural study of music. Occasional paper. Centre for Contemporary Cultural Studies, Birmingham, England.

Braidotti, Rosi. 1991. *Patterns of dissonance.* Trans. E. Guild. New York: Routledge.

Brantlinger, Patrick. 1990. *Crusoe's footprints*. New York: Routledge.

Braudel, F. 1981. *The structures of everyday life*. Vol. 1, *The limits of the possible*. Trans. S. Reynolds. New York: Harper & Row.

Brookeman, Christopher. 1984. *American culture and society since the 1930s*. London: Macmillan.

Brunsdon, Charlotte, and David Morley. 1978. *Everyday television: "Nationwide."* London: British Film Institute.

Burke, Kenneth. 1945. *A grammar of motives*. Englewood Cliffs: Prentice-Hall.

Carey, James W. 1975a. A cultural approach to communication. *Communication* 2: 1–22.

——. 1975b. Canadian communication theory: Extensions and interpretations of Harold Innis. In *Studies in Canadian communications*. Ed. Gertrude J. Robinson and Donald F. Theall. Montreal: McGill University. 27–60.

——. 1975c. Communication and culture. *Communications Research* 2: 173–91.

——. 1977. Mass communication research and cultural studies: An American view. In *Mass communication and society*. Ed. James Curran et al. London: Edward Arnold. 409–26.

——. 1989a. *Communication as culture: Essays on media and society*. Boston: Unwin Hyman.

——. 1989b. Communication and the progressives. *Critical Studies in Mass Communication* 6: 264–82.

——. 1995. American cultural studies and the history of broadcasting. Paper presented at Across Disciplines and Beyond Boundaries Conference. Urbana, IL.

Castells, Manuel. 1989. *The informational city*. Oxford: Blackwells.

Centre for Contemporary Cultural Studies. 1966–67. *Report*. Birmingham, England.

——. 1969–71. *Report*. Birmingham, England.

——. 1972–74. *Report*. Birmingham, England.

——. 1971–77. *Working Papers in Cultural Studies*. Birmingham, England.

——. 1982. *The empire strikes back: Race and racism in 70s Britain*. London: Hutchinson.

Certeau, Michel de. 1984. *The practice of everyday life*. Trans. Steven R. Rendall. Berkeley: University of California Press.

Chambers, Iain. 1981. Pop music: A teaching perspective. *Screen Education* 39: 35–46.

——. 1986. *Popular culture: The metropolitan experience*. London: Methuen.

Chambers, Iain, et al. 1978. Marxism and culture. *Screen* 19: 109–19.

Chambers, Iain, and Lidia Curti, eds. 1996. *The question of postcolonialism*. London: Routledge.

Chan, Stephen. 1992. Otherwise Hong Kong: The impossibilities of engaging culture. Paper presented at Trajectories: Toward an Internationalist Cultural Studies conference. Taipei, Taiwan. July 1992.

Chen, Kuan-Hsing. 1996. Not yet the colonial era: The (super) nation-state and transnationalism of cultural studies. *Cultural Studies* 10: 37–70.

Clarke, John. 1991. *New times and old enemies*. London: Routledge.

Clarke, John, et al. 1975. Subcultures, cultures and class: A theoretical overview. *Working Papers in Cultural Studies*, nos. 7/8: 9–74.

Clifford, James. 1986. Introduction: Partial truths. In *Writing culture*. Ed. James Clifford and George E. Marcus. Berkeley: University of California Press. 1–26.

——. 1988. *The predicament of culture: Twentieth century ethnography, literature and art.* Cambridge: Harvard University Press.

——. 1994. Diasporas. *Cultural Anthropology.* 302–38.

Clifford, James, and George E. Marcus, eds. 1986. *Writing culture: The poetics and politics of ethnography.* Berkeley: University of California Press.

Collins, Ava. 1994. Intellectuals, power and quality television. In *Between borders.* Ed. Henry Giroux and Peter McLaren. New York: Routledge. 56–73.

Corrigan, Philip, and Paul Willis. 1980. Cultural forms and class mediations. *Media Culture and Society* 2: 297–312.

Coward, Rosalind. 1977. Class, "culture," and the social formation. *Screen* 18: 75–105.

Coward, Rosalind, and John Ellis. 1977. *Language and materialism: Developments in semiology and the theory of the subject.* London: Routledge and Kegan Paul.

Crapanzano, Vincent. 1986. Hermes dilemma: The masking of subversion in ethnographic description. In *Writing culture.* Ed. James Clifford and George E. Marcus. Berkeley: University of California Press. 51–76.

"Culture, policy and beyond." Spring 1992. Special issue, *Meanjin* 51.

Davis, Mike. 1985. Urban renaissance and the spirit of postmodernism. *New Left Review,* no. 143: 106–13.

Deetz, Stanley. 1973. Words without things: Towards a social phenomenology of language. *Quarterly Journal of Speech* 59: 40–51.

Deleuze, Gilles. 1988. *Foucault.* Trans. S. Hand. Minneapolis: University of Minnesota Press.

Deleuze, Gilles, and Felix Guattari. 1977. *Anti-Oedipus: Capitalism and schizophrenia.* Trans. Robert Hurley et al. New York: Viking Press.

——. 1981. Rhizome. *I & C,* no. 8: 49–71.

——. 1987. *A thousand plateaus: Capitalism and schizophrenia.* Trans. Brian Massumi. Minneapolis: University of Minnesota Press.

Denning, Michael. 1992. The academic Left and the rise of cultural studies. *Radical History Review* 54:21–48.

Derrida, Jacques. 1976. *Of grammatology.* Trans. Gayatri Chakravorty Spivak. Baltimore: Johns Hopkins University Press.

——. 1978. *Writing and difference.* Trans. A. Bass. London: Routledge.

——. 1981. *Dissemination.* Trans. Barbara Johnson. Chicago: University of Chicago Press.

Dewey, John. 1927. *The public and its problems.* New York: Henry Holt and Co.

——. 1954. *The public and its problems.* Chicago: Swallow Press.

Dhareshwar, Vivek. 1989. Toward a narrative epistemology of the postcolonial predicament. *Inscriptions* 5.

——. 1990. The predicament of theory. In *Theory between the disciplines.* Ed. M. Kreisworth and M. A. Cheetham. Ann Arbor: University of Michigan Press.

Diawara, Manthia. 1992. Black studies, cultural studies: Performative acts. *Afterimage* 20: 6–7.

Dorfman, Ariel, and Armand Mattelart. 1975. *How to read Donald Duck: Imperialist ideology in the Disney comic.* Trans. D. Kunzle. New York: International General.

Dyson, Michael Eric. 1994. Be like Mike: Michael Jordan and the pedagogy of desire. In *Between borders.* Ed. Henry Giroux and Peter McLaren. New York: Routledge. 119–26.

Eco, Umberto. 1976. *A theory of semiotics*. Bloomington: Indiana University Press.

Education Group, Centre for Contemporary Cultural Studies. 1981. *Unpopular education: Schooling and social democracy in England since 1944*. London: Hutchinson.

Education Group II. 1990. *Education Ltd.: Schooling, training and the New Right in England since 1979*. London: Routledge.

Faules, Donald F., and Dennis C. Alexander. 1978. *Communication and social behavior: A symbolic interaction perspective*. Reading: Addison-Wesley.

Finn, Dan. 1987. *Training without jobs: New deals and broken promises*. London: Macmillan.

Foss, Paul, and Meaghan Morris, eds. 1978. *Language, sexuality and subversion*. Darlington: Feral Publications.

Foucault, Michel. 1970. *The order of things: An archaeology of the human sciences*. New York: Pantheon.

———. 1972. *The archeology of knowledge and the discourse on language*. Trans. A. M. Sheridan Smith. New York: Pantheon.

———. 1977a. *Discipline and punish: The birth of the prison*. Trans. Alan Sheridan. New York: Pantheon.

———. 1977b. Power and sex: An interview. *Telos* 32: 152–61.

———. 1978a. *The history of sexuality: An introduction*. Trans. R. Hurley. New York: Pantheon.

———. 1978b. Politics and the study of discourse. *Ideology and Consciousness* 4: 7–26.

———. 1979a. *Power, truth, strategy*. Ed. Meaghan Morris and Paul Patton. Sydney: Feral Publications.

———. 1979b. My body, this paper, this fire. *Oxford Literary Review* 4: 9–28.

———. 1979c. Governmentality. *Ideology and Consciousness* 6: 5–21.

———. 1980a. *Power/knowledge: Selected interviews and other writings 1972–1977*. Ed. Colin Gordon. New York: Pantheon.

———. 1980b. War in the filigree of peace. *Oxford Literary Review* 4: 15–19.

———. 1980c. Two lectures. In *Power/knowledge: selected interviews and other writings 1972–1977*. Ed. Colin Gordon. New York: Pantheon.

———. 1981a. Questions of method: An interview. *I & C*, no. 8: 3–14.

———. 1981b. Is it useless to revolt? *Philosophy and Social Criticism* 8: 5–9.

———. 1986. Of other spaces. *Diacritics* 16: 22–28.

Fraser, Nancy. 1994. Rethinking the public sphere: A contribution to the critique of actually existing democracy. In *Between borders*. Ed. Henry Giroux and Peter McLaren. New York: Routledge. 74–98.

Frow, J. and M. Morris. 1993. Introduction. In *Australian cultural studies: A reader*. Ed. J. Frow and M. Morris. Urbana: University of Illinois Press, vii–xxxii.

Fry, Tony. 1988. From (sun)light to sin. In *It's a sin*. Ed. Lawrence Grossberg. Sydney: Power Publications. 72–82.

Frye, Northrop. 1957. *Anatomy of criticism*. New York: Atheneum.

Gadamer, Hans-George. 1975. *Truth and methods*. New York: Seabury.

Garnham, Nicholas. 1995. Political economy and cultural studies: Reconciliation or divorce? *Critical Studies in Mass Communication* 12: 62–71.

Gerbner, George. 1972. Communication and social environment. In *Communication: A Scientific American book*. San Francisco: W. H. Freeman. 111–20.

——, ed. 1983. *Ferment in the field. Journal of Communication* 33.

Giddens, Anthony. 1979. *Central problems in social theory.* Berkeley: University of California Press.

Gilroy, Paul. 1987. *There ain't no black in the Union Jack.* London: Hutchinson.

——. 1992. Cultural studies and ethnic absolutism. In *Cultural studies.* Ed. Lawrence Grossberg, Cary Nelson, and Paula Treichler. New York: Routledge. 187–97.

——. 1993. *The black Atlantic: Modernity and double consciousness.* Cambridge: Harvard University Press.

Giroux, Henry A. 1992. *Border crossings: Cultural workers and the politics of education.* New York: Routledge.

——. 1994. Living dangerously: Identity politics and the new cultural racism. In *Between borders.* Ed. Henry Giroux and Peter McLaren. New York: Routledge. 29–55.

——. 1996. *Fugitive cultures: Race violence and youth.* New York: Routledge.

Giroux, Henry, and Peter McLaren, eds. 1994. *Between borders: Pedagogy and the Politics of Cultural Studies.* New York: Routledge.

Gitlin, Todd. 1980. *The whole world is watching.* Berkeley: University of California Press.

Gorman, Robert, ed. 1985. *The biographical dictionary of neo-marxism.* Westport: Greenwood Press.

Gouldner, Alvin W. 1976. *The dialectic of ideology and technology.* London: Macmillan.

Gramsci, Antonio. 1971. *Selections from the prison notebooks.* Trans. Q. Hoare and G. Nowell-Smith. New York: International Publishers.

Greimas, A. J. 1966. *Semantique structurale.* Paris: Larousse.

Grossberg, Lawrence. 1977. Cultural interpretation and mass communication. *Communication Research* 4: 339–60.

——. 1979a. Language and theorizing in the human sciences. In *Studies in symbolic interaction.* Vol. 2. Ed. Norman K. Denzin. Greenwich: J.A.I. Press. 189–231.

——. 1979b. Interpreting the "crisis" of culture in communication theory. *Journal of Communication* 29: 56–68.

——. 1982a. Experience, signification, and reality: The boundaries of cultural semiotics. *Semiotica* 41: 73–106.

——. 1982b. Does communication theory need intersubjectivity? Towards an immanent philosophy of interpersonal relations. In *Communication Yearbook 6.* Ed. Michael Burgoon. 171–205.

——. 1982c. Intersubjectivity and the conceptualization of communication. *Human Studies* 5: 213–35.

——. 1982d. The ideology of communication: Poststructuralism and the limits of communication. *Man and World* 15: 83–101.

——. 1983. Cultural studies revisited and revised. In *Communications in transition.* Ed. Mary S. Mander. New York: Praeger. 39–70.

——. 1983–84. The politics of youth culture: Some observations on rock and roll in American culture. *Social Text* 8: 104–26.

——. 1984a. Another boring day in paradise: Rock and roll and the empowerment of everyday life. *Popular Music* 4: 225–57.

——. 1984b. Strategies of marxist cultural interpretation. *Critical Studies in Mass Communication* 1: 392–421.

——. 1984c. "I'd rather feel bad than not feel anything at all": Rock and roll, pleasure and power. *Enclitic* 8: 94–111.

——. 1985a. Michel Foucault. In *The biographical dictionary of neo-marxism*. Ed. Robert Gorman. Westport: Greenwood Press. 143–46.

——. 1985b. Stuart Hall. In *The biographical dictionary of neo-marxism*. Ed. Robert Gorman. Westport: Greenwood Press. 197–200.

——. 1986. History, politics and postmodernism: Stuart Hall and cultural studies. *Journal of Communication Inquiry* 10:61–77.

——. 1987a. The in-difference of television. *Screen* 28 (Spring): 28–45.

——. 1987b. Critical theory and the politics of empirical research. *Mass Communication Review Yearbook* 6: 86–106.

——. 1988a. Wandering audiences, nomadic critics. *Cultural Studies* 2: 377–91.

——. 1988b. *It's a sin: Essays on postmodernism, politics and culture.* Sydney: Power Publications.

——. 1989a. The contexts of audiences and the politics of difference. *Australian Journal of Communication*, no. 16: 13–36.

——. 1989b. The formation(s) of cultural studies: An American in Birmingham. *Strategies*, no. 2: 114–49.

——. 1989c. The circulation of cultural studies. *Critical Studies in Mass Communication* 6: 413–21.

——. 1989d. On the road with three ethnographers. *Journal of Communication Inquiry* 13: 23–26.

——. 1992. *We gotta get out of this place: Popular conservatism and postmodern culture.* New York: Routledge.

——. 1993a. Cultural studies in/and new worlds. *Critical Studies in Mass Communication* 10: 1–22.

——. 1993b. Can cultural studies find true happiness in communication? *Journal of Communication* 43: 89–97.

——. 1993c. Cultural studies and new worlds. In *Race, identity and representation*. Ed. C. McCarthy and W. Crichlow. New York: Routledge. 89–105.

——. 1994a. Bringing it all back home: Cultural studies and education (an introduction). In *Between borders*. Ed. Henry Giroux and Peter McLaren. New York: Routledge. 1–25.

——. 1994b. Something is happening here and you don't know what it is, do you Mr. Jones? A foreword. *South East Asian Journal of Social Science* 22: v–x.

——. 1995a. Cultural studies and political economy: Is anybody else bored with this debate? *Critical Studies in Mass Communication* 122: 72–81.

——. 1995b. Cultural studies: What's in a name (one more time)? *Taboo* 1: 1–37.

——. 1996a. The space of culture, the power of space. In *The question of postcolonialism*. Ed. Iain Chambers and Lidia Curti. London: Routledge. 169–88.

——. 1996b. Identity and cultural studies: Is that all there is? In *Questions of cultural identity*. Ed. Stuart Hall and Paul duGay. London: Sage. 88–107.

——. 1996c. Toward a genealogy of the state of cultural studies. In *Disciplinarity and dissent in cultural studies.* Ed. Cary Nelson and Dilip Gaonkar. New York: Routledge. 131–47.

——. 1997. *Dancing in spite of myself: Essays on popular culture.* Durham: Duke University Press.

——. Forthcoming. Cultural studies, modern logics and globalization. In *New directions in cultural studies.* Ed. Angela McRobbie. Manchester: Manchester University Press.

Grossberg, Lawrence, Cary Nelson, and Paula Treichler, eds. 1992. *Cultural studies.* New York: Routledge.

Guattari, Felix. 1974. Interview. *Diacritics* 4:38–41.

——. 1979a. *L'inconscient machinique.* Paris: Recherches.

——. 1979b. A liberation of desire. In *Homosexualities and French literature.* Ed. George Stambolian and Elaine Marks. Ithaca: Cornell University Press.

——. 1984. *Molecular revolution: Psychiatry and politics.* Trans. Rosemary Sheed. New York: Penguin.

——. 1986. The postmodern dead end. *FlashArt.* 128 (May): 40–41.

Habermas, Jürgen. 1968. *Knowledge and human interests.* Trans. Jeremy J. Shapiro. Boston: Beacon.

——. 1970. Towards a theory of communicative competence." In *Recent sociology 2.* Ed. Hans Peter Dreitzel. New York: Macmillan. 114–48.

——. 1976. *Legitimation crisis.* London: Heinemann Educational Books.

Hage, Ghassan. 1994. Locating multiculturalism's other. *New Formations,* no. 24: 19–34.

Hall, Stuart. 1969. The hippies, an American moment. In *Student power.* Ed. J. Nagel. London: Merlin Press.

——. 1969–70. Introduction to *The annual report of the Centre for Contemporary Cultural Studies.* Birmingham, England.

——. 1971. Response to People and Culture. *Working Papers in Cultural Studies,* no. 1: 97–102.

——. 1972. The social eye of the Picture Post. *Working Papers in Cultural Studies,* no. 2.

——. 1973. Encoding and decoding in the television discourse. Occasional paper. Centre for Contemporary Cultural Studies, Birmingham, England.

——. 1974. Marx's notes on method. *Working Papers in Cultural Studies,* no. 6: 132–70.

——. 1976. Introduction to *An eye on China.* By D. Selbourne. London: Black Liberation Press.

——. 1977. Culture, the media and the "ideological effect." In *Mass communication and society.* Ed. J. Curran et al. London: Edward Arnold. 315–48.

——. 1980a. Cultural studies and the Centre: Some problematics and problems. In *Culture, media, language.* Ed. Stuart Hall et al. London: Hutchinson. 15–47.

——. 1980b. Encoding/decoding. In *Culture, media, language.* Ed. Stuart Hall et al. London: Hutchinson. 128–38.

——. 1980c. Cultural studies: Two paradigms. *Media Culture and Society* 2: 57–72.

——. 1980d. Popular-democratic vs authoritarian populism: Two ways of taking democracy seriously. In *Marxism and democracy.* Ed. A. Hunt. London: Lawrence and Wishart. 157–85.

——. 1980e. Recent developments in theories of language and ideology: A critical note. In *Culture, media, language*. Ed. Stuart Hall et al. London: Hutchinson. 157–62.

——. 1981. Notes on deconstructing "the popular." In *People's history and socialist theory*. Ed. Ralph Samuel. Boston: Routledge and Kegan Paul.

——. 1982. The rediscovery of ideology: Return of the repressed in media studies. In *Culture, society and the media*. Ed. M. Gurevitch et al. New York: Methuen. 56–90.

——. 1983a. The meaning of new times. In *New times: The changing face of politics in the 1990s*. Ed. Stuart Hall and Martin Jacques. London: Lawrence and Wishart. 116–34.

——. 1983b. The problem of ideology: Marxism without guarantees. In *Marx 100 years on*. Ed. B. Matthews. London: Lawrence and Wishart.

——. 1984a. The culture gap. *Marxism Today* (January): 18–23.

——. 1984b. Reconstruction work. *Ten-8*, no. 16: 2–9.

——. 1984c. Mass culture. Unpublished lecture delivered at the University of Wisconsin at Milwaukee.

——. 1985a. Signification, representation, ideology: Althusser and the post-structuralist debates. *Critical Studies in Mass Communication* 2: 87–114.

——. 1985b. Authoritarian populism: A reply to Jessop et al. *New Left Review*, no. 151: 115–24.

——. 1986a. The problem of ideology: Marxism without guarantees. *Journal of Communication Inquiry* 10: 28–44.

——. 1986b. On postmodernism and articulation: An interview. *Journal of Communication Inquiry* 10: 45–60.

——. 1986c. Gramsci's relevance for the study of race and ethnicity. *Journal of Communication Inquiry* 10: 5–27.

——. 1987. Minimal selves. In *Identity: The real me*. In ICA Document 6. London: Institute of Contemporary Arts. 44–46.

——. 1988a. *The hard road to renewal: Thatcherism and the crisis of the Left*. London: Verso.

——. 1988b. Thatcher's lessons. *Marxism Today* (March): 20–27.

——. 1988c. The toad in the garden: Thatcherism amongst the theorists. In *Marxism and the interpretation of culture*. Ed. Cary Nelson and Lawrence Grossberg. Urbana: University of Illinois Press. 35–57.

——. 1988d. Questions and answers. In *Marxism and the interpretation of culture*. Ed. Cary Nelson and Lawrence Grossberg. Urbana: University of Illinois Press. 58–73.

——. 1990a. The emergence of cultural studies and the crisis of the humanities. *October* 53: 11–23.

——. 1990b. Cultural identity and diaspora. In *Identity, community, culture, difference*. Ed. J. Rutherford. London: Lawrence and Wishart. 222–37.

——. 1991a. The local and the global: Globalization and ethnicity." In *Culture globalization and the world system*. Ed. Anthony D. King. London: Macmillan. 19–39.

——. 1991b. Old and new identities, old and new ethnicities. In *Culture globalization and the world-system*. Ed. Anthony D. King. London: Macmillan. 41–68.

——. 1992a. Cultural studies and its theoretical legacies. In *Cultural studies*. Ed. Lawrence Grossberg, Cary Nelson, and Paula Treichler. New York: Routledge. 277–94.

——. 1992b. The West and the rest. In *Formations of modernity*. Ed. S. Hall and B. Gieben. Cambridge: Polity Press. 275–331.

——. 1992c. Race, culture and communications: Looking backward and forward at cultural studies. *Rethinking Marxism* 5: 10–18.

——. 1992d. The question of cultural identity. In *Modernity and its futures*. Ed. Stuart Hall, David Held, and Tony McGrew. Cambridge: Polity. 273–325.

——. 1995. New cultures for old. In *A place in the world? Places, cultures and globalization*. Ed. Doreen Massey and Pat Jess. Oxford: Oxford University Press and Open University. 175–215.

——. n.d. Cultural analyses. Centre for Contemporary Cultural Studies, Birmingham, England.

——. Unpublished. Cultural studies and psychoanalysis.

Hall, Stuart, Chas Critcher, Tony Jefferson, John Clarke, and Brian Roberts. 1978. *Policing the crisis: Mugging, the state, and law and order*. New York: Holmes and Meier.

Hall, Stuart, Dorothy Hobson, Andrew Lowe, and Paul Willis, eds. 1980. *Culture, media, language*. London: Hutchinson.

Hall, Stuart, and Tony Jefferson, eds. 1976. *Resistance through rituals*. London: Hutchinson.

Hall, Stuart, Bob Lumley, and Greg McLennan. 1977. Politics and ideology: Gramsci. In *On Ideology*. Centre for Contemporary Cultural Studies. London: Hutchinson.

Haraway, Donna J. 1991. *Simians, cyborgs, and women: The reinvention of nature*. New York: Routledge.

Harvey, David. 1989. *The condition of modernity*. Oxford: Blackwells.

——. 1995. Militant particularism and global ambition. *Social Text*, no. 42: 69–98.

Hawes, Leonard. 1973. Elements of a model for communication processes. *Quarterly Journal of Speech* 59: 11–21.

——. 1977. Toward a hermeneutic phenomenology of communication. *Communication Quarterly* 25: 30–41.

Hay, James. 1993. Invisible cities/visible geographies: Toward a cultural geography of Italian television in the 90s. *Quarterly Review of Film and Video* 14: 35–47.

Heath, Stephen. 1981. *Questions of cinema*. Bloomington: Indiana University Press.

Hebdige, Dick. 1979. *Subculture: The meaning of style*. London: Routledge.

——. 1981a. Toward a cartography of taste 1935–1962. *Block* 4: 39–56.

——. 1981b. Object as image: The Italian scooter cycle. *Block* 5: 44–64.

——. 1982. Posing . . . threats, striking . . . poses: Youth surveillance and display. *SubStance* 37/38: 68–88.

——. 1983. In poor taste. *Block* 8: 54–68.

——. 1987. Digging for Britain: An excavation in seven parts. In *The British Edge*. Boston: Institute of Contemporary Art. 35–69.

——. 1988. *Hiding in the light: On images and things*. London: Routledge.

——. 1993. The machine is *unheimlich*: Krzysztof Wodiczko's homeless vehicle project. *Cultural Studies* 7: 173–223.

Henderson, Mae G., ed. 1996. Rethinking Black (cultural) studies. *Callaloo* 19: 56–93.

Henriques, Julian, Wendy Looway, Cathy Urwin, Couze Venn, and Valerie Walkerdine. 1984. *Changing the subject: Psychology, social regulation and subjectivity*. London: Methuen.

Hoggart, Richard. 1957. *The uses of literacy*. London: Essential Books.

——. 1967. The literary imagination and the study of society. Occasional paper. Centre for Contemporary Cultural Studies, Birmingham, England.

——. 1969. Contemporary cultural studies. Occasional paper. Centre for Contemporary Cultural Studies, Birmingham, England.

——. 1970. Schools of English and contemporary society. In *Speaking to each other.* Vol. 2. New York: Oxford University Press. 246–59.

Hunter, Ian. 1988. *Culture and government: The emergence of literary education.* London: Macmillan.

Huntington, Samuel. 1993. The clash of civilization. *Foreign Affairs* (n.v.).

Huyssen, Andreas. 1986. *After the great divide: Modernism, mass culture, postmodernism.* Bloomington: University of Indiana Press.

Innis, Harold. 1951. *The bias of communication.* Toronto: University of Toronto Press.

——. 1952. *Changing concepts of time.* Toronto: University of Toronto Press.

Jameson, Fredric. 1972. *The prison house of language.* Princeton: Princeton University Press.

——. 1977. Imaginary and symbolic in Lacan: Marxism, psychoanalytic criticism, and the problem of the subject. *Yale French Studies* 55/56: 338–95.

——. 1979a. Reification and utopia in mass culture. *Social Text* 1: 130–48.

——. 1979b. Class and allegory in contemporary mass culture: *Dog Day Afternoon* as a political film. *Screen Education* 30: 75–92.

——. 1979c. *Fables of aggression: Wyndham Lewis, the modernist as fascist.* Berkeley: University of California Press.

——. 1981. *The political unconscious: Narrative as a socially symbolic act.* Ithaca: Cornell University Press.

——. 1993. On "cultural studies." *Social Text,* no. 34: 17–52.

Johnson, Richard. 1986–87. What is cultural studies anyway? *Social Text* 16: 38–80.

Kellert, Stephen H. 1993. *In the wake of chaos.* Chicago: University of Chicago Press.

Kristeva, Julia. 1969. *Semiotike: Recherches pur une semanalyse.* Trans. T. Gora, A. Jardine, and L. S. Roudiez. Paris: Seuil.

——. 1973. The semiotic activity. *Screen* 14: 25–39.

——. 1974a. La revolution du langage poetique. Paris: Seuil.

——. 1974b. Four types of signifying practice. *Semiotexte* 1: 65–74.

——. 1975a. The system and the speaking subject. In *The tell-tale sign: A survey of semiotics.* Ed. Thomas Sebeok. Lisse: Peter de Ridder Press. 47–56.

——. 1975b. The subject in signifying practice. *Semiotexte* 1: 19–26.

——. 1976. Signifying practice and mode of production. *Edinburgh Magazine* 1: 64–76.

——. 1980. *Desire in language: A semiotic approach to literature and art.* New York: Columbia University Press.

Kuhn, Annette. 1982. *Women's pictures: Feminism and cinema.* Boston: Routledge and Kegan Paul.

Lacan, Jacques. 1977. *Ecrits: A selection.* Trans. Alan Sheridan. New York: Norton.

Laclau, Ernesto. 1977. *Politics and ideology in marxist theory.* London: Verso.

Laclau, Ernesto, and Chantal Mouffe. 1985. *Hegemony and socialist strategy: Towards a radical democratic politics.* London: Verso.

Lanigan, Richard. 1979. Communication models in philosophy: Review and commentary. *Communication Yearbook* 3: 29–49.

Lasswell, Harold D. 1971. The structure and function of communication in society. In *The Processes and Effects of Mass Communication.* Ed. Wilbur Schramm and Donald F. Roberts. Urbana: University of Illinois Press. 84–99.

Lefebvre, Henri. 1984. *Everyday life in the modern world.* Trans. Sacha Rabinovitch. New Brunswick: Transaction.

——. 1991. *The production of space.* Trans. D. Nicholson-Smith. Oxford: Blackwells.

Lévi-Strauss, Claude. 1963. *Structural anthropology.* Trans. C. Jacobson and B. G. Schoepf. New York: Basic Books.

Lukacs, Georg. 1971. *History and class consciousness.* Trans. Rodney Livingstone. Cambridge: MIT Press.

Lyons, John. 1977. *Semantics I.* Cambridge: Cambridge University Press.

Lyotard, Jean-François. 1977a. The unconscious as mise-en-scène. In *Performance in postmodern culture.* Ed. Michel Benamou and Charles Caramello. Madison: Coda Press. 87–98.

——. 1977b. Energumen capitalism. *Semiotexte* 6: 11–26.

——. 1990. *Heidegger and "the jews."* Trans. A. Michel and R. Roberts. Minneapolis: University of Minnesota.

Mann, M. 1973. *Consciousness and action among the western working class.* London: Macmillan.

Marx, Karl. 1973. *Grundrisse.* Trans. M. Nicolaus. New York: Vintage.

Massey, Doreen. 1991. A global sense of place. *Marxism Today* (June): 24–29.

——. 1992. Politics and space/time. *New Left Review,* no. 196.

——. 1994. *Space, place and gender.* London: Polity.

Massumi, Brian. Forthcoming. *The waxing of affect.*

McLuhan, Marshall. 1967. *Understanding media.* London: Sphere.

McRobbie, Angela. 1980. Settling accounts with subcultures: A feminist critique. *Screen Education* 34: 37–49.

——. 1982a. The politics of feminist research: Between talk, text and action. *Feminist Review* 12: 46–57.

——. 1982b. Jackie: An ideology of adolescent femininity. In *Popular culture: Past and present.* Ed. Bernard Waites et al. London: Croom Helm. 263–83.

——. 1986. Dance and social fantasy. In *Gender and generation.* Ed. Angela McRobbie and Mica Nava. London: Methuen.

——. 1996. Looking back at *New Times* and its critics. In *Stuart Hall.* Ed. David Morley and Kuan-Hsing Chen. London: Routledge.

McRobbie, Angela, and Mica Nava, eds. 1986. *Gender and generation.* London: Methuen.

Mercer, Kobena. 1992a. "1968": Periodizing postmodern politics and identity. In *Cultural studies.* Ed. Lawrence Grossberg, Cary Nelson, and Paula Treichler. New York: Routledge. 424–38.

——. 1992b. Back to my routes: A postscript to the 80s. In *Critical decade.* Ed. David Bailey and Stuart Hall. *Ten-8* 2(3): 32–39.

Michaels, Eric. 1994. *Bad aboriginal art: Tradition, media and technological horizons*. Minneapolis: University of Minnesota Press.

Miller, Toby. 1993. *The well-tempered self: Formations of the cultural subject*. Baltimore: Johns Hopkins University Press.

Mohanty, Chandra Talpade. 1994. On race and voice: Challenges for liberal education in the 1990s. In *Between borders*. Ed. Henry Giroux and Peter McLaren. New York: Routledge. 145–66.

Morley, David. 1980. *The "Nationwide" audience: Structure and decoding*. London: BFI.

———. 1981. The "Nationwide" audience: A critical postscript. *Screen Education* 39: 3–14.

———. 1986. *Family television: Cultural power and domestic leisure*. London: Comedia.

———. 1992. *Television audiences and cultural studies*. London: Routledge.

Morley, David, and Kuan-Hsing Chen. 1996. *Stuart Hall: Critical dialogues in cultural studies*. London: Routledge.

Morris, Meaghan. 1988a. At Henry Parkes Motel. *Cultural Studies* 2 (1): 1–47.

———. 1988b. *The pirate's fiancée: Feminism reading postmodernism*. London: Verso.

———. 1988c. Tooth and claw: Tales of survival, and *Crocodile Dundee*. In *The Pirate's Fiancée*. 241–69.

———. 1988d. Banality in cultural studies. *Discourse* 10: 3–29.

———. 1990. Banality in cultural studies. In *Logics of television*. Ed. P. Mellancamp. Bloomington: Indiana University. 14–43.

———. 1990a. Money and real estate. Paper delivered at the conference Cultural Studies Now and in the Future, Urbana, IL.

———. 1992a. On the beach. In *Cultural studies*. Ed. Lawrence Grossberg, Cary Nelson, and Paula Treichler. New York: Routledge. 453–72.

———. 1992b. The man in the mirror: David Harvey's "condition" of postmodernity. *Theory, Culture & Society* 9: 253–79.

———. 1995. A question of cultural studies. Unpublished paper.

———. Forthcoming. *Upward mobility: Popular genres and cultural change*. Bloomington: Indiana University Press.

Mortenson, C. David. 1972. *Communication: The study of human interaction*. New York: McGraw Hill.

Mostern, Kenneth. 1994. Decolonization as learning: Practice and pedagogy in Frantz Fanon's revolutionary narrative. In *Between borders*. Ed. Henry Giroux and Peter McLaren. New York: Routledge. 253–71.

Murdock, Graham. 1978. Blindspots about western marxism: A reply to Dallas Smythe. *Canadian Journal of Political and Social Theory* 2: 109–19.

Nelson, Cary. 1976. Reading criticism. *PMLA* 91: 801–15.

———. 1978. The psychology of criticism, or what can be said. In *Psychoanalysis and the question of the text*. Ed. G. Hartmann. Baltimore: Johns Hopkins University Press. 45–61.

———. 1980. Soliciting self-knowledge: The rhetoric of Susan Sontag's criticism. *Critical Inquiry* 6: 707–26.

———. 1981. On whether criticism is literature. In *What is criticism?* Ed. Paul Hernadi. Bloomington: Indiana University Press. 253–67.

Nelson, Cary, and Lawrence Grossberg, eds. 1988. *Marxism and the interpretation of culture.* Urbana: University of Illinois Press.

Nelson, Cary, Paula Treichler, and Lawrence Grossberg. 1992. Introduction to *Cultural studies.* Ed. Lawrence Grossberg, Cary Nelson, and Paula Treichler. New York: Routledge. 1–22.

Nofsinger, Robert E. 1975. The demand ticket: A conversational device for getting the floor. *Speech Monographs* 42:1–9.

O'Connor, Alan. 1989. The problem of American cultural studies. *Critical Studies in Mass Communication* 6: 405–13.

O'Hanlon, Rosalind. 1988. Recovering the subject: Subaltern studies and histories of resistance in colonial South Asia. *Modern Asian Studies* 22: 189–224.

O'Keefe, Barbara, Jess Delia, and Daniel J. O'Keefe. 1983. Interaction analysis and the analysis of interactional organization. In *Studies in Symbolic Interaction* 3. Ed. Norman K. Denzin. Greenwich: J.A.I. Press.

Park, Robert E. 1967. *Robert E. Park on Social Control and Collective Behavior.* Ed. Ralph H. Turner. Chicago: University of Chicago Press.

Parkin, Frank. 1971. *Class inequality and political order.* London: Macgibbon and Kee.

Parmar, Pratibha. 1989. Other kinds of dreams. *Feminist Review,* no. 31: 55–65.

Parry, Benita. 1987. Problems in current theories of colonial discourse. *Oxford Literary Review* 9: 27–58.

——. 1992. Overlapping territories and intertwined histories: Edward Said's postcolonial cosmopolitanism. In *Edward Said: A critical reader.* Ed. M. Sprinker. Oxford: Blackwell.

Pfister, Joel. 1991. The Americanization of cultural studies. *Yale Journal of Criticism* 4: 199–229.

Poggeler, Otto. 1975. Being as appropriation. *Philosophy Today* 19: 152–78.

Poulantzas, Nicos. 1975. *Political power and social class.* London: New Left Books.

Probyn, Elspeth. 1989. Take my word for it: Ethnography and autobiography. *Journal of Communication Inquiry* 13: 18–22.

Propp, V. 1968. *The morphology of the folk tale.* Trans. L. Scott. Austin: University of Texas Press.

Radway, Janice. 1988. Reception study: Ethnography and the problems of dispersed audiences and nomadic subjects. *Cultural Studies* 2: 359–76.

Radway, Janice, and Lawrence Grossberg. Unpublished. Inside and outside popular culture or, in search of the lost fan.

Ricoeur, Paul. 1970. *Freud and philosophy: An essay on interpretation.* Trans. D. Savage. New Haven: Yale University Press.

Rimmon-Kenan, S. 1984. *Narrative fiction: Contemporary poetics.* London: Methuen.

Robbins, Bruce. 1993. *Secular vocations: Intellectuals, professionalism, culture.* London: Verso.

Robins, Kevin. 1991. Prisoners of the city, whatever could a postmodern city be?" *New Formations,* no. 15: 1–22.

Rommetveit, Ragnar. 1978. On negative rationalism in scholarly studies of verbal communication and dynamic residuals in the construction of human intersubjectivity. In *The social contexts of method.* Ed. Michael Brenner et al. London: Croom Helm. 16–32.

Rooney, Ellen. 1990. Discipline and vanish: Feminism, the resistance to theory, and the politics of cultural studies. *Differences* 2: 14–27.

Rorty, Richard. 1982. Method, social science and social hope. In *Consequences of Pragmatism*. Minneapolis: University of Minnesota Press. 191–210.

Rosaldo, Renato. 1989. *Culture and truth: The remaking of social analysis.* Boston: Beacon Press.

Ross, Andrew. 1989. *No respect: Intellectuals and popular culture.* New York: Routledge.

Rowland, Willard D. 1982. *The politics of TV violence.* Beverly Hills: Sage Publications.

Said, Edward W. 1978. *Orientalism.* New York: Vintage.

Saussure, Ferdinand de. 1954. *The course in general linguistics.* Trans. W. Baskin. New York: Philosophical Library.

Schrag, Calvin O. 1980. *Radical reflection and the origin of the human sciences.* West Lafayette: Purdue University Press.

Schramm, Wilbur. 1971. The nature of communication between humans. In *The processes and effects of mass communication.* Ed. Wilbur Schramm and Donald F. Roberts. Urbana: University of Illinois Press. 3–53.

Schwarz, Bill. 1994. Where is cultural studies? *Cultural Studies* 8: 377–93.

Sedgwick, Eve Kosofsky. 1990. *Epistemology of the closet.* Berkeley: University of California Press.

Segal, Lynne. 1987. *Is the future female?* London: Virago.

Shore, Larry. 1983. The crossroads of business and music: The music industry in the United States and internationally. Unpublished manuscript.

Simon, Roger I. 1994. Forms of insurgency in the production of popular memories: The Columbus quincentenary and the pedagogy of countercommemoration. In *Between borders.* Ed. Henry Giroux and Peter McLaren. New York: Routledge. 127–42.

Slack, Jennifer Daryl. 1984. *Communication technologies and society: Conceptions of causality and the politics of technological intervention.* Norwood: Ablex.

——. 1989. Contextualising technology. In *Rethinking communication.* Vol. 2, *Paradigm exemplars.* Ed. Brenda Dervin et al. Newbury Park: Sage. 329–45.

Smith, A. C. H. 1975. *Paper voices: The popular press and social change.* London: Chatto and Windus.

Smith, Neil. 1992. Geography, difference and the politics of scale. In *Postmodernism and the social sciences.* Ed. J. Doherty, E. Graham, and M. Malek. London: Macmillan.

Smith, Paul. 1988. *Discerning the subject.* Minneapolis: University of Minnesota Press.

Smythe, Dallas. 1977. Communications: Blindspot of western marxism. *Canadian Journal of Political and Social Theory* 1: 1–27.

Soja, Edward W. 1989. *Postmodern geographies: The reassertion of space in critical social theory.* London: Verso.

Spivak, Gayatri Chakravorty. 1987. *In other worlds: Essays in cultural politics.* New York: Routledge.

——. 1988. Can the subaltern speak? In *Marxism and the interpretation of culture.* Ed. Cary Nelson and Lawrence Grossberg. Urbana: University of Illinois Press. 272–313.

Steele, Shelby. 1989. The recoloring of campus life. *Esquire.* February: 47–55.

Stivale, Charles. 1981. Gilles Deleuze and Felix Guattari: Schizoanalysis and literary discourse. *SubStance* 29: 46–57.

Theall, Donald F. 1975. Communication theory and the marginal culture: The socio-aesthetic dimensions of communication study. In *Studies in Canadian communications*. Ed. Gertrude J. Robinson and Donald F. Theall. Montreal: McGill University Press. 7–26.

Thompson, E. P. 1961. The long revolution. *New Left Review*, no. 9: 24–29 and 10: 34–39.

Trend, David. 1994. Nationalities, pedagogies, and media. In *Between borders*. Ed. Henry Giroux and Peter McLaren. New York: Routledge. 225–41.

Turner, Graeme. 1990. *British cultural studies: An introduction*. Boston: Unwin Hyman.

——, ed. 1993. *Nation, culture, text*. London: Routledge.

Tyler, Stephen A. 1986. Post-modern ethnography: From document of the occult to occult document. In *Writing culture*. Ed. James Clifford and George E. Marcus. Berkeley: University of California Press.

Valaskakis, Gail Guthrie. 1988. The Chippewa and the other: Living the heritage of Lac du Flambeau. *Cultural Studies* 2: 267–93.

Viswanathan, Gauri. 1991. Raymond Williams and British colonialism. *Yale Journal of Criticism* 4: 47–66.

Volosinov, V. N. 1973. *Marxism and the philosophy of language*. Trans. L. Matejka and I. R. Titunki. New York: Seminar Press.

Wahl, M. François. 1979. Appendix: Toward a critique of the sign. In *Encyclopedic dictionary of the sciences of language*. Ed. Oswald Ducrot and Tzvetan Todorov. Baltimore: Johns Hopkins University Press. 3478–365.

Walkerdine, Valerie. 1986. Video replay: Families, films and fantasies. In *Formations of fantasy*. Ed. Victor Burgin, James Donald, and Cora Caplan. London: Methuen. 167–99.

Wallace, Michele. 1994. Multiculturalism and oppositionality. In *Between borders*. Ed. Henry Giroux and Peter McLaren. New York: Routledge. 180–91.

Wark, McKenzie. 1992. Speaking trajectories: Meaghan Morris, antipodean theory and Australian cultural studies. *Cultural Studies* 6: 433–48.

——. 1994. *Virtual geography: Living with global media events*. Bloomington: Indiana University Press.

Warshow, Robert. 1974. *The immediate experience*. New York: Atheneum.

Wartella, Ellen, and Byron Reeves. 1987. Historical trends in research on children and the media: 1900–1960. In *Mass Communication Review Yearbook* 6. Ed. M. Gurevitch and M. R. Levy. Newbury Park: Sage Publications. 160–75.

West, Cornel. 1992a. The postmodern crisis of black intellectuals. In *Cultural Studies*. Ed. Lawrence Grossberg, Cary Nelson, and Paula Treichler. New York: Routledge. 689–96.

——. 1992b. Diverse new world. In *Debating P.C.* Ed. P. Berman. New York: Dell. 326–32.

White, Allon. 1977. L'eclatement du suject: The theoretical work of Julia Kristeva. Occasional paper. Centre for Contemporary Cultural Studies, Birmingham, England.

Williams, Raymond. 1958. *Culture and society 1780–1950*. New York: Harper & Row.

——. 1965. *The long revolution*. Middlesex: Penguin.

——. 1968. Culture and revolution. In *From culture to revolution*. Ed. Terry Eagleton and Brian Wicker. London: Sheed and Ward.

——. 1970. *The English novel from Dickens to Lawrence*. New York: Oxford University Press.

——. 1973a. Base and superstructure in marxist theory. *New Left Review*, no. 82: 3–16.

——. 1973b. *The country and the city.* New York: Oxford University Press.

——. 1974. *Television: Technology and cultural form.* London: Fontana.

——. 1976. *Communications.* Harmondsworth Penguin.

——. 1978. *Second generation.* London: Chatto and Windus.

——. 1979. *Politics and letters.* London: New Left Books.

——. 1989. The future of cultural studies. In *The politics of modernism: Against the new conformists.* London: Verso. 151–62.

Willis, Paul. 1977. *Learning to labour: How working class kids get working class jobs.* Westmead: Saxon House.

——. 1978. *Profane culture.* London: Routledge and Kegan Paul.

——. 1990. *Common culture.* Boulder: Westview.

Winkler, K. 1994. Cultural-studies adherents wonder if field lost sight of goals. *Chronicle of Higher Education.* 4 November.

Wolf, Eric R. 1982. *Europe and the people without history.* Berkeley: University of California.

Young, Robert. 1990. *White mythologies: Writing history and the West.* London: Routledge.

Index

Lawrence Grossberg is Morris Davis Professor of Communication
Studies at the University of North Carolina at Chapel Hill. He is the
author of *We Gotta Get Out of This Place: Popular Conservatism and
Postmodern Culture,* and has coedited many volumes including
Cultural Studies (with Cary Nelson and Paula A. Treichler).

Library of Congress Cataloging-in-Publication Data
Grossberg, Lawrence.
Bringing it all back home : essays on cultural studies / Lawrence
Grossberg.
Includes bibliographical references (p.   ) and index.
ISBN 0-8223-1911-X (cloth : alk. paper). —
ISBN 0-8223-1916-0 (paper : alk. paper)
1. Culture—Study and teaching.   2. Popular culture—Study and
teaching.   I. Title.
HM101.G8335   1997
306'.07—dc21   96-50114 CIP